# Solaris™ Performance and Tools

# Solaris™ Performance and Tools

## DTrace and MDB Techniques for Solaris 10 and OpenSolaris

Richard McDougall
Jim Mauro
Brendan Gregg

Sun Microsystems Press

PRENTICE
HALL

Upper Saddle River, NJ • Boston • Indianapolis • San Francisco
New York • Toronto • Montreal • London • Munich • Paris • Madrid
Capetown • Sydney • Tokyo • Singapore • Mexico City

The publisher offers excellent discounts on this book when ordered in quantity for bulk purchases or special sales, which may include electronic versions and/or custom covers and content particular to your business, training goals, marketing focus, and branding interests. For more information, please contact: U.S. Corporate and Government Sales, (800) 382-3419, corpsales@pearsontechgroup.com.

For sales outside the U.S., please contact International Sales, international@pearsoned.com.

Visit us on the Web: www.prenhallprofessional.com

---

**This Book Is Safari Enabled**

The Safari® Enabled icon on the cover of your favorite technology book means the book is available through Safari Bookshelf. When you buy this book, you get free access to the online edition for 45 days.

Safari Bookshelf is an electronic reference library that lets you easily search thousands of technical books, find code samples, download chapters, and access technical information whenever and wherever you need it.

To gain 45-day Safari Enabled access to this book:

• Go to http://www.prenhallprofessional.com/safarienabled

• Complete the brief registration form

• Enter the coupon code YXM9-9VPM-QQBK-52MT-GPBD

If you have difficulty registering on Safari Bookshelf or accessing the online edition, please e-mail customer-service@safaribooksonline.com.

---

*Library of Congress Cataloging-in-Publication Data*
McDougall, Richard.
    Solaris performance and tools : DTrace and MDB techniques for
 Solaris 10 and OpenSolaris / Richard McDougall, Jim Mauro,
 Brendan Gregg.
        p. cm.
    Includes bibliographical references and index.
    ISBN 0-13-156819-1 (hardback : alk. paper)
    1. Solaris (Computer file)  2. Operating systems (Computers)
 I. Mauro, Jim.  II. Gregg, Brendan.  III. Title.
 QA76.76.O63M3957 2006
 005.4'32—dc22
                                    200602013

Pearson Education, Inc.
Rights and Contracts Department
One Lake Street
Upper Saddle River, NJ 07458
Fax: (201) 236-3290

ISBN  0-13-156819-1
Text printed in the United States on recycled paper at Courier in Westford, Massachusetts.
First printing, July 2006

*For Traci, Madi, and Boston—*
*for your love, encouragement, and support . . .*
                                        *—Richard*

*Once again . . .*
*For Donna, Frank, and Dominick.*
*All my love, always . . .*
                                        *Jim*

# Contents

# APPENDICES

# Foreword

Over the past decade, a regrettable idea took hold: Operating systems, while interesting, were a finished, solved problem. The genesis of this idea is manifold, but the greatest contributing factor may simply be that operating systems were not understood; they were largely delivered not as transparent systems, but rather as proprietary black boxes, welded shut to even the merely curious. This is anathema to understanding; if something can't be taken apart—if its inner workings remain hidden—its intricacies can never be understood nor its engineering nuances appreciated. This is especially true of software systems, which can't even be taken apart in the traditional sense. Software is, despite the metaphors, information, not machine, and a closed software system is just about as resistant to understanding as an engineered system can be.

This was the state of Solaris circa 2000, and it was indeed not well understood. Its internals were publicly described only in arcane block comments or old USENIX papers, its behavior was opaque to existing tools, and its source code was cloistered in chambers unknown. Starting in 2000, this began to change (if slowly) —heralded in part by the first edition of the volume that you now hold in your hands: Jim Mauro and Richard McDougall's *Solaris™ Internals*. Jim and Richard had taken on an extraordinary challenge—to describe the inner workings of a system so complicated that no one person actually understands all of it. Over the course of working on their book, Jim and Richard presumably realized that no one book could contain it either. Despite scaling back their ambition to (for example) not include networking, the first edition of *Solaris™ Internals* still weighed in at over six hundred pages.

The publishing of *Solaris™ Internals* marked the beginning of change that accelerated through the first half of the decade, as the barriers to using and understanding Solaris were broken down. Solaris became free, its engineers began to talk about its implementation extensively through new media like blogs, and most important, Solaris itself became open source in June 2005, becoming the first operating system to leap the chasm from proprietary to open. At the same time, the mechanics of Solaris became much more interesting as several revolutionary new technologies made their debut in Solaris 10. These technologies have swayed many a naysayer, and have proved that operating systems are alive after all. Furthermore, there are still hard, important problems to be solved.

If 2000 is viewed as the beginning of the changes in Solaris, 2005 may well be viewed as the end of the beginning. By the end of 2005, what was a seemingly finished, proprietary product had been transformed into an exciting, open source system, alive with potential and possibility. It is especially fitting that these changes are welcomed with this second edition of *Solaris™ Internals*. Faced with the impossible task of reflecting a half-decade of massive engineering change, Jim and Richard made an important decision—they enlisted the explicit help of the engineers that designed the subsystems and wrote the code. In several cases these engineers have wholly authored the chapter on their "baby." The result is a second edition that is both dramatically expanded and highly authoritative—and very much in keeping with the new Solaris zeitgeist of community development and authorship.

On a personal note, it has been rewarding to see Jim and Richard use DTrace, the technology that Mike Shapiro, Adam Leventhal, and I developed in Solaris 10. Mike, Adam, and I were all teaching assistants for our university operating systems course, and an unspoken goal of ours was to develop a pedagogical tool that would revolutionize the way that operating systems are taught. I therefore encourage you not just to read *Solaris™ Internals*, but to *download* Solaris, *run* it on your desktop or laptop or under a virtual machine, and *use* DTrace yourself to see the concepts that Jim and Richard describe—live, and on your own machine!

Be you student or professional, reading for a course, for work, or for curiosity, it is my pleasure to welcome you to your guides through the internals of Solaris. Enjoy your tour, and remember that Solaris is not a finished work, but rather a living, evolving technology. If you're interested in accelerating that evolution—or even if you just have questions on using or understanding Solaris—please join us in the many communities at http://www.opensolaris.org. Welcome!

Bryan Cantrill
San Francisco, California
June 2006

# Preface

Welcome to the second edition of *Solaris™ Internals* and its companion volume, *Solaris™ Performance and Tools*. It has been almost five years since the release of the first edition, during which time we have had the opportunity to communicate with a great many Solaris users, software developers, system administrators, database administrators, performance analysts, and even the occasional kernel hacker. We are grateful for all the feedback, and we have made specific changes to the format and content of this edition based on reader input. Read on to learn what is different. We look forward to continued communication with the Solaris community.

## About These Books

These books are about the internals of Sun's Solaris Operating System—specifically, the SunOS kernel. Other components of Solaris, such as windowing systems for desktops, are not covered. The first edition of *Solaris™ Internals* covered Solaris releases 2.5.1, 2.6, and Solaris 7. These volumes focus on Solaris 10, with updated information for Solaris 8 and 9.

In the first edition, we wanted not only to describe the internal components that make the Solaris kernel tick, but also to provide guidance on putting the information to practical use. These same goals apply to this work, with further emphasis on the use of bundled (and in some cases unbundled) tools and utilities that can be used to examine and probe a running system. Our ability to illustrate more of the kernel's inner workings with observability tools is facilitated in no small part by the inclusion of some revolutionary and innovative technology in Solaris 10—DTrace, a dynamic kernel tracing framework. DTrace is one of many new technologies in Solaris 10, and is used extensively throughout this text.

In working on the second edition, we enlisted the help of several friends and colleagues, many of whom are part of Solaris kernel engineering. Their expertise and guidance contributed significantly to the quality and content of these books. We also found ourselves expanding topics along the way, demonstrating the use of `dtrace(1)`, `mdb(1)`, `kstat(1)`, and other bundled tools. So much so that we decided early on that some specific coverage of these tools was necessary, and chapters were written to provide readers with the required background information on the tools and utilities. From this, an entire chapter on using the tools for performance and behavior analysis evolved.

As we neared completion of the work, and began building the entire manuscript, we ran into a bit of a problem—the size. The book had grown to over 1,500 pages. This, we discovered, presented some problems in the publishing and production of the book. After some discussion with the publisher, it was decided we should break the work up into two volumes.

***Solaris™ Internals.*** This represents an update to the first edition, including a significant amount of new material. All major kernel subsystems are included: the virtual memory (VM) system, processes and threads, the kernel dispatcher and scheduling classes, file systems and the virtual file system (VFS) framework, and core kernel facilities. New Solaris facilities for resource management are covered as well, along with a new chapter on networking. New features in Solaris 8 and Solaris 9 are called out as appropriate throughout the text. Examples of Solaris utilities and tools for performance and analysis work, described in the companion volume, are used throughout the text.

***Solaris™ Performance and Tools.*** This book contains chapters on the tools and utilities bundled with Solaris 10: `dtrace(1)`, `mdb(1)`, `kstat(1)`, etc. There are also extensive chapters on using the tools to analyze the performance and behavior of a Solaris system.

The two texts are designed as companion volumes, and can be used in conjunction with access to the Solaris source code on

```
http://www.opensolaris.org
```

Readers interested in specific releases before Solaris 8 should continue to use the first edition as a reference.

# Intended Audience

We believe that these books will serve as a useful reference for a variety of technical staff members working with the Solaris Operating System.

**Application developers** can find information in these books about how Solaris OS implements functions behind the application programming interfaces. This information helps developers understand performance, scalability, and implementation specifics of each interface when they develop Solaris applications. The system overview section and sections on scheduling, interprocess communication, and file system behavior should be the most useful sections.

**Device driver and kernel module developers** of drivers, STREAMS modules, loadable system calls, etc., can find herein the general architecture and implementation theory of the Solaris OS. The Solaris kernel framework and facilities portions of the books (especially the locking and synchronization primitives chapters) are particularly relevant.

**Systems administrators, systems analysts, database administrators, and Enterprise Resource Planning (ERP) managers** responsible for performance tuning and capacity planning can learn about the behavioral characteristics of the major Solaris subsystems. The file system caching and memory management chapters provide a great deal of information about how Solaris behaves in real-world environments. The algorithms behind Solaris tunable parameters are covered in depth throughout the books.

**Technical support staff** responsible for the diagnosis, debugging, and support of Solaris will find a wealth of information about implementation details of Solaris. Major data structures and data flow diagrams are provided in each chapter to aid debugging and navigation of Solaris systems.

**System users who just want to know more** about how the Solaris kernel works will find high-level overviews at the start of each chapter.

Beyond the technical user community, those in academia studying operating systems will find that this text will work well as a reference. Solaris OS is a robust, feature-rich, volume production operating system, well suited to a variety of workloads, ranging from uniprocessor desktops to very large multiprocessor systems with large memory and input/output (I/O) configurations. The robustness and scalability of Solaris OS for commercial data processing, Web services, network applications, and scientific workloads is without peer in the industry. Much can be learned from studying such an operating system.

## OpenSolaris

In June 2005, Sun Microsystems introduced OpenSolaris, a fully functional Solaris operating system release built from open source. As part of the OpenSolaris initiative, the Solaris source was made generally available through an open license offering. This has some obvious benefits to this text. We can now include Solaris source directly in the text where appropriate, as well as refer to full source listings made available through the OpenSolaris initiative.

With OpenSolaris, a worldwide community of developers now has access to Solaris source code, and developers can contribute to whatever component of the operating system they find interesting. Source code accessibility allows us to structure the books such that we can cross-reference specific source files, right down to line numbers in the source tree.

OpenSolaris represents a significant milestone for technologists worldwide; a world-class, mature, robust, and feature-rich operating system is now easily accessible to anyone wishing to use Solaris, explore it, and contribute to its development.

Visit the Open Solaris Website to learn more about OpenSolaris:

```
http://www.opensolaris.org
```

The OpenSolaris source code is available at:

```
http://cvs.opensolaris.org/source
```

Source code references used throughout this text are relative to that starting location.

## How the Books Are Organized

We organized the *Solaris™ Internals* volumes into several logical parts, each part grouping several chapters containing related information. Our goal was to provide a building block approach to the material by which later sections could build on information provided in earlier chapters. However, for readers familiar with particular aspects of operating systems design and implementation, the individual parts and chapters can stand on their own in terms of the subject matter they cover.

## Volume 1: *Solaris™ Internals*

## Updates and Related Material

To complement these books, we created a Web site at which we will place updated material, tools we refer to, and links to related material on the topics covered. We will regularly update the Web site (http://www.solarisinternals.com) with information about this text and future work on *Solaris™ Internals*. The Web site will be enhanced to provide a forum for Frequently Asked Questions (FAQs) related to the text, as well as general questions about Solaris internals, performance, and behavior. If bugs are discovered in the text, we will post errata on the Web site as well.

# Notational Conventions

Table P.1 describes the typographic conventions used throughout these books, and Table P.2 shows the default system prompt for the utilities we describe.

**Table P.1** Typographic Conventions

| Typeface or Symbol | Meaning | Example |
| --- | --- | --- |
| AaBbCc123 | Command names, file names, and data structures. | The vmstat command. The <sys/proc.h> header file. The proc structure. |
| AaBbCc123() | Function names. | page_create_va() |
| AaBbCc123(2) | Manual pages. | Please see vmstat(1M). |
| **AaBbCc123** | Commands you type within an example. | $ **vmstat**<br>r b w   swap   free   re   mf 0 0 0<br>464440 18920   1   13 |
| *AaBbCc123* | New terms as they are introduced. | A *major page fault* occurs when… |
| MDB | The modular debuggers, including the user-mode debugger (mdb) and the kernel in-situ debugger (kmdb). | Examples that are applicable to both the user-mode and the in-situ kernel debugger. |
| mdb | The user-mode modular debugger. | Examples that are applicable the user-mode debugger. |
| kmdb | The in-situ debugger | Examples that are applicable to the in-situ kernel debugger. |

**Table P.2** Command Prompts

| Shell | Prompt |
| --- | --- |
| Shell prompt | minimum-osversion$ |
| Shell superuser prompt | minimum-osversion# |
| The mdb debugger prompt | > |
| The kmdb debugger prompt | [cpu]> |

## A Note from the Authors

Once again, a large investment in time and energy proved enormously rewarding for the authors. The support from Sun's Solaris kernel development group, the Solaris user community, and readers of the first edition has been extremely gratifying. We believe we have been able to achieve more with the second edition in terms of providing Solaris users with a valuable reference text. We certainly extended our knowledge in writing it, and we look forward to hearing from readers.

# About the Authors

Had **Richard McDougall** lived 100 years ago, he would have had the hood open on the first four-stroke internal combustion-powered vehicle, exploring new techniques for making improvements. He would be looking for simple ways to solve complex problems and helping pioneering owners understand how the technology worked to get the most from their new experience. These days, Richard uses technology to satisfy his curiosity. He is a Distinguished Engineer at Sun Microsystems, specializing in operating systems technology and systems performance.

**Jim Mauro** is a Senior Staff Engineer in the Performance, Architecture, and Applications Engineering group at Sun Microsystems, where his most recent efforts have focused on Solaris performance on Opteron platforms, specifically in the area of file system and raw disk IO performance. Jim's interests include operating systems scheduling and thread support, threaded applications, file systems, and operating system tools for observability. Outside interests include reading and music— Jim proudly keeps his turntable in top working order, and still purchases and plays 12-inch vinyl LPs. He lives in New Jersey with his wife and two sons. When Jim's not writing or working, he's handling trouble tickets generated by his family on issues they're having with home networking and getting the printer to print.

**Brendan Gregg** is a Solaris consultant and instructor teaching classes for Sun Microsystems across Australia and Asia. He is also an OpenSolaris contributor and community leader, and has written numerous software packages, including the DTraceToolkit. A fan of many sports, he trains as a fencer when he is home in Sydney.

# Acknowledgments

## The *Solaris™ Internals* Community Authors

Although there are only three names on the cover of these books, the effort was truly that of a community effort. Several of our friends went above and beyond the call of duty, and gave generously of their time, expertise, and energy by contributing material to the book. Their efforts significantly improved the content, allowing the books to cover a broader range of topics, as well as giving us a chance to hear from specific subject matter experts. Our sincerest thanks to the following.

**Frank Batschulat.** For help updating the UFS chapter. Frank has been a software engineer for 10 years and has worked at Sun Microsystems for a total of 7 years. At Sun he is a member of the Solaris File Systems Group primarily focused on UFS and the generic VFS/VNODE layer.

**Russell Blaine.** For x86 system call information. Russell Blaine has been juggling various parts of the kernel since joining Sun straight out of Princeton in 2000.

**Joe Bonasera.** For the x64 HAT description. Joe is an engineer in the Solaris kernel group, working mostly on core virtual memory support. Joe's background includes working on optimizing compilers and parallel database engines. His recent efforts have been around the AMD64 port, and porting OpenSolaris to run under the Xen virtualization software, specifically in the areas of virtual and physical memory management, and the boot process.

**Jeff Bonwick.** For a description of the vmem Allocator. Jeff is a Distinguished Engineer in Solaris kernel development. His many contributions include the original kernel memory slab allocator, and updated kernel vmem framework. Jeff's most recent work is the architecture, design, and implementation of the Zetabyte Filesystem, ZFS.

**Peter Boothby.** For the kstats overview. Peter Boothby worked at Sun for 11 years in a variety of roles: Systems Engineer; SAP Competence Centre manager for Australia and New Zealand; Sun's performance engineer and group manager at SAP in Germany; Staff Engineer in Scotland supporting European ISVs in their Solaris and Java development efforts. After a 2-year sabbatical skiing in France, racing yachts on Sydney Harbor, and sailing up and down the east coast of Australia, Peter returned to the Sun fold by founding a consulting firm that assists Sun Australia in large-scale consolidation and integration projects.

**Rich Brown.** For text on the file system interfaces as part of the File System chapters. Rich Brown has worked in the Solaris file system area for 10 years. He is currently looking at ways to improve file system observability.

**Bryan Cantrill.** For the overview of the cyclics subsystem. Bryan is a Senior Software Engineer in Solaris kernel engineering. Among Bryan's many contributions are the cyclics subsystem, and interposing on the trap table to gather trap statistics. More recently, Bryan developed Solaris Dynamic Tracing, or DTrace.

**Jonathan Chew.** For help with the dispatcher NUMA and CMT sections. Jonathan Chew has been a software engineer in the Solaris kernel development group at Sun Microsystems since 1995. During that time, he has focused on Uniform Memory Access (NUMA) machines and chip multithreading. Prior to joining Sun, Jonathan was a research systems programmer in the Computer Systems Laboratory at Stanford University and the computer science department at Carnegie Mellon University.

**Todd Clayton.** For information on the large-page architectural changes. Todd is an engineer in Solaris kernel development, where he works on (among other things) the virtual memory code and AMD64 Solaris port.

**Sankhyayan (Shawn) Debnath.** For updating the UFS chapter with Sarah, Frank, Karen, and Dworkin. Sankhyayan Debnath is a student at Purdue University majoring in computer science and was an intern for the file systems group at Sun Microsystems. When not hacking away at code on the computer, you can find him racing his car at the local tracks or riding around town on his motorcycle.

**Casper Dik.** For material that was used to produce the process rights chapter. Casper is an engineer in Solaris kernel development, and has worked extensively in the areas of security and networking. Among Casper's many contributions are the design and implementation of the Solaris 10 Process Rights framework.

**Andrei Dorofeev.** For guidance on the dispatcher chapter. Andrei is a Staff Engineer in the Solaris Kernel Development group at Sun Microsystems. His interests include multiprocessor scheduling, chip multithreading architectures, resource management, and performance. Andrei received an M.S. with honors in computer science from Novosibirsk State University in Russia.

**Roger Faulkner.** For suggestions about the process chapter. Roger is a Senior Staff Engineer in Solaris kernel development. Roger did the original implementation of the process file system for UNIX System V, and his numerous contributions include the threads implementation in Solaris, both past and current, and the unified process model.

**Brendan Gregg.** For significant review contributions and joint work on the performance and debugging volume. Brendan has been using Solaris for around a decade, and has worked as a programmer, a system administrator and a consultant. He is an OpenSolaris contributor, and has written software such as the DTrace toolkit. He teaches Solaris classes for Sun Microsystems.

**Phil Harman.** For the insights and suggestions to the process and thread model descriptions. Phil is an engineer in Solaris kernel development, where he focuses on Solaris kernel performance. Phil's numerous contributions include a generic framework for measuring system call performance called libMicro. Phil is an acknowledged expert on threads and developing multi-threaded applications.

**Jonathan Haslam.** For the DTrace chapter. Jon is an engineer in Sun's performance group, and is an expert in application and system performance. Jon was a very early user of DTrace, and contributed significantly to identifying needed features and enhancements for the final implementation.

**Stephen Hahn.** For original material that is used in the projects, tasks, and resource control chapters. Stephen is an engineer in Solaris kernel development, and has made significant contributions to the kernel scheduling code and resource management implementation, among other things.

**Sarah Jelinek.** For 12 years of software engineering experience, 8 of these at Sun Microsystems. At Sun she has worked on systems management, file system management, and most recently in the file system kernel space in UFS. Sarah holds a B.S. in computer science and applied mathematics, and an M.S. in computer science, both from the University of Colorado, Colorado Springs.

**Alexander Kolbasov.** For the description of task queues. Alexander works in the Solaris Kernel Performance group. Interests include the scheduler, Solaris NUMA implementation, kernel observability, and scalability of algorithms.

**Tariq Magdon-Ismail.** For the updates to the SPARC section of the HAT chapter. Tariq is a Staff Engineer in the Performance, Availability and Architecture Engineering group with over 10 years of Solaris experience. His areas of contribution include large system performance, kernel scalability, and memory management architecture. Tariq was the recipient of the Sun Microsystems Quarterly Excellence Award for his work in the area of memory management. Tariq holds a B.S. with honors in computer science from the University of Maryland, College Park.

**Stuart Maybee.** For information on the file system mount table description. Stuart is an engineer in Sun's kernel development group.

**Dworkin Muller.** For information on the UFS on disk format. Dworkin was a UFS file system developer while at Sun.

**David Powell.** For the System V IPC update. Dave is an engineer in Solaris kernel development, and his many contributions include a rewrite of the System V IPC facility to use new resource management framework for setting thresholds, and contributing to the development of the Solaris 10 Service Management Facility (SMF).

**Karen Rochford.** For her contributions and diagrams for UFS logging. Karen Rochford has 15 years of software engineering experience, with her past 3 years being at Sun. Her focus has been in the area of I/O, including device drivers, SCSI, storage controller firmware, RAID, and most recently UFS and NFS. She holds a B.S. in computer science and mathematics from Baldwin-Wallace College in Berea, Ohio, and an M.S. in computer science from the University of Colorado, Colorado Springs. In her spare time, Karen can be found training her dogs, a briard and a bouvier, for obedience and agility competitions.

**Eric Saxe.** For contributions to the dispatcher, NUMA, and CMT chapters. Eric Saxe has been with Sun for 6 years and is a development engineer in the Solaris Kernel Performance Group. When Eric isn't at home with his family, he spends his time analyzing and enhancing the performance of the kernel's scheduling and virtual memory subsystems on NUMA, CMT, and other large system architectures.

**Eric Schrock.** For the system calls appendix. Eric is an engineer in Solaris kernel development. His most recent efforts have been the development and implementation of the Zetabyte File System, ZFS.

**Michael Shapiro.** For contributions on kmem debugging and introductory text for MDB. Mike Shapiro is a Distinguished Engineer and architect for RAS features in Solaris kernel development. He led the effort to design and build the Sun architecture for Predictive Self-Healing, and is the cocreator of DTrace. Mike is the author of the DTrace compiler, D programming language, kernel panic subsystem, fmd(1M), mdb(1M), dumpadm(1M), pgrep(1), pkill(1), and numerous enhancements to the /proc filesystem, core files, crash dumps, and hardware error handling. Mike has been a member of the Solaris kernel team for 9 years and holds an M.S. in computer science from Brown University.

**Denis Sheahan.** For information on Java in the tools chapter. Denis is a Senior Staff Engineer in the Sun Microsystems UltraSPARC T1 Architecture Group. During his 12 years at Sun, Denis has focused on application software and Solaris OS performance, with an emphasis on database, application server, and Java technology products. He is currently working on UltraSPARC T1 performance for current and future products. Denis holds a B.S. degree in computer science from Trinity College Dublin, Ireland. He received the Sun Chairman's Award for innovation in 2003.

**Tony Shoumack.** For contributions to the performance volume, and numerous reviews. Tony has been working with UNIX and Solaris for 12 years and he is an Engineer in Sun's Client Solutions organization where he specializes in commercial applications, databases and high-availability clustered systems.

**Bart Smaalders.** For numerous good ideas, and introductory text in the NUMA chapter. Bart is a Senior Staff Engineer in Solaris kernel development, and spends his time making Solaris faster.

**Sunay Tripathi.** For authoring the networking chapter. Sunay is the Senior Staff Engineer in Solaris Core Technology group. He has designed, developed and led major projects in Sun Solaris for the past 9 years in kernel/network environment to provide new functionality, performance, and scalability. Before coming to Sun, Sunay was a researcher at Indian Institute of Technology, Delhi, for 4 years and served a 2-year stint at Stanford where he was involved with Center of Design Research, creating smart agents and part of the Mosquito Net group experimenting with mobility in IP networks.

**Andy Tucker.** For the introductory text on zones. Andy has been a Principal Engineer at VMware since 2005, working on the VMware ESX product. Prior to that he spent 11 years at Sun Microsystems working in a variety of areas related to the Solaris Operating System, particularly scheduling, resource management, and virtualization. He received a Ph.D. in computer science from Stanford University in 1994.

## The Reviewers

A special thanks to Dave Miller and Dominic Kay, copy-reviewer extraordinaires. Dave and Dominic meticulously reviewed vast amounts of material, and provided detailed feedback and commentary, through all phases of the book's development.

The following gave generously of their time and expertise reviewing the manuscripts. They found bugs, offered suggestions and comments that considerably improved the quality of the final work—Lori Alt, Roch Bourbonnais, Rich Brown, Alan Hargreaves, Ben Humphreys, Dominic Kay, Eric Lowe, Giri Mandalika, Jim Nissen, Anton Rang, Damian Reeves, Marc Strahl, Michael Schuster, Rich Teer, and Moriah Waterland.

Tony Shoumack and Allan Packer did an amazing eleventh-hour scramble to help complete the review process and apply several improvements.

## Personal Acknowledgments from Richard

Without a doubt, this book has been a true team collaboration—when we look through the list, there are actually over 30 authors for this edition. I've enjoyed working with all of you, and now have the pleasure of thanking you for your help to bring these books to life.

First I'd like to thank my family, starting with my wife Traci, for your unbelievable support and patience throughout this multiyear project. You kept me focused on getting the job done, and during this time you gave me the wonderful gift of our new son, Boston. My 4-year-old daughter Madison is growing up so fast to be the most amazing little lady. I'm so proud of you—and that you've been so interested in this project, and for the artwork you so confidently drew for the cover pages. Yes, Madi, we can finally say the book's done!

For our friends and family who have been so patient while I've been somewhat absent. I owe you several years' worth of camping, dinners, and well, all the other social events I should have been at!

My co-conspirator in crime, Jim Mauro—hey, Jim, we did it! Thank you for being such a good friend and keeping me sane all the way through this effort!

Thanks, Phil Harman, for being the always-available buddy on the other side of IM to keep me company and bounce numerous ideas off. And of course for the many enjoyable photo-taking adventures.

I'd very much like to thank Brendan Gregg for joining in the fold and working jointly on the second volume on performance and tools. Your insights, thoughts, and tools make this volume something that it could not have been without your involvement.

Mary Lou Nohr, our copy editor, for whom I have the greatest respect—you had the patience to work with us as this project grew from 700 pages to 1,600 and then from one book to two. For completing with incredible detail everything we sent your way, in record time. Without you this book would have not been what it is today.

Thank you to the Solaris development team, for the countless innovations that make writing about Solaris so much fun. Thanks to Bart Smaalders, Solaris Kernel performance lead, for the insights, comments, suggestions, and guidance along the way on this and many other projects.

To all the guest authors who helped, thanks for contributing—your insights and words bring a welcome completion to this Solaris story.

For my colleagues within the Sun Performance, Availability, and Architecture group in Sun. So much of the content of these books is owed to your hard efforts.

Thanks to my senior director, Ganesh Ramamurthy, for standing behind this project 100%, and giving us his full support and resources to get the job done.

Richard McDougall
Menlo Park, California
June 2006

## Personal Acknowledgments from Jim

Thanks a million to Greg Doench, our Senior Editor at Prentice Hall, for waiting an extra two years for the updated edition, and jumping through hoops at the eleventh hour when we handed him two books instead of one.

Thanks to Mary Lou Nohr, our copy editor, for doing such an amazing job in record time.

My thanks to Brendan Gregg for a remarkable effort, making massive contributions to the performance book, while at the same time providing amazing feedback on the internals text.

Marc Strahl deserves special recognition. Marc was a key reviewer for the first edition of *Solaris™ Internals* (as well as the current edition). In a first edition eleventh-hour scramble, I somehow managed to get the wrong version of the acknowledgements copy in for the final typesetting, and Marc was left out. I truly appreciate his time and support on both editions.

Solaris Kernel Engineering. Everyone. All of you. The support and enthusiasm was simply overwhelming, and all while continuing to innovate and create the best operating system on the planet. Thanks a million.

My manager, Keng-Tai Ko, for his support, patience, and flexibility, and my senior director, Ganesh Ramamurthy, for incredible support.

My good friends Phil Harman and Bob Sneed, for a lot of listening, ideas, and opinions, and pulling me out of the burn-out doldrums many, many times.

My good mate Richard McDougall, for friendship, leadership, vision, and one hundred great meals and one thousand glasses of wine in the Bay Area. Looking forward to a lot more.

Lastly, my wife Donna, and my two sons, Frank and Dominick, for their love, support, encouragement, and putting up with two-plus years of—"I can't. I have to work on the book."

Jim Mauro
Green Brook, New Jersey
June 2006

## Personal Acknowledgements from Brendan

I'd like to thank Jim and Richard for writing *Solaris™ Internals* in the first place. I studied the first edition from cover to cover, and was amazed at what a unique and valuable reference it was. It has become a constant companion over the years.

Many thanks to Bryan Cantrill, Mike Shapiro—and Adam Leventhal—for both writing DTrace and encouraging me to get involved during the development of Solaris 10. Thanks to my friends, both inside and outside of Sun, for their support and expertise. They include Boyd Adamson, Nathan Kroenert (who encouraged me to read the first edition), Gunther Feuereisen, Gary Riseborough, Dr. Rex di Bona, and Karen Love.

Thanks to the OpenSolaris project for the source code, and the OpenSolaris community for their support. This includes James Dickens, Alan Hargreaves, and Ben Rockwood, who keep us all informed about events. And finally for Claire, thanks for the love, support, and coffee.

Brendan Gregg
Sydney, Australia
March, 2006

# PART ONE

# Observability Methods

# Introduction to Observability Tools

Bryan Cantrill's foreword describes operating systems as "proprietary black boxes, welded shut to even the merely curious." Bryan paints a realistic view of the not-too-distant past when only a small amount of the software stack was visible or observable. Complexity faced those attempting to understand why a system wasn't meeting its prescribed service level and response-time goals. The problem was that the performance analyst had to work with only a small set of hardwired performance statistics, which, ironically, were chosen some decades ago by kernel developers as a means to debug the kernel's implementation. As a result, performance measurement and diagnosis became an art of inferencing and, in some cases, guessing.

Today, Solaris has a rich set of observability facilities, aimed at the administrator, application developer, and operating systems developer. These facilities are built on a flexible observability framework and, as a result, are highly customizable. You can liken this to the Tivo[1] revolution that transformed television viewing: Rather than being locked into a fixed set of program schedules, viewers can now watch *what* they want, *when* they want; in other words, Tivo put the viewer in control instead of the program provider. In a similar way, the Solaris observability tools can be targeted at specific problems, converging on what's important to solve each particular problem quickly and concisely.

---

1. Tivo was among the first digital media recorders for home media. It automatically records programs to hard disk according to users' viewing and selection preferences.

In Part One we describe the methods we typically use for measuring system utilization and diagnosing performance problems. In Part Two we introduce the frameworks upon which these methods build. In Part Three we discuss the facilities for debugging within Solaris.

This chapter previews the material explored in more detail in subsequent chapters.

## 1.1 Observability Tools

The commands, tools, and utilities used for observing system performance and behavior can be categorized in terms of the information they provide and the source of the data. They include the following.

- **Kernel-statistics-gathering tools.** Report kstats, or kernel statistics, collected by means of counters. Examples are `vmstat`, `mpstat`, and `netstat`.
- **Process tools.** Provide system process listings and statistics for individual processes and threads. Examples are `prstat`, `ptree`, and `pfiles`.
- **Forensic tools.** Track system calls and perform in-depth analysis of targets such as applications, kernels, and core files. Examples are `truss` and MDB.
- **Dynamic tools.** Fully instrument-running applications and kernels. DTrace is an example.

In combination, these utilities constitute a rich set of tools that provide much of the information required to find bottlenecks in system performance, debug troublesome applications, and even help determine what caused a system to crash—after the fact! But which tool is right for the task at hand? The answer lies in determining the information needed and matching it to the tools available. Sometimes a single tool provides this information. Other times you may need to turn detective, using one set of tools, say, DTrace, to dig out the information you need in order to zero in on specific areas where other tools like MDB can perform in-depth analysis.

Determining which tool to use to find the relevant information about the system at hand can sometimes be as confusing to the novice as the results the tool produces. Which particular command or utility to use depends both on the nature of the problem you are investigating and on your goal. Typically, a systemwide view is the first place to start (the "stat" commands), along with a full process view (`prstat(1)`). Drilling-down on a specific process or set of processes typically involves the use of several of the commands, along with `dtrace` and/or MDB.

## 1.1.1 Kstat Tools

The system kernel statistics utilities (kstats) extract information continuously maintained in the kernel Kstats framework as counters that are incremented upon the occurrence of specific events, such as the execution of a system call or a disk I/O. The individual commands and utilities built on kstats can be summarized as follows. (Consult the individual man pages and the following chapters for information on the use of these commands and the data they provide.)

- **mpstat(1M).** Per-processor statistics and utilization.
- **vmstat(1M).** Memory, run queue, and summarized processor utilization.
- **iostat(1M).** Disk I/O subsystem operations, bandwidth, and utilization.
- **netstat(1M).** Network interface packet rates, errors, and collisions.
- **kstat(1M).** Name-based output of kstat counter values.
- **sar(1).** Catch-all reporting of a broad range of system statistics; often regularly scheduled to collect statistics that assist in producing reports on such vital signs as daily CPU utilization.

The utilities listed above extract data values from the underlying kstats and report per-second counts for a variety of system events. Note that the exception is netstat(1), which does not normalize values to per-second rates but rather to the per-interval rates specified by the sampling interval used on the command line. With these tools, you can observe the utilization level of the system's hardware resources (processors, memory, disk storage, network interfaces) and can track specific events systemwide, to aid your understanding of the load and application behavior.

## 1.1.2 Process Tools

Information and data on running processes are available with two tools and their options.

- **ps(1).** Process status. List the processes on the system, optionally displaying extended per-process information.
- **prstat(1M).** Process status. Monitor processes on the system, optionally displaying process and thread-level microstate accounting and per-project statistics for resource management.

Per-process information is available through a set of tools collectively known as the ptools, or process tools. These utilities are built on the process file system, procfs, located under /proc.

- **pargs(1).** Display process argument list.
- **pflags(1).** Display process flags.
- **pcred(1).** Display process credentials.
- **pldd(1).** Display process shared object library dependencies.
- **psig(1).** Display process signal dispositions.
- **pstack(1).** Display process stack.
- **pmap(1).** Display process address space mappings.
- **pfiles(1).** Display process opened files with names and flags.
- **ptree(1).** Display process family tree.
- **ptime(1).** Time process execution.
- **pwdx(1).** Display process working directory.

Process control is available with various ptools.

- **pgrep(1).** Search for a process name string, and return the PID.
- **pkill(1).** Send a kill signal or specified signal to a process or process list.
- **pstop(1).** Stop a process.
- **prun(1).** Start a process that has been stopped.
- **pwait(1).** Wait for a process to terminate.
- **preap(1).** Reap a zombie (defunct) process.

## 1.1.3 Forensic Tools

Powerful process- and thread-level tracing and debugging facilities included in Solaris 10 and OpenSolaris provide another level of visibility into process- or thread-execution flow and behavior.

- **truss(1).** Trace functions and system calls.
- **mdb(1).** Debug or control processes.
- **dtrace(1M).** Trace, analyze, control, and debug processes.
- **plockstat(1M).** Track user-defined locks in processes and threads.

Several tools enable you to trace, observe, and analyze the kernel and its interaction with applications.

- **dtrace(1M).** Trace, monitor, and observe the kernel.
- **lockstat(1M).** Track kernel locks and profile the kernel.
- **mdb(1)** and **kmdb(1).** Analyze and debug the running kernel, applications, and core files.

Last, specific utilities track hardware-specific counters and provide visibility into low-level processor and system utilization and behavior.

- **cputrack(1).** Track per-processor hardware counters for a process.
- **cpustat(1M).** Track per-processor hardware counters.
- **busstat(1M).** Track interconnect bus hardware counters.

## 1.2 Drill-Down Analysis

To see how these tools may be used together, let us introduce the strategy of *drill-down analysis* (also called drill-down monitoring). This is where we begin examining the entire system and then narrow down to specific areas based on our findings. The following steps describe a drill down analysis strategy.

1. **Monitoring.** Using a system to record statistics over time. This data may reveal long term patterns that may be missed when using the regular stat tools. Monitoring may involve using SunMC, SNMP or sar.

2. **Identification.** For narrowing the investigation to particular resources, and identifying possible bottlenecks. This may include kstat and procfs tools.

3. **Analysis.** For further examination of particular system areas. This may make use of truss, DTrace, and MDB.

Note that there is no one tool to rule them all; while DTrace has the capability for both monitoring and identifying problems, it is best suited for deeper analysis. Identification may be best served by the kstat counters, which are already available and maintained.

It is also important to note that many sites may have critical applications where it may be appropriate to use additional tools. For example, it may not be suitably effective to monitor a critical Web server using ping(1M) alone, instead a tool that simulates client activity while measuring response time and expected content may prove more effective.

## 1.3  About Part One

In this book, we present specific examples of how and when to use the various tools and utilities in order to understand system behavior and identify problems, and we introduce some of our analysis concepts. We do not attempt to provide a comprehensive guide to performance analysis; rather, we describe the various tools and utilities listed previously, provide extensive examples of their use, and explain the data and information produced by the commands.

We use terms like *utilization* and *saturation* to help quantify resource consumption. Utilization measures how busy a resource is and is usually represented as a percentage average over a time interval. Saturation is often a measure of work that has queued waiting for the resource and can be measured as both an average over time and at a particular point in time. For some resources that do not queue, saturation may be synthesized by error counts. Other terms that we use include *throughput* and *hit ratio*, depending on the resource type.

Identifying which terms are appropriate for a resource type helps illustrate their characteristics. For example, we can measure CPU utilization and CPU cache hit ratio. Appropriate terms for each resource discussed are defined.

We've included tools from three primary locations; the reference location for these tools is at `http://www.solarisinternals.com`.

- Tools bundled with Solaris: based on Kstat, `procfs`, DTrace, etc.
- Tools from `solarisinternals.com`: *Memtool* and others.
- Tools from Brendan Gregg: *DTraceToolKit* and *K9Toolkit*.

### 1.3.1  Chapter Layout

The next chapters on performance tools cover the following key topics:

- Chapter 2, "CPUs"
- Chapter 3, "Processes"
- Chapter 4, "Disk Behavior and Analysis"
- Chapter 5, "File Systems"
- Chapter 6, "Memory"

- Chapter 7, "Networks"
- Chapter 8, "Performance Counters"
- Chapter 9, "Kernel Monitoring"

This list can also serve as an overall checklist of possible problem areas to consider. If you have a performance problem and are unsure where to start, it may help to work through these sections one by one.

# CPUs

Key resources to any computer system are the central processing units (CPUs). Many modern systems from Sun boast numerous CPUs or virtual CPUs (which may be cores or hardware threads). The CPUs are shared by applications on the system, according to a policy prescribed by the operating system and scheduler (see Chapter 3 in *Solaris™ Internals*).

If the system becomes CPU resource limited, then application or kernel threads have to wait on a queue to be scheduled on a processor, potentially degrading system performance. The time spent on these queues, the length of these queues and the utilization of the system processor are important metrics for quantifying CPU-related performance bottlenecks. In addition, we can directly measure CPU utilization and wait states in various forms by using DTrace.

## 2.1 Tools for CPU Analysis

A number of different tools analyze CPU activity. The following summarizes both these tools and the topics covered in this section.

- **Utilization.** Overall CPU utilization can be determined from the idle (id) field from vmstat, and the user (us) and system (sy) fields indicate the type of activity. Heavy CPU saturation is more likely to degrade performance than is CPU utilization.

- **Saturation.** The run queue length from `vmstat` (`kthr:r`) can be used as a measure of CPU saturation, as can CPU latency time from `prstat -m`.

- **Load averages.** These numbers, available from both the `uptime` and `prstat` commands, provide 1-, 5-, and 15-minute averages that combine both utilization and saturation measurements. This value can be compared to other servers if divided by the CPU count.

- **History.** `sar` can be activated to record historical CPU activity. This data can identify long-term patterns; it also provides a reference for what CPU activity is "normal."

- **Per-CPU utilization.** `mpstat` lists statistics by CPU, to help identify application scaling issues should CPU utilization be unbalanced.

- **CPU by process.** Commands such as `ps` and `prstat` can be used to identify CPU consumption by process.

- **Microstate accounting.** High-resolution time counters track several states for user threads; `prstat -m` reports the results.

- **DTrace analysis.** DTrace can analyze CPU consumption in depth and can measure events in minute detail.

Table 2.1 summarizes the tools covered in this chapter, cross-references them, and lists the origin of the data that each tool uses.

**Table 2.1** Tools for CPU Analysis

| Tool | Uses | Description | Reference |
|------|------|-------------|-----------|
| vmstat | Kstat | For an initial view of overall CPU behavior | 2.2 and 2.12.1 |
| psrinfo | Kstat | For physical CPU properties | 2.5 |
| uptime | getloadavg() | For the load averages, to gauge recent CPU activity | 2.6 and 2.12.2 |
| sar | Kstat, sadc | For overall CPU behavior, and dispatcher queue statistics; sar also allows historical data collection | 2.7 and 2.12.1 |
| mpstat | Kstat | For per-CPU statistics | 2.9 |
| prstat | procfs | To identify process CPU consumption | 2.10 and 2.11 |
| dtrace | DTrace | For detailed analysis of CPU activity, including scheduling events and dispatcher analysis | 2.13, 2.14, and 2.15 |

## 2.2 vmstat Tool

The vmstat tool provides a glimpse of the system's behavior on one line and is often the first command you run to familiarize yourself with a system. It is useful here because it indicates both CPU utilization and saturation on one line.

```
$ vmstat 5
 kthr      memory            page            disk          faults      cpu
 r b w   swap   free  re  mf pi po fr de sr dd f0 s1 --   in   sy   cs us sy id
 0 0 0 1324808 319448  1   2  2  0  0  0  0  0  0  0  0  403   21   54  0  1 99
 2 0 0 1318528 302696 480  6 371  0  0  0  0 73  0  0  0  550 5971  190 84 16  0
 3 0 0 1318504 299824 597  0 371  0  0  0  0 48  0  0  0  498 8529  163 81 19  0
 2 0 0 1316624 297904  3   0 597  0  0  0  0 91  0  0  0  584 2009  242 84 16  0
 2 0 0 1311008 292288  2   0 485  0  0  0  0 83  0  0  0  569 2357  252 77 23  0
 2 0 0 1308240 289520  2   0 749  0  0  0  0 107 0  0  0  615 2246  290 82 18  0
 2 0 0 1307496 288768  5   0 201  0  0  0  0 58  0  0  0  518 2231  210 79 21  0
...
```

The first line is the summary since boot, followed by samples every five seconds. vmstat reads its statistics from kstat, which maintains CPU utilization statistics for each CPU. The mechanics behind this are discussed in Section 2.12.

Two columns are of greatest interest in this example. On the far right is cpu:id for percent idle, which lets us determine how utilized the CPUs are; and on the far left is kthr:r for the total number of threads on the ready to run queues, which is a measure of CPU saturation.

In this vmstat example, the idle time for the five-second samples was always 0, indicating 100% utilization. Meanwhile, kthr:r was mostly 2 and sustained, indicating a modest saturation for this single CPU server.

vmstat provides other statistics to describe CPU behavior in more detail, as listed in Table 2.2

**Table 2.2** CPU Statistics from the vmstat Command

| Counter | Description |
| --- | --- |
| kthr | |
| r | Total number of runnable threads on the dispatcher queues; used as a measure of CPU saturation |
| faults | |
| in | Number of interrupts per second |
| sy | Number of system calls per second |
| cs | Number of context switches per second, both voluntary and involuntary |

*continues*

**Table 2.2** CPU Statistics from the `vmstat` Command (*continued*)

| Counter | Description |
|---------|-------------|
| **cpu** | |
| us | Percent user time; time the CPUs spent processing user-mode threads |
| sy | Percent system time; time the CPUs spent processing system calls on behalf of user-mode threads, plus the time spent processing kernel threads |
| id | Percent idle; time the CPUs are waiting for runnable threads. This value can be used to determine CPU utilization |

The following sections discuss CPU utilization and saturation in greater detail.

## 2.3  CPU Utilization

You can calculate CPU utilization from `vmstat` by subtracting `id` from 100 or by adding `us` and `sy`. Keep in mind the following points when considering CPU utilization.

- 100% utilized may be fine—it can be the price of doing business.

- When a Solaris system hits 100% CPU utilization, there is no sudden dip in performance; the performance degradation is gradual. Because of this, CPU saturation is often a better indicator of performance issues than is CPU utilization.

- The measurement interval is important: 5% utilization sounds close to idle; however, for a 60-minute sample it may mean 100% utilization for 3 minutes and 0% utilization for 57 minutes. It is useful to have both short- and long-duration measurements.

- An server running at 10% CPU utilization sounds like 90% of the CPU is available for "free," that is, it could be used without affecting the existing application. This isn't quite true. When an application on a server with 10% CPU utilization wants the CPUs, they will almost always be available immediately. On a server with 100% CPU utilization, the same application will find that the CPUs are already busy—and will need to preempt the currently running thread or wait to be scheduled. This can increase latency (which is discussed in more detail in Section 2.11).

## 2.4 CPU Saturation

The `kthr:r` metric from `vmstat` is useful as a measure for CPU saturation. However, since this is the total across all the CPU run queues, divide `kthr:r` by the CPU count for a value that can be compared with other servers.

Any sustained non-zero value is likely to degrade performance. The performance degradation is gradual (unlike the case with memory saturation, where it is rapid).

Interval time is still quite important. It is possible to see CPU saturation (`kthr:r`) while a CPU is idle (`cpu:idl`). To understand how this is possible, either examine the `%runocc` from `sar -q` or measure the run queues more accurately by using DTrace. You may find that the run queue is quite long for a short period of time, followed by idle time. Averaging over the interval gives both a non-zero run queue length and idle time.

## 2.5 `psrinfo` Command

To determine the number of processors in the system and their speed, use the `psrinfo -v` command. In Solaris 10, `-vp` prints additional information.

```
$ psrinfo -vp
The physical processor has 1 virtual processor (0)
  UltraSPARC-III+ (portid 0 impl 0x15 ver 0x23 clock 900 MHz)
The physical processor has 1 virtual processor (1)
  UltraSPARC-III+ (portid 1 impl 0x15 ver 0x23 clock 900 MHz)
```

## 2.6 `uptime` Command

The `uptime` command is a quick way to print the CPU load averages.[1]

```
$ uptime
12:29am  up 274 day(s), 6 hr(s),  7 users,  load average: 2.00, 1.07, 0.46
```

The numbers are the 1-, 5-, and 15-minute load averages. They represent both utilization and saturation of the CPUs. Put simply, a value equal to your CPU

---

1.  w -u prints the same line of output, perhaps not surprising since w is a hard link to uptime.

count usually means 100% utilization; less than your CPU count is proportionally less than 100% utilization; and greater than your CPU count is a measure of saturation. To compare a load average between servers, divide the load average by the CPU count for a consistent metric.

By providing the 1-, 5-, and 15-minute averages, recently increasing or decreasing CPU load can be identified. The previous uptime example demonstrates an increasing profile (2.00, 1.07, 0.46).

The calculation used for the load averages is often described as the average number of runnable and running threads, which is a reasonable description.[2] As an example, if a single CPU server averaged one running thread on the CPU and two on the dispatcher queue, then the load average would be 3.0. A similar load for a 32-CPU server would involve an average of 32 running threads plus 64 on the dispatcher queues, resulting in a load average of 96.0.

A consistent load average higher than your CPU count may cause degraded application performance. CPU saturation is something that Solaris handles very well, so it is possible that a server can run at some level of saturation without a noticeable effect on performance.

The system actually calculates the load averages by summing high-resolution user time, system time, and thread wait time, then processing this total to generate averages with exponential decay. Thread wait time measures CPU latency. The calculation no longer samples the length of the dispatcher queues, as it did with older Solaris. However, the effect of summing thread wait time provides an average that is usually (but not always) similar to averaging queue length anyway. For more details, see Section 2.12.2.

It is important not to become too obsessed with load averages: they condense a complex system into three numbers and should not be used for anything more than an initial approximation of CPU load.

## 2.7 sar Command

The system activity reporter (sar) can provide live statistics or can be activated to record historical CPU statistics. This can be of tremendous value because you may identify long-term patterns that you might have missed when taking a quick look at the system. Also, historical data provides a reference for what is "normal" for your system.

---

2. This was the calculation, but now it has changed (see 2.12.2); the new way often produces values that resemble those of the old way, so the description still has some merit.

## 2.7.1 `sar` Default Output

The following example shows the default output of sar, which is also the -u option
to sar. An interval of 1 second and a count of 5 were specified.

```
$ sar 1 5

SunOS titan 5.11 snv_16 sun4u    02/27/2006

03:20:42    %usr     %sys     %wio     %idle
03:20:43     82       17        0         1
03:20:44     92        8        0         0
03:20:45     91        9        0         0
03:20:46     94        6        0         0
03:20:47     93        7        0         0

Average      91        9        0         0
```

sar has printed the user (%usr), system (%sys), wait I/O (%wio), and idle times
(%idle). User, system, and idle are also printed by the vmstat command and are
defined in 2.2. The following are some additional points.

- **%usr, %sys (user, system).** A commonly expected ratio is 70% usr and 30%
  sys, but this depends on the application. Applications that use I/O heavily,
  for example a busy Web server, can cause a much higher %sys due to a large
  number of system calls. Applications that spend time processing userland
  code, for example, compression tools, can cause a higher %usr. Kernel mode
  services, such as the NFS server, are %sys based.

- **%wio (wait I/O).** This was supposed to be a measurement of the time spent
  waiting for I/O events to complete.[3] The way it was measured was not very
  accurate, resulting in inconsistent values and much confusion. This statistic
  has now been deliberately set to zero in Solaris 10.

- **%idle (idle).** There are different mentalities for percent idle. One is that percent idle equals wasted CPU cycles and should be put to use, especially when
  server consolidation solutions such as Solaris Zones are used. Another is that
  some level of %idle is healthy (anywhere from 20% to 80%) because it leaves
  "head room" for short increases in activity to be dispatched quickly.

---

3. Historically, this metric was useful on uniprocessor systems as a way of indicating how much
time was spent waiting for I/O. In a multiprocessor system it's not possible to make this simple
approximation, which led to a significant amount of confusion (basically, if %wio was non-zero,
then the only useful information that could be gleaned is that at least one thread somewhere was
waiting for I/O. The magnitude of the %wio value is related more to how much time the system is
idle than to waiting for I/O. You can get a more accurate waiting-for-I/O measure by measuring
individual thread, and you can obtain it by using DTrace.

## 2.7.2 `sar -q`

The `-q` option for `sar` provides statistics on the run queues (dispatcher queues).

```
$ sar -q 5 5

SunOS titan 5.11 snv_16 sun4u      02/27/2006

03:38:43 runq-sz %runocc swpq-sz %swpocc
03:38:48    0.0       0    0.0       0
03:38:53    1.0      80    0.0       0
03:38:58    1.6      99    0.0       0
03:39:03    2.4     100    0.0       0
03:39:08    3.4     100    0.0       0

Average     2.2      76    0.0       0
```

There are four fields.

- **runq-sz (run queue size).** Equivalent to the `kthr:r` field from `vmstat`; can be used as a measure of CPU saturation.[4]
- **%runocc (run queue occupancy).** Helps prevent a danger when intervals are used, that is, short bursts of activity can be averaged down to unnoticeable values. The run queue occupancy can identify whether short bursts of run queue activity occurred.[5]
- **swpq-sz (swapped-out queue size).** Number of swapped-out threads. Swapping out threads is a last resort for relieving memory pressure, so this field will be zero unless there was a dire memory shortage.
- **%swpocc (swapped out occupancy).** Percentage of time there were swapped out threads.

## 2.7.3 Capturing Historical Data

To activate `sar` to record statistics in Solaris 10, use `svcadm enable sar`.[6] The defaults are to take a one-second sample every hour plus every twenty minutes during business hours. This should be customized because a one-second sample every hour isn't terribly useful (the man page for `sadc` suggests it should be

---

4. `sar` seems to have a blind spot for a run queue size between 0.0 and 1.0.
5. A value of 99% for short intervals is usually a rounding error. Another error can be due to drifting intervals and measuring the statistic after an extra update; this causes `%runocc` to be reported as over 100% (e.g., 119% for a 5-second interval).
6. Pending bug 6302763; the description contains a workaround.

greater than five seconds). You can change it by placing an interval and a count after the `sa1` lines in the crontab for the sys user (`crontab -e sys`).

## 2.8 Clock Tick Woes

At some point in a discussion on CPU statistics it is obligatory to lament the inaccuracy of a 100 hertz sample: What if each sample coincided with idle time, misrepresenting the state of the server?

Once upon a time, CPU statistics were gathered every clock tick or every hundredth of a second.[7] As CPUs became faster, it became increasingly possible for fleeting activity to occur between clock ticks, and such activity would not be measured correctly. Now we use *microstate accounting*. It uses high-resolution time-stamps to measure CPU statistics for every event, producing extremely accurate statistics. See Section 2.10.3 in *Solaris™ Internals*

If you look through the Solaris source, you will see high-resolution counters just about everywhere. Even code that expects clock tick measurements will often source the high-resolution counters instead. For example:

```
cpu_sys_stats_ks_update(kstat_t *ksp, int rw)
{
...
        csskd->cpu_ticks_idle.value.ui64 =
            NSEC_TO_TICK(csskd->cpu_nsec_idle.value.ui64);
        csskd->cpu_ticks_user.value.ui64 =
            NSEC_TO_TICK(csskd->cpu_nsec_user.value.ui64);
        csskd->cpu_ticks_kernel.value.ui64 =
            NSEC_TO_TICK(csskd->cpu_nsec_kernel.value.ui64),
...
```

*See uts/common/os/cpu.c*

In this code example, `NSEC_TO_TICK` converts from the microstate accounting value (which is in nanoseconds) to a ticks count. For more details on CPU microstate accounting, see Section 2.12.1.

While most counters you see in Solaris are highly accurate, sampling issues remain in a few minor places. In particular, the run queue length as seen from `vmstat` (`kthr:r`) is based on a sample that is taken every second. Running `vmstat` with an interval of 5 prints the average of five samples taken at one-second intervals. The following (somewhat contrived) example demonstrates the problem.

---

7. In fact, once upon a time statistics were gathered every 60th of a second.

```
$ vmstat 2 5
 kthr        memory              page              disk          faults        cpu
 r b w   swap   free  re  mf pi po fr de sr cd s0 -- --   in   sy   cs us sy id
 0 0 23 1132672 198460 34 47 96 2  2  0 15  6  0  0  0  261  392  170  2  1 97
 0 0 45 983768 120944 1075 4141 0 0 0  0  0  0  0  0  0  355 2931  378  7 25 67
 0 0 45 983768 120944 955 3851 0 0 0   0  0  0  0  0  0  342 1871  279  4 22 73
 0 0 45 983768 120944 940 3819 0 0 0   0  0  0  0  0  0  336 1867  280  4 22 73
 0 0 45 983768 120944 816 3561 0 0 0   0  0  0  0  0  0  338 2055  273  5 20 75

$ uptime
  4:50am  up 14 day(s), 23:32,  4 users,  load average: 4.43, 4.31, 4.33
```

For this single CPU server, vmstat reports a run queue length of zero. However, the load averages (which are now based on microstate accounting) suggest considerable load. This was caused by a program that deliberately created numerous short-lived threads every second, such that the one-second run queue sample usually missed the activity.

The runq-sz from sar -q suffers from the same problem, as does %runocc (which for short-interval measurements defeats the purpose of %runocc).

These are all minor issues, and a valid workaround is to use DTrace, with which statistics can be created at any accuracy desired. Demonstrations of this are in Section 2.14.

## 2.9 mpstat Command

The mpstat command summarizes the utilization statistics for each CPU. The following output is an example from a system with 32 CPUs.

```
$ mpstat 1

CPU minf mjf xcal  intr ithr  csw icsw migr smtx  srw syscl  usr sys  wt idl
  0    0   0  279   267  112  106    7    7   85    0   219   85   2   0  13
  1    1   0  102    99    0  177    9   15  119    2   381   72   3   0  26
  2    2   0   75   130    0  238   19   11   98    5   226   70   3   0  28
  3    1   0   94    32    0   39    8    6   95    2   380   81   2   0  17
  4    1   0   70    75    0  128   11    9   96    1   303   66   2   0  32
  5    1   0   88    62    0   99    7   11   89    1   370   74   2   0  24
  6    4   0   78    47    0   85   24    6   67    8   260   86   2   0  12
  7    2   0   73    29    0   45   21    5   57    7   241   85   1   0  14
  8    2   0   94    21    0   17   10    3   73    0   392   86   2   0  12
  9    3   0   64   106    0  198   23   12   85    7   209   66   2   0  32
 10    2   0   23   164    0  331   20   13   85    7    89   17   2   0  81
 11    3   0   31   105    0  200   14   11   63    4   144   33   2   0  66
 12    0   0   47   129    0  260    3    8   86    0   248   33   2   0  65
 13    4   0   76    48    0   90   25    5   77    8   255   75   2   0  24
 14    5   0   39   130    0  275   17    9   83   10   158   36   2   0  62
 15    2   0   67    99    0  183   18    5  101    4   207   72   2   0  25
 16    3   0   79    61    0  103   20    2   89    3   252   83   2   0  15
 17    2   0   17    64    0  123    8    7   38    2    65   18   1   0  81
```

*continues*

| CPU | minf | mjf | xcal | intr | ithr | csw | icsw | migr | smtx | srw | syscl | usr | sys | wt | idl |
|-----|------|-----|------|------|------|-----|------|------|------|-----|-------|-----|-----|----|-----|
| 18 | 4 | 0 | 86 | 22 | 0 | 21 | 21 | 0 | 98 | 4 | 283 | 98 | 2 | 0 | 0 |
| 19 | 1 | 0 | 10 | 75 | 0 | 148 | 9 | 5 | 38 | 1 | 47 | 9 | 3 | 0 | 88 |
| 20 | 1 | 0 | 49 | 108 | 1 | 208 | 4 | 6 | 85 | 0 | 252 | 29 | 2 | 0 | 69 |
| 21 | 5 | 0 | 90 | 46 | 0 | 77 | 29 | 1 | 75 | 8 | 277 | 92 | 2 | 0 | 6 |
| 22 | 2 | 0 | 56 | 98 | 0 | 186 | 15 | 5 | 71 | 3 | 176 | 59 | 2 | 0 | 39 |
| 23 | 5 | 0 | 37 | 156 | 0 | 309 | 19 | 6 | 75 | 4 | 136 | 39 | 2 | 0 | 59 |
| 24 | 0 | 0 | 32 | 51 | 0 | 97 | 2 | 3 | 32 | 1 | 198 | 15 | 1 | 0 | 83 |
| 25 | 8 | 0 | 82 | 56 | 0 | 142 | 13 | 8 | 87 | 13 | 294 | 82 | 2 | 0 | 16 |
| 26 | 2 | 0 | 66 | 40 | 0 | 75 | 12 | 3 | 66 | 2 | 237 | 73 | 2 | 0 | 25 |
| 27 | 6 | 0 | 80 | 33 | 0 | 57 | 21 | 5 | 89 | 3 | 272 | 86 | 2 | 0 | 13 |
| 28 | 1 | 0 | 97 | 35 | 0 | 56 | 7 | 3 | 94 | 2 | 369 | 76 | 2 | 0 | 22 |
| 29 | 4 | 0 | 83 | 44 | 0 | 79 | 27 | 3 | 69 | 7 | 286 | 89 | 2 | 0 | 9 |
| 30 | 1 | 0 | 95 | 41 | 1 | 69 | 8 | 4 | 105 | 1 | 382 | 80 | 2 | 0 | 18 |
| 31 | 5 | 0 | 16 | 31 | 2 | 99 | 5 | 9 | 20 | 15 | 97 | 9 | 1 | 0 | 90 |
| ... | | | | | | | | | | | | | | | |

For each CPU, a set of event counts and utilization statistics are reported. The first output printed is the summary since boot. After vmstat is checked, the mpstat processor utilization metrics are often the next point of call to ascertain how busy the system CPUs are.

Processor utilization is reported by percent user (usr), system (sys), wait I/O (wt) and idle (idl) times, which have the same meanings as the equivalent columns from vmstat (Section 2.2) and sar (Section 2.7). The syscl field provides additional information for understanding why system time was consumed.

- **syscl (system calls).** System calls per second. See Section 2.13 for an example of how to use DTrace to investigate the impact and cause of system call activity.

The scheduling related statistics reported by mpstat are as follows.

- **csw (context switches).** This field is the total of voluntary and involuntary context switches. Voluntary context switches occur when a thread performs a blocking system call, usually one performing I/O when the thread voluntarily sleeps until the I/O event has completed.

- **icsw (number of involuntary context switches).** This field displays the number of threads involuntarily taken off the CPU either through expiration of their quantum or preemption by a higher-priority thread. This number often indicates if there were generally more threads ready to run than physical processors. To analyze further, a DTrace probe, dequeue, fires when context switches are made, as described in Section 2.15.

- **migr (migrations of threads between processors).** This field displays the number of times the OS scheduler moves ready-to-run threads to an idle processor. If possible, the OS tries to keep the threads on the last processor on which it ran. If that processor is busy, the thread migrates. Migrations on traditional CPUs are bad for performance because they cause a thread to pull its working set into cold caches, often at the expense of other threads.

- **`intr` (interrupts).** This field indicates the number of interrupts taken on the CPU. These may be hardware- or software-initiated interrupts. See Section 3.11 in *Solaris™ Internals* for further information.

- **`ithr` (interrupts as threads).** The number of interrupts that are converted to real threads, typically as a result of inbound network packets, blocking for a mutex, or a synchronization event. (High-priority interrupts won't do this, and interrupts without mutex contention typically interrupt the running thread and complete without converting to a full thread). See Section 3.11 in *Solaris™ Internals* for further information.

The locking-related statistics reported by `mpstat` are as follows.

- **`smtx` (kernel mutexes).** This field indicates the number of mutex contention events in the kernel. Mutex contention typically manifests itself first as system time (due to busy spins), which results in high system (`%sys`) time, which don't show in `smtx`. More useful lock statistics are available through `lockstat(1M)` and the DTrace `lockstat` provider (see Section 9.3.5 and Chapter 17 in *Solaris™ Internals*).

- **`srw` (kernel reader/writer mutexes).** This field indicates the number of reader-writer lock contention events in the kernel. Excessive reader/writer lock contention typically results in nonscaling performance and systems that are unable to use all the available CPU resources (symptom is idle time). More useful lock statistics are available with **`lockstat(1M)` and the DTrace lockstat provider**—See Section 9.3.5 and Chapter 17 in *Solaris™ Internals*.

See Chapter 3 in *Solaris™ Internals*, particularly Section 3.8.1, for further information.

## 2.10  Who Is Using the CPU?

The `prstat` command was introduced in Solaris 8 to provide real-time process status in a meaningful way (it resembles `top`, the original freeware tool written by William LeFebvre). `prstat` uses `procfs`, the `/proc` file system, to fetch process details (see `proc(4)`), and the `getloadavg()` syscall to get load averages.

```
$ prstat
   PID USERNAME  SIZE   RSS STATE  PRI NICE      TIME  CPU PROCESS/NLWP
 25639 rmc      1613M   42M cpu22    0   10   0:33:10 3.1% filebench/2
 25655 rmc      1613M   42M cpu23    0   10   0:33:10 3.1% filebench/2
 25659 rmc      1613M   42M cpu30    0   10   0:33:11 3.1% filebench/2
 25644 rmc      1613M   42M cpu14    0   10   0:33:10 3.1% filebench/2
 25658 rmc      1613M   42M cpu16    0   10   0:33:10 3.1% filebench/2
 25636 rmc      1613M   42M cpu21    0   10   0:33:10 3.1% filebench/2
 25646 rmc      1613M   42M cpu15    0   10   0:33:10 3.1% filebench/2
 25661 rmc      1613M   42M cpu8     0   10   0:33:11 3.1% filebench/2
 25652 rmc      1613M   42M cpu20    0   10   0:33:09 3.1% filebench/2
 25647 rmc      1613M   42M cpu0     0   10   0:33:10 3.1% filebench/2
 25641 rmc      1613M   12M cpu27    0   10   0:33:10 3.1% filebench/2
 25656 rmc      1613M   42M cpu7     0   10   0:33:10 3.1% filebench/2
 25634 rmc      1613M   42M cpu11    0   10   0:33:11 3.1% filebench/2
 25637 rmc      1613M   42M cpu17    0   10   0:33:10 3.1% filebench/2
 25643 rmc      1613M   42M cpu12    0   10   0:33:10 3.1% filebench/2
 25648 rmc      1613M   42M cpu1     0   10   0:33:10 3.1% filebench/2
 25640 rmc      1613M   42M cpu26    0   10   0:33:10 3.1% filebench/2
 25651 rmc      1613M   42M cpu31    0   10   0:33:10 3.1% filebench/2
 25654 rmc      1613M   42M cpu29    0   10   0:33:10 3.1% filebench/2
 25650 rmc      1613M   42M cpu5     0   10   0:33:10 3.1% filebench/2
 25653 rmc      1613M   42M cpu10    0   10   0:33:10 3.1% filebench/2
 25638 rmc      1613M   42M cpu18    0   10   0:33:10 3.1% filebench/2
Total: 91 processes, 521 lwps, load averages: 29.06, 28.84, 26.68
```

The default output from the `prstat` command shows one line of output per process, including a value that represents recent CPU utilization. This value is from `pr_pctcpu` in `procfs` and can express CPU utilization before the `prstat` command was executed (see Section 2.12.3).

The system load average indicates the demand and queuing for CPU resources averaged over a 1-, 5-, and 15-minute period. They are the same numbers as printed by the `uptime` command (see Section 2.6). The output in our example shows a load average of 29 on a 32-CPU system. An average load average that exceeds the number of CPUs in the system is a typical sign of an overloaded system.

## 2.11  CPU Run Queue Latency

The microstate accounting system maintains accurate time counters for threads as well as CPUs. Thread-based microstate accounting tracks several meaningful states per thread in addition to user and system time, which include trap time, lock time, sleep time, and latency time. The process statistics tool, prstat, reports the per-thread microstates for user processes.

```
$ prstat -mL
   PID USERNAME  USR  SYS TRP TFL DFL LCK SLP LAT VCX  ICX SCL SIG PROCESS/LWPID
 25644 rmc        98  1.5 0.0 0.0 0.0 0.0 0.0 0.1   0   36 693   0 filebench/2
 25660 rmc        98  1.7 0.1 0.0 0.0 0.0 0.0 0.1   2   44 693   0 filebench/2
 25650 rmc        98  1.4 0.1 0.0 0.0 0.0 0.0 0.1   0   45 699   0 filebench/2
 25655 rmc        98  1.4 0.1 0.0 0.0 0.0 0.0 0.2   0   46 693   0 filebench/2
 25636 rmc        98  1.6 0.1 0.0 0.0 0.0 0.0 0.2   1   50 693   0 filebench/2
 25651 rmc        98  1.6 0.1 0.0 0.0 0.0 0.0 0.2   0   54 693   0 filebench/2
 25656 rmc        98  1.5 0.1 0.0 0.0 0.0 0.0 0.2   0   60 693   0 filebench/2
 25639 rmc        98  1.5 0.1 0.0 0.0 0.0 0.0 0.2   1   61 693   0 filebench/2
 25634 rmc        98  1.3 0.1 0.0 0.0 0.0 0.0 0.4   0   63 693   0 filebench/2
 25654 rmc        98  1.3 0.1 0.0 0.0 0.0 0.0 0.4   0   67 693   0 filebench/2
 25659 rmc        98  1.7 0.1 0.0 0.0 0.0 0.0 0.4   1   68 693   0 filebench/2
 25647 rmc        98  1.5 0.1 0.0 0.0 0.0 0.0 0.4   0   73 693   0 filebench/2
 25648 rmc        98  1.6 0.1 0.0 0.0 0.0 0.0 0.3 0.2   2   48 693   0 filebench/2
 25643 rmc        98  1.6 0.1 0.0 0.0 0.0 0.0 0.0 0.5   0   75 693   0 filebench/2
 25642 rmc        98  1.4 0.1 0.0 0.0 0.0 0.0 0.0 0.5   0   80 693   0 filebench/2
 25638 rmc        98  1.4 0.1 0.0 0.0 0.0 0.0 0.0 0.6   0   76 693   0 filebench/2
 25657 rmc        97  1.8 0.1 0.0 0.0 0.0 0.4 0.3   6   64 693   0 filebench/2
 25646 rmc        97  1.7 0.1 0.0 0.0 0.0 0.0 0.6   6   83 660   0 filebench/2
 25645 rmc        97  1.6 0.1 0.0 0.0 0.0 0.0 0.9   0   55 693   0 filebench/2
 25652 rmc        97  1.7 0.2 0.0 0.0 0.0 0.0 0.9   2  106 693   0 filebench/2
 25658 rmc        97  1.5 0.1 0.0 0.0 0.0 0.0 1.0   0   72 693   0 filebench/2
 25637 rmc        97  1.7 0.1 0.0 0.0 0.0 0.3 0.6   4   95 693   0 filebench/2
Total: 91 processes, 510 lwps, load averages: 28.94, 28.66, 24.39
```

By specifying the -m (show microstates) and -L (show per-thread) options, we can observe the per-thread microstates. These microstates represent a time-based summary broken into percentages for each thread. The columns USR through LAT sum to 100% of the time spent for each thread during the prstat sample. The important microstates for CPU utilization are USR, SYS, and LAT. The USR and SYS columns are the user and system time that this thread spent running on the CPU. The LAT (latency) column is the amount of time spent waiting for CPU. A non-zero number means there was some queuing for CPU resources. This is an extremely useful metric—we can use it to estimate the potential speedup for a thread if more CPU resources are added, assuming no other bottlenecks obstruct the way. In our example, we can see that on average the filebench threads are waiting for CPU about 0.2% of the time, so we can conclude that CPU resources for this system are not constrained.

Another example shows what we would observe when the system is CPU-resource constrained. In this example, we can see that on average each thread is waiting for CPU resource about 80% of the time.

```
$ prstat -mL
   PID USERNAME USR SYS TRP TFL DFL LCK SLP LAT VCX  ICX SCL SIG PROCESS/LWPID
 25765 rmc       22 0.3 0.1 0.0 0.0 0.0 0.0  77   0   42 165   0 filebench/2
 25833 rmc       22 0.3 0.3 0.0 0.0 0.0 0.0  77   0  208 165   0 filebench/2
 25712 rmc       20 0.2 0.1 0.0 0.0 0.0 0.0  80   0   53 132   0 filebench/2
 25758 rmc       20 0.3 0.1 0.0 0.0 0.0 0.0  80   0   84 148   0 filebench/2
 25715 rmc       20 0.3 0.1 0.0 0.0 0.0 0.0  80   0   56 132   0 filebench/2
 25812 rmc       19 0.2 0.1 0.0 0.0 0.0 0.0  81   0   50 132   0 filebench/2
 25874 rmc       19 0.2 0.0 0.0 0.0 0.0 0.0  81   0   22 132   0 filebench/2
 25842 rmc       19 0.2 0.2 0.0 0.0 0.0 0.0  81   1   92 132   0 filebench/2
 25732 rmc       19 0.2 0.1 0.0 0.0 0.0 0.0  81   0   54  99   0 filebench/2
 25714 rmc       18 0.3 0.1 0.0 0.0 0.0 0.0  81   0   84 165   0 filebench/2
 25793 rmc       18 0.3 0.1 0.0 0.0 0.0 0.0  81   0   30 132   0 filebench/2
 25739 rmc       18 0.3 0.3 0.0 0.0 0.0 0.0  81   0  150 115   0 filebench/2
 25849 rmc       18 0.3 0.0 0.0 0.0 0.0 0.0  81   1   19 132   0 filebench/2
 25788 rmc       18 0.2 0.1 0.0 0.0 0.0 0.0  81   0   77  99   0 filebench/2
 25760 rmc       18 0.2 0.0 0.0 0.0 0.0 0.0  82   0   26 132   0 filebench/2
 25748 rmc       18 0.3 0.1 0.0 0.0 0.0 0.0  82   0   58 132   0 filebench/2
 25835 rmc       18 0.3 0.1 0.0 0.0 0.0 0.0  82   0   65 132   0 filebench/2
 25851 rmc       18 0.2 0.1 0.0 0.0 0.0 0.0  82   0   87  99   0 filebench/2
 25811 rmc       18 0.3 0.2 0.0 0.0 0.0 0.0  82   0  129 132   0 filebench/2
 25767 rmc       18 0.2 0.1 0.0 0.0 0.0 0.0  82   1   25 132   0 filebench/2
 25740 rmc       18 0.3 0.2 0.0 0.0 0.0 0.0  82   0  118 132   0 filebench/2
 25770 rmc       18 0.2 0.1 0.0 0.0 0.0 0.0  82   0   68 132   0 filebench/2
Total: 263 processes, 842 lwps, load averages: 201.45, 192.26, 136.16
```

We can further investigate which threads are consuming CPU within each process by directing prstat to examine a specific process.

```
$ prstat -Lm -p 25691
   PID USERNAME USR SYS TRP TFL DFL LCK SLP LAT VCX ICX SCL SIG PROCESS/LWPID
 25691 rmc      17  0.2 0.2 0.0 0.0 0.0 0.0  83   0  74  99   0 filebench/2
 25691 rmc      0.0 0.0 0.0 0.0 0.0 0.0 100 0.0   0   0   0   0 filebench/1
```

The example shows us that thread number two in the target process is using the most CPU, and spending 83% of its time waiting for CPU. We can further look at information about thread number two with the pstack command.

```
$ pstack 25691/2
25691:  shadow -a shadow -i 2 -s ffffffff10000000 -m /var/tmp/fbenchJDailY
----------------- lwp# 2 / thread# 2 --------------------
 000000010001ae90 flowoplib_hog (30d40, ffffffff6518dc60, 30d40, ffffffff37352c88, 1,
2570d) + 68
 00000001000194a4 flowop_start (ffffffff37352c88, 0, 1, 0, 1, 1000000b0) + 108
 ffffffff7e7ccea0 _lwp_start (0, 0, 0, 0, 0, 0)
```

In this example, we've taken a snapshot of the stack of thread number two of our target process. At the time the snapshot was taken, we can see that the function `flowop_start` was calling `flowoplib_hog`. It's sometimes worth taking several snapshots to see if a pattern is exhibited. DTrace can analyze this further.

## 2.12 CPU Statistics Internals

The following is a brief reference for how some of the CPU statistics are maintained by the kernel.

### 2.12.1 usr, sys, idl Times

The percent user, system and idle times printed by `vmstat`, `sar`, and `mpstat` are retrieved from kstat statistics. These statistics are updated by CPU microstate counters, which are kept in each CPU struct as `cpu->cpu_acct[NCMSTATES]`; these measure cumulative time in each CPU microstate as high-resolution time counters (`hrtime_t`). There are three CPU microstates, `CMS_USER`, `CMS_SYSTEM`, and `CMS_IDLE` (there is also a fourth, `CMS_DISABLED`, which isn't used for microstate accounting).

These per CPU microstate counters are incremented by functions such as `new_cpu_mstate()` and `syscall_mstate()` from `uts/common/os/msacct.c`. When the CPU state changes, a timestamp is saved in `cpu->cpu_mstate_start` and the new state is saved in `cpu->cpu_mstate`. When the CPU state changes next, the current time is fetched (`curtime`) so that the elapsed time in that state can be calculated with `curtime - cpu_mstate_start` and then added to the appropriate microstate counter in `cpu_acct[]`.

These microstates are then saved in `kstat` for each CPU as part of the `cpu_sys_stats_ks_data` struct defined in `uts/common/os/cpu.c` and are given the names `cpu_nsec_user`, `cpu_nsec_kernel`, and `cpu_nsec_idle`. Since userland code expects these counters to be in terms of clock ticks, they are rounded down using `NSEC_TO_TICK` (see Section 2.8), and resaved in `kstat` with the names `cpu_ticks_user`, `cpu_ticks_kernel`, and `cpu_ticks_idle`.

Figure 2.1 summarizes the flow of data from the CPU structures to userland tools through `kstat`

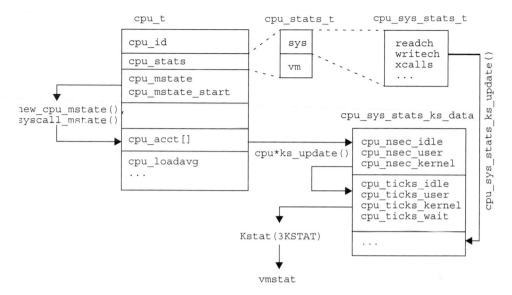

**Figure 2.1** CPU Statistic Data Flow

This is the code from `cpu.c` which copies the `cpu_acct[]` values to `kstat`.

```
static int
cpu_sys_stats_ks_update(kstat_t *ksp, int rw)
{

        css = &cp->cpu_stats.sys;

        bcopy(&cpu_sys_stats_ks_data_template, ksp->ks_data,
            sizeof (cpu_sys_stats_ks_data_template));
        csskd->cpu_ticks_wait.value.ui64 = 0;
        csskd->wait_ticks_io.value.ui64 = 0;
        csskd->cpu_nsec_idle.value.ui64 = cp->cpu_acct[CMS_IDLE];
        csskd->cpu_nsec_user.value.ui64 = cp->cpu_acct[CMS_USER];
        csskd->cpu_nsec_kernel.value.ui64 = cp->cpu_acct[CMS_SYSTEM];
...
```

Note that `cpu_ticks_wait` is set to zero; this is the point in the code where wait I/O has been deprecated.

An older location for tick-based statistics is `cpu->cpu_stats.sys`, which is of `cpu_sys_stats_t`. These are defined in `/usr/include/sys/sysinfo.h`, where original tick counters of the style `cpu_ticks_user` are listed. The remaining statistics from `cpu->cpu_stats.sys` (for example, `readch`, `writech`) are copied directly into kstat's `cpu_sys_stats_ks_data`.

Tools such as vmstat fetch the tick counters from kstat, which provides them under cpu:#:sys: for each CPU. Although these counters use the term "ticks," they are extremely accurate because they are rounded versions of the nsec counters; which are copied from the CPU microstate counters. The mpstat command prints individual CPU statistics (Section 2.9) and the vmstat command aggregates statistics across all CPUs (Section 2.2).

## 2.12.2  Load Averages

The load averages that tools such as uptime print are retrieved using system call getloadavg(), which returns them from the kernel array of signed ints called avenrun[]. They are actually maintained in a high precision uint64_t array called hp_avenrun[], and then converted to avenrun[] to meet the original API. The code that maintains these arrays is in the clock() function from uts/common/os/clock.c, and is run once per second. It involves the following.

The loadavg_update() function is called to add user + system + thread wait (latency) microstate accounting times together. This value is stored in an array within a struct loadavg_s, one of which exists for each CPU, each CPU partition, and for the entire system. These arrays contain the last ten seconds of raw data. Then genloadavg() is called to process both CPU partition and the system wide arrays, and return the average for the last ten seconds. This value is fed to calcloadavg(), which applies exponential decays for the 1-, 5-, 15-minute values, saving the results in hp_avenrun[] or cp_hp_avenrun[] for the CPU partitions. hp_avenrun[] is then converted into avenrun[].

This means that these load averages are damped more than once. First through a rolling ten second average, and then through exponential decays. Apart from the getloadavg() syscall, they are also available from kstat where they are called avenrun_1min, avenrun_5min, avenrun_15min. Running kstat -s avenrun\* prints the raw unprocessed values, which must be divided by FSCALE to produce the final load averages.

## 2.12.3  pr_pctcpu Field

The CPU field that prstat prints is pr_pctcpu, which is fetched by user-level tools from procfs. It is maintained for each thread as thread->t_pctcpu by the cpu_update_pct() function in common/os/msacct.c. This takes a high-resolution timestamp and calculates the elapsed time since the last measurement, which was stored in each thread's t_hrtime. cpu_update_pct() is called by scheduling events, producing an extremely accurate measurement as this is based on events and not ticks. cpu_update_pct() is also called by procfs when a pr_pctcpu value is read, at which point every thread's t_pctcpu is aggregated into pr_pctcpu.

The cpu_update_pct() function processes t_pctcpu as a decayed average by using two other functions: cpu_grow() and cpu_decay(). The way this behaves may be quite familiar: If a CPU-bound process begins, the reported CPU value is not immediately 100%; instead it increases quickly at first and then slows down, gradually reaching 100. The algorithm has the following comment above the cpu_decay() function.

```
/*
 * Given the old percent cpu and a time delta in nanoseconds,
 * return the new decayed percent cpu:  pct * exp(-tau),
 * where 'tau' is the time delta multiplied by a decay factor.
 * We have chosen the decay factor (cpu_decay_factor in param.c)
 * to make the decay over five seconds be approximately 20%.
 *
...
```

This comment explains that the rate of t_pctcpu change should be 20% for every five seconds (and the same for pr_pctcpu).

User-level commands read pr_pctcpu by reading /proc/<pid>/psinfo for each process, which contains pr_pctcpu in a psinfo struct as defined in /usr/include/sys/procfs.h.

## 2.13  Using DTrace to Explain Events from Performance Tools

DTrace can be exploited to attribute the source of events noted in higher-level tools such as mpstat(1M). For example, if we see a significant amount of system time (%sys) and a high system call rate (syscl), then we might want to know who or what is causing those system calls.

```
# mpstat 2
CPU minf mjf xcal  intr ithr  csw icsw migr smtx  srw syscl  usr sys  wt idl
  0  117   0 1583   883  111 1487  593  150 6104   64 11108    7  92   0   1
  1  106   0  557   842    0 1804  694  150 6553   84 10684    6  93   0   1
  2  112   0  664   901    0 1998  795  143 6622   64 11227    6  93   0   1
  3   95   0  770  1035    0 2232  978  131 6549   59 11769    7  92   0   1
^C
# dtrace -n 'syscall:::entry { @[execname] = count(); }'
dtrace: description 'syscall:::entry ' matched 229 probes
^C

  inetd                                                            1
  svc.configd                                                      1
  fmd                                                              2
  snmpdx                                                           2
  utmpd                                                            2
```

*continues*

```
svc.startd                                                   13
sendmail                                                     30
snmpd                                                        36
nscd                                                        105
dtrace                                                     1311
filebench                                              3739725
```

Using the DTrace syscall provider, we can quickly identify which process is causing the most system calls. This `dtrace` one-liner measures system calls by process name. In this example, processes with the name `filebench` caused 3,739,725 system calls during the time the `dtrace` command was running.

We can then drill deeper by matching the syscall probe only when the exec name matches our investigation target, `filebench`, and counting the syscall name.

```
# dtrace -n 'syscall:::entry /execname == "filebench"/ { @[probefunc] = count(); }'
dtrace: description 'syscall:::entry ' matched 229 probes
^C

  lwp_continue                                                4
  lwp_create                                                  4
  mmap                                                        4
  schedctl                                                    4
  setcontext                                                  4
  lwp_sigmask                                                 8
  nanosleep                                                  24
  yield                                                     554
  brk                                                       1590
  pwrite                                                    80795
  lwp_park                                                 161019
  read                                                     324159
  pread                                                    898401
  semsys                                                  1791717
```

Ah, so we can see that the `semsys` syscall is hot in this case. Let's look at what is calling `semsys` by using the `ustack()` DTrace action.

```
# dtrace -n 'syscall::semsys:entry /execname == "filebench"/ { @[ustack()] = count();}'
dtrace: description 'syscall::semsys:entry ' matched 1 probe
^C
              libc.so.1`_syscall6+0x1c
              filebench`flowop_start+0x408
              libc.so.1`_lwp_start
          10793

              libc.so.1`_syscall6+0x1c
              filebench`flowop_start+0x408
              libc.so.1`_lwp_start
          10942

              libc.so.1`_syscall6+0x1c
              filebench`flowop_start+0x408
              libc.so.1`_lwp_start
          11084
```

We can now identify which system call, and then even obtain the hottest stack trace for accesses to that system call. We conclude by observing that the `filebench` `flowop_start` function is performing the majority of `semsys` system calls on the system.

## 2.14 DTrace Versions of `runq-sz`, `%runocc`

Existing tools often provide useful statistics, but not quite in the way that we want. For example, the `sar` command provides measurements for the length of the run queues (`runq-sz`), and a percent run queue occupancy (`%runocc`). These are useful metrics, but since they are sampled only once per second, their accuracy may not be satisfactory. DTrace allows us to revisit these measurements, customizing them to our liking.

**runq-sz**: DTrace can measure run queue length for each CPU and produce a distribution plot.

```
# dtrace -n 'profile-1000hz { @[cpu] = lquantize(      curthread->t_cpu->cpu_disp->disp_
nrunnable, 0, 64, 1); }'
dtrace: description 'profile-1000hz ' matched 1 probe
^C

       0
          value        -------- Distribution ------------- count
           < 0 |                                                0
             0 |@@@@@@@@@@@@@@@@@@@@@@@@@@@@@@@@@@@@@@@@@@        4665
             1 |@@@@                                             489
             2 |                                                 41
             3 |                                                 25
             4 |                                                 4
             5 |                                                 0
```

Rather than sampling once per second, this `dtrace` one-liner[8] samples at 1000 hertz. The example shows a single CPU system with some work queuing on its run queue, but not a great deal. A value of zero means no threads queued (no saturation); however, the CPU may still be processing a user or kernel thread (utilization).

What is actually measured by DTrace is the value of `disp_nrunnable` from the `disp_t` for the current CPU.

---

8. This exists in the DTraceToolkit as `dispqlen.d`.

```
typedef struct _disp {
...
        pri_t           disp_maxrunpri; /* maximum run priority */
        pri_t           disp_max_unbound_pri;    /* max pri of unbound threads */

        volatile int    disp_nrunnable; /* runnable threads in cpu dispq */

        struct cpu      *disp_cpu;       /* cpu owning this queue or NULL */
} disp_t;
                                                    See /usr/include/sys/disp.h
```

**%runocc:** Measuring run queue occupancy is achieved in a similar fashion. disp_nrunnable is also used, but this time just to indicate the presence of queued threads.

```
#!/usr/sbin/dtrace -s
#pragma D option quiet

profile-1000hz
/curthread->t_cpu->cpu_disp->disp_nrunnable/
{
        @qocc[cpu] = count();
}

profile:::tick-1sec
{
        normalize(@qocc, 10);
        printf("\n%8s %8s\n", "CPU", "%runocc");
        printa("%8d %@8d\n", @qocc);
        clear(@qocc);
}
```

This script samples at 1000 hertz and uses a DTrace normalization of 10 to turn the 1000-count into a percentage. We ran this script on a busy 4-CPU server.

```
# ./runocc.d

    CPU   %runocc
      3        39
      1        49
      2        65
      0        97

    CPU   %runocc
      1         2
      3         8
      2        99
      0       100
...
```

Each CPU has an occupied run queue, especially CPU 0.

These examples of sampling activity at 1000 hertz are simple and possibly suffi-ciently accurate (certainly better than the original 1 hertz statistics). While DTrace can *sample* activity, it may be is better suited to *trace* activity, measuring nanosecond timestamps for each event. The sched provider exists to facilitate the tracing of scheduling events. With sched, runq-sz and %runocc can be mea-sured with a much higher accuracy.

## 2.15  DTrace Probes for CPU States

The sched provider makes available probes related to CPU scheduling. Because CPUs are the one resource that all threads must consume, the sched provider is very useful for understanding systemic behavior. For example, using the sched provider, you can understand when and why threads sleep, run, change priority, or wake other threads.

As an example, one common question you might want answered is which CPUs are running threads and for how long. You can use the on-cpu and off-cpu probes to easily answer this question systemwide as shown in the following example.

```
#!/usr/sbin/dtrace -s

sched:::on-cpu
{
        self->ts = timestamp;
}

sched:::off-cpu
/self->ts/
{
        @[cpu] = quantize(timestamp - self->ts);
        self->ts = 0;
}
```

The CPU overhead for the tracing of the probe events is proportional to their frequency. The on-cpu and off-cpu probes occur for each context switch, so the CPU overhead increases as the rate of context switches per second increases. Com-pare this to the previous DTrace scripts that sampled at 1000 hertz—their probe frequency is fixed. Either way, the CPU cost for running these scripts should be negligible.

The following is an example of running this script.

```
# ./where.d
dtrace: script './where.d' matched 5 probes
^C

     0
         value  ------------- Distribution ------------- count
          2048 |                                          0
          4096 |@@                                        37
          8192 |@@@@@@@@@@@@                              212
         16384 |@                                         30
         32768 |                                          10
         65536 |@                                         17
        131072 |                                          12
        262144 |                                          9
        524288 |                                          6
       1048576 |                                          5
       2097152 |                                          1
       4194304 |                                          3
       8388608 |@@@@                                      75
      16777216 |@@@@@@@@@@@                               201
      33554432 |                                          6
      67108864 |                                          0

     1
         value  ------------- Distribution ------------- count
          2048 |                                          0
          4096 |@                                         6
          8192 |@@@@                                      23
         16384 |@@@                                       18
         32768 |@@@@                                      22
         65536 |@@@@                                      22
        131072 |@                                         7
        262144 |                                          5
        524288 |                                          2
       1048576 |                                          3
       2097152 |@                                         9
       4194304 |                                          4
       8388608 |@@@                                       18
      16777216 |@@@                                       19
      33554432 |@@@                                       16
      67108864 |@@@@                                      21
     134217728 |@@                                        14
     268435456 |                                          0
```

The `value` is nanoseconds, and the `count` is the number of occurrences a thread ran for this duration without leaving the CPU. The floating integer above the Distribution plot is the CPU ID.

For CPU 0, a thread ran for between 8 and 16 microseconds on 212 occasions, shown by a small spike in the distribution plot. The other spike was for the 16 to 32 millisecond duration (sounds like TS class quanta—see Chapter 3 in *Solaris™ Internals*), for which threads ran 201 times.

The `sched` provider is discussed in Section 10.6.3.

# 3

# Processes

*Contributions from Denis Sheahan*

**M**onitoring process activity is a routine task during the administration of systems. Fortunately, a large number of tools examine process details, most of which make use of procfs. Many of these tools are suitable for troubleshooting application problems and for analyzing performance.

## 3.1 Tools for Process Analysis

Since there are so many tools for process analysis, it can be helpful to group them into general categories.

- **Overall status tools.** The prstat command immediately provides a by-process indication of CPU and memory consumption. prstat can also fetch microstate accounting details and by-thread details. The original command for listing process status is ps, the output of which can be customized.

- **Control tools.** Various commands, such as pkill, pstop, prun and preap, control the state of a process. These commands can be used to repair application issues, especially runaway processes.

- **Introspection tools.** Numerous commands, such as pstack, pmap, pfiles, and pargs inspect process details. pmap and pfiles examine the memory and file resources of a process; pstack can view the stack backtrace of a process and its threads, providing a glimpse of which functions are currently running.

- **Lock activity examination tools.** Excessive lock activity and contention can be identified with the `plockstat` command and DTrace.
- **Tracing tools.** Tracing system calls and function calls provides the best insight into process behavior. Solaris provides tools including `truss`, `apptrace`, and `dtrace` to trace processes.

Table 3.1 summarizes and cross-references the tools covered in this section.

**Table 3.1**  Tools for Process Analysis

| Tool | Description | Reference |
|------|-------------|-----------|
| `prstat` | For viewing overall process status | 3.2 |
| `ps` | To print process status and information | 3.3 |
| `ptree` | To print a process ancestry tree | 3.4 |
| `pgrep`; `pkill` | To match a process name; to send a signal | 3.4 |
| `pstop`; `prun` | To freeze a process; to continue a process | 3.4 |
| `pwait` | To wait for a process to finish | 3.4 |
| `preap` | To reap zombies | 3.4 |
| `pstack` | For inspecting stack backtraces | 3.5 |
| `pmap` | For viewing memory segment details | 3.5 |
| `pfiles` | For listing file descriptor details | 3.5 |
| `ptime` | For timing a command | 3.5 |
| `psig` | To list signal handlers | 3.5 |
| `pldd` | To list dynamic libraries | 3.5 |
| `pflags`; `pcred` | To list tracing flags; to list process credentials | 3.5 |
| `pargs`; `pwdx` | To list arguments, env; to list working directory | 3.5 |
| `plockstat` | For observing lock activity | 3.6 |
| `truss` | For tracing system calls and signals, and tracing function calls with primitive details | 3.7 |
| `apptrace` | For tracing library calls with processed details | 3.7 |
| `dtrace` | For safely tracing any process activity, with minimal effect on the process and system | 3.7 |

Many of these tools read statistics from the `/proc` file system, `procfs`. See Section 2.10 in *Solaris™ Internals*, which discusses `procfs` from introduction to implementation. Also refer to `/usr/include/sys/procfs.h` and the `proc(4)` man page.

## 3.2 Process Statistics Summary: `prstat`

The process statistics utility, `prstat`, shows us a top-level summary of the processes that are using system resources. The `prstat` utility summarizes this information every 5 seconds by default and reports the statistics for that period.

```
$ prstat
   PID USERNAME  SIZE   RSS STATE   PRI NICE      TIME  CPU PROCESS/NLWP
 25646 rmc      1613M   42M cpu15     0   10   0:33:10 3.1% filebench/2
 25661 rmc      1613M   42M cpu8      0   10   0:33:11 3.1% filebench/2
 25652 rmc      1613M   42M cpu20     0   10   0:33:09 3.1% filebench/2
 25647 rmc      1613M   42M cpu0      0   10   0:33:10 3.1% filebench/2
 25641 rmc      1613M   42M cpu27     0   10   0:33:10 3.1% filebench/2
 25656 rmc      1613M   42M cpu7      0   10   0:33:10 3.1% filebench/2
 25634 rmc      1613M   42M cpu11     0   10   0:33:11 3.1% filebench/2
 25637 rmc      1613M   42M cpu17     0   10   0:33:10 3.1% filebench/2
 25643 rmc      1613M   42M cpu12     0   10   0:33:10 3.1% filebench/2
 25648 rmc      1613M   42M cpu1      0   10   0:33:10 3.1% filebench/2
 25640 rmc      1613M   42M cpu26     0   10   0:33:10 3.1% filebench/2
 25651 rmc      1613M   42M cpu31     0   10   0:33:10 3.1% filebench/2
 25654 rmc      1613M   42M cpu29     0   10   0:33:10 3.1% filebench/2
 25650 rmc      1613M   42M cpu5      0   10   0:33:10 3.1% filebench/2
 25653 rmc      1613M   42M cpu10     0   10   0:33:10 3.1% filebench/2
 25638 rmc      1613M   42M cpu18     0   10   0:33:10 3.1% filebench/2
 25660 rmc      1613M   42M cpu13     0   10   0:33:10 3.1% filebench/2
 25635 rmc      1613M   42M cpu25     0   10   0:33:10 3.1% filebench/2
 25642 rmc      1613M   42M cpu28     0   10   0:33:10 3.1% filebench/2
 25649 rmc      1613M   42M cpu19     0   10   0:33:08 3.1% filebench/2
 25645 rmc      1613M   42M cpu3      0   10   0:33:10 3.1% filebench/2
 25657 rmc      1613M   42M cpu4      0   10   0:33:09 3.1% filebench/2
Total: 91 processes, 521 lwps, load averages: 29.06, 28.84, 26.68
```

The default output for `prstat` shows one line of output per process. Entries are sorted by CPU consumption. The columns are as follows:

- **PID.** The process ID of the process.
- **USERNAME.** The real user (login) name or real user ID.
- **SIZE.** The total virtual memory size of mappings within the process, including all mapped files and devices.
- **RSS.** Resident set size. The amount of physical memory mapped into the process, including that shared with other processes. See Section 6.7.
- **STATE.** The state of the process. See Chapter 3 in *Solaris™ Internals*.
- **PRI.** The priority of the process. Larger numbers mean higher priority. See Section 3.7 in *Solaris™ Internals*.
- **NICE.** Nice value used in priority computation. See Section 3.7 in *Solaris™ Internals*.

- **TIME.** The cumulative execution time for the process, printed in CPU hours, minutes, and seconds.

- **CPU.** The percentage of recent CPU time used by the process.

- **PROCESS/NLWP.** The name of the process (name of executed file) and the number of threads in the process.

## 3.2.1 Thread Summary: `prstat -L`

The `-L` option causes `prstat` to show one thread per line instead of one process per line.

```
$ prstat -L
  PID USERNAME  SIZE    RSS STATE  PRI NICE      TIME  CPU PROCESS/LWPID
25689 rmc      1787M   217M sleep   59    0   0:00:08 0.1% filebench/1
25965 rmc      1785M   214M cpu22   60   10   0:00:00 0.1% filebench/2
26041 rmc      1785M   214M cpu4    60   10   0:00:00 0.0% filebench/2
26016 rmc      1785M   214M sleep   60   10   0:00:00 0.0% filebench/2
    9 root       10M  9648K sleep   59    0   0:00:14 0.0% svc.configd/14
    9 root       10M  9648K sleep   59    0   0:00:26 0.0% svc.configd/12
26174 rmc      5320K  5320K cpu30   59    0   0:00:00 0.0% prstat/1
    9 root       10M  9648K sleep   59    0   0:00:36 0.0% svc.configd/10
    7 root       19M    17M sleep   59    0   0:00:11 0.0% svc.startd/9
   93 root     2600K  1904K sleep   59    0   0:00:00 0.0% syseventd/12
   93 root     2600K  1904K sleep   59    0   0:00:00 0.0% syseventd/11
   93 root     2600K  1904K sleep   59    0   0:00:00 0.0% syseventd/10
   93 root     2600K  1904K sleep   59    0   0:00:00 0.0% syseventd/9
   93 root     2600K  1904K sleep   59    0   0:00:00 0.0% syseventd/8
   93 root     2600K  1904K sleep   59    0   0:00:00 0.0% syseventd/7
   93 root     2600K  1904K sleep   59    0   0:00:00 0.0% syseventd/6
   93 root     2600K  1904K sleep   59    0   0:00:00 0.0% syseventd/5
...
```

The output is similar to the previous example, but the last column is now represented by process name and thread number:

- **PROCESS/LWPID.** The name of the process (name of executed file) and the lwp ID of the lwp being reported.

## 3.2.2 Process Microstates: `prstat -m`

The process microstates can be very useful to help identify why a process or thread is performing suboptimally. By specifying the `-m` (show microstates) and `-L` (show per-thread) options, you can observe the per-thread microstates. The microstates represent a time-based summary broken into percentages of each thread. The columns USR through LAT sum to 100% of the time spent for each thread during the `prstat` sample.

```
$ prstat -mL
   PID USERNAME USR SYS TRP TFL DFL LCK SLP LAT VCX ICX SCL SIG PROCESS/LWPID
 25644 rmc       98 1.5 0.0 0.0 0.0 0.0 0.0 0.1   0  36 693   0 filebench/2
 25660 rmc       98 1.7 0.1 0.0 0.0 0.0 0.0 0.1   2  44 693   0 filebench/2
 25650 rmc       98 1.4 0.1 0.0 0.0 0.0 0.0 0.1   0  45 699   0 filebench/2
 25655 rmc       98 1.4 0.1 0.0 0.0 0.0 0.0 0.2   0  46 693   0 filebench/2
 25636 rmc       98 1.6 0.1 0.0 0.0 0.0 0.0 0.2   1  50 693   0 filebench/2
 25651 rmc       98 1.6 0.1 0.0 0.0 0.0 0.0 0.2   0  54 693   0 filebench/2
 25656 rmc       98 1.5 0.1 0.0 0.0 0.0 0.0 0.2   0  60 693   0 filebench/2
 25639 rmc       98 1.5 0.1 0.0 0.0 0.0 0.0 0.2   1  61 693   0 filebench/2
 25634 rmc       98 1.3 0.1 0.0 0.0 0.0 0.0 0.4   0  63 693   0 filebench/2
 25654 rmc       98 1.3 0.1 0.0 0.0 0.0 0.0 0.4   0  67 693   0 filebench/2
 25659 rmc       98 1.7 0.1 0.0 0.0 0.0 0.0 0.4   1  68 693   0 filebench/2
 25647 rmc       98 1.5 0.1 0.0 0.0 0.0 0.0 0.4   0  73 693   0 filebench/2
 25648 rmc       98 1.6 0.1 0.0 0.0 0.0 0.3 0.2   2  48 693   0 filebench/2
 25643 rmc       98 1.6 0.1 0.0 0.0 0.0 0.0 0.5   0  75 693   0 filebench/2
 25642 rmc       98 1.4 0.1 0.0 0.0 0.0 0.0 0.5   0  80 693   0 filebench/2
 25638 rmc       98 1.4 0.1 0.0 0.0 0.0 0.0 0.6   0  76 693   0 filebench/2
 25657 rmc       97 1.8 0.1 0.0 0.0 0.0 0.4 0.3   6  64 693   0 filebench/2
 25646 rmc       97 1.7 0.1 0.0 0.0 0.0 0.0 0.6   6  83 660   0 filebench/2
 25645 rmc       97 1.6 0.1 0.0 0.0 0.0 0.0 0.9   0  55 693   0 filebench/2
 25652 rmc       97 1.7 0.2 0.0 0.0 0.0 0.0 0.9   2 106 693   0 filebench/2
 25658 rmc       97 1.5 0.1 0.0 0.0 0.0 0.0 1.0   0  72 693   0 filebench/2
 25637 rmc       97 1.7 0.1 0.0 0.0 0.0 0.3 0.6   4  95 693   0 filebench/2
Total: 91 processes, 510 lwps, load averages: 28.94, 28.66, 24 39
```

As discussed in Section 2.11, you can use the USR and SYS states to see what percentage of the elapsed sample interval a process spent on the CPU, and LAT as the percentage of time waiting for CPU. Likewise, you can use the TFL and DTL to determine if and by how much a process is waiting for memory paging—see Section 6.6.1. The remainder of important events such as disk and network waits are bundled into the SLP state, along with other kernel wait events. While SLP column is inclusive of disk I/O, other types of blocking can cause time to be spent in the SLP state. For example, kernel locks or condition variables also accumulate time in this state.

### 3.2.3 Sorting by a Key: `prstat -s`

The output from `prstat` can be sorted by a set of keys, as directed by the `-s` option. For example, if we want to show processes with the largest physical memory usage, we can use `prstat -s rss`.

```
$ prstat -s rss
   PID USERNAME  SIZE    RSS STATE  PRI NICE      TIME  CPU PROCESS/NLWP
 20340 ftp       183M   176M sleep   59    0   0:00:24 0.0% httpd/1
  4024 daemon     11M    10M sleep   59    0   0:00:06 0.0% nfsmapid/19
  2632 daemon     11M  9980K sleep   59    0   0:00:06 0.0% nfsmapid/5
     7 root       10M  9700K sleep   59    0   0:00:05 0.0% svc.startd/14
     9 root     9888K  8880K sleep   59    0   0:00:08 0.0% svc.configd/46
 21091 ftp        13M  8224K sleep   59    0   0:00:00 0.0% httpd/1
   683 root     7996K  7096K sleep   59    0   0:00:07 0.0% svc.configd/16
   680 root     7992K  7096K sleep   59    0   0:00:07 0.0% svc.configd/15
```

*continues*

```
    PID USERNAME  SIZE   RSS STATE  PRI NICE      TIME  CPU PROCESS/NLWP
    671 root     7932K 7068K sleep   59    0   0:00:04 0.0% svc.startd/13
    682 root     7956K 7064K sleep   59    0   0:00:07 0.0% svc.configd/43
    668 root     7924K 7056K sleep   59    0   0:00:03 0.0% svc.startd/13
    669 root     7920K 7056K sleep   59    0   0:00:03 0.0% svc.startd/15
    685 root     7876K 6980K sleep   59    0   0:00:07 0.0% svc.configd/15
    684 root     7824K 6924K sleep   59    0   0:00:07 0.0% svc.configd/16
    670 root     7796K 6924K sleep   59    0   0:00:03 0.0% svc.startd/12
    687 root     7712K 6816K sleep   59    0   0:00:07 0.0% svc.configd/17
    664 root     7668K 6756K sleep   59    0   0:00:03 0.0% svc.startd/12
    681 root     7644K 6752K sleep   59    0   0:00:08 0.0% svc.configd/13
    686 root     7644K 6744K sleep   59    0   0:00:08 0.0% svc.configd/17
    ...
```

The following are valid keys for sorting:

- **cpu.** Sort by process CPU usage. This is the default.
- **pri.** Sort by process priority.
- **rss.** Sort by resident set size.
- **size.** Sort by size of process image.
- **time.** Sort by process execution time.

The -S option sorts by ascending order, rather than descending.

## 3.2.4 User Summary: `prstat -t`

A summary by user ID can be printed with the -t option.

```
$ prstat -t
NPROC USERNAME  SIZE   RSS MEMORY      TIME  CPU
  233 root      797M  477M    48%   0:05:31 0.4%
   50 daemon    143M   95M   9.6%   0:00:12 0.0%
   14 40000     112M   28M   2.8%   0:00:00 0.0%
    2 rmc      9996K 3864K   0.4%   0:00:04 0.0%
    2 ftp       196M  184M    19%   0:00:24 0.0%
    2 50000    4408K 2964K   0.3%   0:00:00 0.0%
   18 nobody    104M   51M   5.2%   0:00:00 0.0%
    8 webservd   48M   21M   2.1%   0:00:00 0.0%
    7 smmsp      47M   10M   1.0%   0:00:00 0.0%
Total: 336 processes, 1201 lwps, load averages: 0.02, 0.01, 0.01
```

## 3.2.5 Project Summary: `prstat -J`

A summary by project ID can be generated with the -J option. This is very useful for summarizing per-project resource utilization. See Chapter 7 in *Solaris™ Internals* for information about using projects.

```
$ prstat -J
    PID USERNAME  SIZE   RSS STATE  PRI NICE     TIME  CPU PROCESS/NLWP
  21130 root     4100K 3264K cpu0    59    0  0:00:00 0.2% prstat/1
  21109 root     7856K 2052K sleep   59    0  0:00:00 0.0% sshd/1
  21111 root     1200K  952K sleep   59    0  0:00:00 0.0% ksh/1
   2632 daemon     11M 9980K sleep   59    0  0:00:06 0.0% nfsmapid/5
    118 root     3372K 2372K sleep   59    0  0:00:06 0.0% nscd/24

 PROJID   NPROC  SIZE   RSS MEMORY     TIME  CPU PROJECT
      3       8   39M   18M   1.8%  0:00:00 0.2% default
      0     323 1387M  841M    85%  0:05:58 0.0% system
     10       3   18M 8108K   0.8%  0:00:04 0.0% group.staff
      1       2   19M 6244K   0.6%  0:00:09 0.0% user.root

Total: 336 processes, 1201 lwps, load averages: 0.02, 0.01, 0.01
```

## 3.2.6 Zone Summary: `prstat -Z`

The -Z option provides a summary per zone. See Chapter 6 in *Solaris™ Internals* for more information about Solaris Zones.

```
$ prstat -Z
    PID USERNAME  SIZE   RSS STATE  PRI NICE     TIME  CPU PROCESS/NLWP
  21132 root     2952K 2692K cpu0    49    0  0:00:00 0.1% prstat/1
  21109 root     7856K 2052K sleep   59    0  0:00:00 0.0% sshd/1
   2179 root     4952K 2480K sleep   59    0  0:00:21 0.0% automountd/3
  21111 root     1200K  952K sleep   49    0  0:00:00 0.0% ksh/1
   2236 root     4852K 2368K sleep   59    0  0:00:06 0.0% automountd/3
   2028 root     4912K 2428K sleep   59    0  0:00:10 0.0% automountd/3
    118 root     3372K 2372K sleep   59    0  0:00:06 0.0% nscd/24

 ZONEID   NPROC  SIZE   RSS MEMORY     TIME  CPU ZONE
      0      47  177M  104M    11%  0:00:31 0.1% global
      5      33  302M  244M    25%  0:01:12 0.0% gallory
      3      40  161M   91M   9.2%  0:00:40 0.0% nakos
      4      43  171M   94M   9.5%  0:00:44 0.0% mcdougallfamily
      2      30   96M   56M   5.6%  0:00:23 0.0% shared
      1      32  113M   60M   6.0%  0:00:45 0.0% packer
      7      43  203M   87M   8.7%  0:00:55 0.0% si
Total: 336 processes, 1202 lwps, load averages: 0.02, 0.01, 0.01
```

## 3.3 Process Status: `ps`

The standard command to list process information is ps, process status. Solaris ships with two versions: /usr/bin/ps, which originated from SVR4; and /usr/ucb/ps, originating from BSD. Sun has enhanced the SVR4 version since its inclusion with Solaris, in particular allowing users to select their own output fields.

### 3.3.1 `/usr/bin/ps` Command

The `/usr/bin/ps` command lists a line for each process.

```
$ ps -ef
    UID    PID   PPID    C     STIME TTY          TIME CMD
   root      0      0    0    Feb 08 ?           0:02 sched
   root      1      0    0    Feb 08 ?           0:15 /sbin/init
   root      2      0    0    Feb 08 ?           0:00 pageout
   root      3      0    1    Feb 08 ?         163:12 fsflush
 daemon    238      1    0    Feb 08 ?           0:00 /usr/lib/nfs/statd
   root      7      1    0    Feb 08 ?           4:58 /lib/svc/bin/svc.startd
   root      9      1    0    Feb 08 ?           1:35 /lib/svc/bin/svc.configd
   root    131      1    0    Feb 08 ?           0:39 /usr/sbin/pfild
 daemon    236      1    0    Feb 08 ?           0:11 /usr/lib/nfs/nfsmapid
...
```

`ps -ef` prints every process (`-e`) with full details (`-f`).
The following fields are printed by `ps -ef`:

- **UID.** The user name for the effective owner UID.
- **PID.** Unique process ID for this process.
- **PPID.** Parent process ID.
- **C.** The man page reads "Processor utilization for scheduling (obsolete)." This value now is recent percent CPU for a thread from the process and is read from `procfs` as `psinfo->pr_lwp->pr_cpu`. If the process is single threaded, this value represents recent percent CPU for the entire process (as with `pr_pctcpu`; see Section 2.12.3). If the process is multithreaded, then the value is from a recently running thread (selected by `prchoose()` from `uts/common/fs/proc/prsubr.c`); in that case, it may be more useful to run `ps` with the `-L` option, to list all threads.
- **STIME.** Start time for the process. This field can contain either one or two words, for example, `03:10:02` or `Feb 15`. This can annoy shell or Perl programmers who expect `ps` to produce a simple whitespace-delimited output. A fix is to use the `-o stime` option, which uses underscores instead of spaces, for example, `Feb_15`; or perhaps a better way is to write a C program and read the `procfs` structs directly.
- **TTY.** The controlling terminal for the process. This value is retrieved from `procfs` as `psinfo->pr_ttydev`. If the process was not created from a terminal, such as with daemons, `pr_ttydev` is set to `PRNODEV` and the `ps` command prints "?". If `pr_ttydev` is set to a device that `ps` does not understand, `ps` prints "??". This can happen when `pr_ttydev` is a `ptm` device (pseudo tty-master), such as with `dtterm` console windows.

- **TIME.** CPU-consumed time for the process. The units are in minutes and seconds of CPU runtime and originate from microstate accounting (user + system time). A large value here (more than several minutes) means either that the process has been running for a long time (check STIME) or that the process is hogging the CPU, possibly due to an application fault.

- **CMD.** The command that created the process and arguments, up to a width of 80 characters. It is read from procfs as psinfo->pr_psargs, and the width is defined in /usr/include/sys/procfs.h as PRARGSZ. The full command line does still exist in memory; this is just the truncated view that procfs provides.

For reference, Table 3.2 lists useful options for /usr/bin/ps.

**Table 3.2** Useful /usr/bin/ps Options

| Option | Description |
| --- | --- |
| -c | Print scheduling class and priority. |
| -e | List every process. |
| -f | Print full details; this is a standard selection of columns. |
| -l | Print long details, a different selection of columns. |
| -L | Print details by lightweight process (LWP). |
| -o format | Customize output fields. |
| -p proclist | Only examine these PIDs. |
| -u uidlist | Only examine processes owned by these user names or UIDs. |
| -z | Print zone name. |

Many of these options are straightforward. Perhaps the most interesting is -o, with which you can customize the output by selecting which fields to print. A quick list of the selectable fields is printed as part of the usage message.

```
$ ps -o
ps: option requires an argument -- o
usage: ps [ -aAdeflcjLPyZ ] [ -o format ] [ -t termlist ]
        [ -u userlist ] [ -U userlist ] [ -G grouplist ]
        [ -p proclist ] [ -g pgrplist ] [ -s sidlist ] [ -z zonelist ]
  'format' is one or more of:
        user ruser group rgroup uid ruid gid rgid pid ppid pgid sid taskid ctid
        pri opri pcpu pmem vsz rss osz nice class time etime stime zone zoneid
        f s c lwp nlwp psr tty addr wchan fname comm args projid project pset
```

The following example demonstrates the use of -o to produce an output similar to /usr/ucb/ps aux, along with an extra field for the number of threads (NLWP).

```
$ ps -eo user,pid,pcpu,pmem,vsz,rss,tty,s,stime,time,nlwp,comm
   USER   PID %CPU %MEM  VSZ  RSS TT    S    STIME       TIME NLWP COMMAND
   root     0  0.0  0.0    0    0 ?     T    Feb_08     00:02    1 sched
   root     1  0.0  0.1 2384  408 ?     S    Feb_08     00:15    1 /sbin/init
   root     2  0.0  0.0    0    0 ?     S    Feb_08     00:00    1 pageout
   root     3  0.4  0.0    0    0 ?     S    Feb_08  02:45:59    1 fsflush
 daemon   238  0.0  0.0 2672    8 ?     S    Feb_08     00:00    1 /usr/lib/nfs/statd
...
```

A brief description for each of the selectable fields is in the man page for ps. The following extra fields were selected in this example:

- **%CPU.** Percentage of recent CPU usage. This is based on pr_pctcpu, See Section 2.12.3.

- **%MEM.** Ratio of RSS over the total number of usable pages in the system (total_pages). Since RSS is an approximation that includes shared memory, this percentage is also an approximation and may overcount memory. It is possible for the %MEM column to sum to over 100%.

- **VSZ.** Total virtual memory size for the mappings within the process, including all mapped files and devices, in kilobytes.

- **RSS.** Approximation for the physical memory used by the process, in kilobytes. See Section 6.7.

- **S.** State of the process: on a processor (O), on a run queue (R), sleeping (S), zombie (Z), or being traced (T).

- **NLWP.** Number of lightweight processes associated with this process; since Solaris 9 this equals the number of user threads.

The -o option also allows the headers to be set (for example, -o user=USERNAME).

## 3.3.2 /usr/ucb/ps

This version of ps is often used with the following options.

```
$ /usr/ucb/ps aux
USER       PID %CPU %MEM   SZ  RSS TT      S   START  TIME COMMAND
root         3  0.5  0.0    0    0 ?       S   Feb 08 166:25 fsflush
root     15861  0.3  0.2 1352  920 pts/3   O 12:47:16  0:00 /usr/ucb/ps aux
root     15862  0.2  0.2 1432 1048 pts/3   S 12:47:16  0:00 more
root      5805  0.1  0.3 2992 1504 pts/3   S   Feb 16  0:03 bash
root         7  0.0  0.5 7984 2472 ?       S   Feb 08  5:03 /lib/svc/bin/svc.s
root       542  0.0  0.1 7328  176 ?       S   Feb 08  4:25 /usr/apache/bin/ht
root         1  0.0  0.1 2384  408 ?       S   Feb 08  0:15 /sbin/init
...
```

Here we listed all processes (a), printed user-focused output (u), and included processes with no controlling terminal (x). Many of the columns print the same details (and read the same `procfs` values) as discussed in Section 3.3.1. There are a few key differences in the way this `ps` behaves:

- The output is sorted on `%CPU`, with the highest `%CPU` process at the top.
- The COMMAND field is truncated so that the output fits in the terminal window. Using `ps auxw` prints a wider output, truncated to a maximum of 132 characters. Using `ps auxww` prints the full command-line arguments with no truncation (something that `/usr/bin/ps` cannot do). This is fetched, if permissions allow, from `/proc/<pid>/as`.
- If the values in the columns are large enough they can collide. For example:

```
$ /usr/ucb/ps aux
USER       PID %CPU %MEM    3%  RES TT       S    START  TIME COMMAND
user1     3132  5.2  4.33132422084 pts/4     S    Feb 16 132:26 Xvnc :1 -desktop X
user1     3153  1.2  2.93544414648 ?         R    Feb 16 21:45 gnome-terminal --s
user1    16865  1.0 10.87992055464 pts/18    S    Mar 02 42:46 /usr/sfw/bin/../li
user1     3145  0.9  1.422216 7240 ?         S    Feb 16 17:37 metacity --sm-save
user1     3143  0.5  0.3 7988 1568 ?         S    Feb 16 12:09 gnome-smproxy --sm
user1     3159  0.4  1.425064 6996 ?         S    Feb 16 11:01 /usr/lib/wnck-appl
...
```

This can make both reading and postprocessing the values quite difficult.

## 3.4 Tools for Listing and Controlling Processes

Solaris provides a set of tools for listing and controlling processes. The general syntax is as follows:

```
$ ptool pid
$ ptool pid/lwpid
```

The following is a summary for each. Refer to the man pages for additional details.

### 3.4.1 Process Tree: `ptree`

The process parent-child relationship can be displayed with the `ptree` command. By default, all processes within the same process group ID are displayed. See

Section 2.12 in *Solaris™ Internals* for information about how processes are grouped in Solaris.

```
$ ptree 22961
301   /usr/lib/ssh/sshd
  21571 /usr/lib/ssh/sshd
    21578 /usr/lib/ssh/sshd
      21580 -ksh
        22961 /opt/filebench/bin/filebench
          22962 shadow -a shadow -i 1 -s ffffffff10000000 -m /var/tmp/fbench9Ca
          22963 shadow -a shadow -i 2 -s ffffffff10000000 -m /var/tmp/fbench9Ca
          22964 shadow -a shadow -i 3 -s ffffffff10000000 -m /var/tmp/fbench9Ca
          22965 shadow -a shadow -i 4 -s ffffffff10000000 -m /var/tmp/fbench9Ca
...
```

## 3.4.2 Grepping for Processes: `pgrep`

The `pgrep` command provides a convenient way to produce a process ID list matching certain criteria.

```
$ pgrep filebench
22968
22961
22966
22979
...
```

The search term will do partial matching, which can be disabled with the `-x` option (exact match). The `-l` option lists matched process names.

## 3.4.3 Killing Processes: `pkill`

The `pkill` command provides a convenient way to send signals to a list or processes matching certain criteria.

```
$ pkill -HUP in.named
```

If the signal is not specified, the default is to send a SIGTERM.

Typing `pkill d` by accident as root may have a disastrous effect; it will match every process containing a "d" (which is usually quite a lot) and send them all a SIGTERM. Due to the way `pkill` doesn't use `getopt()` for the signal, aliasing isn't perfect; and writing a shell function is nontrivial.

### 3.4.4 Temporarily Stop a Process: `pstop`

A process can be temporarily suspended with the `pstop` command.

```
$ pstop 22961
```

### 3.4.5 Making a Process Runnable: `prun`

A process can be made runnable with the `prun` command.

```
$ prun 22961
```

### 3.4.6 Wait for Process Completion: `pwait`

The `pwait` command blocks and waits for termination of a process.

```
$ pwait 22961
(sleep...)
```

### 3.4.7 Reap a Zombie Process: `preap`

A zombie process can be reaped with the `preap` command, which was added in
Solaris 9.

```
$ preap 22961
(sleep...)
```

## 3.5 Process Introspection Commands

Solaris provides a set of utilities for inspecting the state of processes. Most of the
introspection tools can be used either on a running process or postmortem on a
core file resulting from a process dump. The general syntax is as follows:

```
$ ptool pid
$ ptool pid/lwpid
$ ptool core
```

See the man pages for each of these tools for additional details.

## 3.5.1 Process Stack: `pstack`

The stacks of all or specific threads within a process can be displayed with the `pstack` command.

```
$ pstack 23154
23154:  shadow -a shadow -i 193 -s ffffffff10000000 -m /var/tmp/fbench9Cai2S
----------------- lwp# 1 / thread# 1 --------------------
 ffffffff7e7ce0f4 lwp_wait (2, ffffffff7fffe9cc)
 ffffffff7e7c9528 _thrp_join (2, 0, 0, 1, 100000000, ffffffff7fffe9cc) + 38
 0000000100018300 threadflow_init (ffffffff3722f1b0, ffffffff10000000, 10006a658, 0, 0,
1000888b0) + 184
 00000001000172f8 procflow_exec (6a000, 10006a000, 0, 6a000, 5, ffffffff3722f1b0) + 15c
 0000000100026558 main (a3400, ffffffff7ffff948, ffffffff7fffeff8, a4000, 0, 1) + 414
 000000010001585c _start (0, 0, 0, 0, 0, 0) + 17c
----------------- lwp# 2 / thread# 2 --------------------
 000000010001ae90 flowoplib_hog (30d40, ffffffff651f3650, 30d40, ffffffff373aa3b8, 1,
2e906) + 68
 00000001000194a4 flowop_start (ffffffff373aa3b8, 0, 1, 0, 1, 1000888b0) + 408
 ffffffff7e7ccea0 _lwp_start (0, 0, 0, 0, 0, 0)
```

The `pstack` command can be very useful for diagnosing process hangs or the status of core dumps. By default it shows a stack backtrace for all the threads within a process. It can also be used as a crude performance analysis technique; by taking a few samples of the process stack, you can often determine where the process is spending most of its time.

You can also dump a specific thread's stacks by supplying the lwpid on the command line.

```
sol8$ pstack 26258/2
26258:  shadow -a shadow -i 62 -s ffffffff10000000 -m /var/tmp/fbenchI4aGkZ
----------------- lwp# 2 / thread# 2 --------------------
 ffffffff7e7ce138 lwp_mutex_timedlock (ffffffff10000060, 0)
 ffffffff7e7c4e8c mutex_lock_internal (ffffffff10000060, 0, 0, 1000, ffffffff7e8eef80,
ffffffff7f402400) + 248
 000000010001da3c ipc_mutex_lock (ffffffff10000060, 1000888b0, 100088800, 88800,
100000000, 1) + 4
 0000000100019d94 flowop_find (ffffffff651e2278, 100088800, ffffffff651e2180, 88800,
100000000, 1) + 34
 000000010001b990 flowoplib_sempost (ffffffff3739a768, ffffffff651e2180, 0, 6ac00, 1,
1) + 4c
 00000001000194a4 flowop_start (ffffffff3739a768, 0, 1, 0, 1, 1000888b0) + 408
 ffffffff7e7ccea0 _lwp_start (0, 0, 0, 0, 0, 0)
```

## 3.5.2 Process Memory Map: `pmap -x`

The `pmap` command inspects a process, displaying every mapping within the process's address space. The amount of resident, nonshared anonymous, and locked memory is shown for each mapping. This allows you to estimate shared and private memory usage.

```
sol9$ pmap -x 102908
102908:   sh
Address    Kbytes Resident   Anon  Locked Mode   Mapped File
00010000       88       88      -       - r-x--  sh
00036000        8        8      8       - rwx--  sh
00038000       16       16     16       - rwx--   [ heap ]
FF260000       16       16      -       - r-x--  en_.so.2
FF272000       16       16      -       - rwx--  en_US.so.2
FF280000      664      624      -       - r-x--  libc.so.1
FF336000       32       32      8       - rwx--  libc.so.1
FF360000       16       16      -       - r-x--  libc_psr.so.1
FF380000       24       24      -       - r-x--  libgen.so.1
FF396000        8        8      -       - rwx--  libgen.so.1
FF3A0000        8        8      -       - r-x--  libdl.so.1
FF3B0000        8        8      8       - rwx--   [ anon ]
FF3C0000      152      152      -       - r-x--  ld.so.1
FF3F6000        8        8      8       - rwx--  ld.so.1
FFBFE000        8        8      8       - rw---   [ stack ]
--------  ------  ------  ------  ------
total Kb     1072     1032     56       -
```

This example shows the address space of a Bourne shell, with the executable at the top and the stack at the bottom. The total `Resident` memory is 1032 Kbytes, which is an approximation of physical memory usage. Much of this memory will be shared by other processes mapping the same files. The total `Anon` memory is 56 Kbytes, which is an indication of the private memory for this process instance.

You can find more information on interpreting `pmap -x` output in Section 6.8.

### 3.5.3 Process File Table: `pfiles`

A list of files open within a process can be obtained with the `pfiles` command.

```
sol10# pfiles 21571
21571:  /usr/lib/ssh/sshd
  Current rlimit: 256 file descriptors
   0: S_IFCHR mode:0666 dev:286,0 ino:6815752 uid:0 gid:3 rdev:13,2
      O_RDWR|O_LARGEFILE
      /devices/pseudo/mm@0:null
   1: S_IFCHR mode:0666 dev:286,0 ino:6815752 uid:0 gid:3 rdev:13,2
      O_RDWR|O_LARGEFILE
      /devices/pseudo/mm@0:null
   2: S_IFCHR mode:0666 dev:286,0 ino:6815752 uid:0 gid:3 rdev:13,2
      O_RDWR|O_LARGEFILE
      /devices/pseudo/mm@0:null
   3: S_IFCHR mode:0000 dev:286,0 ino:38639 uid:0 gid:0 rdev:215,2
      O_RDWR FD_CLOEXEC
      /devices/pseudo/crypto@0:crypto
   4: S_IFIFO mode:0000 dev:294,0 ino:13099 uid:0 gid:0 size:0
      O_RDWR|O_NONBLOCK FD_CLOEXEC
   5: S_IFDOOR mode:0444 dev:295,0 ino:62 uid:0 gid:0 size:0
      O_RDONLY|O_LARGEFILE FD_CLOEXEC  door to nscd[89]
      /var/run/name_service_door
   6: S_IFIFO mode:0000 dev:294,0 ino:13098 uid:0 gid:0 size:0
      O_RDWR|O_NONBLOCK FD_CLOEXEC
```

*continues*

```
   7:  S_IFDOOR mode:0644 dev:295,0 ino:55 uid:0 gid:0 size:0
       O_RDONLY FD_CLOEXEC  door to keyserv[169]
       /var/run/rpc_door/rpc_100029.1
   8:  S_IFCHR mode:0000 dev:286,0 ino:26793 uid:0 gid:0 rdev:41,134
       O_RDWR FD_CLOEXEC
       /devices/pseudo/udp@0:udp
   9:  S_IFSOCK mode:0666 dev:292,0 ino:31268 uid:0 gid:0 size:0
       O_RDWR|O_NONBLOCK
         SOCK_STREAM
         SO_REUSEADDR,SO_KEEPALIVE,SO_SNDBUF(49152),SO_RCVBUF(49640)
         sockname: AF_INET6 ::ffff:129.146.238.66  port: 22
         peername: AF_INET6 ::ffff:129.146.206.91  port: 63374
  10:  S_IFIFO mode:0000 dev:294,0 ino:13098 uid:0 gid:0 size:0
       O_RDWR|O_NONBLOCK
  11:  S_IFIFO mode:0000 dev:294,0 ino:13099 uid:0 gid:0 size:0
       O_RDWR|O_NONBLOCK FD_CLOEXEC
```

The Solaris 10 version of `pfiles` prints path names if possible.

## 3.5.4 Execution Time Statistics for a Process: `ptime`

A process can be timed with the `ptime` command for accurate microstate accounting instrumentation.[1]

```
$ ptime sleep 1

real        1.203
user        0.022
sys         0.140
```

## 3.5.5 Process Signal Disposition: `psig`

A list of the signals and their current disposition can be displayed with `psig`.

```
sol8$ psig $$
15481:        -zsh
HUP           caught    0
INT           blocked,caught    0
QUIT          blocked,ignored
ILL           blocked,default
TRAP          blocked,default
ABRT          blocked,default
EMT           blocked,default
FPE           blocked,default
KILL          default
BUS           blocked,default
SEGV          blocked,default
SYS           blocked,default
```

*continues*

---

1.  Most other time commands now source the same microstate-accounting-based times.

```
PIPE             blocked,default
ALRM             blocked,caught    0
TERM             blocked,ignored
USR1             blocked,default
USR2             blocked,default
CLD              caught    0
PWR              blocked,default
WINCH            blocked,caught    0
URG              blocked,default
POLL             blocked,default
STOP             default
```

### 3.5.6 Process Libraries: `pldd`

A list of the libraries currently mapped into a process can be displayed with `pldd`. This is useful for verifying which version or path of a library is being dynamically linked into a process.

```
sol8$ pldd $$
482764: -ksh
/usr/lib/libsocket.so.1
/usr/lib/libnsl.so.1
/usr/lib/libc.so.1
/usr/lib/libdl.so.1
/usr/lib/libmp.so.2
```

### 3.5.7 Process Flags: `pflags`

The `pflags` command shows a variety of status information for a process. Information includes the mode—32-bit or 64-bit—in which the process is running and the current state for each thread within the process (see Section 3.1 in *Solaris™ Internals* for information on thread state). In addition, the top-level function on each thread's stack is displayed.

```
sol8$ pflags $$
482764: -ksh
        data model = _ILP32  flags = PR_ORPHAN
   /1:          flags = PR_PCINVAL|PR_ASLEEP [ waitid(0x7,0x0,0xffbff938,0x7) ]
```

### 3.5.8 Process Credentials: `pcred`

The credentials for a process can be displayed with `pcred`.

```
sol8$ pcred $$
482764: e/r/suid=36413  e/r/sgid=10
        groups: 10 10512 570
```

### 3.5.9 Process Arguments: `pargs`

The full process arguments and optionally a list of the current environment settings can be displayed for a process with the `pargs` command.

```
$ pargs -ae 22961
22961:  /opt/filebench/bin/filebench
argv[0]: /opt/filebench/bin/filebench

envp[0]: _=/opt/filebench/bin/filebench
envp[1]: MANPATH=/usr/man:/usr/dt/man:/usr/local/man:/opt/SUNWspro/man:/ws/on998-
tools/teamware/man:/home/rmc/local/man
envp[2]: VISUAL=/bin/vi
...
```

### 3.5.10 Process Working Directory: `pwdx`

The current working directory of a process can be displayed with the `pwdx` command.

```
$ pwdx  22961
22961:  /tmp/filebench
```

## 3.6  Examining User-Level Locks in a Process

With the process lock statistics command, `plockstat(1M)`, you can observe hot lock behavior in user applications that use user-level locks. The `plockstat` command uses DTrace to instrument and measure lock statistics.

```
# plockstat -p 27088
^C
Mutex block

Count     nsec Lock                      Caller
-------------------------------------------------------------------------------
  102 39461866 libaio.so.1`__aio_mutex    libaio.so.1`_aio_lock+0x28
    4 21605652 libaio.so.1`__aio_mutex    libaio.so.1`_aio_lock+0x28
   11 19908101 libaio.so.1`__aio_mutex    libaio.so.1`_aio_lock+0x28
   12 16107603 libaio.so.1`__aio_mutex    libaio.so.1`_aio_lock+0x28
   10  9000198 libaio.so.1`__aio_mutex    libaio.so.1`_aio_lock+0x28
   14  5833887 libaio.so.1`__aio_mutex    libaio.so.1`_aio_lock+0x28
   10  5366750 libaio.so.1`__aio_mutex    libaio.so.1`_aio_lock+0x28
  120   964911 libaio.so.1`__aio_mutex    libaio.so.1`_aio_lock+0x28
   48   713877 libaio.so.1`__aio_mutex    libaio.so.1`_aio_lock+0x28
   52   575273 libaio.so.1`__aio_mutex    libaio.so.1`_aio_lock+0x28
   89   534127 libaio.so.1`__aio_mutex    libaio.so.1`_aio_lock+0x28
   14   427750 libaio.so.1`__aio_mutex    libaio.so.1`_aio_lock+0x28
    1   348476 libaio.so.1`__aio_mutex    libaio.so.1`_aio_req_add+0x228
```

*continues*

```
Mutex spin

Count    nsec Lock                        Caller
----------------------------------  ---------------------------------------
    1 375967836 0x1000bab58              libaio.so.1`_aio_req_add+0x110
  427    817144 libaio.so.1`__aio_mutex  libaio.so.1`_aio_lock+0x28
   18    272192 libaio.so.1`__aio_mutex  libaio.so.1`_aio_lock+0x28
  176    212839 libaio.so.1`__aio_mutex  libaio.so.1`_aio_lock+0x28
   36    203057 libaio.so.1`__aio_mutex  libaio.so.1`_aio_lock+0x28
   41    197392 libaio.so.1`__aio_mutex  libaio.so.1`_aio_lock+0x28
    3    100364 libaio.so.1`__aio_mutex  libaio.so.1`_aio_lock+0x28

Mutex unsuccessful spin

Count    nsec Lock                        Caller
------------------------------------------------------------------------
  222    323249 libaio.so.1`__aio_mutex  libaio.so.1`_aio_lock+0x28
   60    301223 libaio.so.1`__aio_mutex  libaio.so.1`_aio_lock+0x28
   24    295308 libaio.so.1`__aio_mutex  libaio.so.1`_aio_lock+0x28
   56    286114 libaio.so.1`__aio_mutex  libaio.so.1`_aio_lock+0x28
   99    282302 libaio.so.1`__aio_mutex  libaio.so.1`_aio_lock+0x28
   25    278939 libaio.so.1`__aio_mutex  libaio.so.1`_aio_lock+0x28
    1    241628 libaio.so.1`__aio_mutex  libaio.so.1`_aio_req_add+0x228
```

Solaris has two main types of user-level locks:

- **Mutex lock.** An exclusive lock. Only one person can hold the lock. A mutex lock attempts to spin (busy spin in a loop) while trying obtain the lock if the holder is running on a CPU, or blocks if the holder is not running or after trying to spin for a predetermined period.
- **Reader/Writer Lock.** A shared reader lock. Only one person can hold the write lock, but many people could hold a reader lock while there are no writers.

The statistics show the different types of locks and information about contention for each. In this example, we can see mutex-block, mutex-spin, and mutex-unsuccessful-spin. For each type of lock we can see the following:

- **Count.** The number of contention events for this lock
- **nsec.** The average amount of time for which the contention event occurred
- **Lock.** The address or symbol name of the lock object
- **Caller.** The library and function of the calling function

## 3.7 Tracing Processes

Several tools in Solaris can be used to trace the execution of a process, most notably `truss` and DTrace.

## 3.7.1 Using `truss` to Trace Processes

By default, `truss` traces system calls made on behalf of a process. It uses the `/proc` interface to start and stop the process, recording and reporting information on each traced event.

This intrusive behavior of `truss` may slow a target process down to less than half its usual speed. This may not be acceptable for the analysis of live production applications. Also, when the timing of a process changes, race-condition faults can either be relieved or created. Having the fault vanish during analysis is both annoying and ironic.[2] Worse is when the problem gains new complexities.[3]

`truss` was first written as a clever use of `/proc`, writing control messages to `/proc/<pid>/ctl` to manipulate execution flow for debugging. It has since been enhanced to trace LWPs and user-level functions. Over the years it has been an indispensable tool, and there has been no better way to get at this information.

DTrace now exists and can get similar information more safely. However `truss` will still be valuable for many situations. When you use `truss` for troubleshooting commands, speed is hardly an issue; of more interest are the system calls that failed and why. `truss` also provides many translations from flags into codes, allowing many system calls to be easily understood.

In the following example, we trace the system calls for a specified process ID. The trace includes the user LWP (thread) number, system call name, arguments and return codes for each system call.

```
$ truss -p 26274
/1:     lwp_wait(2, 0xFFFFFFFF7FFFEA4C) (sleeping...)
/2:     pread(11, "\0\0\002\0\0\001\0\0\0\0".., 504, 0) = 504
/2:     pread(11, "\0\0\002\0\0\001\0\0\0\0".., 504, 0) = 504
/2:     semget(16897864, 128, 0)                = 8
/2:     semtimedop(8, 0xFFFFFFFF7DEFBDF4, 2, 0xFFFFFFFF7DEFBDE0) = 0
/2:     pread(11, "\0\0\002\0\0\001\0\0\0\0".., 504, 0) = 504
/2:     pread(11, "\0\0\002\0\0\001\0\0\0\0".., 504, 0) = 504
/2:     semget(16897864, 128, 0)                = 8
/2:     semtimedop(8, 0xFFFFFFFF7DEFBDF4, 2, 0xFFFFFFFF7DEFBDE0) = 0
/2:     semget(16897864, 128, 0)                = 8
/2:     semtimedop(8, 0xFFFFFFFF7DEFBDF4, 2, 0xFFFFFFFF7DEFBDE0) = 0
/2:     semget(16897864, 128, 0)                = 8
/2:     semtimedop(8, 0xFFFFFFFF7DEFBDF4, 2, 0xFFFFFFFF7DEFBDE0) = 0
/2:     semget(16897864, 128, 0)                = 8
/2:     semtimedop(8, 0xFFFFFFFF7DEFBDF4, 2, 0xFFFFFFFF7DEFBDE0) = 0
/2:     semget(16897864, 128, 0)                = 8
/2:     semtimedop(8, 0xFFFFFFFF7DEFBDF4, 2, 0xFFFFFFFF7DEFBDE0) = 0
/2:     semget(16897864, 128, 0)                = 8
/2:     semtimedop(8, 0xFFFFFFFF7DEFBDF4, 2, 0xFFFFFFFF7DEFBDE0) = 0
...
```

---

2. It may lead to the embarrassing situation in which `truss` is left running perpetually.
3. Don't truss Xsun; it can deadlock—we did warn you!

Optionally, we can use the `-c` flag to summarize rather than trace a process's system call activity.

```
$ truss -c -p 26274
^C
syscall               seconds   calls  errors
read                     .002      10
semget                   .012      55
semtimedop               .015      55
pread                    .017      45
                     --------  ------   ----
sys totals:              .047     165      0
usr time:               1.030
elapsed:                7.850
```

The `truss` command also traces functions that are visible to the dynamic linker (this excludes functions that have been locally scoped as a performance optimization—see the *Solaris Linker and Libraries Guide*).

In the following example, we trace the functions within the target binary by specifying the `-u` option (trace functions rather than system calls) and `a.out` (trace within the binary, exclude libraries).

```
$ truss -u a.out -p 26274
/2@2:         -> flowop_endop(0xffffffff3735ef80, 0xffffffff6519c0d0, 0x0, 0x0)
/2:      pread(11, "\0\0\002\0\0\001\0\0\0\0".., 504, 0) = 504
/2@2:         -> filebench_log(0x5, 0x10006a830, 0x0, 0x0)
/2@2:       -> filebench_log(0x3, 0x10006a860, 0xffffffff3735ef80, 0xffffffff6519c0d0)
/2@2:         -> filebench_log(0x3, 0x10006a860, 0xffffffff3735ef80, 0xffffffff6519c380)
/2@2:        -> filebench_log(0x3, 0x10006a888, 0xffffffff3735ef80, 0xffffffff6519c380)
/2@2:         <- flowoplib_hog() = 0xffffffff3735ef80
/2@2:         -> flowoplib_sempost(0xffffffff3735ef80, 0xffffffff6519c380)
/2@2:           -> filebench_log(0x5, 0x10006afa8, 0xffffffff6519c380, 0x1)
/2@2:          -> flowop_beginop(0xffffffff3735ef80, 0xffffffff6519c380)
/2:      pread(11, "\0\0\002\0\0\001\0\0\0\0".., 504, 0) = 504
/2@2:         -> filebench_log(0x5, 0x10006aff0, 0xffffffff651f7c30, 0x1)
/2:      semget(16897864, 128, 0)
/2:      semtimedop(8, 0xFFFFFFFF7DEFBDF4, 2, 0xFFFFFFFF7DEFBDE0) = 0
/2@2:         -> filebench_log(0x5, 0x10006b048, 0xffffffff651f7c30, 0x1)
/2@2:         -> flowop_endop(0xffffffff3735ef80, 0xffffffff6519c380, 0xffffffff651f7c30)
/2:      pread(11, "\0\0\002\0\0\001\0\0\0\0".., 504, 0) = 504
/2@2:         -> filebench_log(0x3, 0x10006a8a8, 0xffffffff3735ef80, 0xffffffff6519c380)
...
```

See `truss(1M)` for further information.

## 3.7.2 Using `apptrace` to Trace Processes

The `apptrace` command was added in Solaris 8 to trace calls to shared libraries while evaluating argument details. In some ways it is an enhanced version of an older command, sotruss. The Solaris 10 version of apptrace has been enhanced further, printing separate lines for the return of each function call.

In the following example, apptrace prints shared library calls from the date command.

```
$ apptrace date
-> date      -> libc.so.1:int atexit(int (*)() = 0xff3c0090)
<- date      -> libc.so.1:atexit()
-> date      -> libc.so.1:int atexit(int (*)() = 0x11558)
<- date      -> libc.so.1:atexit()
-> date      -> libc.so.1:char * setlocale(int = 0x6, const char * = 0x11568 "")
<- date      -> libc.so.1:setlocale() = 0xff05216e
-> date      -> libc.so.1:char * textdomain(const char * = 0x1156c "SUNW_OST_OSCMD")
<- date      -> libc.so.1:textdomain() = 0x23548
-> date      -> libc.so.1:int getopt(int = 0x1, char *const * = 0xffbffd04, const char *
= 0x1157c "a:u")
<- date      -> libc.so.1:getopt() = 0xffffffff
-> date      -> libc.so.1:time_t time(time_t * = 0x225c0)
<- date      -> libc.so.1:time() = 0x440d059e
...
```

To illustrate the capability of apptrace, examine the example output for the call to getopt(). The entry to getopt() can be seen after the library name it belongs to (libc.so.1); then the arguments to getopt() are printed. The option string is displayed as a string, "a:u".

apptrace can evaluate structs for function calls of interest. In this example, full details for calls to strftime() are printed.

```
$ apptrace -v strftime date
-> date      -> libc.so.1:size_t strftime(char * = 0x225c4 "", size_t = 0x400, const char
* = 0xff056c38 "%a %b %e %T %Z %Y", const struct tm * = 0xffbffc54)
        arg0 = (char *) 0x225c4 ""
        arg1 = (size_t) 0x400
        arg2 = (const char *) 0xff056c38 "%a %b %e %T %Z %Y"
        arg3 = (const struct tm *) 0xffbffc54 (struct tm) {
        tm_sec: (int) 0x1
        tm_min: (int) 0x9
        tm_hour: (int) 0xf
        tm_mday: (int) 0x7
        tm_mon: (int) 0x2
        tm_year: (int) 0x6a
        tm_wday: (int) 0x2
        tm_yday: (int) 0x41
        tm_isdst: (int) 0x1
        }
        return = (size_t) 0x1c
<- date      -> libc.so.1:strftime() = 0x1c
Tue Mar  7 15:09:01 EST 2006
$
```

This output provides insight into how an application is using library calls, perhaps identifying faults where invalid data was used.

### 3.7.3 Using DTrace to Trace Process Functions

DTrace can trace system activity by using many different providers, including `syscall` to track system calls, `sched` to trace scheduling events, and `io` to trace disk and network I/O events. We can gain a greater understanding of process behavior by examining how the system responds to process requests. The following sections illustrate this:

- Section 2.15
- Section 4.15
- Section 6.11

However DTrace can drill even deeper: user-level functions from processes can be traced down to the CPU instruction. Usually, however, just the function entry and return probes suffice.

By specifying the provider name as `pidn`, where *n* is the process ID, we can use DTrace to trace process functions. Here we trace function entry and return.

```
# dtrace  -F -p 26274 -n 'pid$target:::entry,pid$target:::return { trace(timestamp); }'
dtrace: description 'pid$target:::entry, pid$target:::return ' matched 8836 probes
CPU FUNCTION
 18   -> flowoplib_sempost                      862876225376388
 18    -> flowoplib_sempost                     862876225406704
 18     -> filebench_log                        862876225479188
 18      -> filebench_log                       862876225505012
 18      <- filebench_log                       862876225606436
 18     <- filebench_log                        862876225668788
 18     -> flowop_beginop                       862876225733408
 18      -> flowop_beginop                      862876225770304
 18       -> pread                              862876225860508
 18        -> _save_nv_regs                     862876225924036
 18        <- _save_nv_regs                     862876226011512
 18        -> _pread                            862876226056292
 18        <- _pread                            862876226780092
 18       <- pread                              862876226867256
 18       -> gethrtime                          862876226940056
 18       <- gethrtime                          862876227018644
 18      <- flowop_beginop                      862876227106272
 18     <- flowop_beginop                       862876227162292
 . . .
```

Unlike `truss`, DTrace does not stop and start the process for each traced function; instead, DTrace collects data in per-CPU buffers which the `dtrace` command asynchronously reads. The overhead when using DTrace on a process does depend on the frequency of traced events but is usually less than that of `truss`.

### 3.7.4 Using DTrace to Aggregate Process Functions

When processes are traced as in the previous example, the output may rush by at an incredible pace. Using aggregations can condense information of interest. In the following example, the dtrace command aggregated the user-level function calls of inetd while a connection was established.

```
# dtrace -n 'pid$target:a.out::entry { @[probefunc] = count(); }' -p 252
dtrace: description 'pid$target:a.out::entry ' matched 159 probes
^C

  ...
  store_rep_vals                                                       2
  store_retrieve_rep_vals                                              2
  make_handle_bound                                                    6
  debug_msg                                                           42
  msg                                                                 42
  isset_pollfd                                                        58
  find_pollfd                                                         71
```

In this example, debug_msg() was called 42 times. The column on the right counts the number of times a function was called while dtrace was running. If we drop the a.out in the probe description, dtrace traces function calls from all libraries as well as inetd.

### 3.7.5 Using DTrace to Peer Inside Processes

One of the powerful capabilities of DTrace is its ability to look inside the address space of a process and dereference pointers of interest. We demonstrate by continuing with the previous inetd example.

A function called debug_msg() sounds interesting if we were troubleshooting a problem. inetd's debug_msg() takes a format string and variables as arguments and prints them to a log file if it exists (/var/adm/inetd.log). Since the log file doesn't exist on our server, debug_msg() tosses out the messages.

Without stopping or starting inetd, we can use DTrace to see what debug_ msg() would have been writing. We have to know the prototype for debug_msg(), so we either read it from the source code or guess.

```
# dtrace -n 'pid$target:a.out:debug_msg:entry { trace(copyinstr(arg0)); }' -p 252
dtrace: description 'pid$target:a.out:debug_msg:entry ' matched 1 probe
CPU     ID                    FUNCTION:NAME
  0   52162                   debug_msg:entry    Exiting poll, returned: %d
  0   52162                   debug_msg:entry    Entering process_terminated_methods
  0   52162                   debug_msg:entry    Entering process_network_events
  0   52162                   debug_msg:entry    Entering process_nowait_req
  0   52162                   debug_msg:entry    Entering accept_connection
```

*continues*

```
CPU     ID                        FUNCTION:NAME
  0   52162                    debug_msg:entry   Entering run_method, instance: %s,
                                                 method: %s
  0   52162                    debug_msg:entry   Entering read_method_context: inst: %s,
                                                 method: %s, path: %s
  0   52162                    debug_msg:entry   Entering passes_basic_exec_checks
  0   52162                    debug_msg:entry   Entering contract_prefork
  0   52162                    debug_msg:entry   Entering contract_postfork
  0   52162                    debug_msg:entry   Entering get_latest_contract
  ...
```

The first argument (arg0) contains the format string, and copyinstr() pulls the string from userland to the kernel, where DTrace is tracing. Although the messages printed in this example are missing their variables, they illustrate much of what inetd is internally doing. It is not uncommon to find some form of debug functions left behind in applications, and DTrace can extract them in this way.

## 3.7.6 Using DTrace to Sample Stack Backtraces

When we discussed the pstack command (Section 3.5.1), we suggested a crude analysis technique, by which a few stack backtraces could be taken to see where the process was spending most of its time. DTrace can turn crude into precise by taking samples at a configurable rate, such as 1000 hertz.

The following example samples user stack backtraces at 1000 hertz, matching on the PID for inetd. This is quite a useful DTrace one-liner.

```
# dtrace -n 'profile-1000hz /pid == $target/ { @[ustack()] = count(); }' -p 252
dtrace: description 'profile-1000hz ' matched 1 probe
^C

...

              libc.so.1`__waitid+0x8
              libc.so.1`waitpid+0x68
              inetd`process_terminated_methods+0x74
              inetd`event_loop+0x19c
              inetd`start_method+0x190
              inetd`_start+0x108
               11

              libc.so.1`__pollsys+0x4
              libc.so.1`poll+0x7c
              inetd`event_loop+0x70
              inetd`start_method+0x190
              inetd`_start+0x108
               28

              libc.so.1`__fork1+0x4
              inetd`run_method+0x27c
              inetd`process_nowait_request+0x1c8
              inetd`process_network_events+0xac
              inetd`event_loop+0x220
              inetd`start_method+0x190
              inetd`_start+0x108
               53
```

The final stack backtrace was sampled the most, 53 times. By reading through the functions, we can determine where inetd was spending its on-CPU time.

Rather than sampling until Ctrl-C is pressed, DTrace allows us to specify an interval with ease. We added a tick-5sec probe in the following to stop sampling and exit after 5 seconds.

```
# dtrace -n 'profile-1000hz /pid == $target/ { @[ustack()] = count(); }
tick-5sec { exit(0); }' -p 252
```

## 3.8 Java Processes

The following sections should shed some light on what your Java applications are doing. Topics such as profiling and tracing are discussed.

### 3.8.1 Process Stack on a Java Virtual Machine: `pstack`

You can use the C++ stack unmangler with Java virtual machine (JVM) targets to show the stacks for Java applications. The c++filt utility is provided with the Sun Workshop compiler tools.

```
$ pstack 27494 |c++filt
27494:  /usr/bin/java -client -verbose:gc -Xbatch -Xss256k -XX:+AggressiveHeap
---------------- lwp# 1 / thread# 1 --------------------
 ff3409b4 pollsys  (0, 0, ffbfe858, 0)
 ff2dcec8 poll     (0, 0, 1d4c0, 10624c00, 0, 0) + 7c
 fed316d4 int os_sleep(long long,int) (0, 1d4c0, 1, ff3, 372c0, 0) + 148
 fed2f6e4 int os::sleep(Thread*,long long,int) (372c0, 0, 1d4c0, 7, 4, ff14f934) + 284
 fedc21e0 JVM_Sleep (2, ff14dd24, 0, 1d4c0, ff1470dc, 372c0) + 260
 f8c0bc20 * java/lang/Thread.sleep(J)V+0
 f8c0bbc4 * java/lang/Thread.sleep(J)V+0
 f8c05764 * spec/jbb/JBButil.SecondsToSleep(J)V+11 (line 740)
 f8c05764 * spec/jbb/Company.displayResultTotals(ZZ)V+235 (line 651)
 f8c05764 * spec/jbb/JBBmain.DoARun(Lspec/jbb/Company;SSII)V+197 (line 277)
 f8c05764 * spec/jbb/JBBmain.DOIT(Lspec/jbb/infra/Factory/Container;)V+186 (line 732)
 f8c05764 * spec/jbb/JBBmain.main([Ljava/lang/String;)V+1220 (line 1019)
 f8c00218 * StubRoutines (1)
 fecd9f00 void JavaCalls::call_helper(JavaValue*,methodHandle*,JavaCallArgu-
ments*,Thread*) (1, 372c0, ffbff018, ffbfef50, ffbff01c, 0) + 5b8
 fedb8e84 jni_CallStaticVoidMethod (ff14dd24, ff1470dc, 3788c, 372c0, 0, 37488) + 514
 000123b4 main     (ff14a040, 576d1a, fed2a6d0, 2, 2, 1d8) + 1314
 00011088 _start   (0, 0, 0, 0, 0, 0) + 108
```

## 3.8.2 JVM Profiling

While the JVM has long included the -Xrunhprof profiling flag, the Java 2 Plat-form, Standard Edition (J2SE) 5.0 and later use the JVMTI for heap and CPU pro-filing. Usage information is obtained with the java -Xrunhprof command. This profiling flag includes a variety of options and returns a lot of data. As a result, using a large number of options can significantly impact application performance.

To observe locks, use the command in the following example. Note that setting monitor=y specifies that locks should be observed. Setting msa=y turns on Solaris microstate accounting (see Section 3.2.2, and Section 2.10.3 in *Solaris™ Internals*), and depth=8 sets the depth of the stack displayed.

```
# java -Xrunhprof:cpu=times,monitor=y,msa=y,depth=8,file=path_to_result_file app_name
MONITOR DUMP BEGIN\
    THREAD 200000, trace 302389, status: CW\
    THREAD 200001, trace 300000, status: R\
    THREAD 201044, trace 302505, status: R\
.....
    MONITOR Ljava/lang/StringBuffer;\
        owner: thread 200058, entry count: 1\
        waiting to enter:\
        waiting to be notified:\
MONITOR DUMP END\
MONITOR TIME BEGIN (total = 2442 ms) Sat Nov  5 11:51:04 2005\
rank    self   accum    count trace monitor\
   1 64.51% 64.51%      364 302089 java.lang.Class (Java)\
   2 20.99% 85.50%      294 302094 java.lang.Class (Java)\
   3  9.94% 95.44%      128 302027 sun.misc.Launcher$AppClassLoader (Java)\
   4  4.17% 99.61%      164 302122 sun.misc.Launcher$AppClassLoader (Java)\
   5  0.30% 99.90%       46 302158 sun.misc.Launcher$AppClassLoader (Java)\
   6  0.05% 99.95%       14 302163 sun.misc.Launcher$AppClassLoader (Java)\
   7  0.03% 99.98%       10 302202 sun.misc.Launcher$AppClassLoader (Java)\
   8  0.02% 100.00%       4 302311 sun.misc.Launcher$AppClassLoader (Java)\
MONITOR TIME END\
```

This command returns verbose data, including all the call stacks in the Java process. Note two sections at the bottom of the output: the MONITOR DUMP and MONITOR TIME sections. The MONITOR DUMP section is a complete snapshot of all the monitors and threads in the system. MONITOR TIME is a profile of monitor con-tention obtained by measuring the time spent by a thread waiting to enter a moni-tor. Entries in this record are ranked by the percentage of total monitor contention time and a brief description of the monitor.

In previous versions of the JVM, one option is to dump all the stacks on the run-ning VM by sending a SIGQUIT (signal number 3) to the Java process with the kill command. This dumps the stacks for all VM threads to the standard error as shown below.

```
# kill -3 <pid>
Full thread dump Java HotSpot(TM) Client VM (1.4.1_06-b01 mixed mode):
"Signal Dispatcher" daemon prio=10 tid=0xba6a8 nid=0x7 waiting on condition
[0..0]
"Finalizer" daemon prio=8 tid=0xb48b8 nid=0x4 in Object.wait()
[f2b7f000..f2b7fc24]
        at java.lang.Object.wait(Native Method)
        - waiting on <f2c00490> (a java.lang.ref.ReferenceQueue$Lock)
        at java.lang.ref.ReferenceQueue.remove(ReferenceQueue.java:111)
        - locked <f2c00490> (a java.lang.ref.ReferenceQueue$Lock)
        at java.lang.ref.ReferenceQueue.remove(ReferenceQueue.java:127)
        at java.lang.ref.Finalizer$FinalizerThread.run(Finalizer.java:159)
"Reference Handler" daemon prio=10 tid=0xb2f88 nid=0x3 in Object.wait()
[facff000..facffc24]
        at java.lang.Object.wait(Native Method)
        - waiting on <f2c00380> (a java.lang.ref.Reference$Lock)
        at java.lang.Object.wait(Object.java:426)
        at java.lang.ref.Reference$ReferenceHandler.run(Reference.java:113)
        - locked <f2c00380> (a java.lang.ref.Reference$Lock)
"main" prio=5 tid=0x2c240 nid=0x1 runnable [ffbfe000..ffbfe5fc]
        at testMain.doit2(testMain.java:12)
        at testMain.main(testMain.java:64)
"VM Thread" prio=5 tid=0xb1b30 nid=0x2 runnable
"VM Periodic Task Thread" prio=10 tid=0xb9408 nid=0x5 runnable
"Suspend Checker Thread" prio=10 tid=0xb9d58 nid=0x6 runnable
```

If the top of the stack for a number of threads terminates in a monitor call, this is the place to drill down and determine what resource is being contended. Sometimes removing a lock that protects a hot structure can require many architectural changes that are not possible. The lock might even be in a third-party library over which you have no control. In such cases, multiple instances of the application are probably the best way to achieve scaling.

## 3.8.3  Tuning Java Garbage Collection

Tuning garbage collection (GC) is one of the most important performance tasks for Java applications. To achieve acceptable response times, you will often have to tune GC. Doing that requires you to know the following:

- Frequency of garbage collection events
- Whether Young Generation or Full GC is used
- Duration of the garbage collection
- Amount of garbage generated

To obtain this data, add the -verbosegc, -XX:+PrintGCTimeStamps, and -XX:+PrintGCDetails flags to the regular JVM command line.

```
1953.954: [GC [PSYoungGen: 1413632K->37248K(1776640K)] 2782033K->1440033K(3316736K),
0.3666410 secs]
2018.424: [GC [PSYoungGen: 1477376K->37584K(1760640K)] 2880161K->1473633K(3300736K),
0.3825016 secs]
2018.806: [Full GC [PSYoungGen: 37584K->0K(1760640K)] [ParOldGen: 1436049K-
>449978K(1540096K)] 147363
3K->449978K(3300736K) [PSPermGen: 4634K->4631K(16384K)], 5.3205801 secs]
2085.554: [GC [PSYoungGen: 1440128K->39968K(1808384K)] 1890106K->489946K(3348480K),
0.2442195 secs]
```

The preceding example indicates that at 2018 seconds a Young Generation GC cleaned 3.3 Gbytes and took .38 seconds to complete. This was quickly followed by a Full GC that took 5.3 seconds to complete.

On systems with many CPUs (or hardware threads), the increased throughput often generates significantly more garbage in the VM, and previous GC tuning may no longer be valid. Sometimes Full GC is generated where previously only Young Generation existed. Dump the GC details to a log file to confirm.

Avoid full GC whenever you can because it severely affects response time. Full GC is usually an indication that the Java heap is too small. Increase the heap size by using the -Xmx and -Xms options until Full GCs are no longer triggered. It is best to preallocate the heap by setting -Xmx and -Xms to the same value. For example, to set the Java heap to 3.5 Gbytes, add the -Xmx3550m, -Xms3550m, -Xmn2g, and -Xss128k options. The J2SE 1.5.0_06 release also introduced parallelism into the old GCs. Add the -XX:+UseParallelOldGC option to the standard JVM flags to enable this feature.

For Young Generation the number of parallel GC threads is the number of CPUs presented by the Solaris OS. On UltraSPARC T1 processor-based systems this equates to the number of threads. It may be necessary to scale back the number of threads involved in Young Generation GC to achieve response time constraints. To reduce the number of threads, you can set XX:ParallelGCThreads=number_of_threads.

A good starting point is to set the GC threads to the number of cores on the system. Putting it all together yields the following flags.

```
-Xmx3550m -Xms3550m -Xmn2g -Xss128k -XX:+UseParallelOldGC -XX:+UseParallelGC -XX:Paral-
lelGCThreads=8
-XX:+PrintGCDetails -XX:+PrintGCTimestamps
```

Older versions of the Java virtual machine, such as 1.3, do not have parallel GC. This can be an issue on CMT processors because GC can stall the entire VM. Parallel GC is available from 1.4.2 onward, so this is a good starting point for Java applications on multiprocessor-based systems.

## 3.8.4 Using DTrace on Java Applications

The J2SE 6 (code-named Mustang) release introduces DTrace support within the Java HotSpot virtual machine. The providers and probes included in the Mustang release make it possible for DTrace to collect performance data for applications written in the Java programming language.

The Mustang release contains two built-in DTrace providers: `hotspot` and `hotspot_jni`. All probes published by these providers are user-level statically defined tracing (USDT) probes, accessed by the PID of the Java HotSpot virtual machine process.

The `hotspot` provider contains probes related to the following Java HotSpot virtual machine subsystems:

- **VM life cycle probes.** For VM initialization and shutdown
- **Thread life cycle probes.** For thread start and stop events
- **Class-loading probes.** For class loading and unloading activity
- **Garbage collection probes.** For systemwide garbage and memory pool collection
- **Method compilation probes.** For indication of which methods are being compiled by which compiler
- **Monitor probes.** For all wait and notification events, plus contended monitor entry and exit events
- **Application probes.** For fine-grained examination of thread execution, method entry/method returns, and object allocation

All hotspot probes originate in the VM library (`libjvm.so`), and as such, are also provided from programs that embed the VM. The `hotspot_jni` provider contains probes related to the Java Native Interface (JNI), located at the entry and return points of all JNI methods. In addition, the DTrace `jstack()` action prints mixed-mode stack traces including both Java method and native function names.

As an example, the following D script (`usestack.d`) uses the DTrace `jstack()` action to print the stack trace.

```
#!/usr/sbin/dtrace -s

BEGIN { this->cnt = 0; }

syscall::pollsys:entry
/pid == $1 && tid == 1/
{
    this->cnt++;
    printf("\n\tTID: %d", tid);
```

*continues*

```
    jstack(50);
}

syscall:::entry
/this->cnt == 1/
{
    exit(0);
}
```

And the stack trace itself appears as follows.

```
# ./usejstack.d 1344 | c++filt
CPU     ID                    FUNCTION:NAME
  0    316                    pollsys:entry
  TID: 1
  libc.so.1`__pollsys+0xa
  libc.so.1`poll+0x52
  libjvm.so`int os_sleep(long long,int)+0xb4
  libjvm.so`int os::sleep(Thread*,long long,int)+0x1ce
  libjvm.so`JVM_Sleep+0x1bc
  java/lang/Thread.sleep
  dtest.method3
  dtest.method2
  dtest.method1
  dtest.main
  StubRoutines (1)
  libjvm.so`void JavaCalls::call_helper(JavaValue*,methodHandle*,JavaCallArgu-
ments*,Thread*)+0x1b5
  libjvm.so`void os::os_exception_wrapper(void(*)(JavaValue*,methodHandle*,JavaCallAr-
guments*,Thread*),JavaValue*,methodHandle*,Ja
vaCallArguments*,Thread*)+0x18
  libjvm.so`void JavaCalls::call(JavaValue*,methodHandle,JavaCallArgu-
ments*,Thread*)+0x2d
  libjvm.so`void jni_invoke_static(JNIEnv_*,JavaValue*,_jobject*,JNICallType,_
jmethodID*,JNI_ArgumentPush er*,Thread*)+0x214
  libjvm.so`jni_CallStaticVoidMethod+0x244
  java`main+0x642
  StubRoutines (1)
```

The command line shows that the output from this script was piped to the
c++filt utility, which demangles C++ mangled names, making the output easier
to read. The DTrace header output shows that the CPU number is 0, the probe
number is 316, the thread ID (TID) is 1, and the probe name is pollsys:entry,
where pollsys is the name of the system call. The stack trace frames appear from
top to bottom in the following order: two system call frames, three VM frames, five
Java method frames, and VMframes in the remainder.

For further information on using DTrace with Java applications, see
Section 10.3.

# Disk Behavior and Analysis

This chapter discusses the key factors used for understanding disk behavior and presents an overview of the analysis tools available.

## 4.1 Terms for Disk Analysis

The following terms are related to disk analysis; the list also summarizes topics covered in this section.

- **Environment.** The first step in disk analysis is to know what the disks are—single disks or a storage array—and what their expected workload is: random, sequential, or otherwise.

- **Utilization.** The percent busy value from `iostat -x` serves as a utilization value for disk devices. The calculation behind it is based on the time a device spends active. It is a useful starting point for understanding disk usage.

- **Saturation.** The average wait queue length from `iostat -x` is a measure of disk saturation.

- **Throughput.** The kilobytes/sec values from `iostat -x` can also indicate disk activity, and for storage arrays they may be the only meaningful metric that Solaris provides.

- **I/O rate.** The number of disk transactions per second can be seen by means of `iostat` or DTrace. The number is interesting because each operation incurs a certain overhead. This term is also known as IOPS (I/O operations per second).

- **I/O sizes.** You can calculate the size of disk transactions from `iostat -x` by using the (kr/s + kw/s) / (r/s + w/s) ratio, which gives average event size; or you can measure the size directly with DTrace. Throughput is usually improved when larger events are used.

- **Service times.** The average wait queue and active service times can be printed from `iostat -x`. Longer service times are likely to degrade performance.

- **History.** `sar` can be activated to archive historical disk activity statistics. Long-term patterns can be identified from this data, which also provides a reference for what statistics are "normal" for your disks.

- **Seek sizes.** DTrace can measure the size of each disk head seek and present this data in a meaningful report.

- **I/O time.** Measuring the time a disk spends servicing an I/O event is valuable because it takes into account various costs of performing an I/O operation: seek time, rotation time, and the time to transfer data. DTrace can fetch event time data.

Table 4.1 summarizes and cross-references tools used in this section.

**Table 4.1**  Tools for Disk Analysis

| Tool | Uses | Description | Reference |
|------|------|-------------|-----------|
| `iostat` | Kstat | For extended disk device statistics | 4.6 |
| `sar` | Kstat, sadc | For disk device statistics and history data archiving | 4.13 |
| `iotrace.d` | DTrace | Simple script for events by device and file name | 4.15.3 |
| `bites.d` | DTrace | Simple script to aggregate disk event size | 4.15.4 |
| `seeks.d` | DTrace | Simple script to measure disk event seek size | 4.15.5 |
| `files.d` | DTrace | Simple script to aggregate size by file name | 4.15.6 |
| `iotop` | DTrace | For a disk statistics by-process summary | 4.17.1 |
| `iosnoop` | DTrace | For a trace of disk events, including process ID, times, block addresses, sizes, etc. | 4.17.2 |

## 4.2 Random vs. Sequential I/O

We frequently use the terms *random* and *sequential* while discussing disk behavior. *Random* activity means the disk accesses blocks from random locations on disk, usually incurring a time penalty while the disk heads seek and the disk itself rotates. *Sequential* activity means the disk accesses blocks one after the other, that is, sequentially.

The following demonstrations compare random to sequential disk activity and illustrate why recognizing this behavior is important.

### 4.2.1 Demonstration of Sequential Disk Activity

While a dd command runs to request heavy sequential disk activity, we examine the output of iostat to see the effect. (The options and output of iostat are covered in detail in subsequent sections.)

```
# dd if=/dev/rdsk/c0d0s0 of=/dev/null bs=64k

$ iostat -xnz 5
                    extended device statistics
    r/s    w/s    kr/s    kw/s wait actv wsvc_t asvc_t  %w  %b device
    1.1    0.7    16.2    18.8  0.3  0.0  144.4    2.7   0   0 c0d0
    0.0    0.0     0.0     0.0  0.0  0.0    0.0    0.2   0   0 jupiter:vold(pid564)
                    extended device statistics
    r/s    w/s    kr/s    kw/s wait actv wsvc_t asvc_t  %w  %b device
  819.6    0.0 52455.3     0.0  0.0  1.0    0.0    1.2   1  97 c0d0
                    extended device statistics
    r/s    w/s    kr/s    kw/s wait actv wsvc_t asvc_t  %w  %b device
  820.9    0.2 52535.2     1.6  0.0  1.0    0.0    1.2   1  97 c0d0
                    extended device statistics
    r/s    w/s    kr/s    kw/s wait actv wsvc_t asvc_t  %w  %b device
  827.8    0.0 52981.2     0.0  0.0  1.0    0.0    1.2   1  97 c0d0
...
```

The disk was 97% busy, for which it delivered over 50 Mbytes/sec.

### 4.2.2 Demonstration of Random Disk Activity

Now for random activity, on the same system and the same disk. This time we use the filebench tool to generate a consistent and configurable workload.

```
filebench> load randomread
filebench> set $nthreads=64
filebench> run 600
 1089: 0.095: Random Read Version 1.8 05/02/17 IO personality successfully loaded
 1089: 0.096: Creating/pre-allocating files
```

*continues*

```
1089: 0.279: Waiting for preallocation threads to complete...
1089: 0.279: Re-using file /filebench/bigfile0
1089: 0.385: Starting 1 rand-read instances
1090: 1.389: Starting 64 rand-thread threads
1089: 4.399: Running for 600 seconds...

$ iostat -xnz 5
                    extended device statistics
    r/s    w/s    kr/s    kw/s wait actv wsvc_t asvc_t  %w  %b device
    1.0    0.7     8.6    18.8  0.3  0.0  154.2    2.8   0   0 c0d0
    0.0    0.0     0.0     0.0  0.0  0.0    0.0    0.2   0   0 jupiter:vold(pid564)
                    extended device statistics
    r/s    w/s    kr/s    kw/s wait actv wsvc_t asvc_t  %w  %b device
  291.6    0.2  1166.5     1.6  0.0  1.0    0.0    3.3   0  97 c0d0
                    extended device statistics
    r/s    w/s    kr/s    kw/s wait actv wsvc_t asvc_t  %w  %b device
  290.0    0.0  1160.1     0.0  0.0  1.0    0.0    3.3   0  97 c0d0
...
```

This disk is also 97% busy, but this time it delivers around 1.2 Mbytes/sec. The random disk activity was over 40 times slower in terms of throughput. This is quite a significant difference.

Had we only been looking at disk throughput, then 1.2 Mbytes/sec may have been of no concern for a disk that can pull 50 Mbytes/sec; in reality, however, our 1.2 Mbytes/sec workload almost saturated the disk with activity. In this case, the percent busy (%b) measurement was far more useful, but for other cases (storage arrays), we may find that throughput has more meaning.

## 4.3 Storage Arrays

Larger environments often use storage arrays: These are usually hardware RAID along with an enormous frontend cache (256 Mbytes to 256+ Gbytes). Rather than the millisecond crawl of traditional disks, storage arrays are fast—often performing like an enormous hunk of memory. Reads and writes are served from the cache as much as possible, with the actual disks updated asynchronously.

If we are writing data to a storage array, Solaris considers it completed when the sd or ssd driver receives the completion interrupt. Storage arrays like to use writeback caching, which means the completion interrupt is sent as soon as the cache receives the data. The service time that iostat reports will be tiny because we did not measure a physical disk event. The data remains in the cache until the storage array flushes it to disk at some later time, based on algorithms such as Least Recently Used. Solaris can't see any of this. Solaris metrics such as utilization may have little meaning; the best metric we do have is throughput—kilobytes written per second—which we can use to estimate activity.

In some situations the cache can switch to writethrough mode, such as in the event of a hardware failure (for example, the batteries die). Suddenly the statistics in Solaris change because writes now suffer a delay as the storage array waits for them to write to disk, before an I/O completion is sent. Service times increase, and utilization values such as percent busy may become more meaningful.

If we are reading data from a storage array, then at times delays occur as the data is read from disk. However, the storage array tries its best to serve reads from (its very large) cache, especially effective if prefetch is enabled and the workload is sequential. This means that usually Solaris doesn't observe the disk delay, and again the service times are small and the percent utilizations have little meaning.

To actually understand storage array utilization, you must fetch statistics from the storage array controller itself. Of interest are cache hit ratios and array controller CPU utilization. The storage array may experience degraded performance as it performs other tasks, such as verification, volume creation, and volume reconstruction. How the storage array has been configured and its underlying volumes and other settings are also of great significance.

The one Solaris metric we can trust for storage arrays is throughput, the data read and written to it. That can be used as an indicator for activity. What happens beyond the cache and to the actual disks we do not know, although changes in average service times may give us a clue that some events are synchronous.

## 4.4 Sector Zoning

Sector zoning, also known as Multiple Zone Recording (MZR), is a disk layout strategy for optimal performance. A track on the outside edge of a disk can contain more sectors than one on the inside because a track on the outside edge has a greater length. Since the disk can read more sectors per rotation from the outside edge than the inside, data stored near the outside edge is faster. Manufacturers often break disks into zones of fixed sector per-track ratios, with the number of zones and ratios chosen for both performance and data density.

Data throughput on the outside edge may also be faster because many disk heads rest at the outside edge, resulting in reduced seek times for data blocks nearby.

A simple way to demonstrate the effect of sector zoning is to perform a sequential read across the entire disk. The following example shows the throughput at the start of the test (outside edge) and at the end of the test (inside edge).

```
# dd if=/dev/rdsk/c0t0d0s2 of=/dev/null bs=128k

$ iostat -xnz 10
...
                    extended device statistics
    r/s    w/s    kr/s    kw/s wait actv wsvc_t asvc_t  %w  %b device
  104.0    0.0 13311.0     0.0  0.0  1.0    0.0    9.5   0  99 c0t0d0
...
                    extended device statistics
    r/s    w/s    kr/s    kw/s wait actv wsvc_t asvc_t  %w  %b device
   71.1    0.0  9100.4     0.0  0.0  1.0    0.0   13.9   0  99 c0t0d0
```

Near the outside edge the speed was around 13 Mbytes/sec, while at the inside edge this has dropped to 9 Mbytes/sec. A common procedure that takes advantage of this behavior is to slice disks so that the most commonly accessed data is positioned near the outside edge.

## 4.5 Max I/O Size

An important characteristic when storage devices are configured is the maximum size of an I/O transaction. For sequential access, larger I/O sizes are better; for random access, I/O sizes should to be picked to match the workload. Your first step when configuring I/O sizes is to know your workload: DTrace is especially good at measuring this (see Section 4.15).

A maximum I/O transaction size can be set at a number of places:

- **maxphys.** Disk driver maximum I/O size. By default this is 128 Kbytes on SPARC systems and 56 Kbytes on x86 systems. Some devices override this value if they can.
- **maxcontig.** UFS maximum I/O size. Defaults to equal maxphys, it can be set during `newfs(1M)` and changed with `tunefs(1M)`. UFS uses this value for read-ahead.
- **stripe width.** Maximum I/O size for a logical volume (hardware RAID or software VM) configured by setting a stripe size (per-disk maximum I/O size) and choosing a number of disks. *stripe width = stripe size × number of disks.*
- **interlace.** SVM stripe size.

Ideally, stripe width is an integer divisor of the average I/O transaction size; otherwise, there is a remainder. Remainders can reduce performance for a few reasons, including inefficient filling of cache blocks; and in the case of RAID5, remainders can compromise write performance by incurring the penalty of a read-modify-write or reconstruct-write operation.

The following is a quick demonstration to show maxphys capping I/O size on Solaris 10 x86.

```
# dd if=/dev/dsk/c0d0s0 of=/dev/null bs=1024k

$ iostat -xnz 5
                    extended device statistics
    r/s    w/s    kr/s    kw/s wait actv wsvc_t asvc_t  %w  %b device
    2.4    0.6    55.9    17.8  0.2  0.0   78.9    1.8   0   0 c0d0
    0.0    0.0     0.0     0.0  0.0  0.0    0.0    0.2   0   0 jupiter:vold(pid564)
                    extended device statistics
    r/s    w/s    kr/s    kw/s wait actv wsvc_t asvc_t  %w  %b device
  943.3    0.0 52822.6     0.0  0.0  1.3    0.0    1.4   3 100 c0d0
                    extended device statistics
    r/s    w/s    kr/s    kw/s wait actv wsvc_t asvc_t  %w  %b device
  959.2    0.0 53716.1     0.0  0.0  1.3    0.0    1.4   3 100 c0d0
                    extended device statistics
    r/s    w/s    kr/s    kw/s wait actv wsvc_t asvc_t  %w  %b device
  949.8    0.0 53186.3     0.0  0.0  1.2    0.0    1.3   3  96 c0d0
...
```

Although we requested 1024 Kbytes per transaction, the disk device delivered 56 Kbytes (52822 ÷ 943), which is the value of maxphys.

The dd command can be invoked with different I/O sizes while the raw (rdsk) device is used so that the optimal size for sequential disk access can be discovered.

## 4.6 iostat Utility

The iostat utility is the official place to get information about disk I/O performance, and it is a classic kstat(3kstat) consumer along with vmstat and mpstat. iostat can be run in a variety of ways.

In the following style, iostat provides single-line summaries for active devices.

```
$ iostat -xnz 5
                    extended device statistics
    r/s    w/s    kr/s    kw/s wait actv wsvc_t asvc_t  %w  %b device
    0.2    0.2     1.1     1.4  0.0  0.0    6.6    6.9   0   0 c0t0d0
    0.0    0.0     0.0     0.0  0.0  0.0    0.0    7.7   0   0 c0t2d0
    0.0    0.0     0.0     0.0  0.0  0.0    0.0    3.0   0   0 mars:vold(pid512)
                    extended device statistics
    r/s    w/s    kr/s    kw/s wait actv wsvc_t asvc_t  %w  %b device
  277.1    0.0 2216.4     0.0  0.0  0.6    0.0    2.1   0  58 c0t0d0
                    extended device statistics
    r/s    w/s    kr/s    kw/s wait actv wsvc_t asvc_t  %w  %b device
   79.8    0.0  910.0     0.0  0.4  1.9    5.1   23.6  41  98 c0t0d0
                    extended device statistics
    r/s    w/s    kr/s    kw/s wait actv wsvc_t asvc_t  %w  %b device
   87.0    0.0  738.5     0.0  0.8  2.0    9.4   22.4  65  99 c0t0d0
                    extended device statistics
    r/s    w/s    kr/s    kw/s wait actv wsvc_t asvc_t  %w  %b device
   92.2    0.6  780.4     2.2  2.1  1.9   22.8   21.0  87  98 c0t0d0
```

*continues*

```
                        extended device statistics
    r/s   w/s    kr/s    kw/s wait actv wsvc_t asvc_t  %w  %b device
   101.4  0.0   826.6     0.0  0.8  1.9    8.0   19.0  46  99 c0t0d0
   ...
```

The first output is the summary since boot, followed by samples every five seconds. Some columns have been highlighted in this example. On the right is %b; this
is percent busy and tells us disk *utilization*,[1] which we explain in the next section.
In the middle is wait, the average wait queue length; it is a measure of disk *saturation*. On the left are kr/s and kw/s, kilobytes read and written per second,
which tells us the current disk *throughput*.

In the iostat example, the first five-second sample shows a percent busy of
58%—fairly moderate utilization. For the following samples, we can see the average wait queue length climb to a value of 2.1, indicating that this disk was becoming saturated with requests.

The throughput in the example began at over 2 Mbytes/sec and fell to less than
1 Mbytes/sec. Throughput can indicate disk activity.

iostat provides other statistics that we discuss later. These utilization, saturation, and throughput metrics are a useful starting point for understanding disk
behavior.

## 4.7 Disk Utilization

When considering disk utilization, keep in mind the following points:

- Any level of disk utilization may degrade application performance because
  accessing disks is a slow activity—often measured in milliseconds.

- Sometimes heavy disk utilization is the price of doing business; this is especially the case for database servers.

- Whether a level of disk utilization actually affects an application greatly
  depends on how the application uses the disks and how the disk devices
  respond to requests. In particular, notice the following:

  - An application may be using the disks synchronously and suffering from
    each delay as it occurs, or an application may be multithreaded or use
    asynchronous I/O to avoid stalling on each disk event.

---

1. iostat -D prints the same statistic and calls it "util" or "percentage disk utilization."

- – Many OS and disk mechanisms provide writeback caching so that although the disk may be busy, the application does not need to wait for writes to complete.

- Utilization values are averages over time, and it is especially important to bear this in mind for disks. Often, applications and the OS access the disks in bursts: for example, when reading an entire file, when executing a new command, or when flushing writes. This can cause short bursts of heavy utilization, which may be difficult to identify if averaged over longer intervals.

- Utilization alone doesn't convey the type of disk activity—in particular, whether the activity was random or sequential.

- An application accessing a disk sequentially may find that a heavily utilized disk often seeks heads away, causing what would have been sequential access to behave in a random manner.

- Storage arrays may report 100% utilization when in fact they are able to accept more transactions. 100% utilization here means that Solaris believes the storage device is fully active during that interval, not that it has no further capacity to accept transactions. Solaris doesn't see what really happens on storage array disks.

- Disk activity is complex! It involves mechanical disk properties, buses, and caching and depends on the way applications use I/O. Condensing this information to a single utilization value verges on oversimplification. The utilization value is useful as a starting point, but it's not absolute.

In summary, for simple disks and applications, utilization values are a meaningful measurement so we can understand disk behavior in a consistent way. However, as applications become more complex, the percent utilization requires careful consideration. This is also the case with complex disk devices, especially storage arrays, for which percent utilization may have little value.

While we may debate the accuracy of percent utilization, it still often serves its purpose as being a "useful starting point," which is followed by other metrics when deeper analysis is desired (especially those from DTrace).

## 4.8 Disk Saturation

A sustained level of disk saturation usually means a performance problem. A disk at saturation is constantly busy, and new transactions are unable to preempt the currently active disk operation in the same way a thread can preempt the CPU. This means that new transactions suffer an unavoidable delay as they queue, waiting their turn.

## 4.9 Disk Throughput

Throughput is interesting as an indicator of activity. It is usually measured in kilo-bytes or megabytes per second. Sometimes it is of value when we discover that too much or too little throughput is happening on the disks for the expected applica-tion workload.

Often with storage arrays, throughput is the only statistic available from `iostat` that is accurate. Knowing utilization and saturation of the storage array's individual disks is beyond what Solaris normally can see. To delve deeper into storage array activity, we must fetch statistics from the storage array controller.

## 4.10 `iostat` Reference

The `iostat` command can print a variety of different outputs, depending on which command-line options were used. Many of the standard options are listed below.[2]

- **-c.** Print the standard system time percentages: `us`, `sy`, `wt`, `id`.
- **-d.** Print classic fields: `kps`, `tps`, `serv`.
- **-D.** "New" style output, print disk utilization with a decimal place.
- **-e.** Print device error statistics.
- **-E.** Print extended error statistics. Useful for quickly listing disk details.
- **-I.** Print raw interval counts, rather than per second.
- **-l n.** Limit number of disks printed to n. Useful when also specifying a disk.
- **-M.** Print throughput in Mbytes/sec rather than Kbytes/sec.
- **-n.** Use logical disk names rather than instance names.
- **-p.** Print per partition statistics as well as per device.
- **-P.** Print partition statics only.
- **-t.** Print terminal I/O statistics.
- **-x.** Extended disk statistics. This prints a line per device and provides the breakdown that includes `r/s`, `w/s`, `kr/s`, `kw/s`, `wait`, `actv`, `svc_t`, `%w`, and `%b`.

---

2. Many of these were actually added in Solaris 2.6. The Solaris 2.5 Synopsis for `iostat` was `/usr/bin/iostat [ -cdDItx ] [ -l n ] [ disk . . . ] [ interval [ count ] ]`

The default options of `iostat` are -cdt, which prints a summary of up to four disks on one line along with CPU and terminal I/O details. This is rarely used.[3]

Several new formatting flags crept in around Solaris 8:

- **-C.** Report disk statistics by controller.
- **-m.** For mounted partitions, print the mount point (useful with -p or -P).
- **-r.** Display data in comma-separated format.
- **-s.** Suppress state change messages.
- **-T d|u.** Print timestamps in date (d) or UNIX time (u) format.
- **-z.** Don't print lines that contain all zeros.

People have their own favorite combination, in much the same way they form habits with the ls command. For small environments -xnmpz may be suitable, and for larger -xnMz. Always type `iostat` -E at some point to check for errors.

The man page for `iostat` suggests that iostat -xcnCXTdz [interval] is particularly useful for identifying problems.

Some of these options are demonstrated one by one in the next subsections. A demonstration for many of them at once is as follows.

```
$ iostat -xncell -Td c0t0d0 5
Sun Feb 19 18:01:24 2006
      cpu
 us sy wt id
  1  1  0 98
                              extended device statistics        ---- errors ---
     r/s    w/s   kr/s   kw/s wait actv wsvc_t asvc_t  %w  %b s/w h/w trn tot device
     0.3    0.2    1.9    1.4  0.0  0.0    6.3    7.0   0   0   0   0   0   0 c0t0d0s0 (/)
Sun Feb 19 18:01:29 2006
      cpu
 us sy wt id
  1 19  0 80
                              extended device statistics        ---- errors ---
     r/s    w/s   kr/s   kw/s wait actv wsvc_t asvc_t  %w  %b s/w h/w trn tot device
   311.3    0.0 2490.2    0.0  0.0  0.8    0.0    2.7   0  84   0   0   0   0 c0t0d0
Sun Feb 19 18:01:34 2006
      cpu
 us sy wt id
  1 21  0 77
                              extended device statistics        ---- errors ---
     r/s    w/s   kr/s   kw/s wait actv wsvc_t asvc_t  %w  %b s/w h/w trn tot device
   213.0   21.0 1704.1  105.8  1.0  1.1    4.3    4.5  19  83   0   0   0   0 c0t0d0
...
```

---

3. If you would like to cling to the original single-line summaries of iostat, try iostat -cnD199 1. Make your screen wide if you have many disks. Add a -P for some real entertainment.

The output columns include the following:

- **wait.** Average number of transactions queued and waiting
- **actv.** Average number of transactions actively being serviced
- **wsvc_t.** Average time a transaction spends on the wait queue
- **asvc_t.** Average time a transaction is active or running
- **%w.** Percent wait, based on the time that transactions were queued
- **%b.** Percent busy, based on the time that the device was active

## 4.10.1 `iostat` Default

By default, `iostat` prints a summary since boot line.

```
$ iostat
      tty          dad1            sd1            nfs1             cpu
 tin tout kps tps serv  kps tps serv  kps tps serv  us sy wt id
   0   1   6   1   11    0   0    8    0   0    3    1  1  0 98
```

The output lists devices by their instance name across the top and provides details such as kilobytes per second (kps), transactions per second (tps), and average service time (serv). Also printed are standard CPU and tty[4] statistics such as percentage user (us), system (sy) and idle (id) time, and terminal in chars (tin) and out chars (tout).

We almost always want to measure what is happening now rather than some dim average since boot, so we specify an interval and an optional count.

```
$ iostat 5 2
      tty          dad1            sd1            nfs1             cpu
 tin tout kps tps serv  kps tps serv  kps tps serv  us sy wt id
   0   1   6   1   11    0   0    8    0   0    3    1  1  0 98
   0  39 342 253    3    0   0    0    0   0    0    4 18  0 79
```

Here the interval was five seconds with a count of two. The first line of output is printed immediately and is still the summary since boot. The second and last line is a five-second sample, showing that some disk activity was occurring on dad1.

---

4. A throwback to when ttys were *real* teletypes, and service times were *real* service times.

## 4.10.2 iostat -D

The source code to iostat flags the default style of output as DISK_OLD. A DISK_NEW is also defined[5] and is printed with the -D option.

```
$ iostat -D 5 2
      dad1            sd1            nfs1
rps wps util   rps wps util   rps wps util
  0   0  0.3     0   0  0.0     0   0  0.0
 72  32 74.9     0   0  0.0     0   0  0.0
```

Now we see reads per second (rps), writes per second (wps), and percent utilization (util). Notice that iostat now drops the tty and cpu summaries. We can see them if needed by using -t and -c. The reduced width of the output leaves room for more disks.

The following was run on a server with over twenty disks.

```
$ iostat -D 5 2
      sd0             sd1             sd6             sd30
rps wps util   rps wps util   rps wps util   rps wps util
  0   0  0.0     0   0  0.0     0   0  0.0     0   0  0.0
370  75 89.3     0   0  0.0     0   0  0.0     0   0  0.0
```

However, by default iostat prints only four disks, selected from the top four in an alphabetically sorted list of I/O devices.[6]

## 4.10.3 iostat -l n

Continuing the previous example, if we want to see more than four disks, we use the -l option. Here we use -l 6 so that six disks are printed.

```
$ iostat -D16 5 2
      sd0             sd1             sd6             sd30            sd31            sd32
rps wps util   rps wps util   rps wps util   rps wps util   rps wps util   rps wps util
  0   0  0.0     0   0  0.0     0   0  0.0     0   0  0.0     0   0  0.0     0   0  0.0
369   9 68.8     0   0  0.0     0   0  0.0     0   0  0.0     0   0  0.0     0   0  0.0
```

---

5. "DISK_NEW" for iostat means sometime before Solaris 2.5.
6. See cmd/stat/common/acquire.c: insert_into() scans a list of I/O devices, calling iodev_cmp() to decide placement. iodev_cmp() initially groups in the following order: controllers, disks/partitions, tapes, NFS, I/O paths, unknown. strcmp() is then used for alphabetical sorting.

If we don't like `iostat`'s choice of disks to monitor, we can specify them on the command line as with the following.

```
$ iostat -D16 sd30 sd31 sd32 sd33 sd34 sd35 5 2
      sd30            sd31            sd32            sd33            sd34            sd35
 rps wps util   rps wps util   rps wps util   rps wps util   rps wps util   rps wps util
   0   0  0.0     0   0  0.0     0   0  0.0     0   0  0.0     0   0  0.0     0   0  0.0
   0   0  0.0     0   0  0.0     0   0  0.0     0   0  0.0     0   0  0.0     0   0  0.0
```

## 4.10.4 `iostat -n`

Often we don't think in terms of device instance names. The `-n` option uses the familiar logical name for the device.

```
$ iostat -n 5 2
     tty          c0t0d0          c0t2d0      mars:vold(pid2       cpu
 tin tout kps tps serv   kps tps serv   kps tps serv   us sy wt id
   0    1   6   1   11     0   0    8     0   0    3    1  1  0 98
   0   39 260 168    4     0   0    0     0   0    0    6 22  0 72
```

## 4.10.5 `iostat -x`

Extended device statistics are printed with the `-x` option, making the output of `iostat` multiline.

```
$ iostat -x 5 2
                extended device statistics
device      r/s     w/s    kr/s    kw/s wait actv   svc_t  %w  %b
dad1        0.5     0.2     4.9     1.4  0.0  0.0    11.1   0   0
fd0         0.0     0.0     0.0     0.0  0.0  0.0     0.0   0   0
sd1         0.0     0.0     0.0     0.0  0.0  0.0     7.7   0   0
nfs1        0.0     0.0     0.0     0.0  0.0  0.0     3.0   0   0
                extended device statistics
device      r/s     w/s    kr/s    kw/s wait actv   svc_t  %w  %b
dad1      109.6     0.0   165.8     0.0  0.0  0.6     5.6   0  61
fd0         0.0     0.0     0.0     0.0  0.0  0.0     0.0   0   0
sd1         0.0     0.0     0.0     0.0  0.0  0.0     0.0   0   0
nfs1        0.0     0.0     0.0     0.0  0.0  0.0     0.0   0   0
```

Now `iostat` is printing a line per device, which contains many of the statistics previously discussed. This includes percent busy (`%b`) and the average wait queue length (`wait`). Also included are reads and writes per second (`r/s`, `w/s`), kilobytes read and written per second (kr/s, kw/s), average active transactions (actv), average event service time (svc_t)—which includes both waiting and active times—and percent wait queue populated (%w).

The -x multiline output is much more frequently used than iostat's original single-line output, which now seems somewhat antiquated.

### 4.10.6 iostat -p, -P

Per-partition (or "slice") statistics can be printed with -p. iostat continues to print entire disk summaries as well, unless the -P option is used. The following demonstrates a combination of a few common options.

```
$ iostat -xnmPz 5
                    extended device statistics
    r/s    w/s    kr/s    kw/s wait actv wsvc_t asvc_t  %w  %b device
    0.5    0.2     4.8     1.4  0.0  0.0    5.2    6.7   0   0 c0t0d0s0 (/)
    0.0    0.0     0.0     0.0  0.0  0.0    0.1   32.0   0   0 c0t0d0s1
    0.0    0.0     0.2     0.0  0.0  0.0    1.1    2.6   0   0 c0t0d0s3 (/extra1)
    0.0    0.0     0.1     0.0  0.0  0.0    3.1    7.7   0   0 c0t0d0s4 (/extra2)
    0.0    0.0     0.0     0.0  0.0  0.0   11.9   17.4   0   0 c0t0d0s5 (/extra3)
    0.0    0.0     0.0     0.0  0.0  0.0   10.3   12.0   0   0 c0t0d0s6 (/extra4)
    0.0    0.0     0.0     0.0  0.0  0.0    0.0    3.0   0   0 mars:vold(pid512)
                    extended device statistics
    r/s    w/s    kr/s    kw/s wait actv wsvc_t asvc_t  %w  %b device
    9.6   88.9    69.0   187.6  3.4  1.9   34.2   19.8  61 100 c0t0d0s0 (/)
...
```

With the extended output (-x), a line is printed for each partition (-P), along with its logical name (-n) and mount point if available (-m). Lines with zero activity are not printed (-z). No count was given, so iostat will continue forever. In this example, only c0t0d0s0 was active.

### 4.10.7 iostat -e

Error statistics can be printed with the -e option.

```
$ iostat -xne
                    extended device statistics       ---- errors ---
    r/s    w/s    kr/s    kw/s wait actv wsvc_t asvc_t  %w  %b s/w h/w trn tot device
    0.5    0.2     5.0     1.4  0.0  0.0    5.0    6.6   0   0   0   0   0   0 c0t0d0
    0.0    0.0     0.0     0.0  0.0  0.0    0.0    0.0   0   0   0   0   0   0 fd0
    0.0    0.0     0.0     0.0  0.0  0.0    0.0    7.7   0   0   0   0   1   1 c0t2d0
    0.0    0.0     0.0     0.0  0.0  0.0    0.0    3.0   0   0   0   0   0   0 mars:vold
```

The errors are soft (s/w), hard (h/w), transport (trn), and a total (tot). The following are examples for each of these errors.

- **Soft disk error.** A disk sector fails its CRC and needs to be reread.
- **Hard disk error.** A disk sector continues to fail its CRC after being reread several times (usually 15) and cannot be read.
- **Transport error.** One reported by the I/O bus.

## 4.10.8 `iostat -E`

All error statistics available can be printed with -E, which is also useful for discovering the existence of disks.

```
$ iostat -E
dad1        Soft Errors: 0 Hard Errors: 0 Transport Errors: 0
Model: ST38420A         Revision: 3.05       Serial No: 7AZ04J9S
Size: 8.62GB <8622415872 bytes>
Media Error: 0 Device Not Ready: 0  No Device: 0 Recoverable: 0
Illegal Request: 0
sd1         Soft Errors: 0 Hard Errors: 0 Transport Errors: 1
Vendor:    LG     Product: CD-ROM CRD-8322B Revision: 1.05 Serial No:
Size: 0.00GB <0 bytes>
Media Error: 0 Device Not Ready: 0 No Device: 0 Recoverable: 0
Illegal Request: 0 Predictive Failure Analysis: 0
```

This example shows a system with an 8.62 gigabyte disk (dad1, ST38420A) and a CD-ROM (sd1). Only one transport error on the CD-ROM device occurred.

## 4.11 Reading `iostat`

Previously we discussed the %b and wait fields of iostat's extended output. Many more fields provide other insights into disk behavior.

### 4.11.1 Event Size Ratio

The extended iostat output includes per-second averages for the number of events and sizes, which are in the first four columns. To demonstrate them, we captured the following output while a find / command was also running.

```
$ iostat -xnz 5
                    extended device statistics
    r/s    w/s    kr/s    kw/s wait actv wsvc_t asvc_t  %w  %b device
    0.2    0.2    1.1     1.5  0.0  0.0    6.5    7.1   0   0 c0t0d0
    0.0    0.0    0.0     0.0  0.0  0.0    0.0    7.7   0   0 c0t2d0
    0.0    0.0    0.0     0.0  0.0  0.0    0.0    3.0   0   0 mairs:vold(pid512)
                    extended device statistics
    r/s    w/s    kr/s    kw/s wait actv wsvc_t asvc_t  %w  %b device
  179.8    0.0  290.4     0.0  0.0  0.6    0.0    3.5   0  64 c0t0d0
                    extended device statistics
    r/s    w/s    kr/s    kw/s wait actv wsvc_t asvc_t  %w  %b device
  227.0    0.0  351.8     0.0  0.0  0.8    0.0    3.7   0  83 c0t0d0
                    extended device statistics
    r/s    w/s    kr/s    kw/s wait actv wsvc_t asvc_t  %w  %b device
  217.2    0.0  358.6     0.0  0.0  0.8    0.0    3.8   0  84 c0t0d0
```

Observe the $r/s$ and $kr/s$ fields when the disk was 83% busy. Let's begin with the fact it is 83% busy and only pulling 351.8 Kbytes/sec; extrapolating from 83% to 100%, this disk would peak at a miserable 420 Kbytes/sec. Now, given that we know that this disk can be driven at over 12 Mbytes/sec,[7] running at a speed of 420 Kbytes/sec (3% of the maximum) is a sign that something is seriously amiss. In this case, it is likely to be caused by the nature of the I/O—heavy random disk activity caused by the find command (which we can prove by using DTrace).

Had we only been looking at volume ($kr/s$ + $kw/s$), then a rate of 351.8 Kbytes/sec may have incorrectly implied that this disk was fairly idle.

Another detail to notice is that there were on average 227 reads per second for that sample. There are certain overheads involved when asking a disk to perform an I/O event, so the number of IOPS (I/O operations per second) is useful to consider. Here we would add $r/s$ and $w/s$.

Finally, we can take the value of $kr/s$ and divide by $r/s$, to calculate the average read size: 351.8 Kbytes / 227 = 1.55 Kbytes. A similar calculation is used for the average write size. A value of 1.55 Kbytes is small but to be expected from the find command because it reads through small directory files and inodes.

## 4.11.2 Service Times

Three service times are available: wsvc_t, for the average time spent on the wait queue; asvc_t, for the average time spent active (sent to the disk device); and svc_t for wsvc_t plus asvc_t. iostat prints these in milliseconds.

---

7. We know this from watching iostat while a simple dd test runs: dd if = /dev/rdsk/c0t0d0s0 of = /dev/null bs = 128K.

The active service time is the most interesting; it is the time from when a disk device accepted the event to when it sent a completion interrupt. The source code behind `iostat` describes active time as "run" time. The following demonstrates small active service times caused by running dd on the raw device.

```
$ iostat -xnz 5
...
                    extended device statistics
    r/s    w/s   kr/s   kw/s wait actv wsvc_t asvc_t  %w  %b device
  549.4    0.0 4394.8    0.0  0.0  1.0    0.0    1.7   0  95 c0t0d0
```

Next, we observe longer active service times while a `find /` runs.

```
$ iostat -xnz 5
...
                    extended device statistics
    r/s    w/s   kr/s   kw/s wait actv wsvc_t asvc_t  %w  %b device
   26.2   64.0  209.6  127.1  2.8  1.5   31.2   16.9  43  80 c0t0d0
```

From the previous discussion on event size ratios, we can see that a dd command pulling 4395 Kbytes/sec at 95% busy is using the disks in a better manner than a `find /` command pulling 337 Kbytes/sec (209.6 + 127.1) at 80% busy.

Now we can consider the average active service times, which have been highlighted (`asvc_t`). For the dd command, this was 1.7 ms, while for the `find /` command, it was much slower at 16.9 ms. Faster is better, so this statistic can directly describe average disk event behavior without any further calculation. It also helps to become familiar with what values are "good" or "bad" for your disks. Note: `iostat(1M)` does warn against believing service times for very idle disks.

Should the disk become saturated with requests, we may also see average wait queue times (`wsvc_t`). This indicates the average time penalty for disk events that have queued, and as such can help us understand the effects of saturation.

Lastly, disk service times are interesting from a disk perspective, but they do not necessarily equal application latency; that depends on what the file system is doing (caching, reading ahead). See Section 5.2, to continue the discussion of application latency from the FS.

# 4.12 `iostat` Internals

`iostat` is a consumer of kstat (the Kernel statistics facility, Chapter 11), which prints statistics for `KSTAT_TYPE_IO` devices. We can use the `kstat(1M)` command to see the data that `iostat` is using.

```
$ kstat -n dad1
module: dad                          instance: 1
name:   dad1                         class:     disk
        crtime                       1.718803613
        nread                        5172183552
        nwritten                     1427398144
        rcnt                         0
        reads                        509751
        rlastupdate                  1006817.75420951
        rlentime                     4727.596773858
        rtime                        3551.281310393
        snaptime                     1006817.75420951
        wcnt                         0
        wlastupdate                  1006817.75420951
        wlentime                     3681.523121192
        writes                       207061
        wtime                        492.453167341
$ kstat -n dad1,error
module: daderror                     instance: 1
name:   dad1,error                   class:     device_error
         No Device                   0
        Device Not Ready             0
        Hard Errors                  0
        Illegal Request              0
        Media Error                  0
        Model                        ST38420A          Revision
        Recoverable                  0
        Revision                     3.05
        Serial No                    7AZ04J9S          Size
        Size                         8622415872
        Soft Errors                  0
        Transport Errors             0
        crtime                       1.718974829
        snaptime                     1006852.93847071
```

This shows a kstat object named `dad1`, which is of `kstat_io_t` and is well documented in `sys/kstat.h`. The `dad1,error` object is a regular `kstat` object.

A sample is below.

```
typedef struct kstat_io {
...
        hrtime_t wtime;          /* cumulative wait (pre-service) time */
        hrtime_t wlentime;       /* cumulative wait length*time product */
        hrtime_t wlastupdate;    /* last time wait queue changed */
        hrtime_t rtime;          /* cumulative run (service) time */
        hrtime_t rlentime;       /* cumulative run length*time product */
        hrtime_t rlastupdate;    /* last time run queue changed */
                                                   See sys/kstat.h
```

Since kstat has already provided meaningful data, it is fairly easy for `iostat` to sample it, run some interval calculations, and then print it. As a demonstration of what `iostat` really does, the following is the code for calculating `%b`.

```
/* % of time there is a transaction running */
t_delta = hrtime_delta(old ? old->is_stats.rtime : 0,
    new->is_stats.rtime);
if (t_delta) {
        r_pct = (double)t_delta;
        r_pct /= hr_etime;
        r_pct *= 100.0;
```
*See ...cmd/stat/iostat.c*

The key statistic, `is_stats.rtime`, is from the `kstat_io struct` and is described as "cumulative run (service) time." Since this is a cumulative counter, the old value of `is_stats.rtime` is subtracted from the new, to calculate the actual cumulative runtime since the last sample (`t_delta`). This is then divided by `hr_etime`—the total elapsed time since the last sample—and then multiplied by 100 to form a percentage.

This approach could be described as saying a service time of 1000 ms is available every one second. This provides a convenient known upper limit that can be used for percentage calculations. If 200 ms of service time was consumed in one second, then the disk is 20% busy. Consider using Kbytes/sec instead for our busy calculation; the upper limit would vary according to random or sequential activity, and determining it would be quite challenging.

How `wait` is calculated in the `iostat.c` source looks identical, this time with `is_stats.wlentime`. `kstat.h` describes this as "cumulative wait length × time product" and discusses when it is updated.

```
* At each change of state (entry or exit from the queue),
* we add the elapsed time (since the previous state change)
* to the active time if the queue length was non-zero during
* that interval; and we add the product of the elapsed time
* times the queue length to the running length*time sum.
...
```
*See kstat.h*

This method, known as a "Riemann sum," allows us to calculate a proportionally accurate average wait queue length, based on the length of time at each queue length.

The comment from `kstat.h` also sheds light on how percent busy is calculated: At each change of disk state the elapsed time is added to the active time if there was activity. This sum of active time is the `rtime` used earlier.

For more information on these statistics and kstat, see Section 11.5.2.

## 4.13 sar -d

`iostat` is not the only kstat disk statistics consumer in Solaris; there is also the system activity reporter, `sar`. This is both a command (`/usr/sbin/sar`) and a background service (in the crontab for `sys`) that archives statistics over time and keeps them under `/var/adm/sa`. In Solaris 10 the service is called `svc:/system/sar:default`. It can be enabled by `svcadm enable sar`.[8]

Gathering statistics over time can be especially valuable for identifying long-term patterns. Such statistics can also help identify what activity is "normal" for your disks and can highlight any change around the same time that performance problems were noticed. The disks may not misbehave the moment you analyze them with `iostat`.[9]

To demonstrate the disk statistics that `sar` uses, we can run it by providing an interval.

```
# sar -d 5

SunOS mars 5.11 snv 16 sun4u     02/21/2006

15:56:55   device        %busy    avque    r+w/s   blks/s   avwait   avserv
15:57:00   dad1            58       0.6      226     1090      0.0      2.7
           dad1,a          58       0.6      226     1090      0.0      2.7
           dad1,b           0       0.0        0        0      0.0      0.0
           dad1,c           0       0.0        0        0      0.0      0.0
           dad1,d           0       0.0        0        0      0.0      0.0
           dad1,e           0       0.0        0        0      0.0      0.0
           dad1,f           0       0.0        0        0      0.0      0.0
           dad1,g           0       0.0        0        0      0.0      0.0
           fd0              0       0.0        0        0      0.0      0.0
           nfs1             0       0.0        0        0      0.0      0.0
           sd1              0       0.0        0        0      0.0      0.0
```

The output of `sar -d` includes many fields that we have previously discussed, including percent busy (`%busy`), average wait queue length (`avque`), average wait

---

8. Pending bug 6302763.
9. Some people do automate `iostat` to run at regular intervals and log the output. Having this sort of comparative data on hand during a crisis can be invaluable.

queue time (avwait), and average service time (avserv). Since sar reads the same Kstats that iostat uses, the values reported should be the same.

sar -d also provides the total of reads + writes per second (r+w/s), and the number of 512 byte blocks per second (blk/s).[10]

The disk statistics from sar are among its most trustworthy. Be aware that sar is an old tool and that many parts of Solaris have changed since sar was written (file system caches, for example). Careful interpretation is needed to make use of the statistics that sar prints.

Some tools plot the sar output,[11] which affords a helpful way to visualize data. So long as we understand what the data really means.

## 4.14 Trace Normal Form (TNF) Tracing for I/O

The TNF tracing facility was added to Solaris 2.5 release. It provided various kernel debugging probes that could be enabled to measure thread activity, syscalls, paging, swapping, and I/O events. The I/O probes could answer questions that iostat and Kstat could not, such as which process was causing disk activity. The probes could measure details such as I/O size, block addresses, and event times.

TNF tracing wasn't for the faint-hearted, and not many people learned how to interpret its terse output. A few tools based on TNF tracing were written, including the TAZ disk tool (Richard McDougall) and psio (Brendan Gregg).

For details on TNF tracing see tracing(3TNF) and tnf_kernel_probes(4).

DTrace supersedes TNF tracing, and is discussed in the next section. DTrace can measure the same events that TNF tracing did, but in an easy and programmable manner.

## 4.15 DTrace for I/O

DTrace was added to the Solaris 10 release; see Chapter 10 for a reference. DTrace can trace I/O events with ease by using the io provider, and tracing I/O with the io provider is often used as a demonstration of DTrace itself.

### 4.15.1 io Probes

The io provider supplies io:::start and io:::done probes, which for disk events represents the initiation and completion of physical I/O.

---

10. It's possible that sar was written before the kilobytes unit was conventional.
11. Solaris 10 does ship with StarOffice™ 7, which can plot interactively.

```
# dtrace -lP io
   ID    PROVIDER            MODULE                 FUNCTION NAME
   60         io            genunix                  biodone done
   61         io            genunix                  biowait wait-done
   62         io            genunix                  biowait wait-start
   71         io            genunix           default_physio start
   72         io            genunix            bdev_strategy start
   73         io            genunix                  aphysio start
  862         io                nfs                 nfs4_bio done
  863         io                nfs                 nfs3_bio done
  864         io                nfs                  nfs_bio done
  865         io                nfs                 nfs4_bio start
  866         io                nfs                 nfs3_bio start
  867         io                nfs                  nfs_bio start
```

In this example, we list the probes from the `io` provider. This provider also tracks NFS events, raw disk I/O events, and asynchronous disk I/O events.

The names for the `io:::start` and `io:::done` probes include the kernel function names. Disk events are likely to use the functions `bdev_strategy` and `biodone`, the same functions that TNF tracing probed. If you are writing DTrace scripts to match only one type of disk activity, then specify the function name. For example, `io::bdev_strategy:start` matches physical disk events.

The probes `io:::wait-start` and `io:::wait-done` trace the time when a thread blocks for I/O and begins to wait and the time when the wait has completed.

Details about each I/O event are provided by three arguments to these `io` probes. Their DTrace variable names and contents are as follows:

- **args[0]: struct bufinfo.** Useful details from the `buf` struct
- **args[1]: struct devinfo.** Details about the device: major and minor numbers, instance name, etc.
- **args[2]: struct fileinfo.** Details about the file name, path name, file system, offset, etc.

Note that the `io` probes fire for all I/O requests to peripheral devices and for all file read and file write requests to an NFS server. However, requests for metadata from an NFS server, for example. `readdir(3C)`, do not trigger `io` probes.

The `io` probes are documented in detail in Section 10.6.1.

## 4.15.2 I/O Size One-Liners

You can easily fetch I/O event details with DTrace. The following one-liner command tracks PID, process name, and I/O event size.

```
# dtrace -n 'io:::start { printf("%d %s %d",pid,execname,args[0]->b_bcount); }'
dtrace: description 'io:::start ' matched 6 probes
CPU     ID                      FUNCTION:NAME
  0     72                      bdev_strategy:start 418 nfsd 36864
  0     72                      bdev_strategy:start 418 nfsd 36864
  0     72                      bdev_strategy:start 418 nfsd 36864
  0     72                      bdev_strategy:start 0 sched 512
  0     72                      bdev_strategy:start 0 sched 1024
  0     72                      bdev_strategy:start 418 nfsd 1536
  0     72                      bdev_strategy:start 418 nfsd 1536
...
```

This command assumes that the correct PID is on the CPU for the start of an I/O event, which in this case is fine. When you use DTrace to trace PIDs, be sure to consider whether the process is synchronous with the event.

Tracing I/O activity as it occurs can generate many screenfuls of output. The following one-liner produces a simple summary instead, printing a report of PID, process name, and IOPS (I/O count). We match on io:genunix::start so that this script matches disk events and not NFS events.

```
# dtrace -n 'io:genunix::start { @[pid, execname] = count(); }'
dtrace: description 'io:genunix::start ' matched 3 probes
^C

    16585   find                                                          420
    16586   tar                                                          2812
    16584   dd                                                          22443
```

From the output, we can see that the dd command requested 22,443 disk events, and find requested 420.

### 4.15.3 A More Elaborate Example

While one-liners can be handy, it is often more useful to write DTrace scripts. The following DTrace script uses the device, buffer, and file name information from the io probes.

```
#!/usr/sbin/dtrace -s
#pragma D option quiet

dtrace:::BEGIN
{
        printf("%10s %58s %2s %8s\n", "DEVICE", "FILE", "RW", "Size");
}

io:::start
{
        printf("%10s %58s %2s %8d\n", args[1]->dev_statname,
            args[2]->fi_pathname, args[0]->b_flags & B_READ ? "R" : "W",
            args[0]->b_bcount);
}
```

When run, it provides a simple tracelike output showing the device, file name, read/write flag, and I/O size.

```
# ./iotrace.d
    DEVICE                                                    FILE RW    SIZE
    cmdk0                            /export/home/rmc/.sh_history  W    4096
    cmdk0                              /opt/Acrobat4/bin/acroread  R    8192
    cmdk0                              /opt/Acrobat4/bin/acroread  R    1024
    cmdk0                              /var/tmp/wscon-:0.0-gLaW9a  W    3072
    cmdk0                       /opt/Acrobat4/Reader/AcroVersion  R    1024
    cmdk0        /opt/Acrobat4/Reader/intelsolaris/bin/acroread  R    8192
    cmdk0        /opt/Acrobat4/Reader/intelsolaris/bin/acroread  R    8192
    cmdk0        /opt/Acrobat4/Reader/intelsolaris/bin/acroread  R    4096
    cmdk0        /opt/Acrobat4/Reader/intelsolaris/bin/acroread  R    8192
    cmdk0        /opt/Acrobat4/Reader/intelsolaris/bin/acroread  R    8192
```

The way this script traces I/O events as they occur is similar to the way the Solaris snoop command traces network packets. An enhanced version of this script, called iosnoop, is discussed later in this chapter.

Since I/O events are generally "slow" (a few hundred per second, depending on activity), the CPU costs for tracing them with DTrace is minimal (often less than 0.1% CPU).

## 4.15.4 I/O Size Aggregation

The following short DTrace script makes for an incredibly useful tool; it is available in the DTraceToolkit as bitesize.d. It traces the requested I/O size by process and prints a report that uses the DTrace quantize aggregating function.

```
#!/usr/sbin/dtrace -s
#pragma D option quiet

dtrace:::BEGIN
{
        printf("Tracing... Hit Ctrl-C to end.\n");
}

io:::start
{
        @size[pid, curpsinfo->pr_psargs] = quantize(args[0]->b_bcount);
}

dtrace:::END
{
        printf("%8s  %s\n", "PID", "CMD");
        printa("%8d  %s\n%@d\n", @size);
}
```

The script was run while a `find /` command executed.

```
# ./bites.d
Tracing... Hit Ctrl-C to end.
^C
    PID   CMD
  14818   find /

         value ------------- Distribution ------------- count
           512 |                                            0
          1024 |@@@@@@@@@@@@@@@@@@@@@@@@@@@@@@@@@@@@@@@@@  2009
          2048 |                                            0
          4096 |                                            0
          8192 |@@@                                       180
         16384 |                                            0
```

The `find` command churned thorough directory files and inodes on disk, causing many small disk events. The distribution plot that DTrace has printed nicely conveys the disk behavior that `find` caused and is read as follows: 2009 disk events were between 1024 and 2047 bytes in size, and 180 disk events were between 8 Kbytes and 15.9 Kbytes. In summary, we measured `find` causing a storm of small disk events.

Such a large number of small events usually indicates random disk activity—a characteristic that DTrace can also accurately measure.

Finding the size of disk events alone can be quite valuable. To demonstrate this further, we ran the same script for a different workload. This time we used a `tar` command to archive the disk.

```
# ./bites.d
Tracing... Hit Ctrl-C to end.
^C
  8122   tar cf /dev/null /

         value ------------- Distribution ------------- count
           512 |                                            0
          1024 |@@@@@@@@@@@@@@@@@@@@@@@@@@                 226
          2048 |@@                                         19
          4096 |@@                                         23
          8192 |@@@@@@@@                                   71
         16384 |                                            3
         32768 |                                            1
         65536 |@                                           8
        131072 |@@@@@                                      52
        262144 |                                            0
```

While `tar` must work through many of the same directory files as `find`, it now also reads through file contents. There are now many events in the 128 to 255 Kbytes bucket because `tar` has encountered some large files.

And finally, we ran the script with a deliberately large sequential workload—a `dd` command with specific options.

```
# ./bites.d
Tracing... Hit Ctrl-C to end.
^C
    PID  CMD
   8112  dd if=/dev/rdsk/c0t0d0s0 of=/dev/null bs=128k

          value  ------------- Distribution ------------- count
          65536 |                                         0
         131072 |@@@@@@@@@@@@@@@@@@@@@@@@@@@@@@@@@@@@@@@@@@ 246
         262144 |                                         0
```

We used the dd command to read 128-Kbyte blocks from the raw device, and that's exactly what happened.

It is interesting to compare raw device behavior with that of the block device. In the following demonstration, we changed the rdsk to dsk and ran dd on a slice that contained a freshly mounted file system.

```
# ./bites.d
Tracing... Hit Ctrl-C to end.
^C
   8169  dd if=/dev/dsk/c0t0d0s3 of=/dev/null bs=128k

          value  ------------- Distribution ------------- count
          32768 |                                         0
          65536 |                                         1
         131072 |@@@@@@@@@@@@@@@@@@@@@@@@@@@@@@@@@@@@@@@@@@ 1027
         262144 |                                         0
```

No difference there, except that when the end of the slice was reached, a smaller I/O event was issued.

This demonstration becomes interesting after the dd command has been run several times on the same slice. The distribution plot then looks like this.

```
# ./bites.d
Tracing... Hit Ctrl-C to end.
^C
   8176  dd if=/dev/dsk/c0t0d0s3 of=/dev/null bs=128k

          value  ------------- Distribution ------------- count
           4096 |                                         0
           8192 |@@@@@@@@@@@@@@@                          400
          16384 |@@@                                      83
          32768 |@                                        29
          65536 |@@                                       46
         131072 |@@@@@@@@@@@@@@@@@@@@@@@@@@                667
         262144 |                                         0
```

The distribution plot has become quite different, with fewer 128-Kbyte events and many 8-Kbyte events. What is happening is that the block device is reclaiming pages from the page cache and is at times going to disk only to fill in the gaps.

We next used a different DTrace one-liner to examine this further, summing the bytes read by two different invocations of dd: the first (PID 8186) on the dsk device and the second (PID 8187) on the rdsk device.

```
# dtrace -n 'io:::start { @[pid, args[1]->dev_statname] = sum(args[0]->b_bcount); }'
dtrace: description 'io:::start ' matched 6 probes
^C

    8186   dad1                                                    89710592
    8187   dad1                                                   134874112
```

The rdsk version read the full slice, 134,874,112 bytes. The dsk version read 89,710,592 bytes, 66.5%.

## 4.15.5 I/O Seek Aggregation

The following script can help identify random or sequential activity by measuring the seek distance for disk events and generating a distribution plot. The script is available in the DTraceToolkit as seeksize.d.

```
#!/usr/sbin/dtrace -s
#pragma D option quiet

self int last[dev_t];

dtrace:::BEGIN
{
        printf("Tracing... Hit Ctrl-C to end.\n");
}

io:genunix::start
/self->last[args[0]->b_edev] != 0/
{
        this->last = self->last[args[0]->b_edev];
        this->dist = (int)(args[0]->b_blkno - this->last) > 0 ?
            args[0]->b_blkno - this->last : this->last - args[0]->b_blkno;
        @size[args[1]->dev_statname] = quantize(this->dist);
}

io:genunix::start
{
        self->last[args[0]->b_edev] = args[0]->b_blkno +
            args[0]->b_bcount / 512;
}
```

Since the buffer struct is available to the io probes, we can examine the block address for each I/O event, provided as args[0]->b_blkno. This address is relative to the slice, so we must be careful to compare addresses only when the events are on the same slice, achieved in the script by matching on args[0]->b_edev.

We are assuming that we can trust the block address and that the disk device did not map it to something strange (or if it did, it was mapped proportionally). We are also assuming that the disk device isn't using a frontend cache to initially avoid seeks altogether, as with storage arrays.

The following example uses this script to examine random activity that was generated with `filebench`.

```
# ./seeks.d
Tracing... Hit Ctrl-C to end.
^C

  cmdk0
          value  ------------- Distribution ------------- count
             -1 |                                          0
              0 |@@@@                                      174
              1 |                                          0
              2 |                                          0
              4 |                                          0
              8 |                                          2
             16 |@@                                        104
             32 |@@@                                       156
             64 |@@                                        98
            128 |@                                         36
            256 |@                                         39
            512 |@@                                        70
           1024 |@@                                        71
           2048 |@@                                        71
           4096 |@                                         55
           8192 |@                                         43
          16384 |@                                         63
          32768 |@@                                        91
          65536 |@@@                                       135
         131072 |@@@@                                      159
         262144 |@@                                        107
         524288 |@@@@                                      183
        1048576 |@@@@                                      174
        2097152 |                                          0
```

And the following is for sequential activity from `filebench`.

```
# ./seeks.d
Tracing... Hit Ctrl-C to end.
^C

  cmdk0
          value  ------------- Distribution ------------- count
             -1 |                                          0
              0 |@@@@@@@@@@@@@@@@@@@@@@@@@@@@@@@@@@@@@@@@@@  27248
              1 |                                          0
              2 |                                          0
              4 |                                          0
              8 |                                          12
             16 |                                          141
             32 |                                          218
             64 |                                          118
            128 |                                          7
            256 |                                          81
            512 |                                          0
```

The difference is dramatic. For the sequential test most of the events incurred a zero length seek, whereas with the random test, the seeks were distributed up to the 1,048,576 to 2,097,151 bucket. The units are called disk blocks (not file system blocks), which are disk sectors (512 bytes).

## 4.15.6 I/O File Names

Sometimes knowing the file name that was accessed is of value. This is another detail that DTrace makes easily available through `args[2]->fi_pathname`, as demonstrated by the following script.

```
#!/usr/sbin/dtrace -s
#pragma D option quiet

dtrace:::BEGIN
{
        printf("Tracing... Hit Ctrl-C to end.\n");
}

io:::start
{
        @files[pid, execname, args[2]->fi_pathname] = sum(args[0]->b_bcount);
}

dtrace:::END
{
        normalize(@files, 1024);
        printf("%6s %-12s %6s %s\n", "PID", "CMD", "KB", "FILE");
        printa("%6d %-12.12s %@6d %s\n", @files);
}
```

Running this script with several files of a known size on a newly mounted file system produces the following.

```
# ./files.d
Tracing... Hit Ctrl-C to end.
^C
   PID CMD             KB FILE
  5797 bash             1 /extra1
  8376 grep             8 /extra1/lost+found
  8376 grep            10 /extra1/testfile_size10k
  8376 grep            20 /extra1/testfile_size20k
  8376 grep            30 /extra1/testfile_size30k
  8376 grep            64 <none>
  8376 grep         10240 /extra1/testfile_size10m
  8376 grep         20480 /extra1/testfile_size20m
  8376 grep         30720 /extra1/testfile_size30m
```

Not only can we see that the sizes match the files (see the file names), we can also see that the `bash` shell has read one kilobyte from the `/extra1` directory—no doubt reading the directory contents. The "`<none>`" file name occurs when file system blocks not related to a file are accessed.

## 4.16 Disk I/O Time

DTrace makes many I/O details available to us so that we can understand disk behavior. The previous examples measured I/O counts, I/O size, or seek distance, by disk, process, or file name. One measurement we haven't discussed yet is disk response time.

The time consumed responding to a disk event takes into account seek time, rotation time, transfer time, controller time, and bus time, and as such is an excellent metric for disk utilization. It also has a known maximum: 1000 ms per second per disk. The trick is being able to measure it accurately.

We are already familiar with one disk time measurement: `iostat`'s percent busy (`%b`), which measures disk active time.

Measuring disk I/O time properly for storage arrays has become a complex topic, one that depends on the vendor and the storage array model. To cover each of them is beyond what we have room for here. Some of the following concepts may still apply for storage arrays, but many will need careful consideration.

### 4.16.1 Simple Disk Event

The time the disk spends satisfying a disk request is often called the service time or the active service time. Ideally, we would be able to read event timestamps from the disk controller itself so that we knew exactly when the heads were seeking, when the sectors were read, and so on. Instead, we have the `bdev_strategy` and `biodone` events from the driver presented to DTrace as `io:::start` and `io:::done`.

> **Terminology**
> We define disk-response-time to describe the time consumed by the disk to service only the event in question. This time starts when the disk begins to service that event, which may mean the heads begin to seek. The time ends when the disk completes the request. The advantage of this measurement is that it provides a known maximum for the disk, 1000 ms of disk response time per second. This helps with the calculation for utilization percentages.

By measuring the time from the `strategy` (`bdev_strategy`) to the `biodone`, we have the driver's view of response time; it's the closest measurement available for the actual disk response time. In reality it includes a little extra time to arbitrate and send the request over the I/O bus, which in comparison to the disk time (which is usually measured in milliseconds) often is negligible. This is illustrated in Figure 4.1 for a simple disk event.

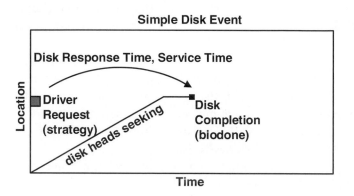

**Figure 4.1** Visualizing a Single Disk Event

The algorithm to measure disk response time is then

$$time(disk\ response) = time(biodone) - time(strategy)$$

We could estimate the total I/O time for a process as a sum of all its disk response times; however, it's not that simple. Modern disks allow multiple events to be sent to the disk, where they are queued. These events can be reordered by the disk so that events can be completed with a minimal sweep of the heads. The following example illustrates the multiple event problem.

## 4.16.2 Concurrent Disk Events

Let's consider that five concurrent disk requests are sent at time = 0 and that they complete at times = 10, 20, 30, 40, and 50 ms, as is represented in Figure 4.2.

The disk is busy processing these events from time = 0 to 50 ms and so is busy for 50 ms. The previous algorithm gives disk response times of 10, 20, 30, 40, and 50 ms. The total would then be 150 ms, implying that the disk has delivered 150 ms of disk response time in only 50 ms. The problem is that we are overcounting response times; just adding them together assumes that the disk processes events one by one, which is not always the case.

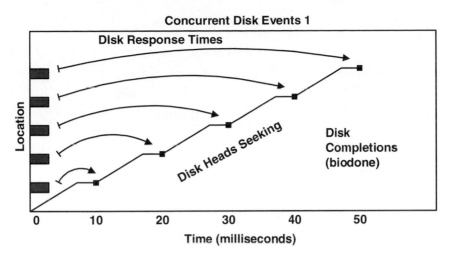

**Figure 4.2** Measuring Concurrent Disk Event Times

Later in this section we measure actual concurrent disk events by using DTrace and then plot it (see Section 4.17.4), which shows that this scenario does indeed occur.

To improve the algorithm for measuring concurrent events, we could treat the end time of the previous disk event as the start time. Time would then be measured from one biodone to the next. That would work nicely for the previous illustration. It doesn't work if disk events are sparse, such that the previous disk event was followed by a period of idle time. We would need to keep track of when the disk was idle to eliminate that problem.

More scenarios exist, too many to list here, that increase the complexity of our algorithm. To cut to the chase, we end up considering the following adaptive disk I/O time algorithm to be suitable for most situations.

### 4.16.3 Adaptive Disk I/O Time Algorithm

To cover simple, concurrent, sparse, and other types of events, we need to be a bit creative:

> *time(disk response) = MIN( time(biodone) – time(previous biodone, same dev),*
> *time(biodone) – time(previous idle -> strategy event, same dev) )*

We achieve the tracking of idle -> strategy events by counting pending events and matching on a strategy event when pending == 0. Both previous times above refer to previous times on the same disk device. This covers all scenarios, and is the algorithm currently used by the DTrace tools in the next section.

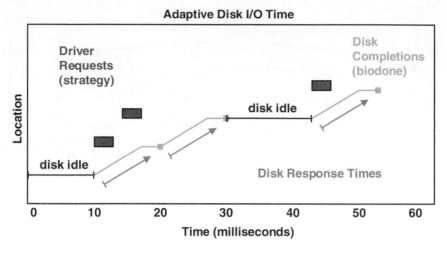

**Figure 4.3** Best Disk Response Times

In Figure 4.3, both concurrent and post-idle events are measured correctly.

There are some bizarre scenarios for which it could be argued that this algorithm is not perfect and that it is only an approximation. If we keep throwing scenarios at our disk algorithm and are fantastically lucky, we'll end up with an elegant algorithm to cover everything in an obvious way. However, there is a greater chance that we'll end up with an overly complex beastlike monstrosity and several contrived scenarios that still don't fit.

So we consider this algorithm presented as sufficient, as long as we remember that at times it may only be a close approximation.

## 4.16.4 Other Response Times

Thread-response time is the response time that the requesting thread experiences. This can be measured from the moment that a read/write system call blocks to its completion, assuming the request made it to disk and wasn't cached. This time includes other factors such as the time spent waiting on the run queue to be rescheduled and the time spent checking the page cache if used.

Application-response time is the time for the application to respond to a client event, often transaction oriented. Such a response time helps us understand why an application may respond slowly.

### 4.16.5  Time by Layer

The relationship between the response times is summarized in Figure 4.4, which depicts a typical sequence of events. This figure highlights both the different layers from which to consider response time and the terminology.

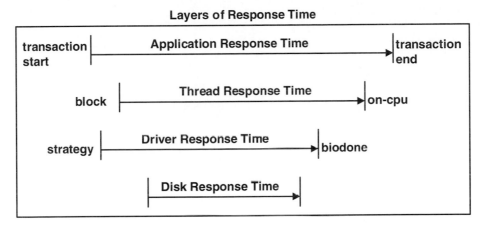

**Figure 4.4**  Relationship among Response Times

The sequence of events in Figure 4.4 is accurate for raw devices but is less meaningful for block devices. Reads on block devices often trigger read-ahead, which at times drives the disks asynchronously to the application reads; and writes often return from the cache and are later flushed to disk.

To understand the performance effect of response times purely from an application perspective, focus on thread and application response times and treat the disk I/O system as a black box. This leaves application latency as the most useful measurement, as discussed in Section 5.3.

## 4.17  DTraceToolkit Commands

The DTraceToolkit is a free collection of DTrace-based tools, some of which analyze disk behavior. We previously demonstrated cut-down versions of two of its scripts, `bitesize.d` and `seeksize.d`. Two of the most popular are `iotop` and `iosnoop`.

## 4.17.1 `iotop` Script

`iotop` uses DTrace to print disk I/O summaries by process, for details such as size (bytes) and disk I/O times. The following demonstrates the default output of `iotop`, which prints size summaries and refreshes the screen every five seconds.

```
# ./iotop
2006 Feb 13 13:38:21,  load: 0.35,  disk_r:  56615 Kb,  disk_w:    637 Kb

  UID    PID   PPID CMD              DEVICE  MAJ MIN D         BYTES
    0  27732  27703 find             cmdk0   102   0 R         38912
    0      0      0 sched            cmdk5   102 320 W        150016
    0      0      0 sched            cmdk2   102 128 W        167424
    0      0      0 sched            cmdk3   102 192 W        167424
    0      0      0 sched            cmdk4   102 256 W        167424
    0  27733  27703 bart             cmdk0   102   0 R      57897984
...
```

In the above output, the `bart` process read approximately 57 Mbytes from disk.

Disk I/O time summaries can also be printed with `-o`, which uses the adaptive disk-response-time algorithm previously discussed. Here we demonstrate this with an interval of ten seconds.

```
# ./iotop -o 10
2006 Feb 13 13:39:19,  load: 0.38,  disk_r:  74885 Kb,  disk_w:   1345 Kb

  UID    PID   PPID CMD              DEVICE  MAJ MIN D      DISKTIME
    1    418      1 nfsd             cmdk3   102 192 W           362
    1    418      1 nfsd             cmdk4   102 256 W           382
    1    418      1 nfsd             cmdk5   102 320 W           460
    1    418      1 nfsd             cmdk2   102 128 W           534
    0      0      0 sched            cmdk5   102 320 W         20643
    0      0      0 sched            cmdk3   102 192 W         25500
    0      0      0 sched            cmdk4   102 256 W         31024
    0      0      0 sched            cmdk2   102 128 W         35166
    0  27732  27703 find             cmdk0   102   0 R        722951
    0  27733  27703 bart             cmdk0   102   0 R       8858818
```

Note that `iotop` prints totals, not per second values. In this example, we read 74,885 Mbytes from disk during those ten seconds (`disk_r`), with the top process `bart` (PID 27733) consuming 8.8 seconds of disk time. For this ten-second interval, 8.8 seconds equates to a utilization value of 88%.

`iotop` can print %I/O utilization with the -P option; this percentage is based on 1000 ms of disk response time per second. The -C option can also be used to prevent the screen from being cleared and to instead provide a rolling output.

```
# ./iotop -CP 1
...
2006 Feb 13 13:40:34,  load: 0.36,  disk_r:   2350 Kb,  disk_w:    1026 Kb

  UID    PID   PPID CMD             DEVICE   MAJ MIN D   %I/O
    0      0      0 sched           cmdk0    102   0 R      0
    0      3      0 fsflush         cmdk0    102   0 W      1
    0  27743  27742 dtrace          cmdk0    102   0 R      2
    0      3      0 fsflush         cmdk0    102   0 R      8
    0      0      0 sched           cmdk0    102   0 W     14
    0  27732  27703 find            cmdk0    102   0 R     19
    0  27733  27703 bart            cmdk0    102   0 R     42
...
```

Figure 4.5 plots %I/O as find and bart read through /usr. This time bart causes heavier %I/O because there are bigger files to read and fewer directories for find to traverse.

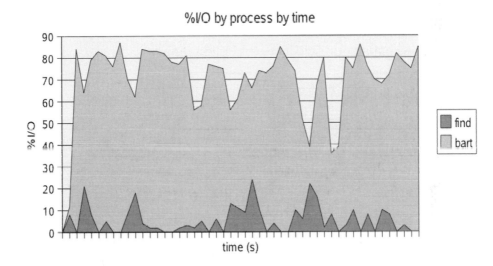

**Figure 4.5** find and bart Read through /usr

Other options for `iotop` can be listed with `-h` (this is version 0.75):

```
# ./iotop -h
USAGE: iotop [-C] [-D|-o|-P] [-j|-Z] [-d device] [-f filename]
             [-m mount_point] [-t top] [interval [count]]

                -C       # don't clear the screen
                -D       # print delta times, elapsed, us
                -j       # print project ID
                -o       # print disk delta times, us
                -P       # print %I/O (disk delta times)
                -Z       # print zone ID
                -d device      # instance name to snoop
                -f filename    # snoop this file only
                -m mount_point # this FS only
                -t top         # print top number only
   eg,
        iotop          # default output, 5 second samples
        iotop 1        # 1 second samples
        iotop -P       # print %I/O (time based)
        iotop -m /     # snoop events on filesystem / only
        iotop -t 20    # print top 20 lines only
        iotop -C 5 12  # print 12 x 5 second samples
```

These options including printing Zone and Project details.

## 4.17.2 `iosnoop` Script

`iosnoop` uses DTrace to monitor disk events in real time. The default output prints details such as PID, block address, and size. In the following example, a `grep` process reads several files from the `/etc/default` directory.

```
# ./iosnoop
  UID   PID D    BLOCK     SIZE       COMM PATHNAME
    0  1570 R   172636     2048       grep /etc/default/autofs
    0  1570 R   102578     1024       grep /etc/default/cron
    0  1570 R   102580     1024       grep /etc/default/devfsadm
    0  1570 R   108310     4096       grep /etc/default/dhcpagent
    0  1570 R   102582     1024       grep /etc/default/fs
    0  1570 R   169070     1024       grep /etc/default/ftp
    0  1570 R   108322     2048       grep /etc/default/inetinit
    0  1570 R   108318     1024       grep /etc/default/ipsec
    0  1570 R   102584     2048       grep /etc/default/kbd
    0  1570 R   102588     1024       grep /etc/default/keyserv
    0  1570 R   973440     8192       grep /etc/default/lu
...
```

The output is printed as the disk events complete.

To see a list of available options for `iosnoop`, use the `-h` option. The options include `-o` to print disk I/O time, using the adaptive disk-response-time algorithm previously discussed. The following is from `iosnoop` version 1.55.

```
# ./iosnoop -h
USAGE: iosnoop [-a|-A|-DeghiNostv] [-d device] [-f filename]
               [-m mount_point] [-n name] [-p PID]
       iosnoop          # default output
               -a       # print all data (mostly)
               -A       # dump all data, space delimited
               -D       # print time delta, us (elapsed)
               -e       # print device name
               -g       # print command arguments
               -i       # print device instance
               -N       # print major and minor numbers
               -o       # print disk delta time, us
               -s       # print start time, us
               -t       # print completion time, us
               -v       # print completion time, string
               -d device       # instance name to snoop
               -f filename     # snoop this file only
               -m mount_point  # this FS only
               -n name         # this process name only
               -p PID          # this PID only
   eg,
       iosnoop -v       # human readable timestamps
       iosnoop -N       # print major and minor numbers
       iosnoop -m /     # snoop events on filesystem / only
```

The block addresses printed are relative to the disk slice, so what may appear to be similar block addresses may in fact be on different slices or disks. The -N option can help ensure that we are examining the same slice since it prints major and minor numbers on which we can be match.

## 4.17.3 Plotting Disk Activity

Using the -t option for iosnoop prints the disk completion time in microseconds. In combination with -N, we can use this data to plot disk events for a process on one slice. Here we fetch the data for the find command, which contains the time (microseconds since boot) and block address. These are our X and Y coordinates. We check that we remain on the same slice (major and minor numbers) and then generate an X/Y plot.

```
# ./iosnoop -tN
TIME             MAJ MIN   UID    PID D   BLOCK    SIZE   COMM PATHNAME
1175384556358    102  0      0  27703 W 3932432    4096   ksh /root/.sh_history
1175384556572    102  0      0  27703 W    3826     512   ksh <none>
1175384565841    102  0      0  27849 R  198700    1024   find /usr/dt
1175384578103    102  0      0  27849 R  770288    3072   find /usr/dt/bin
1175384582354    102  0      0  27849 R  690320    8192   find <none>
1175384582817    102  0      0  27849 R  690336    8192   find <none>
1175384586787    102  0      0  27849 R  777984    2048   find /usr/dt/lib
1175384594313    102  0      0  27849 R  733880    1024   find /usr/dt/lib/amd64
...
```

We ran a `find /` command to generate random disk activity; the results are shown in Figure 4.6. As the disk heads seek to different block addresses, the position of the heads is plotted in red.

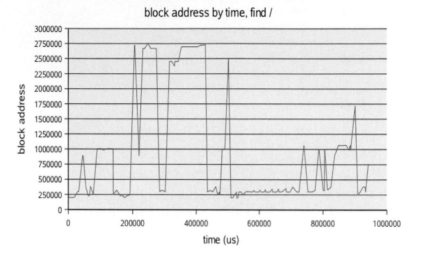

**Figure 4.6** Plotting Disk Activity, a Random I/O Example

Are we really looking at disk head seek patterns? Not exactly. What we are looking at are block addresses for `biodone` functions from the block I/O driver. We aren't using some X-ray vision to look at the heads themselves.

Now, if this is a simple disk device, then the block address probably relates to the disk head location.[12] But if this is a virtual device, say, a storage array, then block addresses could map to anything, depending on the storage layout. However, we could at least say that a large jump in block address probably means a seek at some point (although storage arrays will cache).

The block addresses do help us visualize the pattern of completed disk activity. But remember that "completed" means the block I/O driver *thinks* that the I/O event completed.

### 4.17.4 Plotting Concurrent Activity

Previously, we discussed concurrent disk activity and included a plot (Figure 4.2) to help us understand how these events may occur. Since DTrace can easily trace

12. Even "simple" disks these days map addresses in firmware to an internal optimized layout; all we know is the image of the disk that its firmware presents. The classic example here is sector zoning, as discussed in Section 4.4.

concurrent disk activity, we can include a plot of actual activity. The following DTrace script provides input for a spreadsheet. We match on a device by its major and minor numbers, then print timestamps as the first column and block addresses for `strategy` and `biodone` events in the remaining columns.

```
#!/usr/sbin/dtrace -s
#pragma D option quiet

io:genunix::start
/args[1]->dev_major == 102 && args[1]->dev_minor == 0/
{
        printf("%d,%d,\n", timestamp/1000, args[0]->b_blkno);
}

io:genunix::done
/args[1]->dev_major == 102 && args[1]->dev_minor == 0/
{
        printf("%d,,%d\n", timestamp/1000, args[0]->b_blkno);
}
```

The output of the DTrace script was plotted as Figure 4.7, with timestamps as X-coordinates.

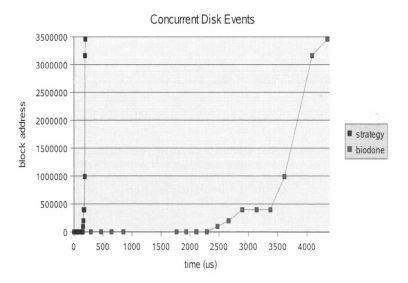

**Figure 4.7** Plotting Raw Driver Events: Strategy and Biodone

Initially, we see many quick `strategies` between 0 and 200 μs, ending in almost a vertical line. This is then followed by slower `biodones` as the disk catches up at mechanical speeds.

## 4.18 DTraceTazTool

TazTool[13] was a GUI disk-analysis tool that used TNF tracing to monitor disk events. It was most notable for its unique disk-activity visualization, which made identifying disk access patterns trivial. This visualization included long-term patterns that would normally be difficult to identify from screenfuls of text.

This visualization technique is returning with the development of a DTrace version of taztool: DTraceTazTool. A screenshot of this tool is shown in Figure 4.8.

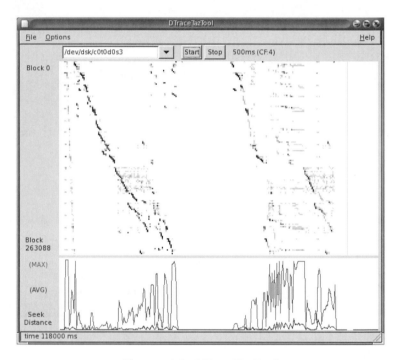

**Figure 4.8** DTraceTazTool

The first section of the plot measures a `ufsdump` of a file system, and the second measures a `tar` archive of the same file system, both times freshly mounted. We can see that the `ufsdump` command caused heavier sequential access (represented by dark stripes in the top graph and smaller seeks in the bottom graph) than did the `tar` command.

It is interesting to note that when the `ufsdump` command begins, disk activity can be seen to span the entire slice—`ufsdump` doing its passes.

---

13. See `http://www.solarisinternals.com/si/tools/taz` for more information.

# 5

# File Systems

File systems are typically observed as a layer between an application and the I/O services providing the underlying storage. When you look at file system performance, you should focus on the latencies observed at the application level. Historically, however, we have focused on techniques that look at the latency and throughput characteristics of the underlying storage and have been flying in the dark about the real latencies seen at the application level.

With the advent of DTrace, we now have end-to-end observability, from the application all the way through to the underlying storage. This makes it possible to do the following:

- Observe the latency and performance impact of file-level requests at the application level.
- Attribute physical I/O by applications and/or files.
- Identify performance characteristics contributed by the file system layer, in between the application and the I/O services.

## 5.1 Layers of File System and I/O

We can observe file system activity at three key layers:

- **I/O layer.** At the bottom of a file system is the I/O subsystem providing the backend storage for the file system. For a disk-based file system, this is typically the block I/O layer. Other file systems (for example, NFS) might use networks or other services to provide backend storage.

- **POSIX libraries and system calls.** Applications typically perform I/O through POSIX library interfaces. For example, an application needing to open and read a file would call open(2) followed by read(2).

    Most POSIX interfaces map directly to system calls, the exceptions being the asynchronous I/O interfaces. These are emulated by user-level thread libraries on top of POSIX pread/pwrite.

    You can trace at this layer with a variety of tools—truss and DTrace can trace the system calls on behalf of the application. truss has significant overhead when used at this level since it starts and stops the application at every system call. In contrast, DTrace typically only adds a few microseconds to each call.

- **VOP layer.** Solaris provides a layer of common entry points between the upper-level system calls and the file system—the file system vnode operations (VOP) interface layer. We can instrument these layers easily with DTrace. We've historically made special one-off tools to monitor at this layer by using kernel VOP-level interposer modules, a practice that adds significant instability risk and performance overhead.

Figure 5.1 shows the end-to-end layers for an application performing I/O through a file system.

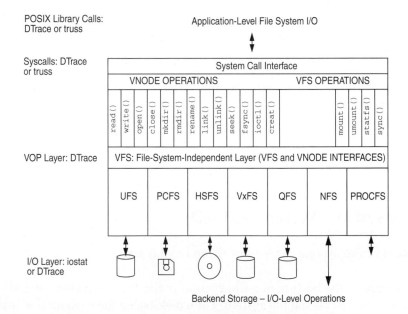

**Figure 5.1** Layers for Observing File System I/O

## 5.2 Observing Physical I/O

The traditional method of observing file system activity is to induce information
from the bottom end of the file system, for example, physical I/O. This can be done
easily with `iostat` or DTrace, as shown in the following `iostat` example and further in Chapter 4.

```
$ iostat -xnczpm 3
      cpu
 us sy wt id
  7  2  8 83
                        extended device statistics
     r/s    w/s    kr/s    kw/s wait actv wsvc_t  asvc_t  %w  %b device
     0.6    3.8    8.0    30.3  0.1  0.2   20.4    37.7   0   3 c0t0d0
     0.6    3.8    8.0    30.3  0.1  0.2   20.4    37.7   0   3 c0t0d0s0 (/)
     0.0    0.0    0.0     0.0  0.0  0.0    0.0    48.7   0   0 c0t0d0s1
     0.0    0.0    0.0     0.0  0.0  0.0    0.0     0.0   0   0 c0t0d0s2
     0.0    0.0    0.0     0.0  0.0  0.0  405.2  1328.5   0   0 c0t1d0
     0.0    0.0    0.0     0.0  0.0  0.0  405.9  1330.8   0   0 c0t1d0s1
     0.0    0.0    0.0     0.0  0.0  0.0    0.0     0.0   0   0 c0t1d0s2
    14.7    4.8  330.8     6.8  0.0  0.3    0.0    13.9   0   8 c4t16d1
    14.7    4.8  330.8     6.8  0.0  0.3    0.0    13.9   0   8 c4t16d1s7 (/export/home)
     1.4    0.4   70.4     4.3  0.0  0.0    0.0    21.8   0   2 c4t16d2
     1.4    0.4   70.4     4.3  0.0  0.0    0.0    21.8   0   2 c4t16d2s7 (/export/home2)
    12.8   12.4   73.5     7.4  0.0  0.1    0.0     2.5   0   3 c4t17d0
    10.8   10.8    0.4     0.4  0.0  0.0    0.0     0.0   0   0 c4t17d0s2
     2.0    1.6   73.1     7.0  0.0  0.1    0.0    17.8   0   3 c4t17d0s7 (/www)
     0.0    2.9    0.0   370.4  0.0  0.1    0.0    19.1   0   6 rmt/1
```

Using `iostat`, we can observe I/O counts, bandwidth, and latency at the device
level, and optionally per-mount, by using the `-m` option (note that this only works
for file systems like UFS that mount only one device). In the above example, we
can see that /export/home is mounted on `c4t16d1s7`. It is generating 14.7 reads
per second and 4.8 writes per second, with a response time of 13.9 milliseconds.
But that's all we know—far too often we deduce too much by simply looking at the
physical I/O characteristics. For example, in this case we could easily assume that
the upper-level application is experiencing good response times, when in fact substantial latency is being added in the file system layer, which is masked by these
statistics. We talk more about common scenarios in which latency is added in the
file system layer in Section 5.4.

By using the DTrace I/O provider, we can easily connect physical I/O events
with some file-system-level information; for example, *file names*. The script from
Section 5.4.3 shows a simple example of how DTrace can display per-operation
information with combined file-system-level and physical I/O information.

```
# ./iotrace.d
    DEVICE                                                   FILE RW      SIZE
    cmdk0                              /export/home/rmc/.sh_history  W      4096
    cmdk0                                 /opt/Acrobat4/bin/acroread  R      8192
    cmdk0                                 /opt/Acrobat4/bin/acroread  R      1024
    cmdk0                                 /var/tmp/wscon-:0.0-gLaW9a  W      3072
    cmdk0                            /opt/Acrobat4/Reader/AcroVersion  R      1024
    cmdk0          /opt/Acrobat4/Reader/intelsolaris/bin/acroread  R      8192
    cmdk0          /opt/Acrobat4/Reader/intelsolaris/bin/acroread  R      8192
    cmdk0          /opt/Acrobat4/Reader/intelsolaris/bin/acroread  R      4096
    cmdk0          /opt/Acrobat4/Reader/intelsolaris/bin/acroread  R      8192
    cmdk0          /opt/Acrobat4/Reader/intelsolaris/bin/acroread  R      8192
```

## 5.3  File System Latency

When analyzing performance, consider the file system as a black box. Look at the latency as it impacts the application and then identify the causes of the latency. For example, if an application is making `read()` calls at the POSIX layer, your first interest should be in how long each `read()` takes as a percentage of the overall application thread-response time. Only when you want to dig deeper should you consider the I/O latency behind the `read()`, such as disk service times—which ironically is where the performance investigation has historically begun. Figure 5.2 shows an example of how you can estimate performance. You can evaluate the percentage of time in the file system (*Tfilesys*) against the total elapsed time (*Ttotal*).

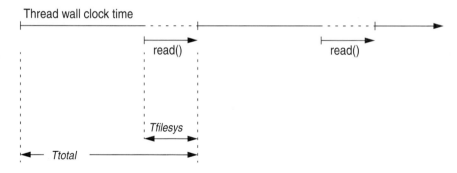

**Figure 5.2**  Estimating File System Performance Impact

Using `truss`, you can examine the POSIX-level I/O calls. You can observe the file descriptor and the size and duration for each logical I/O. In the following example, you can see `read()` and `write()` calls during a `dd` between two files.

```
# dd if=filea of=fileb bs=1024k&

# truss -D -p 13092
13092:    0.0326 read(3, "\0\0\0\0\0\0\0\0\0\0\0\0".., 1048576)  = 1048576
13092:    0.0186 write(4, "\0\0\0\0\0\0\0\0\0\0\0\0".., 1048576)  = 1048576
13092:    0.0293 read(3, "\0\0\0\0\0\0\0\0\0\0\0\0".., 1048576)  = 1048576
13092:    0.0259 write(4, "\0\0\0\0\0\0\0\0\0\0\0\0".., 1048576)  = 1048576
13092:    0.0305 read(3, "\0\0\0\0\0\0\0\0\0\0\0\0".., 1048576)  = 1048576
13092:    0.0267 write(4, "\0\0\0\0\0\0\0\0\0\0\0\0".., 1048576)  = 1048576
13092:    0.0242 read(3, "\0\0\0\0\0\0\0\0\0\0\0\0".., 1048576)  = 1048576
13092:    0.0184 write(4, "\0\0\0\0\0\0\0\0\0\0\0\0".., 1048576)  = 1048576
13092:    0.0368 read(3, "\0\0\0\0\0\0\0\0\0\0\0\0".., 1048576)  = 1048576
13092:    0.0333 write(4, "\0\0\0\0\0\0\0\0\0\0\0\0".., 1048576)  = 1048576
13092:    0.0297 read(3, "\0\0\0\0\0\0\0\0\0\0\0\0".., 1048576)  = 1048576
13092:    0.0175 write(4, "\0\0\0\0\0\0\0\0\0\0\0\0".., 1048576)  = 1048576
13092:    0.0315 read(3, "\0\0\0\0\0\0\0\0\0\0\0\0".., 1048576)  = 1048576
13092:    0.0231 write(4, "\0\0\0\0\0\0\0\0\0\0\0\0".., 1048576)  = 1048576
13092:    0.0338 read(3, "\0\0\0\0\0\0\0\0\0\0\0\0".., 1048576)  = 1048576
13092:    0.0181 write(4, "\0\0\0\0\0\0\0\0\0\0\0\0".., 1048576)  = 1048576
13092:    0.0381 read(3, "\0\0\0\0\0\0\0\0\0\0\0\0".., 1048576)  = 1048576
13092:    0.0177 write(4, "\0\0\0\0\0\0\0\0\0\0\0\0".., 1048576)  = 1048576
13092:    0.0323 read(3, "\0\0\0\0\0\0\0\0\0\0\0\0".., 1048576)  = 1048576
13092:    0.0199 write(4, "\0\0\0\0\0\0\0\0\0\0\0\0".., 1048576)  = 1048576
13092:    0.0364 read(3, "\0\0\0\0\0\0\0\0\0\0\0\0".., 1048576)  = 1048576
13092:    0.0189 write(4, "\0\0\0\0\0\0\0\0\0\0\0\0".., 1048576)  = 1048576
...
```

The truss example shows that read() occurs on file descriptor 3 with an average response time of 30 ms and write() occurs on file descriptor 4 with an average response time of 25 ms. This gives some insight into the high-level activity but no other process statistics with which to formulate any baselines.

By using DTrace, you could gather a little more information about the proportion of the time taken to perform I/O in relation to the total execution time. The following excerpt from the pfilestat DTrace command shows how to sample the time within each system call. By tracing the entry and return from a file system system call, you can observe the total latency as experienced by the application. You could then use probes within the file system to discover where the latency is being incurred.

```
/* sample reads */
syscall::read:entry,
syscall::pread*:entry
/pid == PID && OPT_read/
{
        runstate = READ;
        @logical["running", (uint64_t)0, ""] = sum(timestamp - last);
        totaltime += timestamp - last;
        last = timestamp;

        self->fd = arg0 + 1;
        self->bytes = arg2;
        totalbytes += arg2;
}
```

*continues*

```
fbt::fop_read:entry,
fbt::fop_write:entry
/self->fd/
{
        self->vp = (vnode_t *)arg0;
        self->path = self->vp->v_path == 0 ? "<none>" :
            cleanpath(self->vp->v_path);
}

syscall::read:return,
syscall::pread*:return
/pid == PID && OPT_read/
{
        runstate = OTHER;
        @logical["read", self->fd - 1, self->path] = sum(timestamp - last);
        @bytes["read", self->fd - 1, self->path] = sum(self->bytes);
        totaltime += timestamp - last;
        last = timestamp;
}
```

Using an example target process (tar) with pfilestat, you can observe that tar spends 10% of the time during read() calls of /var/crash/rmcferrari/ vmcore.0 and 14% during write() calls to test.tar out of the total elapsed sample time, and a total of 75% of its time waiting for file system read-level I/O.

```
# ./pfilestat 13092

     STATE    FDNUM      Time Filename
   waitcpu        0        4%
   running        0        9%
      read       11       10% /var/crash/rmcferrari/vmcore.0
     write        3       14% /export/home/rmc/book/examples/test.tar
   sleep-r        0       75%

     STATE    FDNUM      KB/s Filename
      read       11     53776 /var/crash/rmcferrari/vmcore.0
     write        3     53781 /export/home/rmc/book/examples/test.tar

Total event time (ms): 1840   Total Mbytes/sec: 89
```

# 5.4 Causes of Read/Write File System Latency

There are several causes of latency in the file system read/write data path. The simplest is that of latency incurred by waiting for physical I/O at the backend of the file system. File systems, however, rarely simply pass logical requests straight through to the backend, so latency can be incurred in several other ways. For example, one logical I/O event can be fractured into two physical I/O events, resulting in the latency penalty of two disk operations. Figure 5.3 shows the layers that could contribute latency.

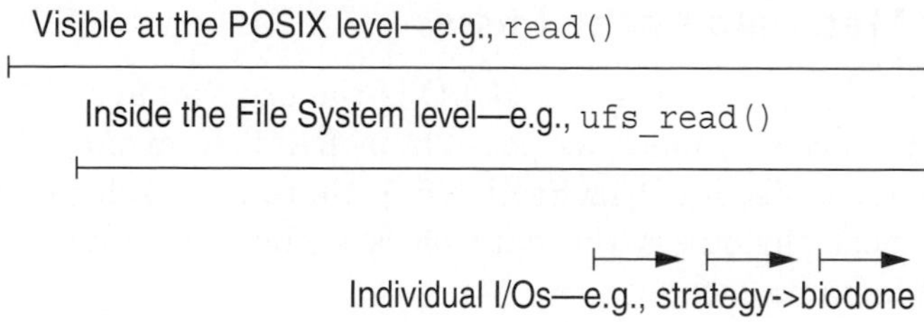

Visible at the POSIX level—e.g., `read()`

Inside the File System level—e.g., `ufs_read()`

Individual I/Os—e.g., strategy->biodone

**Figure 5.3** Layers for Observing File System I/O

Common sources of latency in the file system stack include:

- Disk I/O wait (or network/filer latency for NFS)
- Block or metadata cache misses
- I/O breakup (logical I/Os being fractured into multiple physical I/Os)
- Locking in the file system
- Metadata updates

## 5.4.1 Disk I/O Wait

Disk I/O wait is the most commonly assumed type of latency problem. If the underlying storage is in the synchronous path of a file system operation, then it affects file-system-level latency. For each logical operation, there could be zero (a hit in the block cache), one, or even multiple physical operations.

This `iowait.d` script uses the file name and device arguments in the I/O provider to show us the total latency accumulation for physical I/O operations and the breakdown for each file that initiated the I/O. See Chapter 4 for further information on the I/O provider and Section 10.6.1 for information on its arguments.

```
# ./iowait.d 639
^C
Time breakdown (milliseconds):
 <on cpu>                                           2478
 <I/O wait>                                          6326

I/O wait breakdown (milliseconds):
 file1                                                236
 file2                                                241
 file4                                                244
 file3                                                264
 file5                                                277
 file7                                                330
 ...
```

## 5.4.2 Block or Metadata Cache Misses

Have you ever heard the saying "the best I/O is the one you avoid"? Basically, the file system tries to cache as much as possible in RAM, to avoid going to disk for repetitive accesses. As discussed in Section 5.6, there are multiple caches in the file system—the most obvious is the data block cache, and others include metadata, inode, and file name caches.

## 5.4.3 I/O Breakup

I/O breakup occurs when logical I/Os are fractured into multiple physical I/Os. A common file-system-level issue arises when multiple physical I/Os result from a single logical I/O, thereby compounding latency.

Output from running the following DTrace script shows VOP level and physical I/Os for a file system. In this example, we show the output from a single read(). Note the many page-sized 8-Kbyte I/Os for the single 1-Mbyte POSIX-level read(). In this example, we can see that a single 1-MByte read is broken into several 4-Kbyte, 8-Kbyte, and 56-Kbyte physical I/Os. This is likely due to the file system maximum cluster size (maxcontig).

```
# ./fsrw.d
Event           Device RW     Size Offset Path
sc-read              .  R  1048576      0 /var/sadm/install/contents
 fop_read            .  R  1048576      0 /var/sadm/install/contents
   disk_ra       cmdk0  R     4096     72 /var/sadm/install/contents
   disk_ra       cmdk0  R     8192     96 <none>
   disk_ra       cmdk0  R    57344     96 /var/sadm/install/contents
   disk_ra       cmdk0  R    57344    152 /var/sadm/install/contents
   disk_ra       cmdk0  R    57344    208 /var/sadm/install/contents
   disk_ra       cmdk0  R    49152    264 /var/sadm/install/contents
   disk_ra       cmdk0  R    57344    312 /var/sadm/install/contents
   disk_ra       cmdk0  R    57344    368 /var/sadm/install/contents
   disk_ra       cmdk0  R    57344    424 /var/sadm/install/contents
   disk_ra       cmdk0  R    57344    480 /var/sadm/install/contents
   disk_ra       cmdk0  R    57344    536 /var/sadm/install/contents
   disk_ra       cmdk0  R    57344    592 /var/sadm/install/contents
   disk_ra       cmdk0  R    57344    648 /var/sadm/install/contents
   disk_ra       cmdk0  R    57344    704 /var/sadm/install/contents
   disk_ra       cmdk0  R    57344    760 /var/sadm/install/contents
   disk_ra       cmdk0  R    57344    816 /var/sadm/install/contents
   disk_ra       cmdk0  R    57344    872 /var/sadm/install/contents
   disk_ra       cmdk0  R    57344    928 /var/sadm/install/contents
   disk_ra       cmdk0  R    57344    984 /var/sadm/install/contents
   disk_ra       cmdk0  R    57344   1040 /var/sadm/install/contents
```

## 5.4.4 Locking in the File System

File systems use locks to serialize access within a file (we call these explicit locks) or within critical internal file system structures (implicit locks).

Explicit locks are often used to implement POSIX-level read/write ordering within a file. POSIX requires that writes must be committed to a file in the order in which they are written and that reads must be consistent with the data within the order of any writes. As a simple and cheap solution, many files systems simply implement a per-file reader-writer lock to provide this level of synchronization. Unfortunately, this solution has the unwanted side effect of serializing all accesses within a file, even if they are to non-overlapping regions. The reader-writer lock typically becomes a significant performance overhead when the writes are synchronous (issued with O_DSYNC or O_SYNC) since the writer-lock is held for the entire duration of the physical I/O (typically, in the order of 10 or more milliseconds), blocking all other reads and writes to the same file.

The POSIX lock is the most significant file system performance issue for databases because they typically use a few large files with hundreds of threads accessing them. If the POSIX lock is in effect, then I/O is serialized, effectively limiting the I/O throughput to that of a single disk. For example, if we assume a file system with 10 disks backing it and a database attempting to write, each I/O will lock a file for 10 ms; the maximum I/O rate is around 100 I/Os per second, even though there are 10 disks capable of 1000 I/Os per second (each disk is capable of 100 I/Os per second).

Most file systems using the standard file system page cache (see Section 14.7 in *Solaris™ Internals*) have this limitation. UFS when used with Direct I/O (see Section 5.6.2) relaxes the per-file reader-writer lock and can be used as a high-performance, uncached file system, suitable for applications such as databases that do their own caching.

## 5.4.5 Metadata Updates

File system metadata updates are a significant source of latency because many implementations synchronously update the on-disk structures to maintain integrity of the on-disk structures. There are *logical metadata* updates (file creates, deletes, etc.) and *physical metadata* updates (updating a block map, for example).

Many file systems perform several synchronous I/Os per metadata update, which limits metadata performance. Operations such as creating, renaming, and deleting files often exhibit higher latency than reads or writes as a result. Another area affected by metadata updates is file-extends, which can require a physical metadata update.

## 5.5 Observing File System "Top End" Activity

Applications typically access their data from a file system through the POSIX I/O library and system calls. These accesses are passed into the kernel and into the underlying file system through the VOP layer (see Section 5.1).

Using DTrace function boundary probes, we can trace the VOP layer and monitor file system activity. Probes fired at the entry and exit of each VOP method can record event counts, latency, and physical I/O counts. We can obtain information about the methods by casting the arguments of the VOP methods to the appropriate structures; for example, we can harvest the file name, file system name, I/O size, and the like from these entry points.

The DTrace `vopstat` command instruments and reports on the VOP layer activity. By default, it summarizes each VOP in the system and reports a physical I/O count, a VOP method count, and the total latency incurred for each VOP during the sample period. This utility provides a useful first-pass method of understanding where and to what degree latency is occurring in the file system layer.

The following example shows `vopstat` output for a system running ZFS. In this example, the majority of the latency is being incurred in the VOP_FSYNC method (see Table 14.3 in *Solaris*<sup>TM</sup> *Internals*).

```
# ./vopstat

VOP Physical IO                                         Count
fop_fsync                                                 236

VOP Count                                               Count
fop_create                                                  1
fop_fid                                                     1
fop_lookup                                                  2
fop_access                                                  3
fop_read                                                    3
fop_poll                                                   11
fop_fsync                                                  31
fop_putpage                                                32
fop_ioctl                                                 115
fop_write                                                 517
fop_rwlock                                                520
fop_rwunlock                                              520
fop_inactive                                              529
fop_getattr                                              1057

VOP Wall Time                                        mSeconds
fop_fid                                                     0
fop_access                                                  0
fop_read                                                    0
fop_poll                                                    0
fop_lookup                                                  0
fop_create                                                  0
fop_ioctl                                                   0
fop_putpage                                                 1
fop_rwunlock                                                1
```

*continues*

```
fop_rwlock                                        1
fop_inactive                                      1
fop_getattr                                       2
fop_write                                        22
fop_fsync                                       504
```

## 5.6 File System Caches

File systems make extensive use of caches to eliminate physical I/Os where possible. A file system typically uses several different types of cache, including logical metadata caches, physical metadata caches, and block caches. Each file system implementation has its unique set of caches, which are, however, often logically arranged, as shown in Figure 5.4.

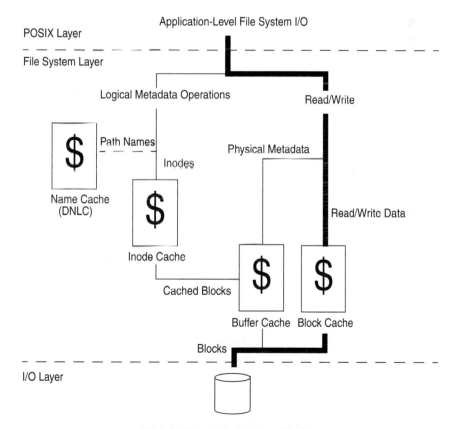

**Figure 5.4** File System Caches

The arrangement of caches for various file systems is shown below:

- **UFS.** The file data is cached in a block cache, implemented with the VM system page cache (see Section 14.7 in *Solaris™ Internals*). The physical metadata (information about block placement in the file system structure) is cached in the buffer cache in 512-byte blocks. Logical metadata is cached in the UFS inode cache, which is private to UFS. Vnode-to-path translations are cached in the central directory name lookup cache (DNLC).

- **NFS.** The file data is cached in a block cache, implemented with the VM system *page cache* (see Section 14.7 in *Solaris™ Internals*). The physical metadata (information about block placement in the file system structure) is cached in the *buffer cache* in 512-byte blocks. Logical metadata is cached in the *NFS attribute cache*, and NFS nodes are cached in the *NFS rnode cache*, which are private to NFS. File name-to-path translations are cached in the central DNLC.

- **ZFS.** The file data is cached in ZFS's *adaptive replacement cache* (ARC), rather than in the page cache as is the case for almost all other file systems.

## 5.6.1 Page Cache

File and directory data for traditional Solaris file systems, including UFS, NFS, and others, are cached in the page cache. The virtual memory system implements a page cache, and the file system uses this facility to cache files. This means that to understand file system caching behavior, we need to look at how the virtual memory system implements the page cache.

The virtual memory system divides physical memory into chunks known as pages; on UltraSPARC systems, a page is 8 kilobytes. To read data from a file into memory, the virtual memory system reads in one page at a time, or "pages in" a file. The page-in operation is initiated in the virtual memory system, which requests the file's file system to page in a page from storage to memory. Every time we read in data from disk to memory, we cause paging to occur. We see the tally when we look at the virtual memory statistics. For example, reading a file will be reflected in `vmstat` as page-ins.

In our example, we can see that by starting a program that does random reads of a file, we cause a number of page-ins to occur, as indicated by the numbers in the `pi` column of `vmstat`.

There is no parameter equivalent to `bufhwm` to limit or control the size of the page cache. The page cache simply grows to consume available free memory. See Section 14.8 in *Solaris™ Internals* for a complete description of how the page cache is managed in Solaris.

```
# ./rreadtest testfile&

# vmstat
 procs      memory            page               disk            faults        cpu
 r b w  swap  free  re  mf  pi  po fr de  sr s0 -- -- --   in   sy   cs us sy id
 0 0 0 50436  2064   5   0  81   0  0  0   0 15  0  0  0  168  361   69  1 25 74
 0 0 0 50508  1336  14   0 222   0  0  0   0 35  0  0  0  210  902  130  2 51 47
 0 0 0 50508   648  10   0 177   0  0  0   0 27  0  0  0  168  850  121  1 60 39
 0 0 0 50508   584  29  57  88 109  0  0   6 14  0  0  0  108 5284  120  7 72 20
 0 0 0 50508   484   0  50 249  96  0  0  18 33  0  0  0  199  542  124  0 50 50
 0 0 0 50508   492   0  41 260  70  0  0  56 34  0  0  0  209  649  128  1 49 50
 0 0 0 50508   472   0  58 253 116  0  0  45 33  0  0  0  198  566  122  1 46 53
```

You can use an MDB command to view the size of the page cache. The macro is included with Solaris 9 and later.

```
sol9# mdb -k
Loading modules: [ unix krtld genunix ip ufs_log logindmux ptm cpc sppp ipc random nfs ]
> ::memstat

Page Summary              Pages                MB   %Tot
------------              -----     ----------------  ----
Kernel                    53444                 208   10%
Anon                     119088                 465   23%
Exec and libs              2299                   8    0%
Page cache                29185                 114    6%
Free (cachelist)            347                   1    0%
Free (freelist)          317909                1241   61%

Total                    522272                2040
Physical                 512136                2000
```

The page-cache-related categories are described as follows:

- **Exec and libs.** The amount of memory used for mapped files interpreted as binaries or libraries. This is typically the sum of memory used for user binaries and shared libraries. Technically, this memory is part of the page cache, but it is page-cache-tagged as "executable" when a file is mapped with PROT_EXEC and file permissions include execute permission.

- **Page cache.** The amount of unmapped page cache, that is, page cache not on the cache list. This category includes the segmap portion of the page cache and any memory mapped files. If the applications on the system are solely using a read/write path, then we would expect the size of this bucket not to exceed segmap_percent (defaults to 12% of physical memory size). Files in /tmp are also included in this category.

- **Free (cache list).** The amount of page cache on the free list. The free list contains unmapped file pages and is typically where the majority of the file system cache resides. Expect to see a large cache list on a system that has large file sets and sufficient memory for file caching. Beginning with Solaris 8, the file system cycles its pages through the cache list, preventing it from stealing memory from other applications unless a true memory shortage occurs.

The complete list of categories is described in Section 6.4.3 and further in Section 14.8 in *Solaris™ Internals*.

With DTrace, we now have a method of collecting one of the most significant performance statistics for a file system in Solaris—the *cache hit ratio* in the file system page cache. By using DTrace with probes at the entry and exit to the file system, we can collect the logical I/O events into the file system and physical I/O events from the file system into the device I/O subsystem.

```
#!/usr/sbin/dtrace -s

#pragma D option quiet

::fop_read:entry
/self->trace == 0 && (((vnode_t *)arg0)->v_vfsp)->vfs_vnodecovered/
{
        vp = (vnode_t*)arg0;
        vfs = (vfs_t *)vp->v_vfsp;
        mountvp = vfs->vfs_vnodecovered;
        uio = (uio_t*)arg1;
        self->path=stringof(mountvp->v_path);
        @rio[stringof(mountvp->v_path), "logical"] = count();
        @rbytes[stringof(mountvp->v_path), "logical"] = sum(uio->uio_resid);
        self->trace = 1;
}

::fop_read:entry
/self->trace == 0 && (((vnode_t *)arg0)->v_vfsp == `rootvfs)/
{
        vp = (vnode_t*)arg0;
        vfs = (vfs_t *)vp->v_vfsp;
        mountvp = vfs->vfs_vnodecovered;
        uio = (uio_t*)arg1;
        self->path="/";
        @rio[stringof("/"), "logical"] = count();
        @rbytes[stringof("/"), "logical"] = sum(uio->uio_resid);
        self->trace = 1;
}

::fop_read:return
/self->trace == 1/
{
        self->trace = 0;
}

io::bdev_strategy:start
/self->trace/
{
        @rio[self->path, "physical"] = count();
        @rbytes[self->path, "physical"] = sum(args[0]->b_bcount);
}
```

*continues*

```
tick-5s
{
        trunc (@rio, 20);
        trunc (@rbytes, 20);
        printf("\033[H\033[2J");
        printf ("\nRead IOPS\n");
        printa ("%-60s %10s %10@d\n", @rio);
        printf ("\nRead Bandwidth\n");
        printa ("%-60s %10s %10@d\n", @rbytes);
        trunc (@rbytes);
        trunc (@rio);
}
```

These two statistics give us insight into how effective the file system cache is, and whether adding physical memory could increase the amount of file-system-level caching.

Using this script, we can probe for the number of logical bytes in the file system through the new Solaris 10 file system fop layer. We count the physical bytes by using the io provider. Running the script, we can see the number of logical and physical bytes for a file system, and we can use these numbers to calculate the hit ratio.

```
Read IOPS
/data1                                                    physical        287
/data1                                                    logical        2401

Read Bandwidth
/data1                                                    physical    2351104
/data1                                                    logical    5101240
```

The /data1 file system on this server is doing 2401 logical IOPS and 287 physical—that is, a hit ratio of 2401 ÷ (2401 + 287) = 89%. It is also doing 5.1 Mbytes/sec logical and 2.3 Mbytes/sec physical.

We can also do this at the file level.

```
#!/usr/sbin/dtrace -s

#pragma D option quiet

::fop_read:entry
/self->trace == 0 && (((vnode_t *)arg0)->v_path)/
{
        vp = (vnode_t*)arg0;
        uio = (uio_t*)arg1;
        self->path=stringof(vp->v_path);
        self->trace = 1;
        @rio[stringof(vp->v_path), "logical"] = count();
        @rbytes[stringof(vp->v_path), "logical"] = sum(uio->uio_resid);
}
```

*continues*

```
::fop_read:return
/self->trace == 1/
{
        self->trace = 0;
}

io::bdev_strategy:start
/self->trace/
{
        @rio[self->path, "physical"] = count();
        @rbytes[self->path, "physical"] = sum(args[0]->b_bcount);
}

tick-5s
{
        trunc (@rio, 20);
        trunc (@rbytes, 20);
        printf("\033[H\033[2J");
        printf ("\nRead IOPS\n");
        printa ("%-60s %10s %10@d\n", @rio);
        printf ("\nRead Bandwidth\n");
        printa ("%-60s %10s %10@d\n", @rbytes);
        trunc (@rbytes);
        trunc (@rio);
}
```

## 5.6.2 Bypassing the Page Cache with Direct I/O

In some cases we may want to do completely unbuffered I/O to a file. A *direct I/O* facility in most file systems allows a direct file read or write to completely bypass the file system page cache. Direct I/O is supported on the following file systems:

- **UFS.** Support for direct I/O was added to UFS starting with Solaris 2.6. Direct I/O allows reads and writes to files in a regular file system to bypass the page cache and access the file at near raw disk performance. Direct I/O can be advantageous when you are accessing a file in a manner where caching is of no benefit. For example, if you are copying a very large file from one disk to another, then it is likely that the file will not fit in memory and you will just cause the system to page heavily. By using direct I/O, you can copy the file through the file system without reading through the page cache and thereby eliminate both the memory pressure caused by the file system and the additional CPU cost of the layers of cache.

  Direct I/O also eliminates the double copy that is performed when the read and write system calls are used. When we read a file through normal buffered I/O, the file system takes two steps: (1) It uses a DMA transfer from the disk controller into the kernel's address space and (2) it copies the data into the buffer supplied by the user in the read system call. Direct I/O eliminates the second step by arranging for the DMA transfer to occur directly into the user's address space.

Direct I/O bypasses the buffer cache only if all the following are true:

- The file is not memory mapped.
- The file does not have holes.
- The read/write is sector aligned (512 byte).

- **QFS.** Support for direct I/O is the same as with UFS.
- **NFS.** NFS also supports direct I/O. With direct I/O enabled, NFS bypasses client-side caching and passes all requests directly to the NFS server. Both reads and writes are uncached and become synchronous (they need to wait for the server to complete). Unlike disk-based direct I/O support, NFS's support imposes no restrictions on I/O size or alignment; all requests are made directly to the server.

You enable direct I/O by mounting an entire file system with the `force-directio` mount option, as shown below.

```
# mount -o forcedirectio /dev/dsk/c0t0d0s6 /u1
```

You can also enable direct I/O for any file with the `directio` system call. Note that the change is file based, and every reader and writer of the file will be forced to use `directio` once it's enabled.

```
int directio(int fildes, DIRECTIO_ON | DIRECTIO_OFF);
                                                      See sys/fcntl.h
```

Direct I/O can provide extremely fast transfers when moving data with big block sizes (>64 kilobytes), but it can be a significant performance limitation for smaller sizes. If an application reads and writes in small sizes, then its performance may suffer since there is no read-ahead or write clustering and no caching.

Databases are a good candidate for direct I/O since they cache their own blocks in a shared global buffer and can cluster their own reads and writes into larger operations.

A set of direct I/O statistics is provided with the `ufs` implementation by means of the `kstat` interface. The structure exported by `ufs_directio_kstats` is shown below. Note that this structure may change, and performance tools should not rely on the format of the direct I/O statistics.

```
struct ufs_directio_kstats {
        uint_t  logical_reads;   /* Number of fs read operations */
        uint_t  phys_reads;      /* Number of physical reads */
        uint_t  hole_reads;      /* Number of reads from holes */
        uint_t  nread;           /* Physical bytes read */
        uint_t  logical_writes;  /* Number of fs write operations */
        uint_t  phys_writes;     /* Number of physical writes */
        uint_t  nwritten;        /* Physical bytes written */
        uint_t  nflushes;        /* Number of times cache was cleared */
} ufs_directio_kstats;
```

You can inspect the direct I/O statistics with a utility from our Web site at `http://www.solarisinternals.com`.

```
# directiostat 3
  lreads lwrites  preads pwrites     Krd    Kwr holdrds  nflush
       0       0       0       0       0      0       0       0
       0       0       0       0       0      0       0       0
       0       0       0       0       0      0       0       0
```

## 5.6.3 The Directory Name Lookup Cache

The directory name cache caches path names for vnodes, so when we open a file that has been opened recently, we don't need to rescan the directory to find the file name. Each time we find the path name for a vnode, we store it in the directory name cache. (See Section 14.10 in *Solaris™ Internals* for further information on the DNLC operation.) The number of entries in the DNLC is set by the system-tuneable parameter, ncsize, which is set at boot time by the calculations shown in Table 5.1. The ncsize parameter is calculated in proportion to the maxusers parameter, which is equal to the number of megabytes of memory installed in the system, capped by a maximum of 1024. The maxusers parameter can also be over-ridden in /etc/system to a maximum of 2048.

**Table 5.1** DNLC Default Sizes

| Solaris Version | Default ncsize Calculation |
|---|---|
| Solaris 2.4, 2.5, 2.5.1 | ncsize = (17 * maxusers) + 90 |
| Solaris 2.6 onwards | ncsize = (68 * maxusers) + 360 |

The size of the DNLC rarely needs to be adjusted, because the size scales with the amount of memory installed in the system. Earlier Solaris versions had a default maximum of 17498 (34906 with `maxusers` set to 2048), and later Solaris versions have a maximum of 69992 (139624 with `maxusers` set to 2048).

Use MDB to determine the size of the DNLC.

```
# mdb -k
> ncsize/D
ncsize:
ncsize:         25520
```

The DNLC maintains housekeeping threads through a task queue. The `dnlc_reduce_cache()` activates the task queue when name cache entries reach `ncsize`, and it reduces the size to `dnlc_nentries_low_water`, which by default is one hundredth less than (or 99% of) `ncsize`. If `dnlc_nentries` reaches `dnlc_max_nentries` (twice `ncsize`), then we know that `dnlc_reduce_cache()` is failing to keep up. In this case, we refuse to add new entries to the `dnlc` until the task queue catches up. Below is an example of DNLC statistics obtained with the `kstat` command.

```
# vmstat -s
        0 swap ins
        0 swap outs
        0 pages swapped in
        0 pages swapped out
   405332 total address trans. faults taken
  1015894 page ins
      353 page outs
  4156331 pages paged in
     1579 pages paged out
  3600535 total reclaims
  3600510 reclaims from free list
        0 micro (hat) faults
   405332 minor (as) faults
   645073 major faults
    85298 copy-on-write faults
   117161 zero fill page faults
        0 pages examined by the clock daemon
        0 revolutions of the clock hand
  4492478 pages freed by the clock daemon
     3205 forks
       88 vforks
     3203 execs
 33830316 cpu context switches
 58808541 device interrupts
   928719 traps
214191600 system calls
 14408382 total name lookups (cache hits 90%)
   263756 user    cpu
   462843 system  cpu
 14728521 idle    cpu
  2335699 wait    cpu
```

The hit ratio of the directory name cache shows the number of times a name was looked up and found in the name cache. A high hit ratio (>90%) typically shows that the DNLC is working well. A low hit ratio does not necessarily mean that the DNLC is undersized; it simply means that we are not always finding the names we want in the name cache. This situation can occur if we are creating a large number of files. The reason is that a `create` operation checks to see if a file exists before it creates the file, causing a large number of cache misses.

The DNLC statistics are also available with `kstat`.

```
$ kstat -n dnlcstats
module: unix                              instance: 0
name:   dnlcstats                         class:    misc
        crtime                            208.832373709
        dir_add_abort                     0
        dir_add_max                       0
        dir_add_no_memory                 0
        dir_cached_current                1
        dir_cached_total                  13
        dir_entries_cached_current        880
        dir_fini_purge                    0
        dir_hits                          463
        dir_misses                        11240
        dir_reclaim_any                   8
        dir_reclaim_last                  3
        dir_remove_entry_fail             0
        dir_remove_space_fail             0
        dir_start_no_memory               0
        dir_update_fail                   0
        double_enters                     6
        enters                            11618
        hits                              1347693
        misses                            10787
        negative_cache_hits               76686
        pick_free                         0
        pick_heuristic                    0
        pick_last                         0
        purge_all                         1
        purge_fs1                         0
        purge_total_entries               3013
        purge_vfs                         158
        purge_vp                          31
        snaptime                          94467.490008162
```

## 5.6.4 Block Buffer Cache

The buffer cache used in Solaris for caching of inodes and file metadata is now also dynamically sized. In old versions of UNIX, the buffer cache was fixed in size by the `nbuf` kernel parameter, which specified the number of 512-byte buffers. We now allow the buffer cache to grow by `nbuf`, as needed, until it reaches a ceiling specified by the `bufhwm` kernel parameter. By default, the buffer cache is allowed to grow until it uses 2% of physical memory. We can look at the upper limit for the buffer cache by using the `sysdef` command.

```
# sysdef
*
* Tunable Parameters
*
 7757824        maximum memory allowed in buffer cache (bufhwm)
    5930        maximum number of processes (v.v_proc)
      99        maximum global priority in sys class (MAXCLSYSPRI)
    5925        maximum processes per user id (v.v_maxup)
      30        auto update time limit in seconds (NAUTOUP)
      25        page stealing low water mark (GPGSLO)
       5        fsflush run rate (FSFLUSHR)
      25        minimum resident memory for avoiding deadlock (MINARMEM)
      25        minimum swapable memory for avoiding deadlock (MINASMEM)
```

Now that we only keep inode and metadata in the buffer cache, we don't need a very large buffer. In fact, we need only 300 bytes per inode and about 1 megabyte per 2 gigabytes of files that we expect to be accessed concurrently (note that this rule of thumb is for UFS file systems).

For example, if we have a database system with 100 files totaling 100 gigabytes of storage space and we estimate that we will access only 50 gigabytes of those files at the same time, then at most we would need $100 \times 300$ bytes = 30 kilobytes for the inodes and about $50 \div 2 \times 1$ megabyte = 25 megabytes for the metadata (direct and indirect blocks). On a system with 5 gigabytes of physical memory, the defaults for `bufhwm` would provide us with a `bufhwm` of 102 megabytes, which is more than sufficient for the buffer cache. If we are really memory misers, we could limit `bufhwm` to 30 megabytes (specified in kilobytes) by setting the `bufhwm` parameter in the `/etc/system` file. To set `bufhwm` smaller for this example, we would put the following line into the `/etc/system` file.

```
*
* Limit size of bufhwm
*
set bufhwm=30000
```

You can monitor the buffer cache hit statistics by using `sar -b`. The statistics for the buffer cache show the number of logical reads and writes into the buffer cache, the number of physical reads and writes out of the buffer cache, and the read/write hit ratios.

```
# sar -b 3 333
SunOS zangief 5.7 Generic sun4u    06/27/99

22:01:51 bread/s lread/s %rcache bwrit/s lwrit/s %wcache pread/s pwrit/s
22:01:54        0    7118     100       0       0     100       0       0
22:01:57        0    7863     100       0       0     100       0       0
22:02:00        0    7931     100       0       0     100       0       0
22:02:03        0    7736     100       0       0     100       0       0
22:02:06        0    7643     100       0       0     100       0       0
22:02:09        0    7165     100       0       0     100       0       0
22:02:12        0    6306     100       8      25      68       0       0
22:02:15        0    8152     100       0       0     100       0       0
22:02:18        0    7893     100       0       0     100       0       0
```

On this system we can see that the buffer cache is caching 100% of the reads and that the number of writes is small. This measurement was taken on a machine with 100 gigabytes of files that were being read in a random pattern. You should aim for a read cache hit ratio of 100% on systems with only a few, but very large, files (for example, database systems) and a hit ratio of 90% or better for systems with many files.

## 5.6.5 UFS Inode Cache

The UFS uses the `ufs_ninode` parameter to size the file system tables for the expected number of inodes. To understand how the `ufs_ninode` parameter affects the number of inodes in memory, we need to look at how the UFS maintains inodes. Inodes are created when a file is first referenced. They remain in memory much longer than when the file is last referenced because inodes can be in one of two states: either the inode is referenced or the inode is no longer referenced but is on an idle queue. Inodes are eventually destroyed when they are pushed off the end of the inode idle queue. Refer to Section 15.3.2 in *Solaris™ Internals* for a description of how `ufs` inodes are maintained on the idle queue.

The number of inodes in memory is dynamic. Inodes will continue to be allocated as new files are referenced. There is no upper bound to the number of inodes open at a time; if one million inodes are opened concurrently, then a little over one million inodes will be in memory at that point. A file is referenced when its reference count is non-zero, which means that either the file is open for a process or another subsystem such as the directory name lookup cache is referring to the file.

When inodes are no longer referenced (the file is closed and no other subsystem is referring to the file), the inode is placed on the idle queue and eventually freed. The size of the idle queue is controlled by the `ufs_ninode` parameter and is limited to one-fourth of `ufs_ninode`. The maximum number of inodes in memory at a given point is the number of active referenced inodes plus the size of the idle queue (typically, one-fourth of `ufs_ninode`). Figure 5.5 illustrates the `inode` cache.

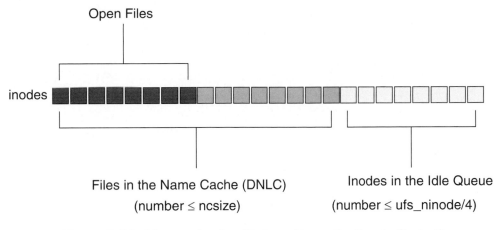

**Figure 5.5** In-Memory Inodes (Referred to as the "Inode Cache")

We can use the `sar` command and inode kernel memory statistics to determine the number of inodes currently in memory. `sar` shows us the number of inodes currently in memory and the number of `inode` structures in the `inode` slab cache. We can find similar information by looking at the `buf_inuse` and `buf_total` parameters in the inode kernel memory statistics.

```
# sar -v 3 3

SunOS devhome 5.7 Generic sun4u    08/01/99

11:38:09  proc-sz    ov  inod-sz      ov  file-sz   ov  lock-sz
11:38:12  100/5930    0  37181/37181   0  603/603    0   0/0
11:38:15  100/5930    0  37181/37181   0  603/603    0   0/0
11:38:18  101/5930    0  37181/37181   0  607/607    0   0/0

# kstat -n ufs_inode_cache
ufs_inode_cache:
buf_size 440 align 8 chunk_size 440 slab_size 8192 alloc 1221573 alloc_fail 0
free 1188468 depot_alloc 19957 depot_free 21230 depot_contention 18 global_alloc 48330
global_free 7823 buf_constructed 3325 buf_avail 3678 buf_inuse 37182
buf_total 40860 buf_max 40860 slab_create 2270 slab_destroy 0 memory_class 0
hash_size 0 hash_lookup_depth 0 hash_rescale 0 full_magazines 219
empty_magazines 332 magazine_size 15 alloc_from_cpu0 579706 free_to_cpu0 588106
buf_avail_cpu0 15 alloc_from_cpu1 573580 free_to_cpu1 571309 buf_avail_cpu1 25
```

The inode memory statistics show us how many inodes are allocated by the `buf_inuse` field. We can also see from the `ufs` inode memory statistics that the size of each inode is 440 bytes on this system See below to find out the size of an inode on different architectures.

```
# mdb -k
Loading modules: [ unix krtld genunix specfs dtrace ...]
> a$d
radix = 10 base ten
> ::sizeof inode_t
sizeof (inode_t) = 0t276
> $q

$ kstat unix::ufs_inode_cache:chunk_size
module: unix                            instance: 0
name:   ufs_inode_cache                 class:     kmem_cache
        chunk_size                      280
```

We can use this value to calculate the amount of kernel memory required for desired number of inodes when setting `ufs_ninode` and the directory name cache size.

The `ufs_ninode` parameter controls the size of the hash table that is used for inode lookup and indirectly sizes the inode idle queue (ufs_ninode ÷ 4). The inode hash table is ideally sized to match the total number of inodes expected to be in memory—a number that is influenced by the size of the directory name cache. By default, `ufs_ninode` is set to the size of the directory name cache, which is approximately the correct size for the inode hash table. In an ideal world, we could set `ufs_ninode` to four-thirds the size of the DNLC, to take into account the size of the idle queue, but practice has shown this to be unnecessary.

We typically set `ufs_ninode` indirectly by setting the directory name cache size (ncsize) to the expected number of files accessed concurrently, but it is possible to set `ufs_ninode` separately in /etc/system.

```
* Set number of inodes stored in UFS inode cache
*
set ufs_ninode = new_value
```

## 5.6.6 Monitoring UFS Caches with `fcachestat`

We can monitor all four key UFS caches by using a single Perl tool: `fcachestat`. This tool measures the DNLC, inode, UFS buffer cache (metadata), and page cache by means of `segmap`.

```
$ ./fcachestat 5
  --- dnlc ---      -- inode ---     -- ufsbuf --     -- segmap --
 %hit     total    %hit     total    %hit     total    %hit     total
99.64    693.4M   59.46      4.9M   99.80     94.0M   81.39    118.6M
66.84     15772   28.30      6371   98.44      3472   82.97      9529
63.72     27624   21.13     12482   98.37      7435   74.70     14699
10.79     14874    5.64     16980   98.45     12349   93.44     11984
11.96     13312   11.89     14881   98.37     10004   93.53     10478
 4.08     20139    5.71     25152   98.42     17917   97.47     16729
 8.25     17171    3.57     20737   98.38     15054   93.64     11154
15.40     12151    6.89     13393   98.37      9403   93.14     11941
 8.26      9047    4.51     10899   98.26      7861   94.70      7186
66.67         6    0.00         3   95.45        44   44.44        18
```

## 5.7 NFS Statistics

The NFS client and server are instrumented so that they can be observed with
`iostat` and `nfsstat`. For client-side mounts, `iostat` reports the latency for read
and write operations per mount, and instead of reporting disk response times,
`iostat` reports NFS server response times (including over-the-write latency). The
`-c` and `-s` options of the `nfsstat` command reports both client- and server-side
statistics for each NFS operation as specified in the NFS protocol.

### 5.7.1 NFS Client Statistics: `nfsstat -c`

The client-side statistics show the number of calls for RPC transport, virtual metadata (also described as attributes), and read/write operations. The statistics are
separated by NFS version number (currently 2, 3, and 4) and protocol options
(TCP or UDP).

```
$ nfsstat -c

Client rpc:
Connection oriented:
calls       badcalls    badxids     timeouts    newcreds    badverfs    timers
202499      0           0           0           0           0           0
cantconn    nomem       interrupts
0           0           0
Connectionless:
calls       badcalls    retrans     badxids     timeouts    newcreds    badverfs
0           0           0           0           0           0           0
timers      nomem       cantsend
0           0           0

Client nfs:
calls       badcalls    clgets      cltoomany
200657      0           200657      7
Version 2: (0 calls)
```

*continues*

```
null        getattr   setattr   root        lookup    readlink read      wrcache
0 0%        0 0%      0 0%      0 0%        0 0%      0 0%     0 0%      0 0%
write       create    remove    rename      link      symlink  mkdir     rmdir
0 0%        0 0%      0 0%      0 0%        0 0%      0 0%     0 0%      0 0%
readdir     statfs
0 0%        0 0%
Version 3: (0 calls)
null        getattr     setattr     lookup      access      readlink
0 0%        0 0%        0 0%        0 0%        0 0%        0 0%
read        write       create      mkdir       symlink     mknod
0 0%        0 0%        0 0%        0 0%        0 0%        0 0%
remove      rmdir       rename      link        readdir     readdirplus
0 0%        0 0%        0 0%        0 0%        0 0%        0 0%
fsstat      fsinfo      pathconf    commit
0 0%        0 0%        0 0%        0 0%
```

## 5.7.2 NFS Server Statistics: `nfsstat -s`

The NFS server-side statistics show the NFS operations performed by the NFS server.

```
$ nfsstat -s

Server rpc:
Connection oriented:
calls       badcalls    nullrecv    badlen      xdrcall     dupchecks   dupreqs
5897288     0           0           0           0           372803      0
Connectionless:
calls       badcalls    nullrecv    badlen      xdrcall     dupchecks   dupreqs
87324       0           0           0           0           0           0

...

Version 4: (949163 calls)
null                    compound
3175 0%                 945988 99%
Version 4: (3284515 operations)
reserved                access                  close                   commit
0 0%                    72954 2%                199208 6%               2948 0%
create                  delegpurge              delegreturn             getattr
4 0%                    0 0%                    16451 0%                734376 22%
getfh                   link                    lock                    lockt
345041 10%              6 0%                    101 0%                  0 0%
locku                   lookup                  lookupp                 nverify
101 0%                  145651 4%               5715 0%                 171515 5%
open                    openattr                open_confirm            open_downgrade
199410 6%               0 0%                    271 0%                  0 0%
putfh                   putpubfh                putrootfh               read
914825 27%              0 0%                    581 0%                  130451 3%
readdir                 readlink                remove                  rename
5661 0%                 11905 0%                15 0%                   201 0%
renew                   restorefh               savefh                  secinfo
30765 0%                140543 4%               146336 4%               277 0%
setattr                 setclientid             setclientid_confirm     verify
23 0%                   26 0%                   26 0%                   10 0%
write                   release_lockowner       illegal
9118 0%                 0 0%                    0 0%
...
```

# 6

# Memory

In this chapter we discuss the major tools used for memory analysis. We detail the methodology behind the use of the tools and the interpretation of the metrics.

## 6.1 Tools for Memory Analysis

Different tools are used for different kinds of memory analyses. Following is a prioritized list of tools for analyzing the various types of problems:

- **Quick memory health check.** First measure the amount of free memory with the `vmstat` command. Then examine the `sr` column of the `vmstat` output to check whether the system is scanning. If the system is short of memory, you can obtain high-level usage details with the MDB `::memstat -d` command.

- **Paging activity.** If the system is scanning, use the `-p` option of `vmstat` to see the types of paging. You would typically expect to see file-related paging as a result of normal file system I/O. Significant paging in of executables or paging in and paging out of anonymous memory suggests that *some* performance is being lost.

- **Attribution.** Using DTrace examples like those in this chapter, show which processes or files are causing paging activity.

- **Time-based analysis.** Estimate the impact of paging on system performance by drilling down with the `prstat` command and then further with DTrace. The `prstat` command estimates the amount of time stalled in datafault waits (typically, anonymous memory/heap page-ins). The DTrace scripts shown in this chapter can measure the exact amount of time spent waiting for paging activity.

- **Process memory usage.** Use the `pmap` command to inspect a process's memory usage, including the amount of physical memory used and an approximation of the amount shared with other processes.

- **MMU/page size performance issues.** Behind the scenes as a secondary issue is the potential performance impact of TLB (Translation Lookaside Buffer) overflows; these can often be optimized through the use of large MMU pages. The `trapstat` utility is ideal for quantifying these issues. We cover more on this advanced topic in the next chapter.

Table 6.1 summarizes and cross-references the tools covered in this chapter.

**Table 6.1** Tools for Memory Analysis

| Tool | Description | Reference |
|------|-------------|-----------|
| DTrace | For drill-down on sources of paging and time-based analysis of performance impact. | 6.11 |
| `kstat` | For access to raw VM performance statistics with command line, C, or Perl to facilitate performance-monitoring scripts. | 6.4, 6.13, 6.14 |
| MDB | For observing major categories of memory allocation. | 6.4 |
| `pmap` | For inspection of per-process memory use and facilitation of capacity planning. | 6.8 |
| `prstat` | For estimating potential performance impact by using microstates. | 6.6.1 |
| `trapstat` | For investigating MMU-related performance impacts. | 6.17 |
| `vmstat` | For determining free memory, scanning and paging rates and types. | 6.2, 6.4.2 |

## 6.2 `vmstat(1M)` Command

The vmstat command summarizes the most significant memory statistics. Included are summaries of the system's free memory, free swap, and paging rates for several classes of usage. Additionally, the -p option shows the paging activity, page-ins, page-outs, and page-frees separated into three classes: file system paging, anonymous memory paging, and executable/shared library paging. You typically use the -p option for a first-pass analysis of memory behavior.

The example below illustrates the vmstat command. Table 6.2 describes the columns. We discuss the definitions and significance of the paging statistics from vmstat in Section 6.18.

```
sol8$ vmstat -p 3
       memory            page           executable      anonymous        filesystem
   swap    free  re  mf  fr  de  sr  epi epo epf  api apo apf  fpi  fpo fpf
 2410424 516556  7  41   0   0   1    0   0   0    0   0   0  127  446   0
 2356376 472424  8   5   0   0   0    0   0   0    0   0   0   12  228   0
 2356376 472032  7   0   0   0   0    0   0   0    0   0   0    0   98   0
 2356376 471800  0   0   0   0   0    0   0   0    0   0   0    0    0   0
 2356376 471712  0   0   0   0   0    0   0   0    0   0   0    0    0   0
```

**Table 6.2** Statistics from the vmstat Command

| Counter | Description |
|---------|-------------|
| swap | Available swap space in Kbytes. |
| free | The amount of free memory as reported by vmstat, which reports the combined size of the cache list and free list. Free memory in Solaris may contain some of the file system cache. |
| re | Page reclaims—The number of pages reclaimed from the cache list. Some of the file system cache is in the cache list, and when a file page is reused and removed from the cache list, a reclaim occurs. File pages in the cache list can be either regular files or executable/library pages. |
| mf | Minor faults—The number of pages attached to an address space. If the page is already in memory, then a minor fault simply reestablishes the mapping to it; minor faults do not incur physical I/O. |
| fr | Page-frees—Kilobytes that have been freed either by the page scanner or by the file system (free-behind). |
| de | The calculated anticipated short-term memory shortfall. Used by the page scanner to free ahead enough pages to satisfy requests. |

*continues*

**Table 6.2** Statistics from the `vmstat` Command (*continued*)

| Counter | Description |
| --- | --- |
| sr | The number of pages scanned by the page scanner per second. |
| epi | Executable and library page-ins—Kilobytes of executable or shared library files paged in. An executable/library page-in occurs whenever a page for the executable binary or shared library is brought back in from the file system. |
| epo | Kilobytes of executable and library page-outs. Should be zero, since executable pages are typically not modified, there is no reason to write them out. |
| epf | Kilobytes of executable and library page-frees—Kilobytes of executable and library pages that have been freed by the page scanner. |
| api | Anonymous memory page-ins—Kilobytes of anonymous (application heap and stack) pages paged in from the swap device. |
| apo | Anonymous memory page-outs—Kilobytes of anonymous (application heap and stack) pages paged out to the swap device. |
| apf | Anonymous memory page-frees—Kilobytes of anonymous (application heap and stack) pages that have been freed after they have been paged out. |
| fpi | Regular file page-ins—Kilobytes of regular files paged in. A file page-in occurs whenever a page for a regular file is read in from the file system (part of the normal file system read process). |
| fpo | Regular file page-outs—Kilobytes of regular file pages that were paged out and freed, usually as a result of being paged out by the page scanner or by write free-behind (when free memory is less than `lotsfree + pages_before_pager`). |
| fpf | Regular file page-frees—Kilobytes of regular file pages that were freed, usually as a result of being paged out by the page scanner or by write free-behind (when free memory is less than `lotsfree + pages_before_pager`). |

## 6.3 Types of Paging

In this section, we quickly review the two major types of "paging": *file I/O paging* and *anonymous memory paging*. Understanding them will help you interpret the system metrics and health. Figure 6.1 puts paging in the context of physical memory's life cycle.

## 6.3.1 File I/O Paging: "Good" Paging

Traditional Solaris file systems (including UFS, VxFS, NFS, etc.) use the virtual memory system as the primary file cache (ZFS is an exception). We cover file systems caching in more detail in Section 14.8 in *Solaris™ Internals*.

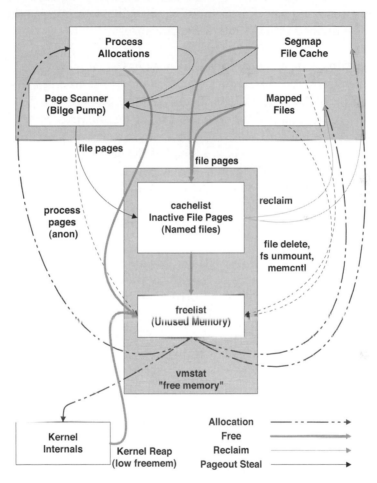

**Figure 6.1** Life Cycle of Physical Memory

File system I/O paging is the term we use for paging reads and writes files through file systems in their default cached mode. Files are read and written in multiples of page-size units to the I/O or to the network device backing the file system. Once a file page is read into memory, the virtual memory system caches that page so that subsequent file-level accesses don't have to reread pages from the device. It's normal to see a substantial amount of paging activity as a result of file I/O. Beginning with Solaris 8, a cyclic file system cache was introduced. The cyclic file system cache recirculates pages from the file system through a central pool known as the cache list, preventing the file system from putting excessive paging pressure on other users of memory within the system. This feature superseded the priority paging algorithms used in Solaris 7 and earlier to minimize these effects.

Paging can be divided into the following categories:

- **Reading files.** File system reads that miss in the file cache are performed as virtual memory page-ins. A new page is taken off the free list, and an I/O is scheduled to fill the page from its backing store. Files read with the system call read(2) are mapped into the segmap cache and are eventually placed back onto the tail of the cache list. The cache list becomes an ordered list of file pages; the oldest cached pages (head of the cache list) are eventually recycled as file system I/O consumes new pages from the free list.

    Smaller I/Os typically exhibit a one-to-one ratio between file system cache misses and page-ins. In some cases, however, the file system will group reads or issue prefetch, resulting in larger or differing relationships between file I/O and paging.

- **Writing files.** The process of writing a file also involves virtual memory operations—updated files are paged out to the backing I/O in multiples of page-size chunks. However, the reporting mechanism exhibits some oddities; for example, only page-outs that hint at discarding the page from cache show as file system page-outs in the kstat and vmstat statistics.

- **Reading executables.** The virtual memory system reads executables (program binaries) into memory upon exec and reads shared libraries into a process's address space. These read operations are basically the same as regular file system reads; however, the virtual memory system marks and tracks them separately to make it easy to isolate program paging from file I/O paging.

Paging of executables is visible through vmstat statistics; executable page-ins, page-outs, and frees are shown in the epi, epo, and epf columns. File page-ins, page-outs, and frees are shown in the fpi, fpo, and fpf columns.

```
$ vmstat -p 3
       memory              page          executable      anonymous       filesystem
   swap   free   re   mf   fr   de   sr   epi  epo  epf  api   apo   apf  fpi  fpo  fpf
 411696  12720   38 35473 15738  0 217112 20 0  848   13 14146 14331  23  377  559
 409356  35344   11  1823 9717  0 141771 104  0   22   96  9376  9389  62  295  306
 345264  26724   53  5234 2329  0  8727   28   0    0  263  2200  2200 103  217  129
 301104  48032   36  7313 8451  0 102271  76   0   75  167  8199  8241  15  157  135
```

## 6.3.2 Anonymous Memory Paging: "Bad" Paging

*Anonymous memory paging* is the term we use when the virtual memory system migrates anonymous pages to the swap device because of a shortage of physical memory. Most often, this occurs when the sum of the process heaps, shared memory, and stacks exceeds the available physical memory, causing the page scanner to begin shifting out to the swap device those pages that haven't recently been used. The next time the owning process references these pages, it incurs a *data fault* and must go to sleep while waiting for the pages to be brought back in from the swap device.

Anonymous paging is visible through the vmstat statistics; page-ins and page-outs are shown in the api and apo columns.

```
$ vmstat -p 3
       memory              page          executable      anonymous       filesystem
   swap   free   re   mf   fr   de   sr   epi  epo  epf  api   apo   apf  fpi  fpo  fpf
 411696  12720   38 35473 15738  0 217112 20 0  848   13 14146 14331  23  377  559
 409356  35344   11  1823 9717  0 141771 104  0   22   96  9376  9389  62  295  306
 345264  26724   53  5234 2329  0  8727   20   0    0  263  2200  2200 103  217  129
 301104  48032   36  7313 8451  0 102271  76   0   75  167  8199  8241  15  157  135
```

Although swap I/O is just another form of file system I/O, it is most often much slower than regular file I/O because of the random movement of memory to and from the swap device. Pages are collected and queued to the swap device in physical page order by the page scanner and are efficiently issued to the swap device (clustering allows up to 1-Mbyte I/Os). However, the owning process typically references the pages semi-sequentially in virtual memory order, resulting in random page-size I/O from the swap device. We know from simple I/O metrics that random 8-Kbyte I/O is likely to yield service times of around 5 milliseconds, significantly affecting performance.

## 6.3.3 Per-Zone Paging Statistics

The DTraceToolkit includes a command to display the vmstat statistics per-zone. It uses the zonename DTrace variable to summarize by zone.

```
# zvmstat 1
      ZONE   re    mf    fr    sr  epi epo epf api apo apf  fpi  fpo  fpf
     global  54   316    1     0    0   0   0   0   0   0    0    1    1
  workzone1   0     0    0     0    0   0   0   0   0   0    0    0    0
      ZONE   re    mf    fr    sr  epi epo epf api apo apf  fpi  fpo  fpf
     global 157   659    1     0   10   0   0   0   0   0    3    2    1
  workzone1 770  1085    0     0   48   0   0   0   0   0  928    0    0
      ZONE   re    mf    fr    sr  epi epo epf api apo apf  fpi  fpo  fpf
     global  56   317    0     0    6   0   0   0   0   0    2    0    0
  workzone1 1478   21    0     0    0   0   0   0   0   0 1635    0    0
                                                        See DTraceToolkit
```

## 6.4 Physical Memory Allocation

You can use the standard Solaris tools to observe the total physical memory configured, memory used by the kernel, and the amount of "free" memory in the system.

### 6.4.1 Total Physical Memory

From the output of the Solaris `prtconf` command, you can ascertain the amount of total physical memory.

```
# prtconf

System Configuration:  Sun Microsystems   i86pc
Memory size: 2048 Megabytes
System Peripherals (Software Nodes):
```

### 6.4.2 Free Memory

Use the `vmstat` command to measure free memory. The first line of output from `vmstat` is an average since boot, so the real free memory figure is available on the second line. The output is in kilobytes. In this example, observe the value of approximately 970 Mbytes of free memory.

```
# vmstat 3
 kthr      memory            page            disk          faults      cpu
 r b w   swap   free  re  mf pi po fr de sr cd cd f0 s0   in   sy   cs us sy id
 0 0 0 1512468 837776 160 20 12 12 12 0  0  0  1  0  0  589 3978  150  2  0 97
54 0 0 1720376 995556  1  13 27  0  0  0  0 20 176 0  0 1144 4948 1580  1  2 97
 0 0 0 1720376 995552  6  65 21  0  0  0  0 22 160 0  0 1191 7099 2139  2  3 95
 0 0 0 1720376 995536  0   0 13  0  0  0  0 21 190 0  0 1218 6183 1869  1  3 96
```

The free memory reported by Solaris includes the cache list portion of the page cache, meaning that you can expect to see a larger free memory size when significant file caching is occurring.

In Solaris 8, free memory did not include pages that were available for use from the page cache, which had recently been added. After a system was booted, the page cache gradually grew and the reported free memory dropped, usually hovering around 8 megabytes. This led to some confusion because Solaris 8 reported low memory even though plenty of pages were available for reuse from the cache. Since Solaris 9, the `free` column of `vmstat` has included the cache list portion and as such is a much more useful measure of free memory.

### 6.4.3 Using the `memstat` Command in MDB

You can use an `mdb` command to view the allocation of the physical memory into the buckets described in previous sections. The macro is included with Solaris 9 and later.

```
sol9# mdb -k
Loading modules: [ unix krtld genunix ip ufs_log logindmux ptm cpc sppp ipc random nfs ]
> ::memstat

Page Summary            Pages                MB   %Tot
------------     ----------------     ----------------   ----
Kernel                  53444                 208   10%
Anon                   119088                 465   23%
Exec and libs            2299                   8    0%
Page cache              29185                 114    6%
Free (cachelist)          347                   1    0%
Free (freelist)        317909                1241   61%

Total                  522272                2040
Physical               512136                2000
```

The categories are described as follows:

- **Kernel.** The total memory used for nonpageable kernel allocations. This is how much memory the kernel is using, excluding anonymous memory used for ancillaries (see Anon in the next paragraph).

- **Anon.** The amount of anonymous memory. This includes user-process heap, stack, and copy-on-write pages, shared memory mappings, and small kernel ancillaries, such as `lwp` thread stacks, present on behalf of user processes.

- **Exec and libs.** The amount of memory used for mapped files interpreted as binaries or libraries. This is typically the sum of memory used for user binaries and shared libraries. Technically, this memory is part of the page cache, but it is page cache tagged as "executable" when a file is mapped with PROT_EXEC and file permissions include execute permission.

- **Page cache.** The amount of unmapped page cache, that is, page cache not on the cache list. This category includes the segmap portion of the page cache and any memory mapped files. If the applications on the system are solely using a read/write path, then we would expect the size of this bucket not to exceed segmap_percent (defaults to 12% of physical memory size). Files in /tmp are also included in this category.

- **Free (cachelist).** The amount of page cache on the free list. The free list contains unmapped file pages and is typically where the majority of the file system cache resides. Expect to see a large cache list on a system that has large file sets and sufficient memory for file caching. Beginning with Solaris 8, the file system cycles its pages through the cache list, preventing it from stealing memory from other applications unless there is a true memory shortage.

- **Free (freelist).** The amount of memory that is actually free. This is memory that has no association with any file or process.

If you want this functionality for Solaris 8, copy the downloadable memory.so library into /usr/lib/mdb/kvm/sparcv9 and then use ::load memory before running ::memstat. (Note that this is not Sun-supported code, but it is considered low risk since it affects only the mdb user-level program.)

```
# wget http://www.solarisinternals.com/si/downloads/memory.so
# cp memory.so /usr/lib/mdb/kvm/sparcv9
# mdb -k
Loading modules: [ unix krtld genunix ip ufs_log logindmux ptm cpc sppp ipc random nfs ]
> ::load memory
> ::memstat
```

## 6.5 Relieving Memory Pressure

When available physical memory becomes exhausted, Solaris uses various mechanisms to relieve memory pressure: the cyclic page cache, the page scanner, and the original swapper. A summary is depicted in Figure 6.2.

The swapper swaps out entire threads, seriously degrading the performance of swapped-out applications. The page scanner selects pages, and is characterized by the scan rate (sr) from vmstat. Both use some form of the Not Recently Used algorithm.

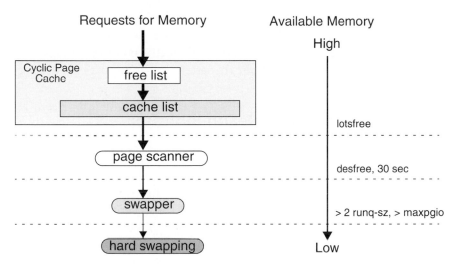

**Figure 6.2** Relieving Memory Pressure

The swapper and the page scanner are only used when appropriate. Since Solaris 8, the cyclic page cache, which maintains lists for a Least Recently Used selection, is preferred.

For more details on these mechanisms, see Chapter 10 in *Solaris™ Internals*. This section focuses on the tools used to observe performance, and Figure 6.2 is an appropriate summary for thinking in terms of tools.

To identify where on Figure 6.2 your system is, use the following tools.

- **free list.** The size of the free list can be examined with `::memstat` from `mdb -k`, discussed in Section 6.4.3. A large `free` column in `vmstat` includes both free list and cache list.

- **cache list.** The size of the cache list can also be examined with `::memstat`.

- **page scanner.** When the page scanner is active, the scan rate (`sr`) field in `vmstat` is non-zero. As the situation worsens, anonymous page-outs will occur and can be observed from `vmstat -p` and `iostat -xnPz` for the swap partition.

- **swapper.** For modern Solaris, it is rare that the swapper is needed. If it is used, the `kthr:w` field from `vmstat` becomes non-zero, to indicate swapped-out threads. This information is also available from `sar -q`. `vmstat -S` can also show swap-ins and swap-outs, as can `sar -w`.

- **hard swapping.** Try typing `echo hardswap/D | mdb -k`, to print a counter that is incremented because of hard swapping. If you are unable to type it in because the system is woefully slow, then you can guess that it is hard swapping anyway. A system that is hard swapping is barely usable. All other alarm bells should also have been triggered by this point (scan rate, heavy anonymous page-outs, swapped-out threads).

## 6.6 Scan Rate as a Memory Health Indicator

Solaris uses a central physical memory manager to reclaim memory from various subsystems when there is a shortage. A single daemon performs serves this purpose: the *page scanner*. The page scanner returns memory to the free list when the amount of free memory falls below a preset level, represented by a preconfigured tunable parameter, lotsfree. Knowing the basics about the page scanner will help you understand and interpret the memory health and performance statistics.

The scanner starts scanning when free memory is lower than lotsfree number of pages free plus a small buffer factor, deficit. The scanner starts scanning at a rate of slowscan pages per second at this point and gets faster as the amount of free memory approaches zero. The system parameter lotsfree is calculated at startup as 1/64th of memory, and the parameter deficit is either zero or a small number of pages—set by the page allocator at times of large memory allocation to let the scanner free a few more pages above lotsfree in anticipation of more memory requests.

Figure 6.3 shows that the rate at which the scanner scans increases linearly as free memory ranges between lotsfree and zero. The scanner starts scanning at the minimum rate set by slowscan when memory falls below lotsfree and then increases to fastscan if memory falls low enough.

The page scanner and its metrics are an important indicator of memory health. If the page scanner is running, there is likely a memory shortage. This is an interesting departure from the behavior you might have been accustomed to on Solaris 7 and earlier, where the page scanner was always running. Since Solaris 8, the file system cache resides on the cache list, which is part of the global free memory count. Thus, if a significant amount of memory is available, even if it's being used as a file system cache, the page scanner won't be running.

The most important metric is the scan rate, which indicates whether the page scanner is running. The scanner starts scanning at an initial rate (slowscan) when freemem falls down to the configured watermark—lotsfree—and then runs faster as free memory gets lower, up to a maximum (fastscan).

You can perform a quick and simple health check by determining whether there is a significant memory shortage. To do this, use vmstat to look at scanning activity and check to see if there is sufficient free memory on the system.

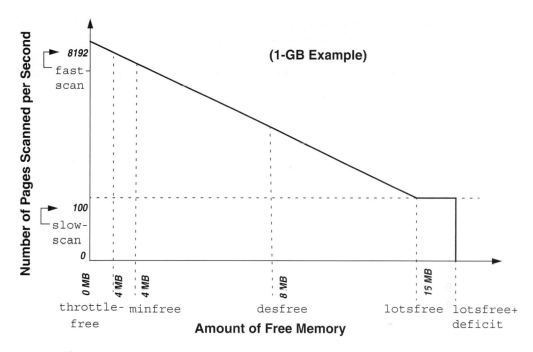

**Figure 6.3** Page Scanner Rate, Interpolated by Number of Free Pages

Let's first look at a healthy system. This system is showing 970 Mbytes of free memory in the free column and a *scan rate* (sr) of zero.

```
$ vmstat -p 3
        memory           page            executable       anonymous         filesystem
    swap   free  re  mf  fr  de  sr  epi epo epf  api apo apf  fpi  fpo  fpf
  1512488 837792 160 20  12   0   0   0   0   0    0   0   0   12   12   12
  1715812 985116  7  82   0   0   0   0   0   0    0   0   0   45    0    0
  1715784 983984  0   2   0   0   0   0   0   0    0   0   0   53    0    0
  1715780 987644  0   0   0   0   0   0   0   0    0   0   0   33    0    0
```

Looking at a second case, we can see two of the key indicators showing a memory shortage—both high scan rates (sr > 50000 in this case) and very low free memory (free < 10 Mbytes).

```
$ vmstat -p 3
        memory           page             executable       anonymous          filesystem
    swap    free   re   mf    fr    de sr    epi epo epf  api  apo   apf  fpi  fpo  fpf
  2276000 1589424 2128 19969   1  0  0     0   0   0    0   0    0     0    1    1
  1087652 388768  12 129675 13879 0 85590   0  0   12    0 3238 3238  10 9391 10630
  608036  51464   20  8853 37303 0 65871   38  0  781   12 19934 19930 95 16548 16591
   94448   8000   17 23674 30169 0 238522  16  0  810   23 28739 28804 56  547  556
```

Given that the page scanner runs only when the free list and cache list are effectively depleted, then any scanning activity is our first sign of memory shortage. Drilling down further with ::memstat (see Section 6.4) shows us where the major allocations are. It's useful to check that the kernel hasn't grown unnecessarily large.

## 6.6.1 Using `prstat` to Estimate Memory Slowdowns

Using the microstate measurement option in prstat, you can observe the percentage of execution time spent in data faults. The microstates show 100% of the execution time of a thread broken down into eight categories; the DFL column shows the percentage of time spent waiting for data faults to be serviced. The following example shows a severe memory shortage. The system was running short of memory, and each thread in filebench is waiting for memory approximately 90% of the time.

```
$ prstat -mL
   PID USERNAME USR SYS TRP TFL DFL LCK SLP LAT VCX ICX SCL SIG PROCESS/LWPID
 15625 rmc      0.1 0.7 0.0 0.0  95 0.0 0.9 3.2  1K 726  88   0 filebench/2
 15652 rmc      0.1 0.7 0.0 0.0  94 0.0 1.8 3.6  1K  1K  10   0 filebench/2
 15635 rmc      0.1 0.7 0.0 0.0  96 0.0 0.5 3.2  1K  1K   8   0 filebench/2
 15626 rmc      0.1 0.6 0.0 0.0  95 0.0 1.4 2.6  1K 813  10   0 filebench/2
 15712 rmc      0.1 0.5 0.0 0.0  47 0.0  49 3.8  1K 831 104   0 filebench/2
 15628 rmc      0.1 0.5 0.0 0.0  96 0.0 0.0 3.1  1K 735   4   0 filebench/2
 15725 rmc      0.0 0.4 0.0 0.0  92 0.0 1.7 5.7 996 736   8   0 filebench/2
 15719 rmc      0.0 0.4 0.0 0.0  40  40  17 2.9  1K 708 107   0 filebench/2
 15614 rmc      0.0 0.3 0.0 0.0  92 0.0 4.7 2.4 874 576  40   0 filebench/2
 15748 rmc      0.0 0.3 0.0 0.0  94 0.0 0.0 5.5 868 646   8   0 filebench/2
 15674 rmc      0.0 0.3 0.0 0.0  86 0.0 9.7 3.2 888 571  62   0 filebench/2
 15666 rmc      0.0 0.3 0.0 0.0  29  46  23 2.1 689 502 107   0 filebench/2
 15682 rmc      0.0 0.2 0.0 0.0  24  43  31 1.9 660 450 107   0 filebench/2
```

## 6.7 Process Virtual and Resident Set Size

A process's memory consumption can be categorized into two major groups: virtual size and resident set size. The virtual size is the total amount of virtual memory used by a process, or more specifically, the sum of the virtual size of the individual mappings constituting its address space. Some or all of a process's virtual memory is backed by physical memory; we refer to that amount as a process's resident set size (RSS).

The basic tools such as ps and prstat show both the process's total virtual size and resident set size (RSS). Take the RSS figure with a grain of salt, since a substantial portion of a process's RSS is shared with other processes in the system.

```
$ ps -eo pid,vsz,rss,args
  PID  VSZ  RSS COMMAND
11896 1040  736 ps -eo pid,vsz,rss,args
11892 1032  768 sh
 3603 1032  768 sh
 2695 1896 1432 telnet donan
 2693 1920 1456 telnet donan
 2433 1920 1440 telnet firefly
 3143 1920 1456 telnet devnull
 2429 1920 1440 telnet firefly.eng
 2134 1920 1440 telnet devnull
```

## 6.8 Using pmap to Inspect Process Memory Usage

You can use the pmap command to show the individual memory mappings that make up a process's address space. You can also use pmap to see the total amount of physical memory used by a process (its RSS) and to gather more information about how a process uses its memory. Since processes share some memory with others through the use of shared libraries and other shared memory mappings, you could overestimate system-wide memory usage by counting the same shared pages multiple times. To help with this situation, consider the amount of nonshared anonymous memory allocated as an estimation of a process's private memory usage, (shown in the Anon column). We cover more on this topic in Section 6.7.

```
solis pmap -x 102908
102908:   sh
Address  Kbytes Resident  Anon Locked Mode  Mapped File
00010000     88       88     -      - r-x--  sh
00036000      8        8     8      - rwx--  sh
00038000     16       16    16      - rwx--   [ heap ]
FF260000     16       16     -      - r-x--  en_.so.2
FF272000     16       16     -      - rwx--  en_US.so.2
FF280000    664      624     -      - r-x--  libc.so.1
FF336000     32       32     8      - rwx--  libc.so.1
FF360000     16       16     -      - r-x--  libc_psr.so.1
FF380000     24       24     -      - r-x--  libgen.so.1
FF396000      8        8     -      - rwx--  libgen.so.1
FF3A0000      8        8     -      - r-x--  libdl.so.1
FF3B0000      8        8     8      - rwx--   [ anon ]
FF3C0000    152      152     -      - r-x--  ld.so.1
FF3F6000      8        8     8      - rwx--  ld.so.1
FFBFE000      8        8     8      - rw---   [ stack ]
--------  -----    -----  ----- ------
total Kb   1072     1032    56      -
```

## 6.9 Calculating Process Memory Usage with `ps` and `pmap`

Recall that the memory use of a process can be categorized into two classes: its virtual memory usage and its physical memory usage (referred to as its resident set size, or RSS). The virtual memory size is the amount of virtual address space that has been allocated to the process, and the physical memory is the amount of real memory pages that has been allocated to a process. You use the `ps` command to display a process's virtual and physical memory usage.

```
$ ps -eo pid,vsz,rss,args
  PID  VSZ  RSS COMMAND
11896 1040  736 ps -eo pid,vsz,rss,args
11892 1032  768 sh
 3603 1032  768 sh
 2695 1896 1432 telnet donan
 2693 1920 1456 telnet donan
 2433 1920 1440 telnet firefly
 3143 1920 1456 telnet devnull
 2429 1920 1440 telnet firefly.eng
 2134 1920 1440 telnet devnull
```

From the `ps` example, you see that the `/bin/sh` shell uses 1032 Kbytes of virtual memory, 768 Kbytes of which have been allocated from physical memory, and that two shells are running. `ps` reports that both shells are using 768 Kbytes of memory each, but in fact, because each shell uses dynamic shared libraries, the total amount of physical memory used by both shells is much less than 768K × 2.

To ascertain how much memory is really being used by both shells, look more closely at the address space within each process. Figure 6.4 shows how the two shells share both the `/bin/sh` binary and their shared libraries. The figure shows each mapping of memory within the shell's address space. We've separated the memory use into three categories:

- **Private.** Memory that is mapped into each process and that is not shared by any other processes.
- **Shared.** Memory that is shared with all other processes on the system, including read-only portions of the binary and libraries, otherwise known as the "text" mappings.
- **Partially shared.** A mapping that is partly shared with other processes. The data mappings of the binary and libraries are shared in this way because they are shared but writable and within each process are private copies of pages that have been modified. For example, the `/bin/sh` data mapping is mapped shared between all instances of `/bin/sh` but is mapped read/write because it contains initialized variables that may be updated during execu-

tion of the process. Variable updates must be kept private to the process, so a private page is created by a "copy on write" operation. (See Section 9.5.2 in *Solaris™ Internals* for further information.)

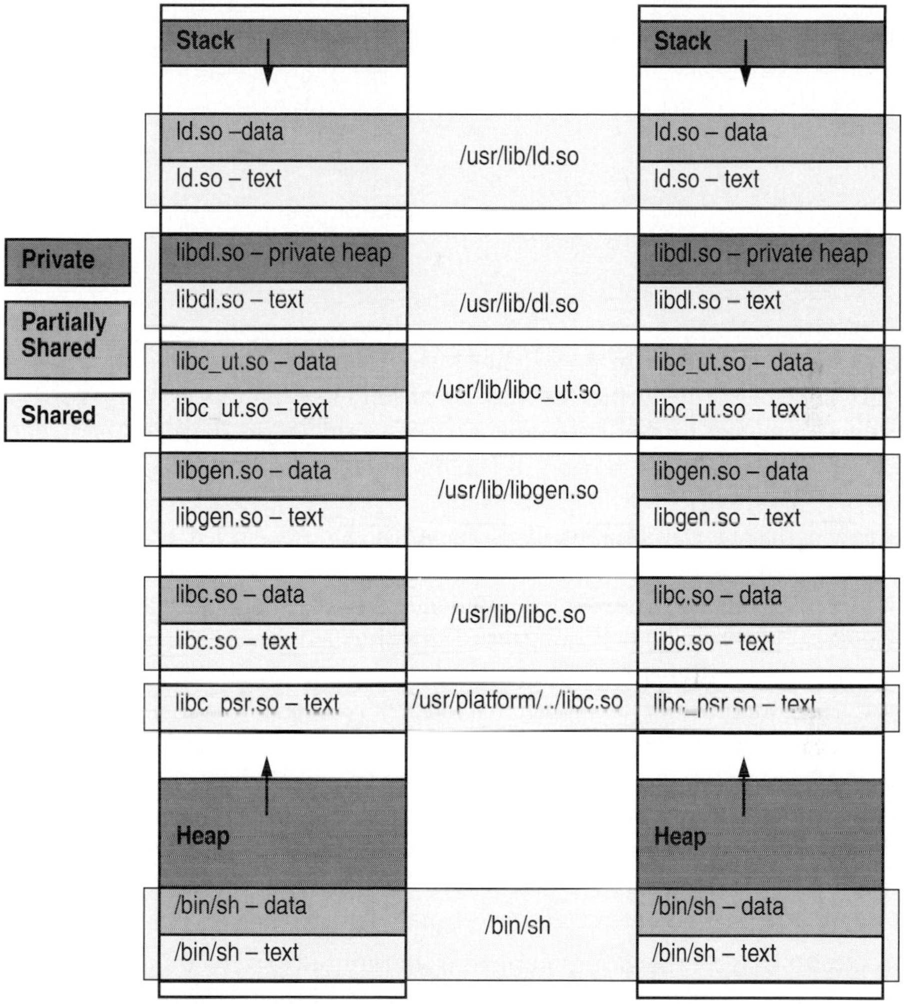

| | Stack ↓ | | Stack ↓ |
|---|---|---|---|
| | ld.so –data | /usr/lib/ld.so | ld.so – data |
| | ld.so – text | | ld.so – text |
| **Private** | libdl.so – private heap | | libdl.so – private heap |
| | libdl.so – text | /usr/lib/dl.so | libdl.so – text |
| **Partially Shared** | libc_ut.so – data | /usr/lib/libc_ut.so | libc_ut.so – data |
| | libc_ut.so – text | | libc_ut.so – text |
| **Shared** | libgen.so – data | /usr/lib/libgen.so | libgen.so – data |
| | libgen.so – text | | libgen.so – text |
| | libc.so – data | /usr/lib/libc.so | libc.so – data |
| | libc.so – text | | libc.so – text |
| | libc_psr.so – text | /usr/platform/../libc.so | libc_psr.so – text |
| | ↑ | | ↑ |
| | Heap ↓ | | Heap ↓ |
| | /bin/sh – data | /bin/sh | /bin/sh – data |
| | /bin/sh – text | | /bin/sh – text |

**Figure 6.4** Process Private and Shared Mappings (/bin/sh Example)

The pmap command displays every mapping within the process's address space, so you can inspect a process and estimate shared and private memory usage. The amount of resident, nonshared anonymous, and locked memory is shown for each mapping.

```
sol9$ pmap -x 102908
102908:    sh
Address   Kbytes Resident   Anon  Locked Mode   Mapped File
00010000      88       88      -      - r-x--  sh
00036000       8        8      8      - rwx--  sh
00038000      16       16     16      - rwx--    [ heap ]
FF260000      16       16      -      - r-x--  en_.so.2
FF272000      16       16      -      - rwx--  en_US.so.2
FF280000     664      624      -      - r-x--  libc.so.1
FF336000      32       32      8      - rwx--  libc.so.1
FF360000      16       16      -      - r-x--  libc_psr.so.1
FF380000      24       24      -      - r-x--  libgen.so.1
FF396000       8        8      -      - rwx--  libgen.so.1
FF3A0000       8        8      -      - r-x--  libdl.so.1
FF3B0000       8        8      8      - rwx--    [ anon ]
FF3C0000     152      152      -      - r-x--  ld.so.1
FF3F6000       8        8      8      - rwx--  ld.so.1
FFBFE000       8        8      8      - rw---    [ stack ]
--------   -----    -----  -----  ------
total Kb    1072     1032     56      -
```

The example output from `pmap` shows the memory map of the /bin/sh command. At the top of the output are the executable text and data mappings. All the executable binary is shared with other processes because it is mapped read-only into each process. A small portion of the data mapping is shared; some is private because of copy-on-write (COW) operations.

You can estimate the amount of incremental memory used by each additional instance of a process by using the resident and anonymous memory counts of each mapping. In the above example, the Bourne shell has a resident memory size of 1032 Kbytes. However, a large amount of the physical memory used by the shell is shared with other instances of the shell. Another identical instance of the shell will share physical memory with the other shell where possible and will allocate anonymous memory for any nonshared portion. In the above example, each additional Bourne shell uses approximately 56 Kbytes of additional physical memory.

A more complex example shows the output format for a process containing different mapping types. In this example, the mappings are as follows:

- **0001000.** Executable text, mapped from `maps` program
- **0002000.** Executable data, mapped from `maps` program
- **0002200.** Program heap
- **0300000.** A mapped file, mapped `MAP_SHARED`
- **0400000.** A mapped file, mapped `MAP_PRIVATE`
- **0500000.** A mapped file, mapped `MAP_PRIVATE | MAP_NORESERVE`
- **0600000.** Anonymous memory, created by mapping /dev/zero

- **0700000.** Anonymous memory, created by mapping /dev/zero with MAP_NORESERVE

- **0800000.** A DISM shared memory mapping, created with SHM_PAGEABLE, with 8 Mbytes locked by mlock(2)

- **0900000.** A DISM shared memory mapping, created with SHM_PAGEABLE, with 4 Mbytes of its pages touched

- **0A00000.** A ISM shared memory mapping, created with SHM_PAGEABLE, with all of its pages touched

- **0B00000.** An ISM shared memory mapping, created with SHM_SHARE_MMU

```
sol9$ pmap -x 15492
15492:   ./maps
 Address   Kbytes      RSS     Anon  Locked Mode   Mapped File
00010000        8        8        -       - r-x--  maps
00020000        8        8        8       - rwx--  maps
00022000    20344    16248    16248       - rwx--  [ heap ]
03000000     1024     1024        -       - rw-s-  dev:0,2 ino:4628487
04000000     1024     1024      512       - rw---  dev:0,2 ino:4628487
05000000     1024     1024      512       - rw--R  dev:0,2 ino:4628487
06000000     1024     1024     1024       - rw---  [ anon ]
07000000      512      512      512       - rw--R  [ anon ]
08000000     8192     8192        -    8192 rwxs-  [ dism shmid=0x5]
09000000     8192     4096        -       - rwxs-  [ dism shmid=0x4]
0A000000     8192     8192        -    8192 rwxsR  [ ism shmid=0x2 ]
0B000000     8192     8192        -    8192 rwxsR  [ ism shmid=0x3 ]
FF280000      680      672        -       - r-x--  libc.so.1
FF33A000       32       32       32       - rwx--  libc.so.1
FF390000        8        8        -       - r-x--  libc_psr.so.1
FF3A0000        8        8        -       - r-x--  libdl.so.1
FF3B0000        8        8        8       - rwx--  [ anon ]
FF3C0000      152      152        -       - r-x--  ld.so.1
FF3F6000        8        8        8       - rwx--  ld.so.1
FFBFA000       24       24       24       - rwx--  [ stack ]
-------- -------- -------- -------- --------
total Kb    50464    42264    18888    16384
```

## 6.10 Displaying Page-Size Information with pmap

You use the -s option to display the hardware translation page sizes for each portion of the address space. (See Chapter 13 in *Solaris™ Internals* for further information on Solaris support for multiple page sizes.) In the example below, you can see that the majority of the mappings use an 8-Kbyte page size and that the heap uses a 4-Mbyte page size. Notice that noncontiguous regions of resident pages of the same page size are reported as separate mappings. In the example below, the libc.so library is reported as separate mappings, since only some of the libc.so text is resident.

```
example$ pmap -xs 15492
15492:  ./maps
 Address   Kbytes     RSS     Anon   Locked Pgsz Mode   Mapped File
00010000        8       8       -       -   8K r-x--  maps
00020000        8       8       8       -   8K rwx--  maps
00022000     3960    3960    3960       -   8K rwx--  [ heap ]
00400000     8192    8192    8192       -   4M rwx--  [ heap ]
00C00000     4096       -       -       -    - rwx--  [ heap ]
01000000     4096    4096    4096       -   4M rwx--  [ heap ]
03000000     1024    1024       -       -   8K rw-s-  dev:0,2 ino:4628487
04000000      512     512     512       -   8K rw---  dev:0,2 ino:4628487
04080000      512     512       -       -    - rw---  dev:0,2 ino:4628487
05000000      512     512     512       -   8K rw--R  dev:0,2 ino:4628487
05080000      512     512       -       -    - rw--R  dev:0,2 ino:4628487
06000000     1024    1024    1024       -   8K rw---  [ anon ]
07000000      512     512     512       -   8K rw--R  [ anon ]
08000000     8192    8192       -    8192    - rwxs-  [ dism shmid=0x5 ]
09000000     4096    4096       -       -   8K rwxs-  [ dism shmid=0x4 ]
0A000000     4096       -       -       -    - rwxs-  [ dism shmid=0x2 ]
0B000000     8192    8192       -    8192   4M rwxsR  [ ism shmid=0x3 ]
FF280000      136     136       -       -   8K r-x--  libc.so.1
FF2A2000      120     120       -       -    - r-x--  libc.so.1
FF2C0000      128     128       -       -   8K r-x--  libc.so.1
FF2E0000      200     200       -       -    - r-x--  libc.so.1
FF312000       48      48       -       -   8K r-x--  libc.so.1
FF31E000       48      40       -       -    - r-x--  libc.so.1
FF33A000       32      32      32       -   8K rwx--  libc.so.1
FF390000        8       8       -       -   8K r-x--  libc_psr.so.1
FF3A0000        8       8       -       -   8K r-x--  libdl.so.1
FF3B0000        8       8       8       -   8K rwx--  [ anon ]
FF3C0000      152     152       -       -   8K r-x--  ld.so.1
FF3F6000        8       8       8       -   8K rwx--  ld.so.1
FFBFA000       24      24      24       -   8K rwx--  [ stack ]
-------- ------- ------- ------- -------
total Kb    50464   42264   18888   16384
```

## 6.11 Using DTrace for Memory Analysis

With the DTrace utility, you can probe more deeply into the sources of activity observed with higher-level memory analysis tools. For example, if you determine that a significant amount of paging activity is due to a memory shortage, you can determine which process is initiating the paging activity. In another example, if you see a significant amount of paging due to file activity, you can drill down to see which process and which file are responsible.

DTrace allows for memory analysis through a vminfo provider, and, optionally, through deeper tracing of virtual memory paging with the fbt provider.

The vminfo provider probes correspond to the fields in the "vm" named kstat. A probe provided by vminfo fires immediately before the corresponding vm value is incremented. Section 10.6.2 lists the probes available from the vm provider; these are further described in Section 10.6.2. A probe takes the following arguments:

- **arg0.** The value by which the statistic is to be incremented. For most probes, this argument is always 1, but for some it may take other values; these probes are noted in Section 10.4.
- **arg1.** A pointer to the current value of the statistic to be incremented. This value is a 64-bit quantity that is incremented by the value in `arg0`. Dereferencing this pointer allows consumers to determine the current count of the statistic corresponding to the probe.

For example, if you should see the following paging activity with `vmstat`, indicating page-in from the swap device, you could drill down to investigate.

```
# vmstat -p 3
      memory              page          executable      anonymous       filesystem
  swap    free   re  mf   fr  de  sr  epi  epo  epf  api  apo  apf  fpi  fpo  fpf
1512400 037792  160  20   12   0   0    0    0    0 8102    0    0   12   12   12
1715812 985116    7  82    0   0   0    0    0    0 7501    0    0   45    0    0
1715784 983984    0   2    0   0   0    0    0    0 1231    0    0   53    0    0
1715780 987644    0   0    0   0   0    0    0    0 2451    0    0   33    0    0

$ dtrace -n anonpgin'{@[execname] = count()}'
dtrace: description 'anonpgin' matched 1 probe
  svc.startd                                                    1
  sshd                                                          2
  ssh                                                           3
  dtrace                                                        6
  vmstat                                                       28
  filebench                                                   913
```

See Section 6.11.1 for examples of how to use dtrace for memory analysis and Section 10.6.2.

## 6.11.1 Using DTrace to Estimate Memory Slowdowns

You can use DTrace to directly measure elapsed time around the page-in probes when a process is waiting for page-in from the swap device, as in this example.

```
#!/usr/sbin/dtrace -s
#pragma D option quiet

dtrace:::BEGIN
{
        trace("Tracing... Hit Ctrl-C to end.\n");
}

sched:::on-cpu
{
        self->on = vtimestamp;
}
```

*continues*

```
sched:::off-cpu
/self->on/
{
        @oncpu[execname] = sum(vtimestamp - self->on);
        self->on = 0;
}

vminfo:::anonpgin
{
        self->anonpgin = 1;
}

fbt::pageio_setup:return
{
        self->wait = timestamp;
}

fbt::pageio_done:entry
/self->anonpgin == 1/
{
        self->anonpgin = 0;
        @pageintime[execname] = sum(timestamp - self->wait);
        self->wait = 0;
}

dtrace:::END
{
        normalize(@oncpu, 1000000);
        printf("Who's on cpu (milliseconds):\n");
        printa("  %-50s %15@d\n", @oncpu);

        normalize(@pageintime, 1000000);
        printf("Who's waiting for pagein (milliseconds):\n");
        printa("  %-50s %15@d\n", @pageintime);

}
```

With an aggregation by execname, you can see who is being held up by paging the most.

```
# ./whospaging.d
Tracing... Hit Ctrl-C to end.
^C
Who's on cpu (milliseconds):
  svc.startd                                             1
  loop.sh                                                2
  sshd                                                   2
  ssh                                                    3
  dtrace                                                 6
  vmstat                                                28
  pageout                                               60
  fsflush                                              120
  filebench                                            913
  sched                                              84562
Who's waiting for pagein (milliseconds):
  filebench                                         230704
```

In the output of whospaging.d, the filebench command spent 913 milliseconds on CPU (doing useful work) and 230.7 seconds waiting for anonymous page-ins.

## 6.12 Obtaining Memory Kstats

Table 6.3 shows the system memory statistics that are available through kstats. These are a superset of the raw statistics used behind the `vmstat` command. Each statistic can be accessed with the `kstat` command or accessed programmatically through C or Perl.

**Table 6.3** Memory-Related Kstats

| Module | Class | Name | Description |
|--------|-------|------|-------------|
| unix | pages | system_pages | Systemwide page count summaries |
| unix | vm | segmap | File system mapping statistics |
| unix | kmem_cache | segvn_cache | Anonymous and memory mapped file statistics |
| unix | hat | sfmmu_global_stat | SPARC sun4u MMU statistics |
| cpu | misc | vm | Systemwide paging statistics |

The `kstat` command shows the metrics available for each named group; invoke the command with the `-n` option and the kstat name, as in Table 6.3. Metrics that reference quantities in page sizes must also take into account the system's base page size. Below is an example.

```
$ kstat -n system_pages
module: unix                          instance: 0
name:   system_pages                  class:    pages
        availrmem                     343567
        crtime                        0
        desfree                       4001
        desscan                       25
        econtig                       4278190080
        fastscan                      256068
        freemem                       248309
        kernelbase                    3556769792
        lotsfree                      8002
        minfree                       2000
        nalloc                        11957763
        nalloc_calls                  9981
        nfree                         11856636
        nfree_calls                   6689
        nscan                         0
        pagesfree                     248309
        pageslocked                   168569
        pagestotal                    512136
        physmem                       522272
```

*continues*

```
        pp_kernel                       64102
        slowscan                        100
        snaptime                        6573953.83957897
$ pagesize
4096
```

## 6.13  Using the Perl Kstat API to Look at Memory Statistics

You can also obtain kstat statistics through the Perl kstat API. With that approach, you can write simple scripts to collect the statistics. For example, below we display statistics for Section 6.4.2 quite easily by using the system_pages statistics.

```
%{$now} = %{$kstats->{0}{system_pages}};
print "$now->{pagesfree}\n";
```

Using a more elaborate script, we read the values for physmem, pp_kernel, and pagesfree and report them at regular intervals.

```
$ wget http://www.solarisinternals.com/si/downloads/prtmem.pl
$ prtmem.pl 10
prtmem started on 04/01/2005 15:46:13 on d-mpk12-65-100, sample interval 5 seconds

                Total       Kernel      Delta       Free        Delta
15:46:18        2040        250         0           972         -12
15:46:23        2040        250         0           968         -3
15:46:28        2040        250         0           968         0
15:46:33        2040        250         0           970         1
...
```

## 6.14  System Memory Allocation Kstats

Use the kstat command to view system memory allocation kstats, as shown below. Table 6.4 describes each statistic.

```
$ kstat -n system_pages
module: unix                        instance: 0
name:   system_pages               class:    pages
        availrmem                   97303
        crtime                      0
        desfree                     1007
        desscan                     25
        econtig                     4275789824
```

*continues*

```
    fastscan                      64455
    freemem                       16780
    kernelbase                    3556769792
    lotsfree                      2014
    minfree                       503
    nalloc                        1682534446
    nalloc_calls                  298799
    nfree                         1681653744
    nfree_calls                   295152
    nscan                         0
    pagesfree                     16780
    pageslocked                   31607
    pagestotal                    128910
    physmem                       128910
    pp_kernel                     32999
    slowscan                      100
    snaptime                      2415909.89921839
```

**Table 6.4** Memory Allocation Kstats with `unix::system_pages`

| Statistic | Description | Units | Reference |
|---|---|---|---|
| availrmem | The amount of unlocked pageable memory available for memory allocation. | Pages | 9.8[a] |
| desfree | If free memory falls below desfree, then the page-out scanner is started 100 times/ second. | Pages | 10.3[a] |
| desscan | Scan rate target for the page scanner. | Pages/s | 10.3[a] |
| econtig | Address of first block of contiguous kernel memory. | Bytes | |
| fastscan | The rate of pages scanned per second when free memory = 0. | Pages/s | 10.3[a] |
| freemem | System free list size. | Pages | 6.4.2 |
| kernelbase | Starting address of kernel mapping. | Bytes | |
| lotsfree | If free memory falls below lotsfree, then the scanner starts stealing anonymous memory pages. | Pages | 10.3[a] |
| minfree | If free memory falls below minfree, then the page scanner is signaled to start every time a new page is created. | Pages | 10.3[a] |
| nalloc | Kernel memory allocator allocations. | Integer | |
| nalloc_calls | Kernel memory allocator calls to alloc(). | Integer | |
| nfree | Kernel memory allocator frees. | Integer | |
| nfree_calls | Kernel memory allocator calls to free(). | Integer | |

*continues*

**Table 6.4** Memory Allocation Kstats with `unix::system_pages` (*continued*)

| Statistic | Description | Units | Reference |
|---|---|---|---|
| nscan | Number of pages scanned by the page scanner at last wake-up. | Pages | 10.3[a] |
| pagesfree | System free list size. | Pages | 6.4.2 |
| pageslocked | Total number of pages locked into memory by the kernel and user processes. | Pages | |
| pagestotal | Total number of pages available to the system after kernel metamanagement memory. | Pages | |
| physmem | Total number of physical pages in the system at boot. | Pages | |
| pp_kernel | Total number of pages used by the kernel. | Pages | |
| slowscan | The rate of pages scanned per second when free memory = `lotsfree`. | Pages/s | 10.3[a] |

a. *Solaris™ Internals, Second Edition*

## 6.15  Kernel Memory with `kstat`

You can determine the amount of kernel memory by using the Solaris `kstat` command and multiplying the `pp_kernel` by the system's base page size. The computed output is in bytes; in this example, the kernel is using approximately 250 Mbytes of memory.

```
$ kstat unix::system_pages:pp_kernel
module: unix                          instance: 0
name:    system_pages                 class:     pages
         pp_kernel                    64102
$ pagesize
4096
$ bc
64102*4096
262561792
```

A general rule is that you would expect the kernel to use approximately 15% of the system's total physical memory. We've seen this to be true in more than 90% of observed situations. Exceptions to the rule are cases, such as an in-kernel Web server cache, in which the majority of the workload is kernel based. Investigate further if you see large kernel memory sizes.

## 6.16 System Paging Kstats

Use the `kstat` command to see the system paging kstats. Table 6.5 describes each statistic.

```
$ kstat -n vm
module: cpu                      instance: 0
name:   vm                       class:    misc
        anonfree                 485085
        anonpgin                 376728
        anonpgout                343517
        as_fault                 5676333
...
```

**Table 6.5** Memory Allocation Kstats from `cpu::vm`

| Statistic | Description | Units |
|---|---|---|
| anonfree | Anonymous memory page-frees—pages of anonymous (application heap and stack) pages that have been freed after they have been paged out. | Pages |
| anonpgin | Anonymous memory page-ins—pages of anonymous (application heap and stack) pages paged in from the swap device. | Pages |
| anonpgout | Anonymous memory page-outs—pages of anonymous (application heap and stack) pages paged out to the swap device. | Pages |
| as_fault | Faults taken within an address space. | Pages |
| cow_fault | Copy-on-write faults | Pages |
| execfree | Pages of executable and library page-frees—pages of executable and library pages that have been freed. | Pages |
| execpgin | Executable and library page-ins—pages of executable or shared library files paged in. An executable/library page-in occurs whenever a page for the executable binary or shared library is brought back in from the file system. | Pages |
| execpgout | Pages of executable and library page-outs. Should be zero. | Pages |
| fsfree | Regular file page-frees—pages of regular file pages that were freed, usually as a result of being paged out by the page scanner or by write free-behind (when free memory is less than `lotsfree` + `pages_before_pager`). | Pages |

*continues*

**Table 6.5** Memory Allocation Kstats from `cpu::vm` (*continued*)

| Statistic | Description | Units |
| --- | --- | --- |
| fspgin | Regular file page-ins—pages of regular files paged in. A file page-in occurs whenever a page for a regular file is read in from the file system (part of the normal file system read process). | Pages |
| fspgout | Regular file page-outs—pages of regular file pages that were paged out and freed, usually as a result of being paged out by the page scanner or by write free-behind (when free memory is less than `lotsfree + pages_before_pager`). | Pages |
| hat_fault | Minor faults—The number of pages attached to an address space. If the page is already in memory, then a minor fault simply reestablishes the mapping to it; minor faults do not incur physical I/O. | Pages |
| kernel_asflt | Translation faults in the kernel address space. | Pages |
| maj_fault | Major faults—the number of faults requiring memory allocation or disk I/O. | Pages |
| pgfrec | Page reclaims—The number of pages reclaimed from the free list. Some of the file system cache is in the free list; when a file page is reused and removed from the free list, a reclaim occurs. File pages in the free list can be either regular files or executable/library pages. | Pages |
| pgin | Total number of page-ins. | Events |
| pgpgin | Total number of pages paged in. | Pages |
| pgout | Total number of page-outs. | Events |
| pgpgout | Total number of pages paged out. | Pages |
| pgrec | Page reclaims from the free list, plus reclaims due to page outs | Pages |
| pgrrun | The number of times the pager was run. | Events |
| pgswapin | The number of pages swapped in. | Pages |
| pgswapout | The number of pages swapped out. | Pages |
| prot_fault | The number of protection faults. | Pages |
| swapin | Total number of swap-ins. | Events |
| swapout | Total number of swap-outs. | Events |
| zfod | Number of pages allocated by zero-fill-on-demand. | Pages |

## 6.17  Observing MMU Performance Impact with `trapstat`

The `trapstat` command provides information about processor exceptions on
UltraSPARC platforms. Since Translation Lookaside Buffer (TLB) misses are serviced in software on UltraSPARC microprocessors, `trapstat` can also provide statistics about TLB misses.

With the `trapstat` command, you can observe the number of TLB misses and
the amount of time spent servicing TLB misses by using the `-t` and `-T` options.
Also with `trapstat`, you can use the amount of time servicing TLB misses to
approximate the potential gains you could make by using a larger page size or by
moving to a platform that uses a microprocessor with a larger TLB.

The `-t` option provides first-level summary statistics. The time spent servicing TLB
misses is summarized in the lower-right corner; in the following example, 46.2% of
the total execution time is spent servicing misses—a significant portion of CPU time.

```
sol9# trapstat -t 1 111
cpu m| itlb-miss %tim itsb-miss %tim | dtlb-miss %tim dtsb-miss %tim |%tim
-----+------------------------------+------------------------------+----
  0 u|     1   0.0      0  0.0 |  2171237 45.7       0  0.0 |45.7
  0 k|     2   0.0      0  0.0 |     3751  0.1       7  0.0 | 0.1
=====+==============================+==============================+====
ttl  |     3   0.0      0  0.0 |  2192238 46.2       7  0.0 |46.2
```

Miss detail is provided for TLB misses in both the instruction (`itlb-miss`) and
data (`dtlb-miss`) portion of the address space. Data is also provided for user-
mode (`u`) and kernel-mode (`k`) misses (the user-mode misses are of most interest
since applications are likely to run in user mode).

The `-T` option breaks down each page size.

```
# trapstat -T 5
cpu m size| itlb miss %tim itsb miss %tim | dtlb miss %tim dtsb miss %tim |%tim
----------+------------------------------+------------------------------+----
  0 u   8k|   2760   0.1    3702  0.7 |   14239  0.7    4386  0.9 | 2.5
  0 u  64k|      0   0.0       0  0.0 |       0  0.0       0  0.0 | 0.0
  0 u 512k|      0   0.0       0  0.0 |       0  0.0       0  0.0 | 0.0
  0 u   4m|      0   0.0       0  0.0 |       0  0.0       0  0.0 | 0.0
- - - - - +- - - - - - - - - - - - - - - + - - - - - - - - - - - - - - +- - -
  0 k   8k|    681   0.1       0  0.0 |  183328  9.9    2992  0.9 |10.8
  0 k  64k|      0   0.0       0  0.0 |      18  0.0       0  0.0 | 0.0
  0 k 512k|      0   0.0       0  0.0 |       0  0.0       0  0.0 | 0.0
  0 k   4m|      0   0.0       0  0.0 |     818  0.1       0  0.0 | 0.1
==========+==============================+==============================+====
     ttl  |   3441   0.2    3702  0.7 |  198403 10.6    7378  1.8 |13.4
```

For further information on large pages and `trapstat`, see Chapter 13 in
*Solaris™ Internals*.

## 6.18 Swap Space

In this section we look at how swap is allocated and then discuss the statistics used for monitoring swap. We refer to swap space as seen by the processes as *virtual swap space* and real (disk or file) swap space as *physical swap space*.

### 6.18.1 Swap Allocation

Swap space allocation goes through distinct stages: reserve, allocate, and swap-out. When you first create a segment, you reserve virtual swap space; when you first touch and allocate a page, you "allocate" virtual swap space for that page; then, if you encounter a memory shortage, you can "swap out" a page to swap space. Table 6.6 summarizes the swap states.

**Table 6.6**  Swap Space Allocation States

| State | Description |
|---|---|
| Reserved | Virtual swap space is reserved for an entire segment. Reservation occurs when a segment is created with private/read/write access. The reservation represents the virtual size of the area being created. |
| Allocated | Virtual swap space is allocated when the first physical page is assigned to it. At that point, a `swapfs vnode` and offset are assigned against the *anon* slot. |
| Swapped out (used swap) | When a memory shortage occurs, a page may be swapped out by the page scanner. Swap-out happens when the page scanner calls `swapfs_putpage` for the page in question. The page is migrated to physical (disk or file) swap. |

Swap space is reserved each time a heap segment is created. The amount of swap space reserved is the entire size of the segment being created. Swap space is also reserved if there is a possibility of anonymous memory being created. For example, mapped file segments that are mapped MAP_PRIVATE (like the executable data segment) reserve swap space because at any time they could create anonymous memory during a copy-on-write operation.

You should reserve virtual swap space up-front so that swap space allocation assignment is done at the time of request, rather than at the time of need. That way, an out-of-swap-space error can be reported synchronously during a system call. If you allocated swap space on demand during program execution rather than when you called malloc(), the program could run out of swap space during execution and have no simple way to detect the out-of-swap-space condition. For example, in the Solaris kernel, we fail a `malloc()` request for memory as it is requested rather than when it is needed later, to prevent processes from failing during seemingly normal execution. (This strategy differs from that of operating systems such as IBM's AIX, where lazy allocation is done. If the resource is exhausted during program execution, then the process is sent a `SIGDANGER` signal.)

The `swapfs` file system includes all available pageable memory as virtual swap space in addition to the physical swap space. That way, you can "reserve" virtual swap space and "allocate" swap space when you first touch a page. When you reserve swap rather than reserving disk space, you reserve virtual swap space from `swapfs`. Disk swap pages are only allocated once a page is paged out.

With `swapfs`, the amount of virtual swap space available is the amount of available unlocked, pageable physical memory plus the amount of physical (disk) swap space available. If you were to run without swap space, then you could reserve as much virtual memory as there is unlocked pageable physical memory available on the system. This would be fine, except that often virtual memory requirements are greater than physical memory requirements, and this case would prevent you from using all the available physical memory on the system.

For example, a process may reserve 100 Mbytes of memory and then allocate only 10 Mbytes of physical memory. The process's physical memory requirement would be 10 Mbytes, but it had to reserve 100 Mbytes of virtual swap, thus using 100 Mbytes of virtual swap allocated from available real memory. If we ran such a process on a 128-Mbyte system, we would likely start only one of these processes before we exhausted our swap space. If we added more virtual swap space by adding a disk swap device, then we could reserve against the additional space, and we would likely get 10 or so of the equivalent processes in the same physical memory.

The process data segment is another good example of a requirement for larger virtual memory than for physical memory. The process data segment is mapped `MAP_PRIVATE`, which means that we need to reserve virtual swap for the whole segment, but we allocate physical memory only for the few pages that we write to within the segment. The amount of virtual swap required is far greater than the physical memory allocated to it, so if we needed to swap pages out to the swap device, we would need only a small amount of physical swap space.

If we had the ideal process that had all of its virtual memory backed by physical memory, then we could run with no physical swap space. Usually, we need something like 0.5 to 1.5 times memory size for physical swap space. It varies, of course, depending on the virtual-to-physical memory ratio of the application. Another consideration is system size. A large multiprocessor Sun Server with 512GB of physical memory is unlikely to require 1TB of swap space. For very large systems with a large amount of physical memory, configured swap can potentially be less than total physical memory. Again, the actual amount of virtual memory required to meet performance goals will be workload dependent.

## 6.18.2 Swap Statistics

The amount of anonymous memory in the system is recorded by the `anon` accounting structures. The `anon` layer keeps track in  the `kanon_info` structure of how anonymous pages are allocated. The `kanon_info` structure, shown below, is defined in the include file `vm/anon.h`.

```
struct k_anoninfo {
        pgcnt_t ani_max;          /* total reservable slots on phys disk swap */
        pgcnt_t ani_free;         /* # of unallocated phys and mem slots */
        pgcnt_t ani_phys_resv;    /* # of reserved phys (disk) slots */
        pgcnt_t ani_mem_resv;     /* # of reserved mem slots */
        pgcnt_t ani_locked_swap;  /* # of swap slots locked in reserved */
                                  /* mem swap */
};
```
                                                                                    *See sys/anon.h*

The `k_anoninfo` structure keeps count of the number of slots reserved on physical swap space and against memory. This information populates the data used for the `swapctl` system call. The `swapctl()` system call provides the data for the `swap` command and uses a slightly different data structure, the `anoninfo` structure, shown below.

```
struct anoninfo {
        pgcnt_t ani_max;
        pgcnt_t ani_free;
        pgcnt_t ani_resv;
};
```
                                                                                    *See sys/anon.h*

The `anoninfo` structure exports the swap allocation information in a platform-independent manner.

## 6.18.3 Swap Summary: `swap -s`

The `swap -s` command output, shown below, summarizes information from the `anoninfo` structure.

```
$ swap -s
total: 108504k bytes allocated + 13688k reserved = 122192k used, 114880k available
```

The output of `swap -s` can be somewhat misleading because it confuses the terms used for swap definition. The output is really telling us that 122,192 Kbytes of virtual swap space have been reserved, 108,504 Kbytes of swap space are allocated to pages that have been touched, and 114,880 Kbytes are free. This information reflects the stages of swap allocation, shown in Figure 6.5. Remember, we reserve swap as we create virtual memory, and then part of that swap is allocated when real pages are assigned to the address space. The balance of swap space remains unused.

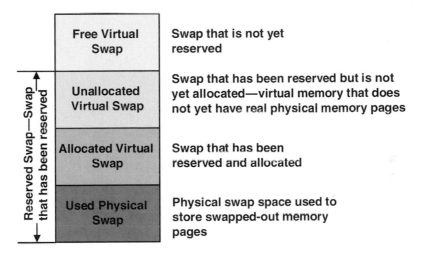

**Figure 6.5** Swap Allocation States

### 6.18.4 Listing Physical Swap Devices: `swap -1`

The `swap -1` command lists the physical swap devices and their levels of physical allocation.

```
$ swap -1
swapfile            dev  swaplo blocks    free
/dev/dsk/c0t0d0s0   136,0     16 1049312 782752
```

The `blocks` and `free` are in units of disk blocks, or sectors (512 bytes). This example shows that some of our physical swap slice has been used.

### 6.18.5 Determining Swapped-Out Threads

The pageout scanner will send clusters of pages to the swap device. However, if it can't keep up with demand, the swapper swaps out entire threads. The number of threads swapped out is either the `kthr:w` column from `vmstat` or `swpq-sz` from `sar -q`.

The following example is the same system from the previous `swap -l` example but it has experienced a dire memory shortage in the past and has swapped out entire threads.

```
$ vmstat 1 2
 kthr       memory            page             disk          faults      cpu
 r b w   swap  free  re  mf pi po fr de sr dd dd f0 s3   in   sy   cs us sy id
 0 0 13 423816 68144  3  16  5  0  0  0  1  0  0  0  0   67   36  136  1  0 98
 0 0 67 375320 43040  0   6  0  0  0  0  0  0  0  0  0  406  354  137  1  0 99

$ sar -q 1

SunOS mars 5.9 Generic_118558-05 sun4u     03/12/2006

05:05:36 runq-sz %runocc swpq-sz %swpocc
05:05:37    0.0       0    67.0      99
```

Our system currently has 67 threads swapped out to the physical swap device. The `sar` command has also provided a `%swpocc` column, which reports the percent swap occupancy. This is the percentage of time that threads existed on the swap device (99% is a rounding error) and is more useful for much longer `sar` intervals.

## 6.18.6 Monitoring Physical Swap Activity

To determine if the physical swap devices are currently busy with I/O transactions, we can use the `iostat` command in the regular manner. We just need to remember that we are looking at the swap slice, not a file system slice.

```
$ iostat -xnPz 1
...
                    extended device statistics
    r/s    w/s    kr/s    kw/s wait actv wsvc_t asvc_t  %w  %b device
    0.0   27.0    0.0  3452.3  2.1  0.7   78.0   24.9  32  34 c0t0d0s1
                    extended device statistics
    r/s    w/s    kr/s    kw/s wait actv wsvc_t asvc_t  %w  %b device
    1.0    0.0    8.0     0.0  0.0  0.0   39.6   36.3   4   4 c0t0d0s0
    0.0   75.1    0.0  9609.3  8.0  1.9  107.1   24.7  88  95 c0t0d0s1
                    extended device statistics
    r/s    w/s    kr/s    kw/s wait actv wsvc_t asvc_t  %w  %b device
    0.0   61.0    0.0  7686.7  5.4  1.4   88.3   23.6  65  73 c0t0d0s1
...
```

Physical memory was quickly exhausted on this system, causing a large number of pages to be written to the physical swap device, `c0t0d0s1`.

Swap activity due to the swapping out of entire threads can be viewed with sar -w. The vmstat -S command prints similar swapping statistics.

### 6.18.7 MemTool `prtswap`

In the following example, we use the prtswap script in MemTool to list the states of swap to find out where the swap is allocated from. We then use the prtswap command without the -l option for just a summary of the swap allocations.

```
# prtswap -l
Swap Reservations:
--------------------------------------------------------------------------
Total Virtual Swap Configured:                          767MB =
RAM Swap Configured:                                        255MB
Physical Swap Configured:                           +       512MB

Total Virtual Swap Reserved Against:                    513MB =
RAM Swap Reserved Against:                                    1MB
Physical Swap Reserved Against:                     +       512MB

Total Virtual Swap Unresv. & Avail. for Reservation:    253MB -
Physical Swap Unresv. & Avail. for Reservations:             0MB
RAM Swap Unresv. & Avail. for Reservations:         +      253MB


Swap Allocations: (Reserved and Phys pages allocated)
--------------------------------------------------------------------------
Total Virtual Swap Configured:                          767MB
Total Virtual Swap Allocated Against:                   467MB

Physical Swap Utilization: (pages swapped out)
--------------------------------------------------------------------------
Physical Swap Free (should not be zero!):               232MB =
Physical Swap Configured:                                   512MB
Physical Swap Used (pages swapped out):             -       279MB
                                                              See MemTool
```

```
# prtswap

Virtual Swap:
-------------------------------------------------------------
Total Virtual Swap Configured:                          767MB
Total Virtual Swap Reserved:                            513MB
Total Virtual Swap Free: (programs will fail if 0)      253MB


Physical Swap Utilization: (pages swapped out)
-------------------------------------------------------------
Physical Swap Configured:                               512MB
Physical Swap Free (programs will be locked in if 0):   232MB
                                                              See MemTool
```

The prtswap script uses the anonymous accounting structure members to establish how swap space is allocated and uses the availrmem counter, the swapfsminfree reserve, and the swap -l command to find out how much swap is used. Table 6.7 shows the anonymous accounting variables stored in the kernel.

**Table 6.7**  Swap Accounting Information

| Field | Description |
|---|---|
| k_anoninfo.ani_max | The total number of reservable slots on physical (disk-backed) swap. |
| k_anoninfo.ani_phys_resv | The number of physical (disk-backed) reserved slots. |
| k_anoninfo.ani_mem_resv | The number of memory reserved slots. |
| k_anoninfo.ani_free | Total number of unallocated physical slots + the number of reserved but unallocated memory slots. |
| availrmem | The amount of unreserved memory. |
| swapfsminfree | The swapfs reserve that won't be used for memory reservations. |

## 6.18.8  Display of Swap Reservations with pmap

The -S option of pmap describes the swap reservations for a process. The amount of swap space reserved is displayed for each mapping within the process. Swap reservations are reported as zero for shared mappings since they are accounted for only once systemwide.

```
sol9$ pmap -S 15492
15492:  ./maps
 Address   Kbytes     Swap Mode   Mapped File
00010000        8        - r-x--  maps
00020000        8        8 rwx--  maps
00022000    20344    20344 rwx--  [ heap ]
03000000     1024        - rw-s-  dev:0,2 ino:4628487
04000000     1024     1024 rw---  dev:0,2 ino:4628487
05000000     1024      512 rw--R  dev:0,2 ino:4628487
06000000     1024     1024 rw---  [ anon ]
07000000      512      512 rw--R  [ anon ]
08000000     8192        - rwxs-  [ dism shmid=0x5]
09000000     8192        - rwxs-  [ dism shmid=0x4]
0A000000     8192        - rwxs-  [ dism shmid=0x2]
0B000000     8192        - rwxsR  [ ism shmid=0x3]
FF280000      680        - r-x--  libc.so.1
FF33A000       32       32 rwx--  libc.so.1
FF390000        8        - r-x--  libc_psr.so.1
FF3A0000        8        - r-x--  libdl.so.1
FF3B0000        8        8 rwx--  [ anon ]
FF3C0000      152        - r-x--  ld.so.1
FF3F6000        8        8 rwx--  ld.so.1
FFBFA000       24       24 rwx--  [ stack ]
-------- ------- -------
total Kb    50464    23496
```

You can use the swap reservation information to estimate the amount of virtual swap used by each additional process. Each process consumes virtual swap from a global virtual swap pool. Global swap reservations are reported by the `avail` field of the `swap(1M)` command.

It is important to stress that while you should consider virtual reservations, you must not confuse them with physical allocations (which is easy to do since many commands just describe them as "swap"). For example:

```
# pmap -S 236
236:    /usr/lib/nfs/nfsmapid
 Address   Kbytes     Swap Mode    Mapped File
00010000       24        - r-x--   nfsmapid
00026000        8        8 rwx--   nfsmapid
00028000     7768     7768 rwx--    [ heap ]
...
FF3EE000        8        8 rwx--   ld.so.1
FFBFE000        8        8 rw---    [ stack ]
-------- ------- -------
total Kb    10344     8272
```

Process ID 236 (`nfsmapid`) has a total Swap reservation of 8 Mbytes. Now we list the state of our physical swap devices on this system:

```
$ swap -l
swapfile             dev  swaplo blocks     free
/dev/dsk/c0t0d0s1    136,9     16 2097632 2097632
```

No physical swap has been used.

7

# 7

# Networks

In this chapter, we review the tools available to monitor networking within and between Solaris systems. We examine tools for systemwide network statistics and per-process statistics.

## 7.1 Terms for Network Analysis

The following list of terms related to network analysis also serves as an overview of the topics in this section.

- **Packets.** Network interface packet counts can be fetched from `netstat -i` and roughly indicate network activity.

- **Bytes.** Measuring throughput in terms of bytes is useful because interface maximum throughput is measured in comparable terms, bits/sec. Byte statistics for interfaces are provided by Kstat, SNMP, `nx.se`, and `nicstat`.

- **Utilization.** Heavy network use can degrade application response. The `nicstat` tool calculates utilization by dividing current throughput by a known maximum.

- **Saturation.** Once an interface is saturated, network applications usually experience delays. Saturation can occur elsewhere on the network.

- **Errors.** `netstat -i` is useful for printing error counts: collisions (small numbers are normal), input errors (bad FCS), and output errors (late collisions).

73

- **Link status.** `link_status` plus `link_speed` and `link_mode` are three values to describe the state of the interface; they are provided by `kstat` or `ndd`.

- **Tests.** There is great value in test driving the network to see what speed it can really manage. Tools such as TTCP can be used.

- **By-process.** Network I/O by process can be analyzed with DTrace. Scripts such as `tcptop` and `tcpsnoop` perform this analysis.

- **TCP.** Various TCP statistics are kept for MIB-II,[1] plus additional statistics. These statistics are useful for troubleshooting and are obtained with `kstat` or `netstat -s`.

- **IP.** Various IP statistics are kept for MIB-II, plus additional statistics. They are obtained with `kstat` or `netstat -s`.

- **ICMP.** Tests, such as the `ping` and `traceroute` commands, that make use of ICMP can inform about the network surroundings. Various ICMP statistics, obtained with `kstat` or `netstat -s`, are also kept.

Table 7.1 summarizes and cross-references the tools discussed in this section.

**Table 7.1** Tools for Network Analysis

| Tool | Uses | Description | Ref. |
|------|------|-------------|------|
| `netstat` | Kstat | Kitchen sink of network statistics. Route table, established connections, interface packet counts, and errors | 7.7.1 |
| `kstat` | Kstat | For fetching raw kstat counters for each network interface and the TCP, IP, and ICMP modules | 7.7.2, 7.9.2, 7.10.2, 7.11.1 |
| `nx.se` | Kstat | For printing network interface and TCP throughput in terms of kilobytes | 7.7.3 |
| `nicstat` | Kstat | For printing network interface utilization | 7.7.4 |
| `snmpnetstat` | SNMP | For network interface statistics from SNMP | 7.7.5 |
| `checkcable` | Kstat, ndd | For network interface status: link speed, link mode, link up availability | 7.7.6 |

*continues*

---

1. Management Information Base, a collection of documented statistics that SNMP uses

**Table 7.1**  Tools for Network Analysis  (*continued*)

| Tool | Uses | Description | Ref. |
|------|------|-------------|------|
| ping | ICMP | To test whether remote hosts are "alive" | 7.7.7 |
| traceroute | UDP, ICMP | To print the path to a remote host, including delays to each hop | 7.7.8 |
| snoop | /dev | To capture network packets | 7.7.9 |
| TTCP | TCP | For applying a network traffic workload | 7.7.10 |
| pathchar | UDP, ICMP | For analysis of the path to a remote host, including speed between hops | 7.7.11 |
| ntop | libpcap | For reporting on sniffed traffic | 7.7.12 |
| nfsstat | Kstat | For viewing NFS client and server statistics | 7.7.13, 7.7.14 |
| tcptop | DTrace | For printing a by-process summary of network usages | 7.8.1 |
| tcpsnoop | DTrace | For tracing network packets by-process | 7.8.2 |
| dtrace | DTrace | For capturing TCP, IP, and ICMP statistics programmatically | 7.9.4, 7.10.4, 7.11.3 |

## 7.2  Packets Are Not Bytes

The official tool in Solaris for monitoring network traffic is the netstat command.

```
$ netstat -i 1
     input    hme0     output              input  (Total)    output
 packets errs  packets errs  colls  packets errs  packets errs   colls
 141461153 29    152961282 0      0          234608752 29    246108881 0       0
 295     0     2192    0     0      299     0     2196    0     0
 296     0     2253    0     0      300     0     2257    0     0
 295     0     2258    0     0      299     0     2262    0     0
 179     0     1305    0     0      183     0     1309    0     0
 ...
```

In the above output, we can see that the hme0 interface had very few errors (which is useful to know) and was sending over 2,000 packets per second. Is 2,000 a lot? We don't know whether this means the interface is at 100% utilization or 1% utilization; all it tells us is that traffic is occurring.

Measuring traffic by using packet counts is like measuring rainfall by listening for rain. Network cards are rated in terms of throughput, 100 Mbits/sec, 1000 Mbits/sec, etc. Measuring the current network traffic in similar terms (by using bytes) helps us understand how utilized the interface really is.

Bytes per second are indeed tracked by Kstat, and `netstat` is a Kstat consumer. However, `netstat` doesn't surrender this information without a fight.[2] These days we are supposed to use `kstat` to get it.

```
$ kstat -p 'hme:0:hme0:*bytes64'
hme:0:hme0:obytes64      51899673435
hme:0:hme0:rbytes64      47536009231
```

This output shows that byte statistics for network interfaces are indeed in Kstat, which will let us calculate a percent utilization. Later, we cover tools that help us do that. For now we discuss why network utilization, saturation, and errors are useful metrics to observe.

## 7.3 Network Utilization

The following points help describe the effects of network utilization.

- Network events, like disk events, are slow. They are often measured in milliseconds. A client application that is heavily network bound will experience delays. Network server applications often obviate these delays by being multithreaded or multiprocess.

- A network card that is at 100% utilization will most likely degrade application performance. However there are times where we expect 100% utilization, such as in bulk network transfers.

- Dividing the current Kbytes/sec by the speed of the network card can provide a useful measure of network utilization.

- Using only Kbytes/sec in a utilization calculation fails to account for per-packet overheads.

- Unexpectedly high utilizations may be caused when auto-negotiation has failed by choosing a much slower speed.

---

2. The secret `-k` option that dumped all kstats has been dropped in Solaris 10 anyway.

## 7.4 Network Saturation

A network card that is sent more traffic than it can send in an interval queues data in various buffers, including the TCP buffer. This causes application delays as the network card clears the backlog.

An important point is that while your system may not be saturated, something else on the network may be. Often your network traffic will pass through several hops, any of which may be experiencing problems.

## 7.5 Network Errors

Errors can occur from network collisions and as such are a normal occurrence. With hubs they occurred so often that various rules were formulated to help us know what really was a problem (> 5% of packet counts).

Three types of errors are visible in the previous `netstat -i` output, examples are:

- **output:colls.** Collisions. Normal in small doses.
- **input:errs.** A frame failed its frame check sequence.
- **output:errs.** Late collisions. A collision occurred after the first 64 bytes were sent.

The last two types of errors can be caused by bad wiring, faulty cards, auto-negotiation problems, and electromagnetic interference. If you are monitoring a microwave link, add "rain fade" and nesting pigeons to the list. And if your Solaris server happens to be on a satellite, you get to mention Solar winds as well.

## 7.6 Misconfigurations

Sometimes poor network performance is due to misconfigured components. This can be difficult to identify because there no error statistic indicates a fault; the misconfiguration might be found only after meticulous scrutiny of all network settings.

Places to check: *all* interface settings (`ifconfig -a`), route tables (`netstat -rn`), interface flags (`link_speed/link_mode`, discussed in Section 7.7.6), name server configurations (`/etc/nsswitch.conf`), DNS resolvers (`/etc/resolv.conf`), `/var/adm/messages`, FMA faults (`fmadm faulty`, `fmdump`), firewall configurations, and configurable network components (switches, routers, gateways).

## 7.7 Systemwide Statistics

The following tools allow us to observe network statistics, including statistics for TCP, IP, and each network interface, throughout the system.

### 7.7.1 `netstat` Command

The Solaris `netstat` command is the catch-all for a number of different network status programs.

```
$ netstat -i
Name  Mtu  Net/Dest      Address      Ipkts     Ierrs Opkts    Oerrs Collis Queue
lo0   8232 localhost     localhost    191       0     191      0     0      0
ipge0 1500 waterbuffalo  waterbuffalo 31152163  0     24721687 0     0      0

$ netstat -i 3
   input    ipge0     output         input  (Total)     output
packets errs  packets errs  colls  packets errs  packets errs  colls
31152218 0    24721731 0    0      31152409 0    24721922 0    0

$ netstat -I ipge0 -i 3
   input    ipge0     output         input  (Total)     output
packets errs  packets errs  colls  packets errs  packets errs  colls
31152284 0    24721797 0    0      31152475 0    24721988 0    0
```

`netstat -i`, mentioned earlier, prints only packet counts. We don't know if they are big packets or small packets, and we cannot use them to accurately determine how utilized the network interface is. Other performance monitoring tools plot this as a "be all and end all" value—this is wrong.

Packet counts may help as an indicator of activity. A packet count of less than 100 per second can be treated as fairly idle; a worst case for Ethernet makes this around 150 Kbytes/sec (based on maximum MTU size).

The `netstat -i` output may be much more valuable for its error counts, as discussed in Section 7.5.

`netstat -s` dumps various network-related counters from kstat. This shows that Kstat does track at least some details in terms of bytes.

```
$ netstat -s | grep Bytes
        tcpOutDataSegs    =37367847   tcpOutDataBytes   =166744792
        tcpRetransSegs    =153437     tcpRetransBytes   =72298114
        tcpInAckSegs      =25548715   tcpInAckBytes     =148658291
        tcpInInorderSegs  =35290928   tcpInInorderBytes =3637819567
        tcpInUnorderSegs  =324309     tcpInUnorderBytes =406912945
        tcpInDupSegs      =152795     tcpInDupBytes     =73998299
        tcpInPartDupSegs  =  7896     tcpInPartDupBytes =5821485
        tcpInPastWinSegs  =    38     tcpInPastWinBytes =971347352
```

However, the byte values above are for TCP in total, including loopback traffic that didn't travel through the network interfaces. These statistics can still be of some value, especially if large numbers of errors are observed. For more details on these and a reference table, see Section 7.9.

netstat -k on Solaris 9 and earlier dumped all kstat counters.

```
$ netstat -k | awk '/^hme0/,/^$/'
hme0:
ipackets 70847004 ierrors 6 opackets 73438793 oerrors 0 collisions 0
defer 0 framing 0 crc 0 sqe 0 code_violations 0 len_errors 0
ifspeed 100000000 buff 0 oflo 0 uflo 0 missed 6 tx_late_collisions 0
retry_error 0 first_collisions 0 nocarrier 0 nocanput 0
allocbfail 0 runt 0 jabber 0 babble 0 tmd_error 0 tx_late_error 0
rx_late_error 0 slv_parity_error 0 tx_parity_error 0 rx_parity_error 0
slv_error_ack 0 tx_error_ack 0 rx_error_ack 0 tx_tag_error 0
rx_tag_error 0 eop_error 0 no_tmds 0 no_tbufs 0 no_rbufs 0
rx_late_collisions 0 rbytes 289601566 obytes 358304357 multircv 558 multixmt 73411
brdcstrcv 3813836 brdcstxmt 1173700 norcvbuf 0 noxmtbuf 0    newfree 0
ipackets64 70847004 opackets64 73438793 rbytes64 47534241822 obytes64 51897911909
align_errors 0
fcs_errors 0   sqe_errors 0 defer_xmts 0 ex_collisions 0
macxmt_errors 0 carrier_errors 0 toolong_errors 0 macrcv_errors 0
link_duplex 0 inits 31 rxinits 0 txinits 0 dmarh_inits 0
dmaxh_inits 0 link_down_cnt 0 phy_failures 0 xcvr_vendor 524311
asic_rev 193 link_up 1
```

From the output we can see that there are byte counters (rbytes64, obytes64) for the hme0 interface, which is just what we need to measure per-interface traffic. However netstat -k was an undocumented switch that has now been dropped in Solaris 10. This is fine since there are better ways to get to kstat, including the C library, which is used by tools such as vmstat.

## 7.7.2 kstat Command

The Solaris Kernel Statistics framework tracks network usage, and as of Solaris 8, the kstat command fetches these details (see Chapter 11). This command has a variety of options for selecting statistics and can be executed by non-root users.

The -m option for kstat matches on a module name. In the following example, we use it to display all available statistics for the networking modules.

```
$ kstat -m tcp
module: tcp                      instance: 0
name:   tcp                      class:     mib2
        activeOpens              803
        attemptFails             312
        connTableSize            56
...
```

continues

```
$ kstat -m ip
module: ip                                    instance: 0
name:   icmp                                  class:    mib2
        crtime                                3.207830752
        inAddrMaskReps                        0
        inAddrMasks                           0
...

$ kstat -m hme
module: hme                                   instance: 0
name:   hme0                                  class:    net
name:   hme0                                  class:    net

        align_errors                          0
        allocbfail                            0
...
```

These commands fetch statistics for ip, tcp, and hme (our Ethernet card). The first group of statistics (others were truncated) from the tcp and ip modules states their class as mib2: These statistic groups are maintained by the TCP and IP code for MIB-II and then copied into kstat during a kstat update.

The following kstat command fetches byte statistics for our network interface, printing output every second.

```
$ kstat -p 'hme:0:hme0:*bytes64' 1
hme:0:hme0:obytes64      51899673435
hme:0:hme0:rbytes64      47536009231

hme:0:hme0:obytes64      51899673847
hme:0:hme0:rbytes64      47536009709
...
```

Using kstat in this manner is currently the best way to fetch network interface statistics with tools currently shipped with Solaris. Other tools exist that take the final step and print this data in a more meaningful way: Kbytes/sec or percent utilization. Two such tools are nx.se and nicstat.

### 7.7.3 nx.se Tool

The SE Toolkit provides a language, SymbEL, that lets us write our own performance monitoring tools. It also contained a collection of example tools, including nx.se which helps us calculate network utilization.

```
$ se nx.se 1
Current tcp RtoMin is 400, interval 1, start Sun Oct  9 10:36:42 2005

10:36:43 Iseg/s Oseg/s InKB/s OuKB/s Rst/s  Atf/s  Ret%  Icn/s  Ocn/s
tcp       841.6    4.0  74.98   0.27  0.00   0.00   0.0   0.00   0.00
Name     Ipkt/s Opkt/s InKB/s OuKB/s IErr/s OErr/s Coll% NoCP/s Defr/s
hme0      845.5  420.8 119.91  22.56  0.000  0.000  0.0   0.00   0.00

10:36:44 Iseg/s Oseg/s InKB/s OuKB/s Rst/s  Atf/s  Ret%  Icn/s  Ocn/s
tcp       584.2    5.0  77.97   0.60  0.00   0.00   0.0   0.00   0.00
Name     Ipkt/s Opkt/s InKB/s OuKB/s IErr/s OErr/s Coll% NoCP/s Defr/s
hme0      579.2  297.1 107.95  16.16  0.000  0.000  0.0   0.00   0.00
```

Having KB/s lets us determine how busy our network interfaces are. Other useful fields include collision percent (Coll%), no-can-puts per second (NoCP/s), and defers per second (Defr/s), which may be evidence of network saturation. nx.se also prints useful TCP statistics above the interface lines.

## 7.7.4 nicstat Tool

nicstat, a tool from the freeware K9Toolkit, reports network utilization and saturation by interface. It is available as a C or Perl kstat consumer.

```
$ nicstat 1
    Time    Int    rKb/s    wKb/s     rPk/s     wPk/s      rAvs     wAvs    %Util    Sat
10:48:30   hme0     4.02     4.39      6.14      6.36    670.73   706.50     0.07   0.00
10:48:31   hme0     0.29     0.50      3.00      4.00     98.00   127.00     0.01   0.00
10:48:32   hme0     1.35     4.23     14.00     15.00     98.70   399.00     0.05   0.00
10:48:33   hme0    67.73    19.08    426.00    207.00    162.81    94.39     0.71   0.00
10:48:34   hme0   315.22   128.91   1249.00    723.00    258.44   182.58     3.64   0.00
10:48:35   hme0   529.96    67.53   2045.00   1046.00    265.37    66.11     4.89   0.00
10:48:36   hme0   454.14    62.16   2294.00   1163.00    202.72    54.73     4.23   0.00
10:48:37   hme0    93.55    15.78    583.00    295.00    164.31    54.77     0.90   0.00
10:48:38   hme0    74.84    32.41    516.00    298.00    148.52   111.38     0.88   0.00
10:48:39   hme0     0.76     4.17      7.00      9.00    111.43   474.00     0.04   0.00
                                            See K9Toolkit; nicstat.c or nicstat.pl
```

In this example output of nicstat, we can see a small amount of network traffic, peaking at 4.89% utilization.

The following are the switches available from version 0.98 of the Perl version of nicestat.

```
$ nicstat -h
USAGE: nicstat [-hsz] [-i int[,int...]] | [interval [count]]
   eg, nicstat              # print a 1 second sample
       nicstat 1            # print continually every 1 second
       nicstat 1 5          # print 5 times, every 1 second
       nicstat -s           # summary output
       nicstat -i hme0      # print hme0 only
```

The utilization measurement is based on the current throughput divided by the maximum speed of the interface (if available through kstat). The saturation measurement is a value that reflects errors due to saturation if kstat found any.

This method for calculating utilization does not account for other per-packet costs, such as Ethernet preamble. These costs are generally minor, and we assume they do not greatly affect the utilization value.

## 7.7.5 SNMP

It's worth mentioning that useful data is also available in SNMP, which is used by software such as MRTG (a popular freeware network utilization plotter). A full install of Solaris 10 provides Net-SNMP, putting many of the commands under /usr/sfw/bin.

Here we demonstrate the use of snmpget to fetch interface statistics.

```
$ snmpget -v1 -c public localhost ifOutOctets.2 ifInOctets.2
IF-MIB::ifOutOctets.2 = Counter32: 10016768
IF-MIB::ifInOctets.2 = Counter32: 11932165
```

The .2 corresponds to our primary interface. These values are the outbound and inbound bytes. In Solaris 10 a full description of the IF-MIB statistics can be found in /etc/sma/snmp/mibs/IF-MIB.txt.

Other software products fetch and present data from the IF-MIB, which is a valid and desirable approach for monitoring network interface activity. Solaris 10's Net-SNMP supports SNMPv3, which provides User-based Security Module (USM) for the creation of user accounts and encrypted sessions; and View-based Access Control Module (VACM) to restrict users to view only the statistics they need. When configured, they greatly enhance the security of SNMP. For information on each, see snmpusm(1M) and snmpvacm(1M).

Net-SNMP also provides a version of netstat called snmpnetstat. Besides the standard output using -i, snmpnetstat has a -o option to print octets (bytes) instead of packets.

```
$ snmpnetstat -v1 -c public -i localhost
Name       Mtu Network    Address          Ipkts Ierrs  Opkts Oerrs Queue
lo0       8232 loopback   localhost         6639     0   6639     0     0
hme0      1500 192.168.1  titan           385635     0  86686     0     0
hme0:1    1500 192.168.1  192.168.1.204        0     0      0     0     0
$
$ snmpnetstat -v1 -c public -o localhost
Name       Network    Address        Ioctets   Ooctets
lo0        loopback   localhost            0         0
hme0       192.168.1  titan         98241462  55500788
hme0:1     192.168.1  192.168.1.204        0         0
```

Input bytes (Ioctets) and output bytes (Ooctets) can be seen. Now all we need is an interval for this information to be of real value.

```
# snmpnetstat -v1 -c public -I hme0 -o localhost 10
    input    (hme0)     output                         input    (Total)     output
   packets     errs    packets     errs    colls      packets     errs    packets     errs     colls
    386946       0      88300        0        0        395919       0      97273        0        0
       452       0        797        0        0           538       0        883        0        0
         0       0          0        0        0             0       0          0        0        0
         0       0          0        0        0             0       0          0        0        0
       844       0       1588        0        0           952       0       1696        0        0
         0       0          0        0        0             0       0          0        0        0
         0       0          0        0        0             0       0          0        0        0
       548       0        965        0        0           656       0       1073        0        0
         0       0          0        0        0             0       0          0        0        0
         0       0          0        0        0             0       0          0        0        0
^C
```

Even though we provided the -o option, by also providing an interval (10 seconds), we caused the snmpnetstat command to revert to printing packet counts. Also, the statistics that SNMP uses are only updated every 30 seconds. Future versions of snmpnetstat may correctly print octets with intervals.

### 7.7.6 checkcable Tool

Sometimes network performance problems can be caused by incorrect auto-negotiation that selects a lower speed or duplex. There is a way to retrieve the settings that a particular network card has chosen, but there is not one way that works for all cards. It usually involves poking around with the ndd command and using a lookup table for your particular card to decipher the output of ndd.

Consistent data for network cards should be available from Kstat, and Sun does have a standard in place. However many of the network drivers were written before the standard existed, and some were written by third-party companies. The state of consistent Kstat data for network cards is improving and at some point in the future should boil down to a few well understood one-liners of the kstat command, such as: kstat -p | grep <interfacename>.

In the meantime, it is not always that easy. Some data is available from kstat, much of it from ndd. The following example demonstrates fetching ndd data for an hme card.

```
# ndd /dev/hme link_status
1
# ndd /dev/hme link_speed
1
# ndd /dev/hme link_mode
1
```

These numbers indicate a connected or unconnected cable (link_status), the current speed (link_speed), and the duplex (link_mode). What 1 or some other number means depends on the card. A list of available ndd variables for this card can be listed with ndd -get /dev/hme \? (the -get is optional).

SunSolve has Infodocs to explain what these numbers mean for various cards. If you have mainly one type of card at your site, you eventually remember what the numbers mean. As a very general rule, "1" is often good, "0" is often bad; so "0" for link_mode probably means half duplex.

The checkcable tool, available from the K9Toolkit, deciphers many card types for you.[3] It uses both kstat and ndd to retrieve the network settings because not all the data is available to either kstat or ndd.

```
# checkcable
Interface   Link Duplex  Speed  AutoNEG
hme0          UP   FULL    100       ON

# checkcable
Interface   Link Duplex  Speed  AutoNEG
hme0        DOWN   FULL    100       ON
```

The first output has the hme0 interface as link-connected (UP), full duplex, 100 Mbits/sec, and auto-negotiation on; the second output was with the cable disconnected. The speed and duplex must be set to what the switch thinks they are set to so that the network link functions correctly.

There are still some cards that checkcable is unable to view. The state of card statistics is slowly getting better; eventually, checkcable will not be needed to translate these numbers.

---

3. checkcable is Perl, which can be read to see supported cards and contribution history.

### 7.7.7 `ping` Tool

`ping` is the classic network probe tool; it uses ICMP messages to test the response time of round-trip packets.

```
$ ping -s mars
PING mars: 56 data bytes
64 bytes from mars (192.168.1.1): icmp_seq=0. time=0.623 ms
64 bytes from mars (192.168.1.1): icmp_seq=1. time=0.415 ms
64 bytes from mars (192.168.1.1): icmp_seq=2. time=0.464 ms
^C
----mars PING Statistics----
3 packets transmitted, 3 packets received, 0% packet loss
round-trip (ms)  min/avg/max/stddev = 0.415/0.501/0.623/0.11
```

So we discover that mars is up and that it responds within 1 millisecond. Solaris 10 enhanced `ping` to print three decimal places for the times. `ping` is handy to see if a host is up, but that's about all.

### 7.7.8 `traceroute` Tool

`traceroute` sends a series of UDP packets with an increasing TTL, and by watching the ICMP time-expired replies, we can discover the hops to a host (assuming the hops actually decrement the TTL):

```
$ traceroute www.sun.com
traceroute: Warning: Multiple interfaces found; using 260.241.10.2 @ hme0:1
traceroute to www.sun.com (209.249.116.195), 30 hops max, 40 byte packets
 1  tpggate (260.241.10.1)  21.224 ms  25.933 ms  25.281 ms
 2  172.31.217.14 (172.31.217.14)  49.565 ms  27.736 ms  25.297 ms
 3  syd-nxg-ero-zeu-2-gi-3-0.tpgi.com.au (220.244.229.9)  25.454 ms  22.066 ms  26.237
ms
 4  syd-nxg-ibo-l3-ge-0-2.tpgi.com.au (220.244.229.132)  42.216 ms *  37.675 ms
 5  220-245-178-199.tpgi.com.au (220.245.178.199)  40.727 ms  38.291 ms  41.468 ms
 6  syd-nxg-ibo-ero-ge-1-0.tpgi.com.au (220.245.178.193)  37.437 ms  38.223 ms  38.373
ms
 7  Gill-2.gw2.syd1.asianetcom.net (202.147.41.193)  24.953 ms  25.191 ms  26.242 ms
 8  po2-1.gw1.nrt4.asianetcom.net (202.147.55.110)  155.811 ms  169.330 ms  153.217 ms
 9  Abovenet.POS2-2.gw1.nrt4.asianetcom.net (203.192.129.42)  150.477 ms  157.173 ms *
10  so-6-0-0.mpr3.sjc2.us.above.net (64.125.27.54)  240.077 ms  239.733 ms  244.015 ms
11  so-0-0-0.mpr4.sjc2.us.above.net (64.125.30.2)  224.560 ms  228.681 ms  221.149 ms
12  64.125.27.102 (64.125.27.102)  241.229 ms  235.481 ms  238.868 ms
13  * *^C
```

The times may provide some idea of where a network bottleneck is. We must also remember that networks are dynamic and that this may not be the permanent path to that host (and could even change as `traceroute` executes).

### 7.7.9 `snoop` Tool

The power to capture and inspect network packets live from the interface is provided by `snoop`, an indispensable tool. When network events don't seem to be working, it can be of great value to verify that the packets are actually arriving in the first place.

`snoop` places a network device in "promiscuous mode" so that all network traffic, addressed to this host or not, is captured. You ought to have permission to be sniffing network traffic, as often `snoop` displays traffic contents—including user names and passwords.

```
# snoop
Using device /dev/hme (promiscuous mode)
      jupiter -> titan        TCP D=22 S=36570 Ack=1602213819 Seq=1929072366 Len=0
Win=49640
       titan -> jupiter     TCP D=36570 S=22 Push Ack=1929072366 Seq=1602213819 Len=128
Win=49640
      jupiter -> titan        TCP D=22 S=36570 Ack=1602213947 Seq=1929072366 Len=0
Win=49640
...
```

The most useful options include the following: don't resolve hostnames (`-r`), change the device (`-d`), output to a capture file (`-o`), input from a capture file (`-i`), print semi-verbose (`-V`, one line per protocol layer), print full-verbose (`-v`, all details), and send packets to `/dev/audio` (`-a`). Packet filter syntax can also be applied.

By using output files, you can try different options when reading them (`-v`, `-V`). Moreover, outputting to a file incurs less CPU overhead than the default live output.

### 7.7.10 TTCP

Test TCP is a freeware tool that tests the throughput between two hops. It needs to be run on both the source and destination, and a Java version of TTCP runs on many different operating systems. Beware, it floods the network with traffic to perform its test.

The following is run on one host as a receiver. The options used here made the test run for a reasonable duration—around 60 seconds.

```
$ java ttcp -r -n 65536
Receive: buflen= 8192  nbuf= 65536 port= 5001
Then the following was run on the second host as the transmitter,

$ java ttcp -t jupiter -n 65536
Transmit: buflen= 8192  nbuf= 65536 port= 5001
Transmit connection:
  Socket[addr=jupiter/192.168.1.5,port=5001,localport=46684].
Transmit: 536870912 bytes in 46010 milli-seconds = 11668.57 KB/sec (93348.56 Kbps).
```

This example shows that the speed between these hosts for this test is around 11.6 megabytes per second.

It is not uncommon for people to test the speed of their network by transferring a large file around. This may be better than it sounds; any test is better than none.

## 7.7.11 `pathchar` Tool

After writing `traceroute`, Van Jacobson wrote `pathchar`, an amazing tool that identifies network bottlenecks. It operates like `traceroute`, but rather than printing response time to each hop, it prints bandwidth between each pair of hops.

```
# pathchar 192.168.1.1
pathchar to 192.168.1.1 (192.168.1.1)
 doing 32 probes at each of 64 to 1500 by 32
 0 localhost
 |     30 Mb/s,    79 us (562 us)
 1 neptune.drinks.com (192.168.2.1)
 |     44 Mb/s,   195 us (1.23 ms)
 2 mars.drinks.com (192.168.1.1)
2 hops, rtt 547 us (1.23 ms), bottleneck  30 Mb/s, pipe 7555 bytes
```

This tool works by sending "shaped" traffic over a long interval and carefully measuring the response times. It doesn't flood the network like TTCP does.

Binaries for `pathchar` can be found on the Internet, but the source code has yet to be released. Some open source versions, based on the ideas from `pathchar`, are in development.

## 7.7.12 `ntop` Tool

`ntop` sniffs network traffic and issues comprehensive reports through a web interface. It is very useful, so long as you can (and are allowed to) snoop the traffic of interest. It is driven from a web browser aimed at localhost:3000.

```
# ntop
ntop v.1.3.1 MT [sparc-sun-solaris2.8] listening on [hme0,hme0:0,hme0:1].
Copyright 1998-2000 by Luca Deri <deri@ntop.org>
Get the freshest ntop from http://www.ntop.org/

Initialising...
Loading plugins (if any)...
WARNING: Unable to find the plugins/ directory.
Waiting for HTTP connections on port 3000...
Sniffying...
```

## 7.7.13 NFS Client Statistics: `nfsstat -c`

```
$ nfsstat -c

Client rpc:
Connection oriented:
calls       badcalls    badxids     timeouts   newcreds   badverfs   timers
202499      0           0           0          0          0          0
cantconn    nomem       interrupts
0           0           0
Connectionless:
calls       badcalls    retrans     badxids    timeouts   newcreds   badverfs
0           0           0           0          0          0          0
timers      nomem       cantsend
0           0           0


Client nfs:
calls       badcalls  clgets      cltoomany
200657      0         200657      7
Version 2: (0 calls)
null      getattr   setattr   root      lookup    readlink  read      wrcache
0 0%      0 0%      0 0%      0 0%      0 0%      0 0%      0 0%      0 0%
write     create    remove    rename    link      symlink   mkdir     rmdir
0 0%      0 0%      0 0%      0 0%      0 0%      0 0%      0 0%      0 0%
readdir   statfs
0 0%      0 0%
Version 3: (0 calls)
null        getattr     setattr     lookup      access      readlink
0 0%        0 0%        0 0%        0 0%        0 0%        0 0%
read        write       create      mkdir       symlink     mknod
0 0%        0 0%        0 0%        0 0%        0 0%        0 0%
remove      rmdir       rename      link        readdir     readdirplus
0 0%        0 0%        0 0%        0 0%        0 0%        0 0%
fsstat      fsinfo      pathconf    commit
0 0%        0 0%        0 0%        0 0%
```

Client statistics printed include retransmissions (`retrans`), unmatched replies (`badxids`), and `timeouts`. See `nfsstat(1M)` for verbose descriptions.

## 7.7.14 NFS Server Statistics: `nfsstat -s`

The server version of `nfsstat` prints a screenful of statistics to pick through. Of interest are the value of `badcalls` and the number of file operation statistics.

```
$ nfsstat -s

Server rpc:
Connection oriented:
calls       badcalls    nullrecv    badlen     xdrcall    dupchecks  dupreqs
5897288     0           0           0          0          372803     0
Connectionless:
calls       badcalls    nullrecv    badlen     xdrcall    dupchecks  dupreqs
87324       0           0           0          0          0          0

...
```

*continues*

```
Version 4: (949163 calls)
null                    compound
3175 0%                 945988 99%
Version 4: (3284515 operations)
reserved        access              close               commit
0 0%            72954 2%            199208 6%           2948 0%
create          delegpurge          delegreturn         getattr
4 0%            0 0%                16451 0%            734376 22%
getfh           link                lock                lockt
345041 10%      6 0%                101 0%              0 0%
locku           lookup              lookupp             nverify
101 0%          145651 4%           5715 0%             171515 5%
open            openattr            open_confirm        open_downgrade
199410 6%       0 0%                271 0%              0 0%
putfh           putpubfh            putrootfh           read
914825 27%      0 0%                581 0%              130451 3%
readdir         readlink            remove              rename
5661 0%         11905 0%            15 0%               201 0%
renew           restorefh           savefh              secinfo
30765 0%        140543 4%           146336 4%           277 0%
setattr         setclientid         setclientid_confirm verify
23 0%           26 0%               26 0%               10 0%
write           release_lockowner   illegal
9118 0%         0 0%                0 0%
...
```

## 7.8  Per-Process Network Statistics

In this section, we explore tools to monitor network usage by process. We build on
DTrace to provide these tools.

In previous versions of Solaris it was difficult to measure network I/O by process, just as it was difficult to measure disk I/O by process. Both of these problems
have been solved with DTrace—disk by process is now trivial with the io provider. However, at the time of this writing, a network provider has yet to be
released. So while network-by-process measurement is possible with DTrace, it is
not straightforward.[4]

### 7.8.1  `tcptop` Tool

`tcptop`, a DTrace-based tool from the freeware DTraceToolkit, summarizes TCP
traffic by system and by process.

---

4.  The DTraceToolkit's TCP tools are the only ones so far to measure tcp/pid events correctly.
The shortest of the tools is over 400 lines. If a net provider is released, that script might be only
12 lines.

```
# tcptop 10
Sampling... Please wait.
2005 Jul  5 04:55:25,  load: 1.11,  TCPin:      2 Kb,  TCPout:     110 Kb

 UID    PID LADDR            LPORT FADDR           FPORT     SIZE NAME
 100  20876 192.168.1.5      36396 192.168.1.1        79     1160 finger
 100  20875 192.168.1.5      36395 192.168.1.1        79     1160 finger
 100  20878 192.168.1.5      36397 192.168.1.1        23     1303 telnet
 100  20877 192.168.1.5        859 192.168.1.1       514   115712 rcp
                                                            See DTraceToolkit
```

The first line of the above report contains the date, CPU load average (one minute), and two TCP statistics, TCPin and TCPout. These are from the TCP (MIB); they track local host traffic as well as physical network traffic.

The rest of the report contains per-process data and includes fields for the PID, local address (LADDR), local port (LPORT), remote address (FADDR[5]), remote port (FPORT), number of bytes transferred during sample (SIZE), and process name (NAME). tcptop retrieves this data by tracing TCP events

This particular version of tcptop captures these per-process details for connections that were established while tcptop was running and could observe the handshake. Since TCPin and TCPout fields are for all traffic, a large discrepancy between them and the per-process details may suggest that we missed observing handshakes for busy sessions.[6]

It turns out to be quite difficult to kludge DTrace to trace network traffic by process such that it identifies all types of traffic correctly 100% of the time. Without a network provider, the events must be traced from fbt. The fbt provider is an unstable interface, meaning that probes may change for minor releases of Solaris.[7]

The greatest problem with using DTrace to trace network traffic by process is that both inbound and outbound traffic are asynchronous to the process, so we can't simply look at the on-CPU PID when the network event occurred. From userland, when the PID is correct, there is no one single way that TCP traffic is generated, such that we could simply trace it then and there. We have to contend with many other issues; for example, when tracing traffic to the telnet server, we would want to identify in.telnetd as the process responsible (principle of least surprise?). However, in.telnetd never steps onto the CPU after establishing the connection, and instead we find that telnet traffic is caused by a plethora of

---

5. We chose the name "FADDR" after looking too long at the connection structure (struct conn_s).
6. A newer version of tcptop is in development to examine all sessions regardless of connection time (and has probably been released by the time you are reading this). The new version has an additional command-line option to revert to the older behavior.
7. Not only can the fbt probes change, but they have done so; a recent change to the kernel has changed TCP slightly, meaning that many of the DTrace TCP scripts need updating.

unlikely suspects: ls, find, date, etc. With enough D code, though, we can solve these issues with DTrace.

### 7.8.2 tcpsnoop Tool

The tcpsnoop tool is the companion to tcptop. It is also from the DTraceToolkit and prints TCP packet details live by process.

```
# tcpsnoop
  UID    PID LADDR            LPORT DR RADDR            RPORT SIZE CMD
  100  20892 192.168.1.5      36398 -> 192.168.1.1         79   54 finger
  100  20892 192.168.1.5      36398 <- 192.168.1.1         79   66 finger
  100  20892 192.168.1.5      36398 -> 192.168.1.1         79   54 finger
  100  20892 192.168.1.5      36398 -> 192.168.1.1         79   56 finger
  100  20892 192.168.1.5      36398 <- 192.168.1.1         79   54 finger
  100  20892 192.168.1.5      36398 <- 192.168.1.1         79  606 finger
  100  20892 192.168.1.5      36398 -> 192.168.1.1         79   54 finger
  100  20892 192.168.1.5      36398 <- 192.168.1.1         79   54 finger
  100  20892 192.168.1.5      36398 -> 192.168.1.1         79   54 finger
  100  20892 192.168.1.5      36398 -> 192.168.1.1         79   54 finger
  100  20892 192.168.1.5      36398 <- 192.168.1.1         79   54 finger
    0    242 192.168.1.5         23 <- 192.168.1.1      54224   54 inetd
    0    242 192.168.1.5         23 -> 192.168.1.1      54224   54 inetd
    0    242 192.168.1.5         23 <- 192.168.1.1      54224   54 inetd
    0    242 192.168.1.5         23 <- 192.168.1.1      54224   78 inetd
    0    242 192.168.1.5         23 -> 192.168.1.1      54224   54 inetd
    0  20893 192.168.1.5         23 -> 192.168.1.1      54224   57 in.telnetd
    0  20893 192.168.1.5         23 <- 192.168.1.1      54224   54 in.telnetd
    0  20893 192.168.1.5         23 -> 192.168.1.1      54224   78 in.telnetd
...
```

In the above output we can see a PID column and packet details, the result of tracking TCP traffic that has travelled on external interfaces. While running, tcpsnoop captured the details of an outbound finger command and an inbound telnet.

As with tcptop, this version of tcpsnoop examines newly connected sessions (while tcpsnoop has been running). This behavior can be useful because when the tcpsnoop tool is run over an existing network session (like ssh), it doesn't trace its own output.

## 7.9 TCP Statistics

The TCP code maintains a large number of statistics for MIB-II, which is used by SNMP. These counters track details such as the number of established connections and the total number of segments sent, received, and retransmitted.

They could be used as an indicator of activity, although you must remember that these statistics usually include loopback traffic. You could also use them when you are troubleshooting networking issues: A large number of retransmissions may be a sign that a network fault is causing packet loss.

TCP statistics can be found in the following places:

- TCP MIB-II statistics, listed in /etc/sma/snmp/mibs/TCP-MIB.txt on Solaris 10 or in RFC 2012; available from both the SNMP daemon and Kstat.
- Solaris additions to TCP MIB-II, listed in /usr/include/inet/mib2.h and available from Kstat.
- Extra Kstat collections maintained by the module.

## 7.9.1 TCP Statistics Internals

To explain how the TCP MIB statistics are maintained, we show tcp.c code that updates two of these statistics.

```
static int
tcp_snmp_get(queue_t *q, mblk_t *mpctl)
{
...
                        tcp = connp->conn_tcp;
                        UPDATE_MIB(&tcp_mib, tcpInSegs, tcp->tcp_ibsegs);
                        tcp->tcp_ibsegs = 0;
                        UPDATE_MIB(&tcp_mib, tcpOutSegs, tcp->tcp_obsegs);
                        tcp->tcp_obsegs = 0;
...
                                                    See uts/common/inet/tcp/tcp.c
```

UPDATE_MIB increases the statistic by the argument specified. Here the tcpIn-Segs and tcpOutSegs statistics are updated. These are from standard TCP MIB-II statistics that the Solaris 10 SNMP daemon[8] makes available; they are defined on Solaris 10 in the TCP-MIB.txt[9] file.

The tcp.c code also maintains additional MIB statistics. For example,

```
void
tcp_rput_data(void *arg, mblk_t *mp, void *arg2)
{
...
                BUMP_MIB(&tcp_mib, tcpInDataInorderSegs);
                UPDATE_MIB(&tcp_mib, tcpInDataInorderBytes, seg_len);
...
                                                    See uts/common/inet/tcp/tcp.c
```

8. The SNMP daemon is based on Net-SNMP.
9. This file from RFC 2012 defines updated TCP statistics for SNMPv2. Also of interest is RFC 1213, the original MIB-II statistics, which include TCP.

BUMP_MIB incremented the tcpInDataInorderSegs statistic by 1, then tcpInDataInorderBytes was updated. These are not standard statistics that are RFC defined, and as such they are not currently made available by the SNMP daemon. They are some of many extra and useful statistics maintained by the Solaris code.

A list of these extra statistics is in mib2.h after the comment that reads /* In addition to MIB-II */.

```
typedef struct mib2_tcp {
...
/* In addition to MIB-II */
...
        /* total # of data segments received in order */
        Counter tcpInDataInorderSegs;
        /* total # of data bytes received in order */
        Counter tcpInDataInorderBytes;
...
                                            See /usr/include/inet/mib2.h
```

Table 7.2 lists all the extra statistics. The kstat view of TCP statistics (see Section 7.7.2) is copied from these MIB counters during each kstat update.

This behavior leads to an interesting situation: Since kstat provides a copy of all the MIB statistics that Solaris maintains, kstat provides a greater number of statistics than does SNMP. So to delve into TCP statistics in greater detail, use Kstat commands such as kstat and netstat -s.

## 7.9.2 TCP Statistics from Kstat

The kstat command can fetch all the TCP MIB statistics.

```
$ kstat -n tcp
module: tcp                             instance: 0
name:   tcp                             class:    mib2
        activeOpens                     812
        attemptFails                    312
        connTableSize                   56
        connTableSize6                  84
        crtime                          3.203529053
        currEstab                       5
        estabResets                     2
...
```

You can print all statistics from the TCP module by specifying -m instead of -n; -m, includes tcpstat, a collection of extra kstats that are not contained in the Solaris TCP MIB. And you can print individual statistics by using -s.

## 7.9.3 TCP Statistics Reference

Table 7.2 lists all the TCP MIB-II statistics and the Solaris additions. This list was taken from `mib2.h`. See `TCP-MIB.txt` for more information about some of these statistics.

**Table 7.2** TCP Kstat/MIB-II Statistics

| Statistic | Description |
|---|---|
| tcpRtoAlgorithm | Algorithm used for transmit timeout value |
| tcpRtoMin | Minimum retransmit timeout (ms) |
| tcpRtoMax | Maximum retransmit timeout (ms) |
| tcpMaxConn | Maximum # of connections supported |
| tcpActiveOpens | # of direct transitions CLOSED -> SYN-SENT |
| tcpPassiveOpens | # of direct transitions LISTEN -> SYN-RCVD |
| tcpAttemptFails | # of direct SIN-SENT/RCVD -> CLOSED/LISTEN |
| tcpEstabResets | # of direct ESTABLISHED/CLOSE-WAIT -> CLOSED |
| tcpCurrEstab | # of connections ESTABLISHED or CLOSE-WAIT |
| tcpInSegs | Total # of segments received |
| tcpOutSegs | Total # of segments sent |
| tcpRetransSegs | Total # of segments retransmitted |
| tcpConnTableSize | Size of `tcpConnEntry_t` |
| tcpOutRsts | # of segments sent with `RST` flag |
| ... | /* In addition to MIB-II */ |
| tcpOutDataSegs | Total # of data segments sent |
| tcpOutDataBytes | Total # of bytes in data segments sent |
| tcpRetransBytes | Total # of bytes in segments retransmitted |
| tcpOutAck | Total # of ACKs sent |
| tcpOutAckDelayed | Total # of delayed ACKs sent |
| tcpOutUrg | Total # of segments sent with the `urg` flag on |
| tcpOutWinUpdate | Total # of window updates sent |
| tcpOutWinProbe | Total # of zero window probes sent |
| tcpOutControl | Total # of control segments sent (`syn`, `fin`, `rst`) |
| tcpOutFastRetrans | Total # of segments sent due to "fast retransmit" |
| tcpInAckSegs | Total # of ACK segments received |
| tcpInAckBytes | Total # of bytes ACKed |

*continues*

**Table 7.2** TCP Kstat/MIB-II Statistics *(continued)*

| Statistic | Description |
| --- | --- |
| `tcpInDupAck` | Total # of duplicate ACKs |
| `tcpInAckUnsent` | Total # of ACKs acknowledging unsent data |
| `tcpInDataInorderSegs` | Total # of data segments received in order |
| `tcpInDataInorderBytes` | Total # of data bytes received in order |
| `tcpInDataUnorderSegs` | Total # of data segments received out of order |
| `tcpInDataUnorderBytes` | Total # of data bytes received out of order |
| `tcpInDataDupSegs` | Total # of complete duplicate data segments received |
| `tcpInDataDupBytes` | Total # of bytes in the complete duplicate data segments received |
| `tcpInDataPartDupSegs` | Total # of partial duplicate data segments received |
| `tcpInDataPartDupBytes` | Total # of bytes in the partial duplicate data segments received |
| `tcpInDataPastWinSegs` | Total # of data segments received past the window |
| `tcpInDataPastWinBytes` | Total # of data bytes received past the window |
| `tcpInWinProbe` | Total # of zero window probes received |
| `tcpInWinUpdate` | Total # of window updates received |
| `tcpInClosed` | Total # of data segments received after the connection has closed |
| `tcpRttNoUpdate` | Total # of failed attempts to update the rtt estimate |
| `tcpRttUpdate` | Total # of successful attempts to update the rtt estimate |
| `tcpTimRetrans` | Total # of retransmit timeouts |
| `tcpTimRetransDrop` | Total # of retransmit timeouts dropping the connection |
| `tcpTimKeepalive` | Total # of keepalive timeouts |
| `tcpTimKeepaliveProbe` | Total # of keepalive timeouts sending a probe |
| `tcpTimKeepaliveDrop` | Total # of keepalive timeouts dropping the connection |
| `tcpListenDrop` | Total # of connections refused because backlog is full on listen |
| `tcpListenDropQ0` | Total # of connections refused because half-open queue (q0) is full |
| `tcpHalfOpenDrop` | Total # of connections dropped from a full half-open queue (q0) |
| `tcpOutSackRetransSegs` | Total # of retransmitted segments by SACK retransmission |
| `tcp6ConnTableSize` | Size of `tcp6ConnEntry_t` |

## 7.9.4 TCP Statistics from DTrace

DTrace can probe TCP MIB statistics as they are incremented, as the `BUMP_MIB` and `UPDATE_MIB` macros were modified to do. The following command lists the TCP MIB statistics from DTrace.

```
# dtrace -ln 'mib:ip::tcp*'
   ID    PROVIDER            MODULE                     FUNCTION NAME
  789         mib                ip          tcp_find_pktinfo tcpInErrs
  790         mib                ip          ip_rput_data_v6 tcpInErrs
  791         mib                ip             ip_tcp_input tcpInErrs
 1163         mib                ip             tcp_ack_timer tcpOutAckDelayed
 1164         mib                ip       tcp_xmit_early_reset tcpOutRsts
 1165         mib                ip            tcp_xmit_ctl tcpOutRsts
...
```

While it can be useful to trace these counters as they are incremented, some needs are still unfulfilled. For example, tracking network activity by PID, UID, project, or zone is not possible with these probes alone: There is no guarantee that they will fire in the context of the responsible thread, so DTrace's variables such as execname and pid sometimes match the wrong process.

DTrace can be useful to capture these statistics during an interval of your choice. The following one-liner does this until you press Ctrl-C.

```
# dtrace -n 'mib:::tcp* { @[probename] = sum(arg0); }'
dtrace: description 'mib:::tcp* ' matched 93 probes
^C

  tcpInDataInorderSegs                                       7
  tcpInAckSegs                                              14
  tcpRttUpdate                                             14
  tcpInDataInorderBytes                                    16
  tcpOutDataSegs                                           16
  tcpOutDataBytes                                        4889
  tcpInAckBytes                                          4934
```

## 7.10 IP Statistics

As with TCP statistics, Solaris maintains a large number of statistics in the IP code for SNMP MIB-II. These often exclude loopback traffic and may be a better indicator of physical network activity than are the TCP statistics. They can also help with troubleshooting as various packet errors are tracked. The IP statistics can be found in the following places:

- IP MIB-II statistics, listed in /etc/sma/snmp/mibs/IP-MIB.txt on Solaris 10 or in RFC 2011; available from both the SNMP daemon and Kstat.
- Solaris additions to IP MIB-II, listed in /usr/include/inet/mib2.h and available from Kstat.
- Extra Kstat collections maintained by the module.

## 7.10.1 IP Statistics Internals

The IP MIB statistics are maintained in the Solaris code in the same way as the TCP MIB statistics (see Section 7.9.1). The Solaris code also maintains additional IP statistics to extend MIB-II.

## 7.10.2 IP Statistics from Kstat

The kstat command can fetch all the IP MIB statistics as follows.

```
$ kstat -n ip
module: ip                          instance: 0
name:   ip                          class:    mib2
        addrEntrySize               96
        crtime                      3.207689216
        defaultTTL                  255
        forwDatagrams               0
        forwProhibits               0
        forwarding                  2
        fragCreates                 0
...
```

You can print all Kstats from the IP module by using -m instead of -n. The -m option includes extra Kstats that are not related to the Solaris IP MIB. You can print individual statistics with -s.

## 7.10.3 IP Statistics Reference

Table 7.3 lists all the IP MIB-II statistics and the Solaris additions. This list was taken from mib2.h. See TCP-MIB.txt for more information about some of these statistics.

**Table 7.3** IP Kstat/MIB-II Statistics

| Statistic | Description |
|---|---|
| ipForwarding | Forwarder? 1 = gateway; 2 = not gateway |
| ipDefaultTTL | Default time-to-live for IPH |
| ipInReceives | # of input datagrams |
| ipInHdrErrors | # of datagram discards for IPH error |
| ipInAddrErrors | # of datagram discards for bad address |
| ipForwDatagrams | # of datagrams being forwarded |
| ipInUnknownProtos | # of datagram discards for unknown protocol |

*continues*

**Table 7.3** IP Kstat/MIB-II Statistics *(continued)*

| Statistic | Description |
|---|---|
| ipInDiscards | # of datagram discards of good datagrams |
| ipInDelivers | # of datagrams sent upstream |
| ipOutRequests | # of outdatagrams received from upstream |
| ipOutDiscards | # of good outdatagrams discarded |
| ipOutNoRoutes | # of outdatagram discards: no route found |
| ipReasmTimeout | Seconds received fragments held for reassembly. |
| ipReasmReqds | # of IP fragments needing reassembly |
| ipReasmOKs | # of datagrams reassembled |
| ipReasmFails | # of reassembly failures (not datagram count) |
| ipFragOKs | # of datagrams fragmented |
| ipFragFails | # of datagram discards for no fragmentation set |
| ipFragCreates | # of datagram fragments from fragmentation |
| ipAddrEntrySize | Size of `mib2_ipAddrEntry_t` |
| ipRouteEntrySize | Size of `mib2_ipRouteEntry_t` |
| ipNetToMediaEntrySize | Size of `mib2_ipNetToMediaEntry_t` |
| ipRoutingDiscards | # of valid route entries discarded |
| ... | /*The following defined in MIB-II as part of TCP and UDP groups */ |
| tcpInErrs | Total # of segments received with error |
| udpNoPorts | # of received datagrams not deliverable (no application.) |
| ... | /* In addition to MIB-II */ |
| ipInCksumErrs | # of bad IP header checksums |
| ipReasmDuplicates | # of complete duplicates in reassembly |
| ipReasmPartDups | # of partial duplicates in reassembly |
| ipForwProhibits | # of packets not forwarded for administrative reasons |
| udpInCksumErrs | # of UDP packets with bad UDP checksums |
| udpInOverflows | # of UDP packets dropped because of queue overflow |
| rawipInOverflows | # of RAW IP packets (all IP protocols except UDP, TCP, and ICMP) dropped because of queue overflow |
| ... | /* The following are private IPSEC MIB */ |
| ipsecInSucceeded | # of incoming packets that succeeded with policy checks |
| ipsecInFailed | # of incoming packets that failed policy checks |
| ipMemberEntrySize | Size of `ip_member_t` |
| ipInIPv6 | # of IPv6 packets received by IPv4 and dropped |
| ipOutIPv6 | # of IPv6 packets transmitted by `ip_wput` |
| ipOutSwitchIPv6 | # of times `ip_wput` has switched to become `ip_wput_v6` |

### 7.10.4 IP Statistics from DTrace

As with TCP, DTrace can trace these statistics as they are updated. The following command lists the probes that correspond to IP MIB statistics whose name begins with "ip" (which is not quite all of them; see Table 7.3).

```
# dtrace -ln 'mib:ip::ip*'
   ID    PROVIDER              MODULE                      FUNCTION NAME
  691         mib                  ip           ndp_input_advert ipv6IfIcmpInBad...
  692         mib                  ip          ndp_input_solicit ipv6IfIcmpInBad...
  693         mib                  ip        ill_frag_free_pkts ipReasmFails
  694         mib                  ip            ill_frag_timeout ipReasmFails
  695         mib                  ip            ill_frag_timeout ipv6ReasmFails
  697         mib                  ip             ip_wput_frag_v6 ipv6OutFragOKs
...
```

And the following one-liner tracks these statistics until Ctrl-C is pressed.

```
# dtrace -n 'mib:::ip* { @[probename] = sum(arg0); }'
dtrace: description 'mib:::ip* ' matched 209 probes
^C

  ipInDelivers                                                  6
  ipInReceives                                                 91
  ipOutRequests                                               153
```

## 7.11 ICMP Statistics

ICMP statistics are maintained by Solaris in the same way as TCP and IP, as explained in the previous two sections. To avoid unnecessary repetition, we list only key points and differences in this section.

The MIB-II statistics are in /etc/sma/snmp/mibs/IP-MIB.txt and in RFC 2011, along with IP. Solaris has a few additions to the ICMP MIB.

### 7.11.1 ICMP Statistics from Kstat

The following command prints all of the ICMP MIB statistics.

```
$ kstat -n icmp
module: ip                              instance: 0
name:   icmp                            class:     mib2
        crtime                          3.207830752
        inAddrMaskReps                  0
        inAddrMasks                     0
...
```

## 7.11.2 ICMP Statistics Reference

Table 7.4 from `mib2.h` lists ICMP MIB-II statistics plus Solaris additions.

**Table 7.4** ICMP Kstat/MIB-II Statistics

| Statistic | Description |
| --- | --- |
| icmpInMsgs | Total # of received ICMP messages |
| icmpInErrors | # of received ICMP messages msgs with errors |
| icmpInDestUnreachs | # of received "dest unreachable" messages |
| icmpInTimeExcds | # of received "time exceeded" messages |
| icmpInParmProbs | # of received "parameter problem" messages |
| icmpInSrcQuenchs | # of received "source quench" messages |
| icmpInRedirects | # of received "ICMP redirect" messages |
| icmpInEchos | # of received "echo request" messages |
| icmpInEchoReps | # of received "echo reply" messages |
| icmpInTimestamps | # of received "timestamp" messages |
| icmpInTimestampReps | # of received "timestamp reply" messages |
| icmpInAddrMasks | # of received "address mask request" messages |
| icmpInAddrMaskReps | # of received "address mask reply" messages |
| icmpOutMsgs | total # of sent ICMP messages |
| icmpOutErrors | # of messages not sent for internal ICMP errors |
| icmpOutDestUnreachs | # of "dest unreachable" messages sent |
| icmpOutTimeExcds | # of "time exceeded" messages sent |
| icmpOutParmProbs | # of "parameter problem" messages sent |
| icmpOutSrcQuenchs | # of "source quench" messages sent |
| icmpOutRedirects | # of "ICMP redirect" messages sent |
| icmpOutEchos | # of "Echo request" messages sent |
| icmpOutEchoReps | # of "Echo reply" messages sent |
| icmpOutTimestamps | # of "timestamp request" messages sent |
| icmpOutTimestampReps | # of "timestamp reply" messages sent |
| icmpOutAddrMasks | # of "address mask request" messages sent |
| icmpOutAddrMaskReps | # of "address mask reply" messages sent |
| . . . | /* In addition to MIB-II */ |
| icmpInCksumErrs | # of received packets with checksum errors |
| icmpInUnknowns | # of received packets with unknown codes |

*continues*

**Table 7.4** ICMP Kstat/MIB-II Statistics (*continued*)

| Statistic | Description |
|---|---|
| `icmpInFragNeeded` | # of received unreachables with "fragmentation needed" |
| `icmpOutFragNeeded` | # of sent unreachables with "fragmentation needed" |
| `icmpOutDrops` | # of messages not sent since original packet was broadcast/multicast or an ICMP error packet |
| `icmpInOverflows` | # of ICMP packets dropped because of queue overflow |
| `icmpInBadRedirects` | # of received "ICMP redirect" messages that are bad and thus ignored |

## 7.11.3 ICMP Statistics from DTrace

The following DTrace one-liner tracks ICMP MIB events.

```
# dtrace -n 'mib:::icmp* { @[probename] = sum(arg0); }'
dtrace: description 'mib:::icmp* ' matched 34 probes
^C

  icmpInEchoReps                                              1
  icmpInEchos                                                 3
  icmpOutEchoReps                                             3
  icmpOutMsgs                                                 3
  icmpInMsgs                                                  4
```

## 7.11.4 Tracing Raw Network Functions

The fbt provider traces raw kernel functions, but its use is not recommended, because kernel functions may change between minor releases of Solaris, breaking DTrace scripts that used them. On the other hand, being able to trace these events is certainly better than not having the option at all.

The following example counts the frequency of TCP/IP functions called for this demonstration.

```
# dtrace -n 'fbt:ip::entry { @[probefunc] = count(); }'
dtrace: description 'fbt:ip::entry ' matched 1757 probes
^C
...
  ip_cksum                                                  519
  tcp_wput_data                                            3058
  tcp_output                                               3165
  tcp_wput                                                 3195
  squeue_enter                                             3203
```

This one-liner matched 1,757 probes for this build of Solaris 10 (the number of matches will vary for other builds). Another line of attack is the network driver itself. Here we demonstrate `hme`.

```
# dtrace -n 'fbt:hme::entry { @[probefunc] = count(); }'
dtrace: description 'fbt:hme::entry ' matched 100 probes
^C
...
  hmewput                                                        221
  hmeintr                                                        320
  hme_check_dma_handle                                           668
  hme_check_acc_handle                                           762
```

The 100 probes provided by this `hme` driver may be sufficient for the task at hand and are easier to use than 1,757 probes. `rtls` provides even fewer probes, 33.

# 8

# Performance Counters

This chapter introduces tools to examine CPU cache activity (cpustat, cputrack) and bus activity (busstat).

## 8.1 Introducing CPU Caches

Figure 8.1 depicts typical caches that a CPU can use.

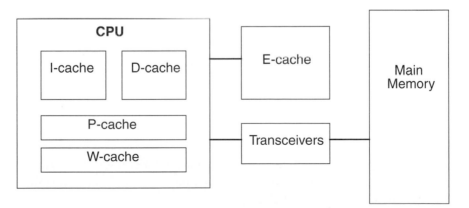

**Figure 8.1** CPU Caches

Caches include the following:

- **I-cache.** Level 1 instruction cache
- **D-cache.** Level 1 data cache
- **P-cache.** Prefetch cache
- **W-cache.** Write cache
- **E-cache.** Level 2 external or embedded cache

These are the typical caches for the content of main memory, depending on the processor. Another framework for caching page translations as part of the Memory Management Unit (MMU) includes the Translation Lookaside Buffer (TLB) and Translation Storage Buffers (TSBs). These translation facilities are discussed in detail in Chapter 12 in *Solaris™ Internals*.

Of particular interest are the I-cache, D-cache, and E-cache, which are often listed as key specifications for a CPU type. Details of interest are their size, their cache line size, and their set-associativity. A greater size improves cache hit ratio, and a larger cache line size can improve throughput. A higher set-associativity improves the effect of the Least Recently Used policy, which can avoid hot spots where the cache would otherwise have flushed frequently accessed data.

Experiencing a low cache hit ratio and a large number of cache misses for the I-, D-, or E-cache is likely to degrade application performance. Section 8.2 demonstrates the monitoring of different event statistics, many of which can be used to determine cache performance.

It is important to stress that each processor type is different and can have a different arrangement, type, and number of caches. For example, the UltraSPARC IV+ has a *Level 3* cache of 32 Mbytes, in addition to its Level 1 and 2 caches.

To highlight this further, the following describes the caches for three recent SPARC processors:

- **UltraSPARC III Cu.** The Level 2 cache is an external cache of either 1, 4, or 8 Mbytes in size, providing either 64-, 256-, or 512-byte cache lines connected by a dedicated bus. It is unified, write-back, allocating, and either one-way or two-way set-associative. It is physically indexed, physically tagged (PIPT).
- **UltraSPARC IIIi.** The Level 2 cache is an embedded cache of 1 Mbyte in size, providing a 64-byte cache line and is on the CPU itself. It is unified, write-back, write-allocate, and four-way set-associative. It is physically indexed, physically tagged (PIPT).
- **UltraSPARC T1.** Sun's UltraSPARC T1 is a chip level multi-processor. Its CMT hardware architecture has eight cores, or individual execution pipelines, per chip, each with four strands or active thread contexts that share a

pipeline in each core. Each cycle of a different hardware strand is scheduled on the pipeline in round robin order. There are 32 threads total per Ultra-SPARC T1 processor.

The cores are connected by a high-speed, low-latency crossbar in silicon. An UltraSPARC T1 processor can be considered SMP on a chip. Each core has an instruction cache, a data cache, an instruction translation-lookaside buffer (iTLB), and a data TLB (dTLB) shared by the four strands. A twelve-way associative unified Level 2 (L2) on-chip cache is shared by all 32 hardware threads. Memory latency is uniform across all cores—uniform memory access (UMA), not non-uniform memory access (NUMA).

Figure 8.2 illustrates the structure of the UltraSPARC T1 processor.

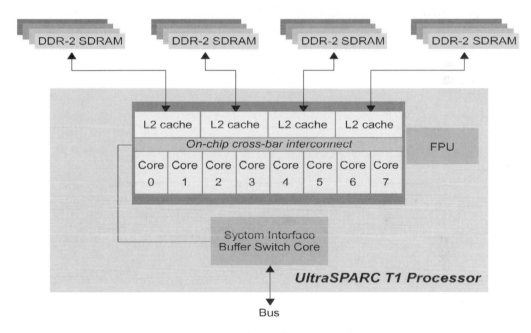

**Figure 8.2** UltraSPARC T1 Caches

For a reference on UltraSPARC caches, see the UltraSPARC Processors Documentation Web site at

```
http://www.sun.com/processors/documentation.html
```

This Web site lists the processor user manuals, which are referred to by the cpustat command in the next section. Other CPU brands have similar documentation that can be found online.

## 8.2 `cpustat` Command

The `cpustat` command monitors the CPU Performance Counters (CPCs), which provide performance details for the CPU hardware caches. These types of hardware counters are known as Performance Instrumentation Counters, or *PICs*, which also exist on other devices. The PICs are programmable and record statistics for different events (*event* is a deliberate term). For example, they can be programmed to track statistics for CPU cache events.

A typical UltraSPARC system might provide two PICs, each of which can be programmed to monitor one event from a list of around twenty. An example of an event is an E-cache hit, the number of which could be counted by a PIC.

Which CPU caches can be measured depends on the type of CPU. Different CPU types not only can have different caches but also can have different available events that the PICs can monitor. It is possible that a CPU could contain a cache with no events associated with it—leaving us with no way to measure cache performance.

The following example demonstrates the use of `cpustat` to measure E-cache (Level 2 cache) events on an UltraSPARC IIi CPU.

```
# cpustat -c pic0=EC_ref,pic1=EC_hit 1 5
  time cpu event        pic0       pic1
 1.005   0 tick        66931      52598
 2.005   0 tick        67871      52569
 3.005   0 tick        65003      50907
 4.005   0 tick        64793      50958
 5.005   0 tick        64574      50904
 5.005   1 total      329172     257936
```

The `cpustat` command has a `-c` eventspec option to configure which events the PICs should monitor. We set `pic0` to monitor `EC_ref`, which is E-cache references; and we set `pic1` to monitor `EC_hit`, which is E-cache hits.

### 8.2.1 Cache Hit Ratio, Cache Misses

If both the cache references and hits are available, as with the UltraSPARC IIi CPU in the previous example, you can calculate the *cache hit ratio*. For that calculation you could also use cache misses and hits, which some CPU types provide. The calculations are fairly straightforward:

$$cache\ hit\ ratio = cache\ hits\ /\ cache\ references$$
$$cache\ hit\ ratio = cache\ hits\ /\ (cache\ hits + cache\ misses)$$

A higher cache hit ratio improves the performance of applications because the latency incurred when main memory is accessed through memory buses is obviated. The cache hit ratio may also indicate the pattern of activity; a low cache hit ratio may indicate a hot spot—where frequently accessed memory locations map to the same cache location, causing frequently used data to be flushed.

Since satisfying each cache miss incurs a certain time cost, the volume of *cache misses* may be of more interest than the cache hit ratio. The number of misses can more directly affect application performance than does changing percent hit ratios since the number of misses is proportional to the total time penalty.

Both cache hit ratios and cache misses can be calculated with a little awk, as the following script, called ecache, demonstrates.[1]

```
#!/usr/bin/sh
#
# ecache - print E$ misses and hit ratio for UltraSPARC IIi CPUs.
#
# USAGE: ecache [interval [count]]      # by default, interval is 1 sec

cpustat -c pic0=EC_ref,pic1=EC_hit ${1-1} $2 | awk '
        BEGIN { pagesize = 20; lines = pagesize }
        lines >= pagesize {
            lines = 0
            printf("%8s %3s %5s %9s %9s %9s %7s\n",\
               "E$ time", "cpu", "event", "total", "hits", "miss", "%hit")
        }
        $1 !~ /time/ {
            total = $4
            hits = $5
            miss = total - hits
            ratio = 100 * hits / total
            printf("%8s %3s %5s %9s %9s %9s %7.2f\n",\
               $1, $2, $3, total, hits, miss, ratio)
            lines++
        }
```

This script is verbose to illustrate the calculations performed, in particular, using extra named variables.[2] nawk or perl would also be suitable for postprocessing the output of cpustat, which itself reads the PICs by using the libcpc library, and binding a thread to each CPU.

---

1. This script is based on E-cache from the freeware CacheKit (Brendan Gregg). See the CacheKit for scripts that support other CPU types and scripts that measure I- and D-cache activity.
2. A one-liner version to add just the %hit column is as follows:
   ` # cpustat -nc pic0=EC_ref,pic1=EC_hit 1 5 | awk '{ printf "%s %.2f\n",$0,$5*100/$4 }' `

The following example demonstrates the extra columns that `ecache` prints.

```
# ecache 1 5
E$  time cpu event    total     hits    miss    %hit
    1.013   0 tick    65856    51684   14172   78.48
    2.013   0 tick    71511    55793   15718   78.02
    3.013   0 tick    69051    54203   14848   78.50
    4.013   0 tick    69878    55082   14796   78.83
    5.013   0 tick    68665    53873   14792   78.46
    5.013   1 total  344961   270635   74326   78.45
```

This tool measures the volume of cache misses (`miss`) and the cache hit ratio (`%hit`) achieved for UltraSPARC II CPUs.

## 8.2.2 Listing PICs and Events

The `-h` option to `cpustat` lists the available events for a CPU type and the PICs that can monitor them.

```
# cpustat -h
Usage:
        cpustat [-c events] [-p period] [-nstD] [interval [count]]

        -c events specify processor events to be monitored
        -n        suppress titles
        -p period cycle through event list periodically
        -s        run user soaker thread for system-only events
        -t        include %tick register
        -D        enable debug mode
        -h        print extended usage information

        Use cputrack(1) to monitor per-process statistics.

        CPU performance counter interface: UltraSPARC I&II

        event specification syntax:
        [picn=]<eventn>[,attr[n][=<val>]] [,[picn=]<eventn>[,attr[n][=<val>]],...]

        event0:  Cycle_cnt Instr_cnt Dispatch0_IC_miss IC_ref DC_rd DC_wr
                 EC_ref EC_snoop_inv Dispatch0_storeBuf Load_use
                 EC_write_hit_RDO EC_rd_hit

        event1:  Cycle_cnt Instr_cnt Dispatch0_mispred EC_wb EC_snoop_cb
                 Dispatch0_FP_use IC_hit DC_rd_hit DC_wr_hit Load_use_RAW
                 EC_hit EC_ic_hit

        attributes: nouser sys

        See the "UltraSPARC I/II User's Manual" (Part No. 802-7220-02) for
        descriptions of these events. Documentation for Sun processors can
        be found at: http://www.sun.com/processors/manuals
```

The `-h` output lists the events that can be monitored and finishes by referring to the reference manual for this CPU. These invaluable manuals discuss the CPU caches in detail and explain what the events really mean.

In this example of `cpustat -h`, the event specification syntax shows that you can set `picn` to measure events from `eventn`. For example, you can set `pic0` to `IC_ref` and `pic1` to `IC_hit`; but not the other way around. The output also indicates that this CPU type provides only two PICs and so can measure only two events at the same time.

## 8.2.3 PIC Examples: UltraSPARC IIi

We chose the UltraSPARC IIi CPU for the preceding examples because it provides a small collection of fairly straightforward PICs. Understanding this CPU type is a good starting point before we move on to more difficult CPUs. For a full reference for this CPU type, see Appendix B of the *UltraSPARC I/II User's Manual*.[3]

The UltraSPARC IIi provides two 32-bit PICs, which are joined as a 64-bit register. The 32-bit counters could wrap around, especially for longer sample intervals. The 64-bit Performance Control Register (PCR) configures those events (statistics) the two PICs will contain. Only one invocation of `cpustat` (or `cputrack`) at a time is possible, since there is only one set of PICs to share.

The available events for measuring CPU cache activity are listed in Table 8.1. This is from the *User's Manual*, where you can find a listing for all events.

**Table 8.1** UltraSPARC IIi CPU Cache Events

| Event | PICs | Description |
|-------|------|-------------|
| `IC_ref` | PIC0 | I-cache references; I-cache references are fetches of up to four instructions from an aligned block of eight instructions. I-cache references are generally prefetches and do not correspond exactly to the instructions executed. |
| `IC_hit` | PIC1 | I-cache hits. |
| `DC_rd` | PIC0 | D-cache read references (including accesses that subsequently trap); non-D-cacheable accesses are not counted. Atomic, block load, "internal" and "external" bad ASIs, quad precision LDD, and MEMBAR instructions also fall into this class. |

*continues*

---

3. This manual is available at `http://www.sun.com/processors/manuals/805-0087.pdf`.

**Table 8.1** UltraSPARC IIi CPU Cache Events *(continued)*

| Event | PICs | Description |
|---|---|---|
| `DC_rd_hit` | PIC1 | D-cache read hits are counted in one of two places:<br>1. When they access the D-cache tags and do not enter the load buffer (because it is already empty)<br>2. When they exit the load buffer (because of a D-cache miss or a nonempty load buffer) |
| `DC_wr` | PIC0 | D-cache write references (including accesses that subsequently trap); non-D-cacheable accesses are not counted. |
| `DC_wr_hit` | PIC1 | D-cache write hits. |
| `EC_ref` | PIC0 | Total E-cache references; noncacheable accesses are not counted. |
| `EC_hit` | PIC1 | total E-cache hits. |
| `EC_write_ hit_RDO` | PIC0 | E-cache hits that do a read for ownership of a UPA transaction. |
| `EC_wb` | PIC1 | E-cache misses that do writebacks. |
| `EC_snoop_ inv` | PIC0 | E-cache invalidates from the following UPA transactions: S_INV_REQ, S_CPI_REQ. |
| `EC_snoop_cb` | PIC1 | E-cache snoop copybacks from the following UPA transactions: S_CPB_REQ, S_CPI_REQ, S_CPD_REQ, S_CPB_MSI_REQ. |
| `EC_rd_hit` | PIC0 | E-cache read hits from D-cache misses. |
| `EC_ic_hit` | PIC1 | E-cache read hits from I-cache misses. |

Reading through the descriptions will reveal many subtleties you need to consider to understand these events. For example, some activity is not cacheable and so does not show up in event statistics for that cache. This includes block loads and block stores, which are not sent to the E-cache since it is likely that this data will be touched only once. You should consider such a point if an application experienced memory latency not explained by the E-cache miss statistics alone.

## 8.2.4  PIC Examples: The UltraSPARC T1 Processor

Each of the 32 UltraSPARC T1 strands has a set of hardware performance counters that can be monitored using the cpustat(1M) command. cpustat can collect two counters in parallel, the second always being the instruction count. For example, to collect iTLB misses and instruction counts for every strand on the chip, type the following:

```
# /usr/sbin/cpustat -c pic0=ITLB_miss,pic1=Instr_cnt,sys 1 10
time cpu event pic0 pic1
2.019 0 tick 6 186595695 # pic0=ITLB_miss,sys,pic1=Instr_cnt,sys
2.089 1 tick 7 192407038 # pic0=ITLB_miss,sys,pic1=Instr_cnt,sys
2.039 2 tick 49 192237411 # pic0=ITLB_miss,sys,pic1=Instr_cnt,sys
2.049 3 tick 15 190609811 # pic0=ITLB_miss,sys,pic1=Instr_cnt,sys
......
```

Both a pic0 and pic1 register must be specified. ITLB_miss is used in the preceding example, although instruction counts are only of interest in this instance.

The performance counters indicate that each strand is executing about 190 million instructions per second. To determine how many instructions are executing per core, aggregate counts from four strands. Strands zero, one, two, and three are in the first core, strands four, five, six, and seven are in the second core, and so on. The preceding example indicates that the system is executing about 760 million instructions per core per second. If the processor is executing at 1.2 Gigahertz, each core can execute a maximum of 1200 million instructions per second, yielding an efficiency rating of 0.63. To achieve maximum throughput, maximize the number of instructions per second on each core and ultimately on the chip.

Other useful cpustat counters for assessing performance on an UltraSPARC T1 processor-based system are detailed in Table 8.2. All counters are per second, per thread. Rather than deal with raw misses, accumulate the counters and express them as a percentage miss rate of instructions. For example, if the system executes 200 million instructions per second on a strand and IC_miss indicates 14 million instruction cache misses per second, then the instruction cache miss rate is seven percent.

**Table 8.2** UltraSPARC-T1 Performance Counters

| Events | Description | High Value | Impact | Potential Remedy |
|--------|-------------|------------|--------|------------------|
| IC_miss | Number of instruction cache misses | >7% | Small impact as latency can be hidden by strands | Compiler flag options to compact the binary. See compiler section. |
| DC_miss | Number of data cache misses | >11% | Small impact as latency can be hidden by strands | Compact data structures to align on 64-byte boundaries. |

*continues*

**Table 8.2** UltraSPARC-T1 Performance Counters (*continued*)

| Events | Description | High Value | Impact | Potential Remedy |
|---|---|---|---|---|
| ITLB_miss | Number of instruction TLB misses | >.001% | Potentially severe impact from TLB thrashing | Make sure text on large pages. See TLB section. |
| DTLB_miss | Number of data TLB misses | >.005% | Potentially severe impact from TLB thrashing | Make sure data segments are on large pages. See TLB section. |
| L1_imiss | Instruction cache misses that also miss L2 | >2% | Medium impact potential for all threads to stall | Reduce conflict with data cache misses if possible. |
| L1_dmiss_ld | Data case misses that also miss L2 | >2% | Medium impact potential for all threads to stall | Potential alignment issues. Offset data structures. |

## 8.2.5 Event Multiplexing

Since some CPUs have only two PICs, only two events can be measured at the same time. If you are looking at a specific CPU component like the I-cache, this situation may be fine. However, sometimes you want to monitor more events than just the PIC count. In that case, you can use the -c option more than once, and the cpustat command will alternate between them. For example,

```
# cpustat -c pic0=IC_ref,pic1=IC_hit -c pic0=DC_rd,pic1=DC_rd_hit -c \
pic0=DC_wr,pic1=DC_wr_hit -c pic0=EC_ref,pic1=EC_hit -p 1 0.25 5
   time cpu event      pic0     pic1
  0.267  0  tick     221423   197095  # pic0=IC_ref,pic1=IC_hit
  0.513  0  tick        105       65  # pic0=DC_rd,pic1=DC_rd_hit
  0.763  0  tick         37       21  # pic0=DC_wr,pic1=DC_wr_hit
  1.013  0  tick        282      148  # pic0=EC_ref,pic1=EC_hit
  1.267  0  tick     213558   190520  # pic0=IC_ref,pic1=IC_hit
  1.513  0  tick        109       62  # pic0=DC_rd,pic1=DC_rd_hit
  1.763  0  tick         37       21  # pic0=DC_wr,pic1=DC_wr_hit
  2.013  0  tick        276      149  # pic0=EC_ref,pic1=EC_hit
  2.264  0  tick     217713   194040  # pic0=IC_ref,pic1=IC_hit
...
```

We specified four different PIC configurations (-c eventspec), and cpustat cycled between sampling each of them. We set the interval to 0.25 seconds and set a period (-p) to 1 second so that the final value of 5 is a cycle count, not a sample count. An extra commented field lists the events the columns represent, which helps a postprocessing script such as awk to identify what the values represent.

Some CPU types provide many PICs (more than eight), usually removing the need for event multiplexing as used in the previous example.

### 8.2.6 Using cpustat with Multiple CPUs

Each example output of cpustat has contained a column for the CPU ID (cpu). Each CPU has its own PIC, so when cpustat runs on a multi-CPU system, it must collect PIC values from every CPU. cpustat does this by creating a thread for each CPU and binding it onto that CPU. Each sample then produces a line for each CPU and prints it in the order received. Thus, some slight shuffling of the output lines occurs.

The following example demonstrates cpustat on a server with four Ultra-SPARC IV CPUs, each of which has two cores.

```
# cpustat -c pic0=DC_rd,pic1=DC_rd_miss 5 1
   time cpu event      pic0      pic1
  5.008 513  tick    355670     25132
  5.008   3  tick   8824184     34366
  5.008 512  tick        11         1
  5.008   2  tick      1127       123
  5.008 514  tick     55337      3908
  5.008   0  tick        10         3
  5.008   1  tick     19833       854
  5.008 515  tick   7360753     36567
  5.008   8 total 16616925    100954
```

The cpu column prints the total CPU count for the last line (total).

### 8.2.7 Cycles per Instruction

The CPC events can monitor more than just the CPU caches. The following example demonstrates the use of the cycle count and instruction count on an Ultra-SPARC IIi to calculate the average number of *cycles per instruction*, printed last.

```
# cpustat -nc pic0=Cycle_cnt,pic1=Instr_cnt 10 1 | \
awk '{ printf "%s %.2f cpi\n",$0,$4/$5; }'
 10.034   0  tick 3554903403 3279712368  1.08 cpi
 10.034   1 total 3554903403 3279712368  1.08 cpi
```

This single 10-second sample averaged 1.08 cycles per instruction. During this test, the CPU was busy running an infinite loop program. Since the same simple instructions are run over and over, the instructions and data are found in the Level-1 cache, resulting in fast instructions.

Now the same test is performed while the CPU is busy with heavy random memory access:

```
# cpustat -nc pic0=Cycle_cnt,pic1=Instr_cnt 10 1 | \
awk '{ printf "%s %.2f cpi\n",$0,$4/$5; }'
 10.036   0  tick 205607856  34023849  6.04 cpi
 10.036   1 total 205607856  34023849  6.04 cpi
```

Since accessing main memory is much slower, the cycles per instruction have increased to an average of 6.04.

## 8.2.8 PIC Examples: UltraSPARC IV

The UltraSPARC IV processor provides a greater number of events that can be monitored. The following example is the output from cpustat -h, which lists these events.

```
# cpustat -h
...
Use cputrack(1) to monitor per-process statistics.

        CPU performance counter interface: UltraSPARC III+ & IV

        events  pic0=<event0>,pic1=<event1>[,sys][,nouser]

        event0: Cycle_cnt Instr_cnt Dispatch0_IC_miss IC_ref DC_rd DC_wr
                EC_ref EC_snoop_inv Dispatch0_br_target Dispatch0_2nd_br
                Rstall_storeQ Rstall_IU_use EC_write_hit_RTO EC_rd_miss
                PC_port0_rd SI_snoop SI_ciq_flow SI_owned SW_count_0
                IU_Stat_Br_miss_taken IU_Stat_Br_count_taken
                Dispatch_rs_mispred FA_pipe_completion MC_reads_0
                MC_reads_1 MC_reads_2 MC_reads_3 MC_stalls_0 MC_stalls_2
                EC_wb_remote EC_miss_local EC_miss_mtag_remote

        event1: Cycle_cnt Instr_cnt Dispatch0_mispred EC_wb EC_snoop_cb
                IC_miss_cancelled Re_FPU_bypass Re_DC_miss Re_EC_miss
                IC_miss DC_rd_miss DC_wr_miss Rstall_FP_use EC_misses
                EC_ic_miss Re_PC_miss ITLB_miss DTLB_miss WC_miss
                WC_snoop_cb WC_scrubbed WC_wb_wo_read PC_soft_hit
                PC_snoop_inv PC_hard_hit PC_port1_rd SW_count_1
                IU_Stat_Br_miss_untaken IU_Stat_Br_count_untaken
                PC_MS_misses Re_RAW_miss FM_pipe_completion MC_writes_0
                MC_writes_1 MC_writes_2 MC_writes_3 MC_stalls_1 MC_stalls_3
                Re_DC_missovhd EC_miss_mtag_remote EC_miss_remote

        See the "SPARC V9 JPS1 Implementation Supplement: Sun
        UltraSPARC-III+"
```

Some of these are similar to the UltraSPARC IIi CPU, but many are additional. The extra events allow memory controller and pipeline activity to be measured.

# 8.3 cputrack Command

While the cpustat command monitors activity for the entire system, the cputrack command allows the same counters to be measured for a single process. This can be useful for focusing on particular applications and determining whether only one process is the cause of performance issues.

The event specification for cputrack is the same as cpustat, except that instead of an interval and a count, cputrack takes either a command or -p PID.

```
# cputrack
Usage:
        cputrack [-T secs] [-N count] [-Defhnv] [-o file]
                 -c events [command [args] | -p pid]

        -T secs    seconds between samples, default 1
        -N count   number of samples, default unlimited
        -D         enable debug mode
        -e         follow exec(2), and execve(2)
        -f         follow fork(2), fork1(2), and vfork(2)
        -h         print extended usage information
        -n         suppress titles
        -t         include virtualized %tick register
        -v         verbose mode
        -o file    write cpu statistics to this file
        -c events  specify processor events to be monitored
        -p pid     pid of existing process to capture

        Use cpustat(1M) to monitor system-wide statistics.
```

The usage message for cputrack ends with a reminder to use cpustat for systemwide statistics.

The following example demonstrates cputrack monitoring the instructions and cycles for a sleep command.

```
# cputrack -c pic0=Instr_cnt,pic1=Cycle_cnt sleep 5
  time lwp       event      pic0       pic1
 1.024   1        tick    188134     629987
 2.023   1        tick         0          0
 3.023   1        tick         0          0
 4.023   1        tick         0          0
 5.023   1        tick         0          0
 5.034   1        exit    196623     682808
```

In the first second, the sleep command initializes and executes 188,134 instructions. Then the sleep command sleeps, reporting zero counts in the output; this shows that cputrack is monitoring our sleep command only and is not reporting on other system activity. The sleep command wakes after five seconds and executes the final instructions, finishing with the total on exit of 196,623 instructions.

As another example, we use `cputrack` to monitor the D-cache activity of PID 19849, which has multiple threads. The number of samples is limited to 20 (`-N`).

```
$ cputrack -N 20 -c pic0=DC_access,pic1=DC_miss -p 19849
   time lwp       event       pic0         pic1
  1.007   1       tick   34543793       824363
  1.007   2       tick          0            0
  1.007   3       tick 1001797338      5153245
  1.015   4       tick  976864106      5536858
  1.007   5       tick 1002880440      5217810
  1.017   6       tick  948543113      3731144
  2.007   1       tick   15425817       745468
  2.007   2       tick          0            0
  2.014   3       tick 1002035102      5110169
  2.017   4       tick  976879154      5542155
  2.030   5       tick 1018802136      5283137
  2.033   6       tick 1013933228      4072636
......
```

This CPU type provides D-cache misses for `pic1`, a useful statistic inasmuch as cache misses incur a certain time cost. Here, lwp 2 appears to be idle, while lwps 3, 4, 5, and 6 are causing many D-cache events. With a little `awk`, we could add another column for D-cache hit ratio.

For additional information on `cputrack`, see `cputrack(1)`.

## 8.4 `busstat` Command

The `busstat` command monitors bus statistics for systems that contain instrumented buses. Such buses contain Performance Instrumentation Counters (PICs), which in some ways are similar to the CPU PICs.

### 8.4.1 Listing Supported Buses

`busstat -l` lists instrumented buses that `busstat` can monitor.

```
# busstat -l
busstat: No devices available in system.
```

If you see the "No devices available" message, then you won't get any further. Find another system (usually a larger system) that responds by listing instance names. The following is from a Sun Enterprise E4500.

```
# busstat -l
Busstat Device(s):
sbus1 ac0 ac1 ac2 ac3 ac4 sbus0 sbus2 sbus3 sbus4
```

The output of busstat -l has now listed six devices that provide PICs for us to use. sbus is for SBus, the interconnect bus for devices including peripherals; ac is for Address Controller.

## 8.4.2  Listing Bus Events

The -e switch for busstat lists events that a bus device can monitor. Here we list events for ac0.

```
# busstat -e ac0
pic0
mem_bank0_rds
mem_bank0_wrs
mem_bank0_stall
mem_bank1_rds
mem_bank1_wrs
mem_bank1_stall
clock_cycles
...

pic1
mem_bank0_rds
mem_bank0_wrs
mem_bank0_stall
mem_bank1_rds
mem_bank1_wrs
mem_bank1_stall
clock_cycles
...
```

The list of events for each PIC is very long; we truncated it so that this example doesn't fill an entire page.

It can help to use the pr command to rework the output into columns. The following example does this for the sbus0.

```
# busstat -e sbus0 | pr -t2
pic0                              pic1
dvma_stream_rd                    dvma_stream_rd
dvma_stream_wr                    dvma_stream_wr
dvma_const_rd                     dvma_const_rd
dvma_const_wr                     dvma_const_wr
dvma_tlb_misses                   dvma_tlb_misses
dvma_stream_buf_mis               dvma_stream_buf_mis
dvma_cycles                       dvma_cycles
dvma_bytes_xfr                    dvma_bytes_xfr
interrupts                        interrupts
upa_inter_nack                    upa_inter_nack
pio_reads                         pio_reads
pio_writes                        pio_writes
sbus_reruns                       sbus_reruns
pio_cycles                        pio_cycles
#
```

The first column lists events for pic0; the second are events for pic1.

Unlike `cpustat`, `busstat` does not finish by listing a reference manual for these events. There is currently little public documentation for bus events[4]; most Internet searches match only the man page for `busstat` and the event names in the OpenSolaris source. Fortunately, many of the event names are self-evident (for example, `mem_bank0_rds` is probably memory bank 0 reads), and some of the terms are similar to those used for CPU PICs, as documented in the CPU manuals.

## 8.4.3 Monitoring Bus Events

Monitoring bus events is similar to monitoring CPU events, except that we must specify which bus instance or instances to examine.

The following example examines `ac1` for memory bank stalls, printing a column for each memory bank. We specified an interval of 1 second and a count of 5.

```
# busstat -w ac1,pic0=mem_bank0_stall,pic1=mem_bank1_stall 1 5
time dev    event0              pic0           event1              pic1
1    ac1    mem_bank0_stall     2653           mem_bank1_stall     0
2    ac1    mem_bank0_stall     2039           mem_bank1_stall     0
3    ac1    mem_bank0_stall     3614           mem_bank1_stall     0
4    ac1    mem_bank0_stall     3213           mem_bank1_stall     0
5    ac1    mem_bank0_stall     2380           mem_bank1_stall     0
```

The second bank is empty, so `pic1` measured no events for it. Memory stall events are interesting—they signify latency suffered when a memory bank is already busy with a previous request.

There are some differences between `busstat` and `cpustat`: There is no total line with `busstat`, and intervals less than one second are not accepted. `busstat` uses a `-w` option to indicate that devices are written to, thereby configuring them so that their PICs will monitor the specified events, whereas `cpustat` itself writes to each CPU's PCR.

By specifying `ac` instead of `ac1`, we now monitor these events across all address controllers.

```
# busstat -w ac,pic0=mem_bank0_stall,pic1=mem_bank1_stall 1 5
time dev    event0              pic0           event1              pic1
1    ac0    mem_bank0_stall     2641           mem_bank1_stall     0
1    ac1    mem_bank0_stall     2766           mem_bank1_stall     0
1    ac2    mem_bank0_stall     0              mem_bank1_stall     0
1    ac3    mem_bank0_stall     0              mem_bank1_stall     0
1    ac4    mem_bank0_stall     0              mem_bank1_stall     0
2    ac0    mem_bank0_stall     2374           mem_bank1_stall     0
```

*continues*

---

4. Probably because no one has asked! `busstat` is not in common use by customers; the main users have been engineers within Sun.

```
time dev    event0               pic0      event1               pic1
2    ac1    mem_bank0_stall      2545      mem_bank1_stall      0
2    ac2    mem_bank0_stall      0         mem_bank1_stall      0
2    ac3    mem_bank0_stall      0         mem_bank1_stall      0
2    ac4    mem_bank0_stall      0         mem_bank1_stall      0
3    ac0    mem_bank0_stall      2133      mem_bank1_stall      0
```

We would study the `dev` column to see which device the line of statistics belongs to.

`busstat` also provides a `-r` option, to read PICs without changing the configured events. This means that we monitor whatever was previously set by `-w`. Here's an example of using `-r` after the previous `-w` example.

```
# busstat -r ac0 1 5
time dev    event0               pic0      event1               pic1
1    ac0    mem_bank0_stall      2039      mem_bank1_stall      0
2    ac0    mem_bank0_stall      1822      mem_bank1_stall      0
3    ac0    mem_bank0_stall      1868      mem_bank1_stall      0
4    ac0    mem_bank0_stall      2109      mem_bank1_stall      0
5    ac0    mem_bank0_stall      1779      mem_bank1_stall      0
```

## 8.4.4 Event Multiplexing

As with using `cpustat` for a limited number of PICs (see Section 8.2.5), you can specify multiple events for `busstat` so that more events than PICs can be monitored. The multiple-event specifications are measured alternately.

The following example demonstrates the use of `busstat` to measure many bus events.

```
# busstat -w ac0,pic0=mem_bank0_rds,pic1=mem_bank0_wrs -w \
ac0,pic0=addr_pkts,pic1=data_pkts -w ac0,pic0=ac_addr_pkts,pic1=ac_data_pkts 1 9
time dev    event0               pic0      event1               pic1
1    ac0    mem_bank0_rds        47692     mem_bank0_wrs        1785
2    ac0    addr_pkts            87753     data_pkts            112209
3    ac0    ac_addr_pkts         126718    ac_data_pkts         141410
4    ac0    mem_bank0_rds        40187     mem_bank0_wrs        4860
5    ac0    addr_pkts            92343     data_pkts            119899
6    ac0    ac_addr_pkts         55964     ac_data_pkts         69573
7    ac0    mem_bank0_rds        39518     mem_bank0_wrs        3050
8    ac0    addr_pkts            84103     data_pkts            108542
9    ac0    ac_addr_pkts         256737    ac_data_pkts         317145
#
```

We specified three pairs of events, with an interval of one second and a count of nine. Each event pair was measured three times, for one second. We would study the `event0` and `event1` columns to see what the `pic` values represent.

For additional information on `busstat`, see `busstat(1M)`.

## 8.4.5 Example: UltraSPARC T1

UltraSPARC T1 processors also have a number of DRAM performance counters, the most important of which are read and write operations to each of the four memory banks. The tool to display DRAM counters is the busstat command. Be sure to type the command on a single line.

```
# busstat -w dram0,pic0=mem_reads,pic1=mem_writes -w dram1,pic0=mem_reads,pic1=mem_
writes
-w dram2,pic0=mem_reads,pic1=mem_writes -w dram3,pic0=mem_reads,pic1=mem_writes
time dev event0 pic0 event1 pic1
1 dram0 mem_reads 16104 mem_writes 8086
1 dram1 mem_reads 15953 mem_writes 8032
1 dram2 mem_reads 15957 mem_writes 8069
1 dram3 mem_reads 15973 mem_writes 8001
```

The counts are of 64-byte lines read or written to memory; to get the total bandwidth, add all four counters together. In the preceding example, the system is roughly reading (4 * 16000 * 64) = 4096000 bytes / 3.9 megabytes per second and writing (4 * 8000 * 64 bytes) = 2048000 bytes / 1.95 megabytes per second.

# Kernel Monitoring

In this chapter, we explore tools that can be used to monitor performance of kernel subsystems, drivers and other loadable kernel modules.

## 9.1 Tools for Kernel Monitoring

There are several tools available in the Solaris environment to measure and optimize the performance of kernel code and device drivers. The following tasks are the most common:

- Identify the reason for high system time (`mpstat %sys`). We can use a kernel profile (DTrace or `lockstat -I`) or trace (DTrace) to produce a ranked list of system calls, functions, modules, drivers, or subsystems that are contributing to system time.

- Identify the reason for nonscalability on behalf of a system call. Typically, our approach is to observe the wall clock time and CPU cycles of a code path as load is increased. We can use DTrace to identify both the CPU cycles and end-to-end wall clock time of a code path and quickly focus on the problem areas.

- Understand the execution path of a subsystem to assist in diagnosis of a performance or functional problem. We can use DTrace to map the code's actual execution graph.

- Identify the performance characteristics and optimize a particular code path. By measuring the CPU consumption of the code path, we can identify costly code or functions and made code-level improvements. The `lockstat` kernel profile can pinpoint CPU cycles down to individual instructions if required. DTrace can help us understand key performance factors for arbitrary code paths.

- Identify the source of lock contention. We can use the `lockstat(1M)` utility and DTrace lockstat provider to quantify and attribute lock contention to source.

- Examine interrupt statistics. We can use `vmstat -i` or `intrstat` (DTrace).

## 9.2 Profiling the Kernel and Drivers

The `lockstat` command and DTrace can profile the kernel and so identify hot functions. We begin by discussing `lockstat`'s kernel profile function (the profile capability is buried inside the lock statistics tool). We then briefly mention how we would use DTrace. For a full description of how to use DTrace, refer to Chapter 10.

### 9.2.1 Profiling the Kernel with `lockstat -I`

The `lockstat` utility contains a kernel profiling capability. By specifying the `-I` option, you instruct the `lockstat` utility to collect kernel function samples from a time-based profile interrupt, rather than from lock contention events. The following profile summarizes sampled instruction addresses and can optionally be reduced to function names or other specific criteria.

```
# lockstat -kIi997 sleep 10
Profiling interrupt: 10596 events in 5.314 seconds (1994 events/sec)
Count indv cuml rcnt     nsec CPU+PIL              Caller
-------------------------------------------------------------------------------
 5122  48%  48% 1.00     1419 cpu[0]               default_copyout
 1292  12%  61% 1.00     1177 cpu[1]               splx
 1288  12%  73% 1.00     1118 cpu[1]               idle
  911   9%  81% 1.00     1169 cpu[1]               disp_getwork
  695   7%  88% 1.00     1170 cpu[1]               i_ddi_splhigh
  440   4%  92% 1.00     1163 cpu[1]+11            splx
  414   4%  96% 1.00     1163 cpu[1]+11            i_ddi_splhigh
  254   2%  98% 1.00     1176 cpu[1]+11            disp_getwork
   27   0%  99% 1.00     1349 cpu[0]               uiomove
   27   0%  99% 1.00     1624 cpu[0]               bzero
   24   0%  99% 1.00     1205 cpu[0]               mmrw
   21   0%  99% 1.00     1870 cpu[0]               (usermode)
    9   0%  99% 1.00     1174 cpu[0]               xcopyout
    8   0%  99% 1.00      650 cpu[0]               ktl0
    6   0%  99% 1.00     1220 cpu[0]               mutex_enter
    5   0%  99% 1.00     1236 cpu[0]               default_xcopyout
    3   0% 100% 1.00     1383 cpu[0]               write
    3   0% 100% 1.00     1330 cpu[0]               getminor
    3   0% 100% 1.00      333 cpu[0]               utl0
    2   0% 100% 1.00      961 cpu[0]               mmread
    2   0% 100% 1.00     2000 cpu[0]+10            read_rtc
```

In the example, we use -I to request a kernel profile at 997 hertz (-i997) and to coalesce instruction addresses into function names (-k). If we didn't specify -k, then we would see samples with instruction level resolution, as function+offset.

In the next example, we request that stack backtraces be collected for each sample, to a depth of 10 (-s 10). With this option, lockstat prints a summary of each unique stack as sampled.

```
# lockstat -i997 -Iks 10 sleep 30
Profiling interrupt: 119800 events in 30.038 seconds (3988 events/sec)
-------------------------------------------------------------------------------
Count indv cuml rcnt     nsec CPU+PIL                Hottest Caller
29919  25%  25% 0.00     5403 cpu[2]                 kcopy

      nsec ------ Time Distribution ------ count     Stack
      1024 |                                2        uiomove
      2048 |                                18       rdip
      4096 |                                25       ufs_read
      8192 |@@@@@@@@@@@@@@@@@@@@@@@@@@@@@@   29853    fop_read
     16384 |                                21       pread64
                                                     sys_syscall32 --------------------
-------------------------------------------------------------------------------
Count indv cuml rcnt     nsec CPU+PIL                Hottest Caller
29918  25%  50% 0.00     5386 cpu[1]                 kcopy

      nsec ------ Time Distribution ------ count     Stack
      4096 |                                38       uiomove
      8192 |@@@@@@@@@@@@@@@@@@@@@@@@@@@@@@   29870    rdip
     16384 |                                10       ufs_read
                                                     fop_read
                                                     pread64
                                                     sys_syscall32
-------------------------------------------------------------------------------
Count indv cuml rcnt     nsec CPU+PIL                Hottest Caller
29893  25%  75% 0.00     5283 cpu[3]                 kcopy

      nsec ------ Time Distribution ------ count     Stack
      1024 |                                140      uiomove
      2048 |                                761      rdip
      4096 |@                               1443     ufs_read
      8192 |@@@@@@@@@@@@@@@@@@@@@@@@@@@@@    27532    fop_read
     16384 |                                17       pread64
                                                     sys_syscall32
-------------------------------------------------------------------------------
```

## 9.3 Analyzing Kernel Locks

Locks are used in the kernel to serialize access to critical regions and data structures. If contention occurs around a lock, a performance problem or scalability limitation can result. Two main tools analyze lock contention in the kernel: lockstat(1M) and the DTrace lockstat provider.

## 9.3.1 Adaptive Locks

Adaptive locks enforce mutual exclusion to a critical section and can be acquired in most contexts in the kernel. Because adaptive locks have few context restrictions, they constitute the vast majority of synchronization primitives in the Solaris kernel. These locks are adaptive in their behavior with respect to contention. When a thread attempts to acquire a held adaptive lock, it determines if the owning thread is currently running on a CPU. If the owner is running on another CPU, the acquiring thread spins. If the owner is not running, the acquiring thread blocks.

To observe adaptive locks, first consider the spin behavior. Locks that spin excessively burn CPU cycles, behavior that is manifested as high system time. If you notice high system time with `mpstat(1M)`, spin locks might be a contributor. You can confirm the amount of system time that results from spinning lock contention by looking at the kernel function profile; spinning locks show up as `mutex_*` functions high in the profile. To identify which lock is spinning and which functions are causing the lock contention, use `lockstat(1M)` and the DTrace `lockstat` provider.

Adaptive locks that block yield the CPU, and excessive blocking results in idle time and nonscalability. To identify which lock is blocking and which functions are causing the lock contention, again use `lockstat(1M)` and DTrace.

## 9.3.2 Spin Locks

Threads cannot block in some kernel contexts, such as high-level interrupt context and any context-manipulating dispatcher state. In these contexts, this restriction prevents the use of adaptive locks. Spin locks are instead used to effect mutual exclusion to critical sections in these contexts. As the name implies, the behavior of these locks in the presence of contention is to spin until the lock is released by the owning thread.

Locks that spin excessively burn CPU cycles, manifested as high system time. If you notice high system time with `mpstat(1M)`, spin locks might be a contributor. You can confirm the amount of system time that results from spinning lock contention by looking at the kernel function profile; spinning locks show up as `mutex_*` functions high in the profile. To identify which lock is spinning and which functions are causing the lock contention, use `lockstat(1M)` and the DTrace `lockstat` provider.

## 9.3.3 Reader/Writer Locks

Readers/writer locks enforce a policy of allowing multiple readers or a single writer—but not both—to be in a critical section. These locks are typically used for structures that are searched more frequently than they are modified and for which there is substantial time in the critical section. If critical section times are short, readers/writer locks implicitly serialize over the shared memory used to implement the lock, giving them no advantage over adaptive locks. See rwlock(9F) for more details on readers/writer locks.

Reader/writer locks that block yield the CPU, and excessive blocking results in idle time and nonscalability. To identify which lock is blocking and which functions are causing the lock contention, use lockstat(1M) and the DTrace lockstat provider.

### 9.3.4 Thread Locks

A thread lock is a special kind of spin lock that locks a thread in order to change thread state.

### 9.3.5 Analyzing Locks with lockstat

The lockstat command provides summary or detail information about lock events in the kernel. By default (without the -I as previously demonstrated), it provides a systemwide summary for lock *contention* events for the duration of a command that is supplied as an argument. For example, to make lockstat sample for 30 seconds, we often use sleep 30 as the command. Note that lockstat doesn't actually introspect the sleep command; it's only there to control the sample window.

We recommend starting with the -P option, which sorts by the product of the number of contention events with the cost of the contention event (this puts the most resource expensive events at the top of the list).

```
# lockstat -P sleep 30

Adaptive mutex spin: 3486197 events in 30.031 seconds (116088 events/sec)

Count indv cuml rcnt     spin Lock                     Caller
-------------------------------------------------------------------------------
1499963 43%  43% 0.00      84 pr_pidlock               pr_p_lock+0x29
1101187 32%  75% 0.00      24 0xffffffff810cdec0       pr_p_lock+0x50
285012   8%  83% 0.00      27 0xffffffff827a9858       rdip+0x506
...
```

For each type of lock, the total number of events during the sample and the length of the sample period are displayed. For each record within the lock type, the following information is provided:

- **Count.** The number of contention events for this lock.
- **indv.** The percentage that this record contributes to the total sample set.
- **cuml.** A cumulative percentage of samples contributing to the total sample set.

- **rcnt.** Average reference count. This will always be 1 for exclusive locks (mutexes, spin locks, rwlocks held as writer) but can be greater than 1 for shared locks (rwlocks held as reader).

- **nsec or spin.** The average amount of time the contention event occurred for block events or the number of spins (spin locks).

- **Lock.** The address or symbol name of the lock object.

- **CPU+PIL.** The CPU ID and the processor interrupt level at the time of the sample. For example, if CPU 4 is interrupted while at PIL 6, this is reported as cpu[4]+6.

- **Caller.** The calling function and the instruction offset within the function.

To estimate the impact of a lock, multiply Count by the cost. For example, if a blocking event on average costs 48,944,759 ns and the event occurs 1,929 times in a 30-second window, we can assert that the lock is blocking threads for a total of 94 seconds during that period (30 seconds). How is this greater than 30 seconds? Multiple threads are blocking, so because of overlapping blocking events, the total blocking time can be larger than the elapsed time of the sample.

The full output from this example with the -P option follows.

```
# lockstat -P sleep 30

Adaptive mutex spin: 3486197 events in 30.031 seconds (116088 events/sec)

Count indv cuml rcnt     spin Lock                      Caller
-------------------------------------------------------------------------------
1499963 43%  43% 0.00      84 pr_pidlock                pr_p_lock+0x29
1101187 32%  75% 0.00      24 0xffffffff810cdec0        pr_p_lock+0x50
 285012  8%  83% 0.00      27 0xffffffff827a9858        rdip+0x506
 212621  6%  89% 0.00      29 0xffffffff827a9858        rdip+0x134
  98531  3%  92% 0.00     103 0xffffffff9321d480        releasef+0x55
  92486  3%  94% 0.00      19 0xffffffff8d5c4990        ufs_lockfs_end+0x81
  89404  3%  97% 0.00      27 0xffffffff8d5c4990        ufs_lockfs_begin+0x9f
  83186  2%  99% 0.00      96 0xffffffff9321d480        getf+0x5d
   6356  0%  99% 0.00     186 0xffffffff810cdec0        clock+0x4e9
   1164  0% 100% 0.00     141 0xffffffff810cdec0        post_syscall+0x352
    294  0% 100% 0.00      11 0xffffffff801a4008        segmap_smapadd+0x77
    279  0% 100% 0.00      11 0xffffffff801a41d0        segmap_getmapflt+0x275
    278  0% 100% 0.00      11 0xffffffff801a48f0        segmap_smapadd+0x77
    276  0% 100% 0.00      11 0xffffffff801a5010        segmap_getmapflt+0x275
    276  0% 100% 0.00      11 0xffffffff801a4008        segmap_getmapflt+0x275
...
Adaptive mutex block: 3328 events in 30.031 seconds (111 events/sec)
Count indv cuml rcnt     nsec Lock                      Caller
-------------------------------------------------------------------------------
   1929 58%  58% 0.00 48944759 pr_pidlock               pr_p_lock+0x29
    263  8%  66% 0.00    47017 0xffffffff810cdec0       pr_p_lock+0x50
    255  8%  74% 0.00 53392369 0xffffffff9321d480       getf+0x5d
    217  7%  80% 0.00    26133 0xffffffff810cdec0       clock+0x4e9
    207  6%  86% 0.00   227146 0xffffffff827a9858       rdip+0x134
    197  6%  92% 0.00    64467 0xffffffff8d5c4990       ufs_lockfs_begin+0x9f
    122  4%  96% 0.00    64664 0xffffffff8d5c4990       ufs_lockfs_end+0x81
    112  3%  99% 0.00   164559 0xffffffff827a9858       rdip+0x506
```

*continues*

```
Spin lock spin: 3491 events in 30.031 seconds (116 events/sec)
Count indv cuml rcnt     spin Lock                  Caller
-------------------------------------------------------------------------------
 2197  63%  63% 0.00     2151 turnstile_table+0xbd8  disp_lock_enter+0x35
  314   9%  72% 0.00     3129 turnstile_table+0xe28  disp_lock_enter+0x35
  296   8%  80% 0.00     3162 turnstile_table+0x888  disp_lock_enter+0x35
  211   6%  86% 0.00     2032 turnstile_table+0x8a8  disp_lock_enter+0x35
  127   4%  90% 0.00      856 turnstile_table+0x9f8  turnstile_interlock+0x171
  114   3%  93% 0.00      269 turnstile_table+0x9f8  disp_lock_enter+0x35
   44   1%  95% 0.00       90 0xffffffff827f4de0     disp_lock_enter_high+0x13
   37   1%  96% 0.00      581 0xffffffff827f4de0     disp_lock_enter+0x35
...
Thread lock spin: 1104 events in 30.031 seconds (37 events/sec)
Count indv cuml rcnt     spin Lock                  Caller
-------------------------------------------------------------------------------
  487  44%  44% 0.00     1671 turnstile_table+0xbd8  ts_tick+0x26
  219  20%  64% 0.00     1510 turnstile_table+0xbd8  turnstile_block+0x387
   92   8%  72% 0.00     1941 turnstile_table+0x8a8  ts_tick+0x26
   77   7%  79% 0.00     2037 turnstile_table+0xe28  ts_tick+0x26
   74   7%  86% 0.00     2296 turnstile_table+0x888  ts_tick+0x26
   36   3%  89% 0.00      292 cpu[0]+0xf8            ts_tick+0x26
   27   2%  92% 0.00       55 cpu[1]+0xf8            ts_tick+0x26
   11   1%  93% 0.00       26 cpu[3]+0xf8            ts_tick+0x26
   10   1%  94% 0.00       11 cpu[2]+0xf8            post_syscall+0x556
```

## 9.4 DTrace `lockstat` Provider

The `lockstat` provider probes help you discern lock contention statistics or understand virtually any aspect of locking behavior. The `lockstat(1M)` command is actually a DTrace consumer that uses the `lockstat` provider to gather its raw data.

The `lockstat` provider makes available two kinds of probes: content-event probes and hold-event probes.

- Contention-event probes correspond to contention on a synchronization primitive; they fire when a thread is forced to wait for a resource to become available. Solaris is generally optimized for the noncontention case, so prolonged contention is not expected. Use these probes to aid your understanding of those cases in which contention does arise. Because contention is relatively rare, enabling contention-event probes generally doesn't substantially affect performance.

- Hold-event probes correspond to acquiring, releasing, or otherwise manipulating a synchronization primitive. These probes can answer arbitrary questions about the way synchronization primitives are manipulated. Because Solaris acquires and releases synchronization primitives very often (on the order of millions of times per second per CPU on a busy system), enabling hold-event probes has a much higher probe effect than does enabling contention-event probes. While the probe effect induced by enabling the probes can be substantial, it is not pathological, so you can enable them with confidence on production systems.

The `lockstat` provider makes available probes that correspond to the different synchronization primitives in Solaris; these primitives and the probes that correspond to them are discussed in Section 10.6.4.

The provider probes are as follows:

- **Adaptive lock probes.** The four lockstat probes are `adaptive-acquire`, `adaptive-block`, `adaptive-spin`, and `adaptive-release`. They are shown for reference in Table 10.7. For each probe, `arg0` contains a pointer to the `kmutex_t` structure that represents the adaptive lock.

  Adaptive locks are much more common than spin locks. The following script displays totals for both lock types to provide data to support this observation.

```
lockstat:::adaptive-acquire
/execname == "date"/
{
        @locks["adaptive"] = count();
}

lockstat:::spin-acquire
/execname == "date"/
{
        @locks["spin"] = count();
}
```

  If we run this script in one window and run a `date(1)` command in another, then when we terminate the DTrace script, we see the following output.

```
# dtrace -s ./whatlock.d
dtrace: script './whatlock.d' matched 5 probes
^C
spin                                                        26
adaptive                                                  2981
```

  As this output indicates, over 99% of the locks acquired from running the `date` command are adaptive locks. It may be surprising that so many locks are acquired in doing something as simple as retrieving a date. The large number of locks is a natural artifact of the fine-grained locking required of an extremely scalable system like the Solaris kernel.

- **Spin lock probes.** The three probes pertaining to spin locks are `spin-acquire`, `spin-spin`, and `spin-release`. They are shown in Table 10.8.
- **Thread locks.** Thread lock hold events are available as spin lock hold-event probes (that is, `spin-acquire` and `spin-release`), but contention events

have their own probe (thread-spin) specific to thread locks. The thread lock
hold-event probe is described in Table 10.9.

- **Readers/writer lock probes.** The probes pertaining to readers/writer locks
  are rw-acquire, rw-block, rw-upgrade, rw-downgrade, rw-release.
  They are shown in Table 10.10. For each probe, arg0 contains a pointer to the
  krwlock_t structure that represents the adaptive lock.

## 9.5 DTrace Kernel Profiling

The profile provider in DTrace identifies hot functions by sampling the kernel
stack activity.

```
# dtrace -n 'profile-997hz / arg0 != 0 / { @ks[stack()]=count() }'
dtrace: description 'profile-997ms ' matched 1 probe
^C

              genunix`syscall_mstate+0x1c7
              unix`sys_syscall32+0xbd
                1

              unix`bzero+0x3
              procfs`pr_read_lwpusage_32+0x2f
              procfs`prread+0x5d
              genunix`fop_read+0x29
              genunix`pread+0x217
              genunix`pread32+0x26
              unix`sys_syscall32+0x101
                1

              unix`kcopy+0x48
              genunix`copyin_nowatch+0x48
              genunix`copyin_args32+0x45
              genunix`syscall_entry+0xcb
              unix`sys_syscall32+0xe1
                1

              unix`sys_syscall32+0xae
                1

              unix`mutex_exit+0x19
              ufs`rdip+0x368
              ufs`ufs_read+0x1a6
              genunix`fop_read+0x29
              genunix`pread64+0x1d7
              unix`sys_syscall32+0x101
                2

              unix`kcopy+0x2c
              genunix`uiomove+0x17f
              ufs`rdip+0x382
              ufs`ufs_read+0x1a6
              genunix`fop_read+0x29
              genunix`pread64+0x1d7
              unix`sys_syscall32+0x101
                13
```

## 9.6 Interrupt Statistics: `vmstat -i`

Another useful measure of kernel activity is the number of received interrupts. A
device may be busy processing a flood of interrupts and consuming significant CPU
time. This CPU time may not appear in the usual by-process view from `prstat`.

The `-i` option of the `vmstat` command obtains interrupt statistics.

```
$ vmstat -i
interrupt              total       rate
------------------------------
clock              272636119        100
hmec0                 726271          0
audiocs                    0          0
fdc0                       8          0
ecppc0                     0          0
------------------------------
Total              273362398        100
```

In this example, the `hmec0` device received 726,271 interrupts. The rate is also
printed, which for the clock interrupt is 100 hertz. This output may be handy,
although the counters that `vmstat` currently uses are of `ulong_t`, which may
wrap and thus print incorrect values if a server is online for several months.

## 9.7 Interrupt Analysis: `intrstat`

The `intrstat` command, new in Solaris 10, uses DTrace. It measures the number
of interrupts and, more importantly, the CPU time consumed servicing interrupts,
by driver instance. This information is priceless and was extremely difficult to
measure on previous versions of Solaris.

In the following example we ran `intrstat` on an UltraSPARC 5 with a 360
MHz CPU and a 100 Mbits/sec interface while heavy network traffic was received.

```
# intrstat 2

      device |       cpu0%tim
-------------+---------------
      hme#0  |       2979 43.5

      device |       cpu0%tim
-------------+---------------
      hme#0  |       2870 42.6
      uata#0 |          0  0.0
...
```

The hme0 instance consumed a whopping 43.5% of the CPU for the first 2-second sample. This value is huge, bearing in mind that the network stack of Solaris 10 is much faster than previous versions. Extrapolating, it seems unlikely that this server could ever drive a gigabit Ethernet card at full speed if one was installed.

The intrstat command should become a regular tool for the analysis of both kernel driver activity and CPU consumption, especially for network drivers.

# PART TWO

# Observability Infrastructure

# 10

# Dynamic Tracing

*Contributed by Jon Haslam*

---

$\mathbb{S}$olaris 10 delivered a revolutionary new subsystem called the Solaris Dynamic Tracing Framework (or DTrace for short). DTrace is an observability technology that allows us, for the first time, to answer virtually every question we ever wanted to ask about the behavior of our systems and applications.

## 10.1 Introduction to DTrace

Before Solaris 10, the Solaris observational toolset was already quite rich; many examples in this book use tools such as truss(1), pmap(1), pstack(1), vmstat(1), iostat(1), and others. However, as rich as each individual tool is, it still provides only limited and fixed insight into one specific area of a system. Not only that, but each of the tools is disjoint in its operation. It's therefore difficult to accurately correlate the events reported by a tool, such as iostat, and the applications that are driving the behavior the tool reports. In addition, all these tools present data in different formats and frequently have very different interfaces. All this conspires to make observing and explaining systemwide behavioral characteristics very difficult indeed.

Solaris dynamic tracing makes these issues a thing of the past. With one subsystem we can observe, quite literally, any part of system and application behavior, ranging from every instruction in an application to the depths of the kernel. A single interface to this vast array of information means that, for the first time ever, subsystem boundaries can be crossed seamlessly, allowing easy observation of cause and effect across an entire system. For example, requests such as "show me the applications that caused writes to a given device" or "display the kernel code path that was executed as a result of a given application function call" are now trivial to fulfill. With DTrace we can ask almost any question we can think of.

With DTrace we can create custom programs that contain arbitrary questions and then dynamically modify application and kernel code to provide immediate answers to these questions. All this can be done on live production environments in complete safety, and by default the subsystem is available only to the superuser (uid 0). When not explicitly enabled, DTrace has zero probe effect and the system acts as if DTrace were not present at all.

DTrace has its own scripting language with which we can express the questions we want to ask; this language is called "D." It provides most of the richness of "C" plus some tracing-specific additions.

The aim of this chapter is not to go into great detail on the language and architecture but to highlight the essential elements that you need to understand when reading this book. For a thorough treatment of the subject, read the *Solaris Dynamic Tracing Guide* available at http://docs.sun.com.

## 10.2 The Basics

As an introduction to DTrace and the D language, let's start with a simple example.

The truss(1) utility, a widely used observational tool, provides a powerful means to observe system and library call activity. However, it has many drawbacks: It operates on one process at a time, with no systemwide capability; it is verbose with fixed-output format; and it offers its users a limited choice of questions. Moreover, because of the way it works, truss can reduce application performance. Every time a thread in a process makes a system call, truss stops the thread through procfs, records the arguments for the system call, and then restarts the thread. When the system call returns, truss again stops the thread, records the return code, and then restarts it. It's not hard to see how this can have quite an impact on performance. DTrace, however, operates completely in the kernel, collecting relevant data at the source. Because the application is no longer controlled through procfs, the impact on the application is greatly minimized.

With DTrace we can surpass the power of truss with our first script, which in itself is almost the simplest script that can be written. Here's a D script, truss.d, that lets us observe all global system call activity.

```
#!/usr/sbin/dtrace -s

syscall:::entry
{
}
```

There are a few important things to note from the above example.
The first line of the program is as follows:

```
#!/usr/sbin/dtrace -s
```

This specifies that the dtrace(1M) program is to be used as the interpreter, and the -s argument tells dtrace that what follows is a D program that it should execute. Note: The interpreter line for all the examples in this chapter is omitted for the sake of brevity, but it is still very much required.

Next follows a description of the events we are interested in looking at. Here we are interested in what happens every time a system call is made.

```
syscall:::entry
```

This is an example of a probe *description*. In DTrace, a *probe* is a place in the system where we want to ask a question and record some pertinent data. Such data might include function arguments, stack traces, timestamps, file names, function names, and the like.

The braces that follow the probe specification contain the *actions* that are to be executed when the associated probe is encountered. Actions are generally focused on recording items of data; we'll see examples of these shortly. This example contains no actions, so the default behavior is to just print the name of the probe that has been hit (or *fired* in tracing parlance) as well as the CPU it executed on and a numerical ID for the probe.

Let's run our simple script.

```
sol10# ./truss.d
dtrace: script './truss.d' matched 225 probes
CPU     ID                FUNCTION:NAME
  0     13                 write:entry
  0    103                 ioctl:entry
  0    317               pollsys:entry
  0     13                 write:entry
  0    103                 ioctl:entry
  0    317               pollsys:entry
^C
```

As you can see from the preceding output, the syscall:::entry probe description enabled 225 different probes in this instance; this is the number of system calls currently available on this system. We don't go into the details now of exactly what this means, but be aware that, when the script is executed, the kernel is *instrumented* according to our script. When we stop the script, the instrumentation is removed and the system acts in the same way as a system without DTrace installed.

The final thing to note here is that the execution of the script was terminated with a Control-C sequence (as shown with the ^C in the above output). A script can itself issue an explicit `exit()` call to terminate; in the absence of this, the user will have to type Control-C.

The preceding script gives a global view of all system call activity. To focus our attention on a single process, we can modify the script to use a *predicate*. A predicate is associated with a probe description and is a set of conditions placed between forward slashes ("/"). For example:

```
#pragma D option quiet

syscall:::entry
/pid == 660/
{
        printf("%-15s: %8x %8x %8x %8x %8x %8x\n",
            probefunc, arg0, arg1, arg2, arg3, arg4, arg5);
}
```

If the expressions within the predicate evaluate to true, then we are interested in recording some data and the associated actions are executed. However, if they evaluate to false, then we choose not to record anything and return. In this case, we want to execute the actions only if the thread making the system call belongs to pid 660.

We made a couple of additions to the D script. The `#pragma` just tells DTrace not to print anything unless it's explicitly asked to do so (the `-q` option to `dtrace(1M)` does the same thing). Second, we added some output formatting to `printf()` to display the name of the system call that was made and its first six arguments, whether the system call has them or not. We look more at output formatting and arguments later. Here is some example output from our script.

```
s10## ./truss.d
write         :       16    841b548           8     0 831de790           8
read          :       16   f942dcc0          20     0 831de790          20
write         :       16    841b548           8     0 831de790           8
read          :       16   f942dcc0          20     0 831de790          20
pollsys       : f942dce0          1   f942dbf0     0 831de790   f942dbf0
write         :        5   feab36b1           1     e 81b31250           1
pollsys       :   8046ef0          2    8046f88     0 81b31250    8046f88
```

With a few lines of D we have created the functional equivalent of `truss -p`.

Now that we've seen a simple example, let's look at some of the basic building blocks of DTrace.

## 10.2.1  D Program Structure

D is a block-structured language similar in layout to `awk`. A program consists of one or more clauses that take the following form:

```
probe
/ optional predicates /
{
        optional action statements;
}
```

Each clause describes one or more probes to enable, an optional predicate, and any actions to associate with the probe specification. When a D program contains several clauses that enable the same probe, the clauses are executed in the order in which they appear in the program. For example:

```
syscall::read:entry
{
        printf("A");
}

syscall::read:entry
{
        printf(" B");
        exit(1);
}
```

The above script contains two clauses; each clause enables the read(2) system call entry probe. When this script is executed, the system is modified dynamically to insert our tracing actions into the read() system call. When any application next makes a read() call, the first clause is executed, causing the character "A" to be displayed. The next clause is executed immediately after the first, and the sequence "B" is also displayed. The exit(1) call terminates the tracing session, an action that in turn causes the enabled probes and their actions to be removed. The system then returns to its default state. Executing the script we see this:

```
sol10# ./read.d
A B
```

The preceding explanation is a huge simplification of what actually happens when we execute a D script. The important thing to note here is the dynamic nature of the modifications that are made when a D script is executed. The modifications made to the system (the "instrumentation") exist just for the lifetime of the script. When no DTrace scripts are running, the system acts just as if DTrace were not installed.

## 10.2.2 Providers and Probes

By default, DTrace provides tens of thousands of probes that you can enable to gain unparalleled insight into the behavior of a system (use `dtrace -l` to list them all). Each probe can be referred to by a unique numerical ID or by a more commonly used human-readable one that consists of four colon-separated fields. These are defined as follows:

```
provider:module:function:name
```

- **Provider.** The name of the DTrace provider that created this probe. A provider is essentially a kernel module that creates groups of probes that are related in some way (for example, kernel functions, an application's functions, system calls, timers).
- **Module.** The name of the module to which this probe belongs if the probe is associated with a program location. For kernel probes, it is the name of the module (for example, `ufs`); for applications, it is a library name (for example, `libc.so`).
- **Function.** The name of the function that this probe is associated with if it belongs to a program location. Kernel examples are `ufs_write()` and `clock()`; a userland (a program running in user-mode) example is the `printf()` function of `libc`.
- **Name.** The name component of the probe. It generally gives an idea of its meaning. Examples include `entry` or `return` for kernel function calls, `start` for an I/O probe, and `on-cpu` for a scheduling probe.

Note two key facts about probe specifications:

- If any field in a probe specification is empty, that field matches any value (that is, it acts like a wildcard).
- `sh(1)`-like pattern matching is supported.

Table 10.1 lists examples of valid probe descriptions.

**Table 10.1** Examples of DTrace Probe Descriptions

| Probe Description | Meaning |
| --- | --- |
| `fbt:ufs:ufs_write:entry` | The `ufs_write()` kernel function's entry point |
| `fbt:nfs::` | All the probes in the kernel `nfs` module |
| `syscall::write:entry` | The `write()` system call entry point |
| `syscall::*read*:entry` | All the matches of `read`, `readlink`, `readv`, `pread`, and `pread64` system calls |
| `syscall:::` | All system call entry and return probes |
| `io:::start` | All the places in the kernel from which a physical I/O can occur |
| `sched:::off-cpu` | All the places in kernel where a currently executing thread is taken off the CPU |

Although it isn't necessary to specify all the fields in a probe, the examples in this book do so in order to remove any ambiguity about which probes are being enabled. Also note that a comma-separated list of probes can be used to associate multiple probes with the same predicate and actions.

In previous examples we saw the syscall provider being used to ask questions concerning system call usage. Exactly what is a provider and what is its relationship to a probe? A provider creates the probes that are essentially the individual system points at which we ask questions. There are a number of providers, each able to instrument a different part of the system.

The following providers are of special interest to us:

- **fbt.** The Function Boundary Tracing provider places probes at the entry and return point of virtually every kernel function. This provider illuminates the operation of the Solaris kernel and is used extensively in this book. Its full power is realized when it is used in conjunction with the Solaris source code.

- **pid.** This provider probes for userland processes at function entry, function return, and even down to the instruction level.

- **syscall.** This provider probes at the entry and return point of every system call.

- **profile.** This provider gives us timer-driven probes. The timers can be specified at any resolution from nanoseconds to days and can interrupt all CPUs or just one.

- **sdt.** The Statically Defined Tracing provider enables programmers to place probes at arbitrary locations in their code and to choose probe names that convey specific meaning. (For example, a probe named `transmit-start` means more to most observers than the function name in which it sits.)

The following providers leverage the `sdt` provider to grant powerful observability into key Solaris functional areas:

- **sched.** This provider affords a group of probes for scheduling-related events. Such events include a thread being placed on the CPU, taken off the CPU, put to sleep, or woken up.
- **io.** This provider probes for I/O-related events. Such events include I/O starts, I/O completion, and I/O waits.
- **proc.** The probes of the `proc` provider examine process creation and life cycle events. Such events include `fork`, `exec`, thread creation, and signal send and receive.
- **vminfo.** The `vminfo` provider is layered on top of the kstat updates to the vm kstat. Every time an update is made to a member of the vm kstat, a probe is fired.
- **sysinfo.** The `sysinfo` provider is also layered on top of the kstat updates, in this case, to the sys kstat. Every time an update is made to a member of the sys kstat, a probe is fired.

## 10.2.3 Aggregations

The `syscall` example used earlier is simple and powerful. However, the output quickly becomes voluminous and overwhelming with thousands of lines generated in seconds. It rapidly becomes difficult to discern patterns of activity in the data, such as might be perceived in a view of all system calls sorted by count. Historically, we would have generated our data and post-processed this by using tools such as `awk(1)` or `perl(1)`, but that approach is laborious and time wasting. DTrace enables us to succinctly specify how to group vast amounts of data so that we can easily observe such patterns. The mechanism that does this is termed an aggregation. We use aggregations to refine our initial script.

```
syscall:::entry
{
        @sys[probefunc] = count();
}
```

And here is the output now.

```
sol10# ./truss.d
dtrace: script './truss.d' matched 225 probes
^C

  <output elided>
  fcntl
  xstat                                                                   1113
  lwp_park                                                                2767
  setcontext                                                              4593
  lwp_sigmask                                                             4599
  write                                                                   7429
  setitimer                                                               8234
  writev                                                                  8444
  ioctl                                                                  17718
  pollsys                                                               135603
  read                                                                  141379
```

Instead of seeing every system call as it is made, we are now presented with a table of system calls sorted by count: over 330,000 system calls presented in several lines!

The concept of an aggregation is simple. We want to associate the value of a function with an arbitrary element in an array. In our example, every time a system call probe is fired, the name of the system call is used (using the *probefunc* built-in variable) to index an associative array. The result of the count() function is then stored in this element of the array (this simply adds 1 to an internal variable for the index in the array and so effectively keeps a running total of the number of times this system call has been entered). In that way, we do not focus on data at individual probe sites but succinctly collate large volumes of data.

An aggregation can be split into two basic components: on the left side, a named associative array that is preceded by the @ symbol; on the right side, an aggregating function.

```
@name [ keys ] = function();
```

An aggregating function has the special property that it produces the same result when applied to a set of data as when applied to subsets of that data and then again to that set of results. A simple example of this is finding the minimum value of the set [5, 12, 4, 7, 18]. Applying the min() function to the whole set gives the result of 4. Equally, computing the minimum value of two subsets [5, 12] and [4, 7, 18] produces 5 and 4. Applying min() again to [5, 4] yields 4.

Several aggregating functions in DTrace and their results are listed below.

- **count.** Returns the number of times called.
- **avg.** Returns the mean of its arguments. The following example displays the average write size that each process makes. The third argument to the write(2) system call is the size of the write being made. Since arguments are indexed from 0, arg2 is therefore the size of the write.

```
syscall::write:entry
{
        @sys[execname] = avg(arg2);
}

sol10# ./avg.d
dtrace: script './avg.d' matched 1 probe
^C

  ls                                                                  101
  egrep                                                               162
  gnome-panel                                                         169
  gnome-terminal                                                      290
  soffice.bin                                                         309
  metacity                                                            334
  battstat-applet-                                                    366
  init                                                                412
  mozilla-bin                                                        1612
  gconfd-2                                                          27763
```

- **sum.** Returns the total value of its arguments.

- **max.** Returns the maximum value of its arguments.

- **min.** Returns the minimum value of its arguments.

- **quantize.** Stores the specified argument in the appropriate bucket in a power-of-2 series.

The following example stores in the appropriate bucket the size of the memory requested in the call to `malloc()`.

```
pid$1:libc:malloc:entry
{
        @["malloc sizes"] = quantize(arg0);
}

sol10# ./malloc.d 658
dtrace: script './malloc.d' matched 1 probe
^C

  malloc sizes
            value  ------------ Distribution ------------ count
                2 |                                         0
                4 |@@                                       405
                8 |@@@@                                     886
               16 |@@@@@@@                                  1673
               32 |@                                        205
               64 |@@@@@@                                   1262
              128 |@@@@@@@                                  1600
              256 |@@@@@@@                                  1632
              512 |                                         3
             1024 |                                         5
             2048 |@@@@                                     866
             4096 |                                         10
             8192 |@@@                                      586
            16384 |                                         0
```

The example shows that 1673 memory allocations between the size of 16 and 31 bytes were requested. The @ character indicates the relative size of each bucket.

- **lquantize.** Linear quantizations are frequently used to drill down on buckets of interest when the quantize() function has previously been used. This time we use a linear range of buckets that goes between two sizes with a specified step size. The example below specifies that calls to malloc() between 4 and 7 bytes in size go in their own bucket.

```
pid$1:libc:malloc:entry
{
        @["malloc sizes"] = lquantize(arg0,4,8,1);
}

sol10# ./lmalloc.d 658
dtrace: script './lmalloc.d' matched 1 probe
^C

  malloc sizes
           value  ---------- - Distribution ------------- count
            < 4 |                                          6
              4 |@                                         423
              5 |                                          0
              6 |@                                         400
              7 |                                          0
           >= 8 |@@@@@@@@@@@@@@@@@@@@@@@@@@@@@@@@@@@@@@@@@  18452
```

## 10.2.4 Variables

Having looked at aggregations, we now come to the two basic data types provided by D: associative arrays and scalar variables. An associative array stores data elements that can be accessed with an arbitrary name, known as a key or an index. This differs from normal, fixed-size arrays in a number of different ways:

- There are no predefined limits on the number of elements in the array.
- The elements can be indexed with an arbitrary key and not just with integer keys.
- The storage for the array is not preallocated or contained in consecutive storage locations.

Associative arrays in D commonly keep a history of events that have occurred in the past to use in controlling flow in scripts. The following example uses an associative array, arr, to keep track of the largest writes made by applications.

```
syscall::write:entry
/arr[execname] < arg2/
{
        printf("%d byte write: %s\n", arg2, execname);
        arr[execname] = arg2;
}
```

The actions of the clause are executed if the write size, stored in `arg2`, is larger than that stored in the associative array `arr` for a given application. If the predicate evaluates to `true`, then this is the largest write seen for this application. The actions record this by first printing the size of the write and then by updating the element in the array with the new maximum write size.

D is similar to languages such as C in its implementation of scalar variables, but a few differences need to be highlighted. The first thing to note is that in the D language, variables do not have to be declared in advance of their use, much the same as in `awk(1)` or `perl(1)`. A variable comes into existence when it first has a value assigned to it; its type is inferred from the assigned value (you are allowed to declare variables in advance but doing so isn't necessary). There is no explicit memory management in D, much as in the Java programming language. The storage for a variable is allocated when the variable is declared, and deallocated when the value of 0 is assigned to the variable.

The D language provides three types of variable scope: global, thread-local, and clause-local. Thread-local variables provide separate storage for each thread for a given variable and are referenced with the `self->` prefix.

```
fbt:ufs:ufs_write:entry
{
        self->in = timestamp;
}
```

In the clause above, every different thread that executes the `ufs_write()` function has its own copy of a variable named `in`. Its type is the same as the timestamp built-in variable, and it holds the value that the timestamp built-in variable had when the thread started executing the actions in the clause. This is a nanosecond value since an arbitrary time in the past.

A common use of thread-local variables is to highlight a sequence of interest for a given thread and also to associate data with a thread during that sequence. The following example uses the `sched` provider to record, by application, all the time that a specified user (UID 1003) spent executing.

```
sched:::on-cpu
/uid == 1003/
{
        self->ts = timestamp;
}

sched:::off-cpu
/self->ts/
{
        @time[execname] = sum(timestamp - self->ts);
        self->ts = 0;
}
```

The above D script contains two clauses. The first one uses the `sched:::on-cpu` probe to enable a probe at every point in the kernel where a thread can be placed onto a processor and run. The predicate attached to this probe specifies that the actions are only to be executed if the uid of the thread is 1003. The action merely stores the current timestamp in nanoseconds by assigning the `timestamp` built-in variable to a thread-local variable, `self->ts`.

The second clause uses the `sched:::off-cpu` probe to enable a probe at every location in the kernel where a thread can be taken off the CPU. The `self->ts` variable in the predicate ensures that only threads owned by uid 1003 that have already been through the `sched:::on-cpu` probe shall execute the following actions. Why couldn't we just predicate on uid == 1003 as in the first clause? Well, we want to ensure that any thread executing the following actions has already been through the first clause so that its `self->ts` variable is set. If it hasn't been set, we will end up storing a huge value in the `@time` aggregation because `self->ts` will be 0! Using a thread-local variable in predicates like this to control flow in a D script is a common technique that we frequently use in this book.

```
sol10# ./sched.d
dtrace: script './sched.d' matched 6 probes
^C

  cat                                                    1247134
  xterm                                                  1830446
  ksh                                                    3909045
  stdlibfilt                                             5499630
  make                                                  60092218
  sh                                                   158049977
  sed                                                  162507340
  CC                                                   304925644
  ir2hf                                                678855289
  sched                                               2600916929
  ube_ipa                                             2851647754
  ccfe                                                5879225939
  ube                                                 7942433397
```

The preceding example can be enhanced with the profile provider to produce output at a given periodic rate. To produce output every 5 seconds, we can just add the following clause:

```
profile:::tick-5s
{
        printa(@time);
        trunc(@time);
}
```

The profile provider sets up a probe that fires every 5 seconds on a single CPU. The two actions used here are commonly used when periodically displaying aggregation data:

- **printa().** This function prints aggregation data. This example uses the default formatting, but we can control output by using modifiers in much the same way as with `printf()`. Note that we refer to the aggregation result (that is, the value returned from the aggregation function) by using the @ formatting character with the appropriate modifier. The above `printa()` could be rewritten with

```
printa("%-56s %@10d", @time);
```

- **trunc().** This function truncates an aggregation or removes its current contents altogether. The `trunc()` action deletes all the keys and the aggregation results if no second, optional, value is given. Specifying a second argument, $n$, removes all the keys and the aggregation values in the aggregation apart from the top $n$ values.

## 10.2.5  Probe Arguments

In DTrace, probe arguments are made available through one or two mechanisms, depending on which provider is responsible for the probe:

- **args[].** The `args[]` array presents a typed array of arguments for the current probe. `args[0]` is the first argument, `args[1]` the second, and so on. The providers whose probe arguments are presented through the `args[]` array include `fbt`, `sched`, `io`, and `proc`.
- **arg0 ... arg9.** The `argn` built-in variables are accessible by all probes. They are raw 64-bit integer quantities and, as such, must be cast to the appropriate type.

For an example of argument usage, let's look at a script based on the `fbt` provider. The Solaris kernel, like any other program, is made up of many functions that offer well-defined interfaces to perform specific operations. We often want to ask pertinent questions upon entry to a function, such as, What was the value of its third argument? or upon exit from a function, What was the return value? For example:

```
fbt:ufs:ufs_read:entry
/uid == 1003/
{
        self->path = stringof(args[0]->v_path);
        self->ts = timestamp;
}

fbt:ufs:ufs_read:return
/self->path != NULL/
{
        @[self->path] = max(timestamp - self->ts);
        self->path = 0;
        self->ts = 0;
}
```

This example looks at all the reads performed through `ufs` file systems by a particular user (UID 1003) and, for each file, records the maximum time taken to carry out the read call. A few new things require further explanation.

The name of the file being read from is stored in the thread-local variable, `self->path`, with the following statement:

```
self->path = stringof(args[0]->v_path);
```

The main point to note here is the use of the `args[]` array to reference the first argument (`args[0]`) of the `ufs_read` function. Using MDB, we can inspect the arguments of `ufs_read`:

```
sol10# mdb -k
Loading modules: [ unix krtld genunix dtrace specfs ufs ip sctp usba uhci fctl s1394 nca
lofs audiosup nfs random sppp crypto ptm ipc ]
> ufs_read::nm -f ctype
C Type
int (*)(struct vnode *, struct uio *, int, struct cred *, struct caller_context *)
```

The first argument to `ufs_read()` is a pointer to a vnode structure (`struct vnode *`). The path name of the file that is represented by that vnode is stored in the `v_path` member of the vnode structure and can be accessed through `args[0]->v_path`. Using MDB again, we inspect the type of the `v_path` member variable.

```
> ::print -t struct vnode v_path
char *v_path
```

The v_path member is a character pointer and needs to be converted to DTrace's native string type. In DTrace a string is a built-in data type. The stringof() action is one of many features that allow easy manipulation of strings. It converts the char * representation of v_path into the DTrace string type.

If the arg0 built-in variable had been used, a cast would be required and would be written as this:

```
self->path = stringof(((struct vnode *)arg0)->v_path);
```

The predicate associated with the ufs_read:return probe ensures that its actions are only executed for files with a non-NULL path name. The action then uses the path name stored in the self->path variable to index an aggregation, and the max() aggregating function tracks the maximum time taken for reads against this particular file. For example:

```
sol10# ./ufs.d
dtrace: script './ufs.d' matched 2 probes
^C

  /lib/ld.so.1                                               3840
  /usr/share/lib/zoneinfo/GB                                 5523
  <output elided>
  /usr/share/man/man1/ls.1                                2599836
  /./usr/bin/more                                         3941344
  /./usr/bin/tbl                                          3988087
  /usr/share/lib/pub/eqnchar                              4397573
  /usr/share/lib/tmac/an                                  5054675
  /./usr/bin/nroff                                        7004599
  /./usr/bin/neqn                                         7021088
  /./usr/bin/col                                          9989462
  /usr/share/man/windex                                  13742938
  /./usr/bin/man                                         17179129
```

Now let's look at a syscall-based example of return probe use. The following script exploits the fact that syscall probes have their return value stored in arg0 and the error code for the call stored in the errno built-in variable.

```
syscall::open*:entry
{
        self->path = arg0;
}
```

*continues*

```
syscall::open*:return
/self->path != NULL && (int)arg0 == -1 && errno == EACCES/
{
        printf("UID %d permission denied to open %s\n",
            uid, copyinstr(self->path));
        self->path = 0;
}
```

The first clause enables probes for the open(2) and open64(2) system calls. It then stores the address of the buffer, which contains the file name to open, in the thread-local variable self->path.

The second clause enables the corresponding syscall return probes. The conditions of interest are laid out in the predicate:

- The stored file name buffer isn't a NULL pointer (self->path != NULL).
- The open failed (arg0 == −1).
- The open failed owing to insufficient permissions (errno == EACCES).

If the above conditions are all true, then a message is printed specifying the UID that induced the condition and the file for which permissions were lacking.

```
sol10# ./open.d
UID 39079 permission denied to open /etc/shadow
```

Finally, a note regarding the copyinstr() action used in the second clause above: All probes, predicates, and associated actions are executed in the kernel, and therefore any data that originates in userland must be copied into the kernel to be used. The buffer that contains the file name to be opened in our example is a buffer that resides in a userland application. For the contents to be printed, the buffer must be copied to the kernel address space and converted into a DTrace string type; this is what copyinstr() does.

## 10.2.6 Mixing Providers

DTrace gives us the freedom to observe interactions across many different subsystems. The following slightly larger script demonstrates how we can follow all the work done in userland and the kernel by a given application function. We can use dtrace -p to attach to and instrument a running process. For example, we can use a script that looks at the function getgr_lookup() in the name services cache daemon. The getgr_lookup() function is called to translate group IDs and group names. Note that here we are interested in the principle of examining a particular function; the actual program and function chosen here are irrelevant.

```
#pragma D option flowindent

pid$target:a.out:getgr_lookup:entry
{
        self->in = 1;
}

pid$target:::entry,
pid$target:::return
/self->in/
{
        printf("(pid)\n");
}

fbt:::entry,
fbt:::return
/self->in/
{
        printf("(fbt)\n");
}

pid$target:a.out:getgr_lookup:return
/self->in/
{
        self->in = 0;
        exit(0);
}
```

The #pragma flowindent directive at the start of the script means that indentation will be increased on entry to a function and reduced on the same function's return. Showing function calls in a nested manner like this makes the output much more readable.

The pid provider instruments userland applications. The process to be instrumented is specified with the $target macro argument, which always expands to the PID of the process being traced when we attach to the process by using the -p option to dtrace(1M).

The second clause enables all the entry and return probes in the nscd process, and the third clause enables every entry and return probe in the kernel. The predicate in both of these clauses specifies that we are only interested in executing the actions if the thread-local self->in variable is set. This variable is set to 1 when nscd's getgr_lookup() function is entered and set to 0 on exit from this function (that is, when the return probe is fired). For example:

```
sol10# dtrace -s ./nscd.d -p `pgrep nscd`
dtrace: script './nscd.d' matched 43924 probes
CPU FUNCTION
  0   -> getgr_lookup                      (pid)
  0     -> mutex_lock                      (pid)
  0       -> mutex_lock_impl               (pid)
  0       <- mutex_lock_impl               (pid)
  0     <- mutex_lock                      (pid)
```

*continues*

```
   0    -> _xstat                          (pid)
   0      -> copyout                       (fbt)
   0      <- kcopy                         (fbt)
   0      -> syscall_mstate                (fbt)
   0         -> gethrtime_unscaled         (fbt)
   0         <- gethrtime_unscaled         (fbt)
   0      <- syscall_mstate                (fbt)
   0      -> syscall_entry                 (fbt)
<output elided>
   0      <- syscall_exit                  (fbt)
   0      -> syscall_mstate                (fbt)
   0         -> gethrtime_unscaled         (fbt)
   0         <- gethrtime_unscaled         (fbt)
   0      <- syscall_mstate                (fbt)
   0    <- _xstat                          (pid)
   0    -> get_hash                        (pid)
   0      -> abs                           (pid)
   0         -> copyout                    (fbt)
   0         <- kcopy                      (fbt)
   0      <- abs                           (pid)
   0    <- get_hash                        (pid)
   0    -> memcpy                          (pid)
   0      -> copyout                       (fbt)
   0      <- kcopy                         (fbt)
   0    <- memcpy                          (pid)
   0    -> mutex_unlock                    (pid)
   0    <- mutex_unlock                    (pid)
   0   | getgr_lookup:return               (pid)
   0  <- getgr_lookup
```

## 10.2.7 Accessing Global Kernel Data

DTrace provides a very useful feature by which we can access symbols defined in the Solaris kernel from within a D script. We can use the backquote character (`) to refer to kernel symbols, and this information can be used to great advantage when we are exploring the behavior of a Solaris kernel. For example, a variable named mpid is declared in the Solaris kernel source to keep track of the last PID that was allocated. It is declared in uts/common/os/pid.c as follows:

```
static pid_t mpid;
```

The following script uses this variable to calculate the rate of process creation on the system and to output a message if it exceeds a given amount (10 processes per second in this case):

```
dtrace:::BEGIN
{
        cnt = `mpid;
}
```

*continues*

```
profile:::tick-1s
/`mpid < cnt+10/
{
        cnt = `mpid;
}

profile:::tick-1s
/`mpid >= cnt+10/
{
        printf("High process creation rate: %d/sec\n", `mpid - cnt);
        cnt = `mpid;
}
```

The first clause uses the BEGIN probe from the dtrace provider to initialize a global variable (cnt) to the current value of the mpid kernel variable.

The BEGIN, END, and ERROR probes are special probes that belong to the dtrace provider. These probes are essentially virtual probes in that they aren't associated with any code location or timer source. The BEGIN probe fires before any other probes when we start the tracing session and allows us to perform tasks such as data initialization. The END probe is called when the tracing session is terminated either with a Control-C or an explicit call to the exit() action. Its main function is to print data collected during the execution of the script. The ERROR probe is less commonly used; it is called upon abnormal termination of the script.

Both of the next two clauses in the previous example enable the profile:::tick-1s probe. The probe fires every second, and the two clauses are executed in the order specified in the script. The important thing to note is that the predicates in the two clauses contain mutually exclusive logic, which ensures that only one of them will be true at any one time—either ten processes have been created in the last second or they haven't!

The predicate in the first profile:::tick-1s clause specifies that its actions should only be executed if fewer than ten processes have been created (the `mpid variable is within ten of its value one second ago as stored in the cnt variable). If fewer than ten processes have been created in the last second, the cnt variable is updated with the current value of mpid.

The actions in the second clause are executed when more than ten processes have been created. If cnt has already been updated in the first clause, then the predicate will be false and the actions are not executed (a message is then printed with the growth rate, and the cnt variable is updated). For example:

```
sol10# ./scope.d
High process creation rate: 30/sec
High process creation rate: 31/sec
High process creation rate: 35/sec
High process creation rate: 35/sec
High process creation rate: 44/sec
High process creation rate: 44/sec
High process creation rate: 20/sec
```

## 10.2.8 Assorted Actions of Interest

DTrace defines numerous actions, only a small percentage of which are used in this book. Actions that you may see used include `normalize()`, `stack()`, and `ustack()`.

- **`normalize()`.** This action effectively divides the values in the aggregation by a supplied normalization factor. A simple example is the use of a `tick-5s` probe to display data that you want displayed as a per-second rate:

```
syscall::read:entry
{
        @reads[probefunc] = count();
}

tick-5s
{
        printa("%s (non normalized) %50@d\n\n", @reads);
        normalize(@reads, 5);
        printa("%s (  normalized  ) %50@d\n", @reads);
        trunc(@reads);
}
```

The above example uses a single aggregation, `@reads`, to store the number of read system calls made. Every 5 seconds the contents of the aggregation are displayed by `printa()` and then divided by 5 to give a per-second value with the `normalize()` action. The normalized aggregation is then printed and its contents are deleted with the `trunc()` action. For example,

```
sol10# ./norm.d
read (non normalized)                                            5012

read (  normalized  )                                            1002
```

- **`stack()`.** This action produces the stack trace of the kernel thread at the time of execution. It commonly indexes aggregations to determine the most common callstacks when at a given probe. It can also be an invaluable tool for learning how the code flow in the kernel works because it gives a ready view of the call sequence up to a given point. The following script and output show the most frequently executed call sequence through the `ufs` file system over a given trace period.

```
fbt:ufs::entry
{
        @ufs[stack()] = count();
}

END
{
        trunc(@ufs, 1);
}

sol10# ./stack.d
dtrace: script './stack.d' matched 419 probes
^C
CPU     ID                              FUNCTION:NAME
  0      2                                    :END


            genunix`fop_lookup+0x18
            genunix`lookuppnvp+0x371
            genunix`lookuppnat+0x11a
            genunix`lookupnameat+0x8b
            genunix`cstatat_getvp+0x16d
            genunix`cstatat64_32+0x48
            genunix`lstat64_32+0x25
            unix`sys_syscall32+0x101
          18650
```

- **ustack().** This action is the equivalent of the stack function for userland applications. The following script and output display the stack trace of the userland application that is generating most of the work in the ufs code.

```
#!/usr/sbin/dtrace -s

fbt:ufs::entry
{
        @ufs[ustack()] = count();
}

END
{
        trunc(@ufs, 1);
}

sol10# ./ustack.d
dtrace: script './stack.d' matched 419 probes
^C
CPU     ID                              FUNCTION:NAME
  0      2                                    :END


            libc.so.1`lstat64+0x7
            libc.so.1`walk+0x44b
            libc.so.1`walk+0x44b
            libc.so.1`walk+0x44b
            libc.so.1`walk+0x44b
            libc.so.1`walk+0x44b
            libc.so.1`nftw64+0x185
            find`main+0x2b6
            find`0x80513d2
          231489
```

The find(1) application is at the top of the list here. The walk() routine is listed multiple times because it is recursively called to walk a file tree.

## 10.3 Inspecting Java Applications with DTrace

This section presents two sample applications that demonstrate the interaction of the Mustang Java HotSpot Virtual Machine and the Solaris 10 DTrace Framework. The first example, Java2Demo, is bundled with the Mustang release and will already be familiar to most developers. Because the hotspot provider is built into the Mustang VM itself, running the application is all that is required to trigger probe activity. The second example is a custom debugging scenario that uses DTrace to find a troublesome line of native code in a Java Native Interface (JNI) application.

The following script, written in the D programming language, defines the set of probes that DTrace will listen to while the Java2Demo application is running. In this case, the only probes of interest are those related to garbage collection.

```
#!/usr/sbin/dtrace -Zs

#pragma D option quiet

self int cnt;

dtrace:::BEGIN
{
        self->cnt = 0;
        printf("Ready..\n");
}

hotspot$1:::gc-begin
/self->cnt == 0/
{
        self->tid = tid;
        self->cnt++;
}

hotspot$1:::*
/self->cnt != 0 /
{
        printf("  tid: %d, Probe: %s\n", tid, probename);
}

hotspot$1:::gc-end
{
        printf("  tid: %d, D-script exited\n", tid);
        exit(0);
}
```

To run this example:

1.  Start the sample application: `java -jar Java2Demo.jar`.
2.  Note the application's PID (11201 for this example).
3.  Start the D script, passing in the PID as its only argument: `hotspot_gc.d 11201`.

The following output shows that DTrace prints the thread ID and probe name as each probe fires in response to garbage collection activity in the VM:

```
Ready..
 tid: 4, Probe: gc-begin
 tid: 4, Probe: mem-pool-gc-begin
 tid: 4, Probe: mem-pool-gc-begin
 tid: 4, Probe: mem-pool-gc-begin
 tid: 4, Probe: mem-pool-gc-begin
 tid: 4, Probe: mem-pool-gc-end
 tid: 4, Probe: mem-pool-gc-end
 tid: 4, Probe: mem-pool-gc-end
 tid: 4, Probe: mem-pool-gc-end
 tid: 4, Probe: mem-pool-gc-begin
 tid: 4, Probe: mem-pool-gc-begin
 tid: 4, Probe: mem-pool-gc-begin
 tid: 4, Probe: mem-pool-gc-begin
 tid: 4, Probe: mem-pool-gc-begin
 tid: 4, Probe: mem-pool-gc-end
 tid: 4, Probe: mem-pool-gc-end
 tid: 4, Probe: mem-pool-gc-end
 tid: 4, Probe: mem-pool-gc-end
 tid: 4, Probe: mem-pool-gc-end
 tid: 4, Probe: gc-end
 tid: 4, D-script exited
```

The next script shows the thread ID (tid) and probe name in all probes; class name, method name and signature in the `"method-compile-begin"` probe; and method name and signature in the `compiled-method-load` probe:

```
#!/usr/sbin/dtrace -Zs

#pragma D option quiet

self int cnt;

dtrace:::BEGIN
{
        self->cnt == 0;
        printf("Ready..\n");
}
```

*continues*

```
hotspot$1:::method-compile-begin
/self->cnt == 0/
{
        self->tid = tid;
        self->cnt++;
        printf(" tid: %d, %21s, %s.%s %s\n", tid, probename,
        copyinstr(arg2), copyinstr(arg4), copyinstr(arg6));
}

hotspot$1:::method-compile-end
/self->cnt > 0/
{
        printf(" tid: %d, %21s\n", tid, probename);
}

hotspot$1:::compiled-method-load
/self->cnt > 0/
{
        printf(" tid: %d, %21s, %s %s\n", tid, probename,
           copyinstr(arg2), copyinstr(arg4));
}

hotspot$1:::vm-shutdown
{
        printf(" tid: %d, %21s\n", tid, probename);
        printf(" tid: %d, D-script exited\n", tid);
        exit(0);
}

hotspot$1:::*
/self->cnt > 0/
{
        printf(" tid: %d, %21s, %s %s\n", tid, probename,
           copyinstr(arg2), copyinstr(arg4));
}
```

## Its output shows:

```
Ready..
tid: 9,    method-compile-begin, sun/java2d/SunGraphics2D.setFont (Ljava/awt/Font;)V
tid: 9,    compiled-method-load, setFont (Ljava/awt/Font;)V
tid: 9,        method-compile-end
tid: 9,    method-compile-begin, sun/java2d/SunGraphics2D validateCompClip
tid: 9,    compiled-method-load, validateCompClip ()V
tid: 9,        method-compile-end
tid: 8,    method-compile-begin, javax/swing/RepaintManager addDirtyRegion0
tid: 8,    compiled-method-load, addDirtyRegion0 (Ljava/awt/Container;IIII)V
tid: 8,        method-compile-end
tid: 9,    method-compile-begin, java/io/BufferedInputStream read
tid: 9,    compiled-method-load, read ()I
tid: 9,        method-compile-end
tid: 8,    method-compile-begin, java/awt/geom/AffineTransform translate
tid: 8,    compiled-method-load, translate (DD)V
tid: 8,        method-compile-end
tid: 9,    method-compile-begin, sun/awt/X11/Native getInt
tid: 9,    compiled-method-load, getInt (J)I
tid: 9,        method-compile-end
tid: 8,    method-compile-begin, sun/java2d/SunGraphics2D setColor
tid: 8,    compiled-method-load, setColor (Ljava/awt/Color;)V
```

*continues*

```
tid: 8,      method-compile-end
tid: 9,      method-compile-begin, sun/reflect/GeneratedMethodAccessor1 invoke
tid: 9,      compiled-method-load, invoke (Ljava/lang/Object;[Ljava/lang/Object;)Ljava/
lang/
Object;
tid: 9,      method-compile-end
tid: 9,      method-compile-begin, sun/java2d/SunGraphics2D constrain
tid: 9,      compiled-method-load, constrain (IIII)V
tid: 9,      method-compile-end
tid: 8,      method-compile-begin, java/awt/Rectangle setLocation
tid: 8,      compiled-method-load, setLocation (II)V
tid: 8,      method-compile-end
tid: 9,      method-compile-begin, java/awt/Rectangle move
tid: 9,      compiled-method-load, move (II)V
tid: 9,      method-compile-end
tid: 8,      method-compile-begin, java/lang/Number <init>
tid: 8,      compiled-method-load, <init> ()V
tid: 8,      method-compile-end
tid: 8,      method-compile-begin, sun/awt/X11/XToolkit getAWTLock
tid: 8,      compiled-method-load, getAWTLock ()Ljava/lang/Object;
tid: 8,      method-compile-end
tid: 17,            vm-shutdown
tid: 17, D-script exited
```

The next example demonstrates a debugging session with the hotspot_jni provider. Consider, if you will, an application that is suspected to be calling JavaTM Native Interface (JNI) functions from within a critical region. A JNI critical region is the space between calls to JNI methods `GetPrimitiveArrayCritical` and `ReleasePrimitiveArrayCritical`. There are some important rules for what is allowed within that space. Chapter 4 of the JNI 5.0 Specification makes it clear that within this region, "Native code should not run for an extended period of time before it calls `ReleasePrimitiveArrayCritical`." In addition, "Native code must not call other JNI functions, or any system call that may cause the current thread to block and wait for another Java thread."

The following D script will inspect a JNI application for this kind of violation:

```
#!/usr/sbin/dtrace -Zs

#pragma D option quiet

self int in_critical_section;

dtrace:::BEGIN
{
        printf("ready..\n");
}

hotspot_jni$1:::ReleasePrimitiveArrayCritical_entry
{
        self->in_critical_section = 0;
}
```

*continues*

```
hotspot_jni$1:::GetPrimitiveArrayCritical_entry

{
        self->in_critical_section = 0;
}

hotspot_jni$1:::*
/self->in_critical_section == 1/
{
        printf("JNI call %s made from JNI critical region\n", probename);
}

hotspot_jni$1:::GetPrimitiveArrayCritical_return
{
        self->in_critical_section = 1;
}

syscall:::entry
/pid == $1 && self->in_critical_section == 1/
{
        printf("system call %s made in JNI critical region\n", probefunc);
}
```

Output:

```
system call brk made in JNI critical section
system call brk made in JNI critical section
system call ioctl made in JNI critical section
system call fstat64 made in JNI critical section
JNI call FindClass_entry made from JNI critical region
JNI call FindClass_return made from JNI critical region
```

From this DTrace output, we can see that the probes FindClass_entry and FindClass_return have fired due to a JNI function call within a critical region. The output also shows some system calls related to calling printf() in the JNI critical region. The native code for this application shows the guilty function:

```
#include "t.h"
/*
 * Class:     t
 * Method:    func
 * Signature: ([I)V
 */
JNIEXPORT void JNICALL Java_t_func
  (JNIEnv *env, jclass clazz, jintArray array) {
    int* value = (int*)env->GetPrimitiveArrayCritical(array, NULL);
    printf("hello world");
    env->FindClass("java/lang/Object");
    env->ReleasePrimitiveArrayCritical(array, value, JNI_ABORT);
}
```

## 10.3.1 Inspecting Applications with the DTrace jstack Action

Mustang is the first release to contain built-in DTrace probes, but support for the DTrace `jstack()` action was actually first introduced in the JavaTM 2 Platform Standard Edition 5.0 Update Release 1. The DTrace `jstack()` action prints mixed-mode stack traces including both Java method and native function names. As an example of its use, consider the following application, which periodically sleeps to mimic hanging behavior:

```
public class dtest{
    int method3(int stop){
        try{Thread.sleep(500);}
        catch(Exception ex){}
        return stop++;
    }
    int method2(int stop){
        int result = method3(stop);
        return result + 1;
    }
    int method1(int arg){
        int stop=0;
        for(int i=1; i>0; i++){
            if(i>arg){stop=i=1;}
            stop=method2(stop);
        }
        return stop;
    }
    public static void main(String[] args) {
        new dtest().method1(10000);
    }
}
```

To find the cause of the hang, the user would want to know the chain of native and Java method calls in the currently executing thread. The expected chain would be something like:

```
<chain of initial VM functions> ->
dtest.main -> dtest.method1 -> dtest.method2 -> dtest.method3 ->
java/lang/Thread.sleep -> <chain of VM sleep functions> ->
<Kernel pool functions>
```

The following D script (`usestack.d`) uses the DTrace `jstack()` action to print the stack trace:

```
#!/usr/sbin/dtrace -s

BEGIN { this->cnt = 0; }
```

*continues*

```
syscall::pollsys:entry
/pid == $1 && tid == 1/
{
    this->cnt++;
    printf("\n\tTID: %d", tid);
    jstack(50);
}

syscall:::entry
/this->cnt == 1/
{
    exit(0);
}
```

And the stack trace itself appears as follows:

```
$ usejstack.d 1344 | c++filt
CPU     ID                      FUNCTION:NAME
  0     316                     pollsys:entry
    TID: 1
    libc.so.1`__pollsys+0xa
    libc.so.1`poll+0x52
    libjvm.so`int os_sleep(long long,int)+0xb4
    libjvm.so`int os::sleep(Thread*,long long,int)+0x1ce
    libjvm.so`JVM_Sleep+0x1bc
    java/lang/Thread.sleep
    dtest.method3
    dtest.method2
    dtest.method1
    dtest.main
    StubRoutines (1)
    libjvm.so`void JavaCalls::call_helper(JavaValue*,methodHandle*,JavaCallArgu-
ments*,Thread*)+0x1b5
    libjvm.so`void os::os_exception_wrapper(void(*)(JavaValue*,methodHandle*,JavaCallAr-
guments*,Thread*),JavaValue*,methodHandle*,Ja
vaCallArguments*,Thread*)+0x18
    libjvm.so`void JavaCalls::call(JavaValue*,methodHandle,JavaCallArgu-
ments*,Thread*)+0x2d
    libjvm.so`void jni_invoke_static(JNIEnv_*,JavaValue*,_jobject*,JNICallType,_
jmethodID*,JNI_ArgumentPush er*,Thread*)+0x214
    libjvm.so`jni_CallStaticVoidMethod+0x244
    java`main+0x642
    StubRoutines (1)
```

The command line shows that the output from this script was piped to the `c++filt` utility, which demangles C++ mangled names making the output easier to read. The DTrace header output shows that the CPU number is 0, the probe number is 316, the thread ID (TID) is 1, and the probe name is `pollsys:entry`, where `pollsys` is the name of the system call. The stack trace frames appear from top to bottom in the following order: two system call frames, three VM frames, five Java method frames, and the remaining frames are VMframes.

It is also worth noting that the DTrace jstack action will run on older releases, such as the Java 2 Platform, Standard Edition version 1.4.2, but hexadecimal addresses will appear instead of Java method names. Such addresses are of little use to application developers.

## 10.3.2 Adding Probes to Pre-Mustang Releases

In addition to the `jstack()` action, it is also possible for pre-Mustang users to add DTrace probes to their release with the help of VM Agents. A VM agent is a shared library that is dynamically loaded into the VM at startup.

VM agents are available for the following releases:

- For The Java 2 Platform, Standard Edition, version 1.4.2, there is a `dvmpi` agent that uses the Java Virtual Machine Profiler Interface (JVMPI).

- For The Java 2 Platform Standard Edition 5.0, there is a `dvmti` agent that uses the JVM Tool Interface (JVM TI).

To obtain the agents, visit the DVM java.net project website at

            `https://solaris10-dtrace-vm-agents.dev.java.net/`

and follow the "Documents and Files" link. The file `dvm.zip` contains both binary and source code versions of the agent libraries.

The following diagram shows an abbreviated view of the resulting directory structure once dvm.zip has been extracted:

```
     build    make    src     test
       |
     ---------------------
      |      |     |      |
    amd64  i386  sparc  sparcv9
      |      |     |      |
     lib    lib   lib    lib
```

Each lib directory contains the pre-built binaries `dvmti.jar`, `libdvmpi.so`, and `libdvmti.so`. If you prefer to compile the libraries yourself, the included README file contains all necessary instructions.

Once unzipped, the VM must be able to find the native libraries on the filesystem. This can be accomplished either by copying the libraries into the release with the other shared libraries, or by using a platform-specific mechanism to help a process find it, such as `LD_LIBRARY_PATH`. In addition, the agent library itself must be able to find all the external symbols that it needs. The ldd utility can be used to verify that a native library knows how to find all required externals.

Both agents accept options to limit the probes that are available, and default to the least possible performance impact. To enable the agents for use in your own applications, run the java command with one of the following additional options:

- `-Xrundvmpi`
- `-Xrundvmti` (for defaults)
- `-Xrundvmpi:all`
- `-Xrundvmti:all` (for all probes)

For additional options, consult the DVM agent `README`. Both agents have their limitations, but `dvmpi` has more, and we recommend using the Java Standard Edition 5.0 Development Kit (JDK 5.0) and the `dvmti` agent if possible.

When using the agent-based approach, keep in mind that:

- The `dvmpi` agent uses JVMPI and only works with one collector. JVMPI has historically been an unstable, experimental interface, and there is a performance penalty associated with using it. JVMPI only works with JDK 5.0 and earlier.
- The `dvmti` agent uses JVM TI and only works with JDK 5.0 and later. It works with all collectors, has little performance impact for most probes, and is a formal and much more stable interface.
- Both agents have some performance penalty for method entry/exit and object alloc/free, less so with the dvmti agent.
- The `dvmti` agent uses BCI (byte code instrumentation), and therefore adds bytecodes to methods (if method entry/exit or object alloc/free probes are active).
- Enabling the allocation event for the JVMTI agent creates an overhead even when DTrace is not attached, and the JVMPI agent severely impacts performance and limits deployment to the serial collector.

Section C.1 provides a D script for testing DVM probes. The DVM agent provider interface, shown in Section C.2, lists all probes provided by `dvmpi` and `dvmti`.

## 10.4 DTrace Architecture

Although DTrace instruments are found at both user and kernel level, the majority of the instrumentation and probe-processing activity take place in the Solaris kernel. This section looks at the basic architecture of DTrace, provides a high-level overview of the process of instrumentation, and examines what happens when this instrumentation is activated.

Figure 10.1 presents the architecture of the DTrace subsystem.

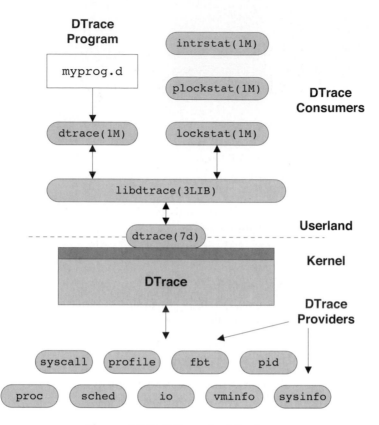

**Figure 10.1** DTrace Architecture

Processes, known as consumers, communicate with the DTrace kernel sub-system through the interfaces provided in the DTrace library, libdtrace(3LIB). Data is transferred between consumers and the kernel by ioctl(2) calls on the dtrace pseudo-device provided by the dtrace(7d) device driver. Several consumers are included in Solaris 10, including lockstat(1M), plockstat(1M), and intrstat(1M), but generalized access to the DTrace facility is provided by the dtrace(1M) consumer. A consumer's basic jobs are to communicate tracing specifications to the DTrace kernel subsystem and to process data resulting from these specifications.

A key component of libdtrace is the D compiler. The role of a compiler is to transform a high-level language into the native machine language of the target processor, the high-level language in this case being D. However, DTrace implements its own virtual machine with its own machine-independent instruction set called DIF (D Intermediate Format), which is the target language for compilation. The tracing scripts we specify are transformed into the DIF language and emulated in the kernel when a probe fires, in much the same way as a Java virtual machine interprets Java bytecodes. One of the most important properties of DTrace is its ability to execute arbitrary code safely on production systems without inducing failure. The use of a runtime emulation environment ensures that errors such as dereferencing null pointers can be caught and dealt with safely.

The basic architecture and flow of the D compiler is shown in Figure 10.2.

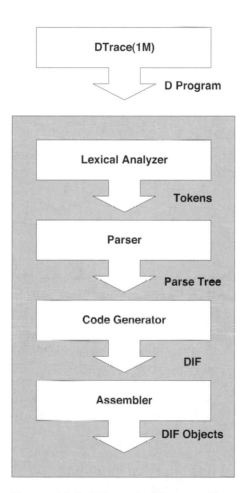

**Figure 10.2** DTrace Architecture Flow

The input D script is split up into tokens by the lexical analyzer; the tokens are used by the parser to build a parse tree. The code generator then makes several passes over the nodes in the parse tree and generates the DIF code for each of the nodes. The assembler then builds DIF Objects (DIFO) for the generated DIF. A

DIFO stores the return type of the D expression encoded by this piece of DIF along with its string and variable tables. All the individual pieces of DIFO that constitute a D program are put together into a file. The format of this file is known as the DTrace Object Format (DOF). This DOF is then injected into the kernel and the system is instrumented.

Take as an example the following D clause:

```
syscall::write:entry
/execname == "foo" && uid == 1001/
{
        self->me = 1;
}
```

This clause contains two DIF objects, one for the predicate and one for the single action. We can use the -S option to dtrace to look at the DIF instructions generated when the clauses are compiled. Three DIF instructions are generated for the single action shown above.

```
OFF OPCODE       INSTRUCTION
00: 25000001     setx DT_INTEGER[0], %r1        ! 0x1
01: 2d050001     stts %r1, DT_VAR(1280)         ! DT_VAR(1280) = "me"
02: 23000001     ret  %r1
```

The DIF virtual machine is a simple RISC-like environment with a limited set of registers and a small instruction set. The first instruction loads register r1 with the first value in a DIFO-specific array of integer constants. The second instruction stores the value that is now in register r1 into the thread-specific variable me, which is referenced through the DIFO-specific variable table. The third instruction returns the value stored in register r1.

The encodings for DIF instructions are called opcodes; it is these that are stored in the DIFO. Each instruction is a fixed 4 bytes, so this DIFO contains 12 bytes of encoded DIF.

The DOF generated by the compilation process is sent to the DTrace kernel subsystem, and the system is instrumented accordingly. When a probe is enabled, an enabling control block (ECB) is created and associated with the probe (see Figure 10.3). An ECB holds some consumer-specific state and also the DIFOs for this probe enabling. If it is the first enabling for this probe, then the framework calls the appropriate provider, instructing it to enable this probe. Each ECB contains the DIFO for the predicates and actions associated with this enabling of the probe. All the enablings for a probe, whether by one or multiple consumers, are represented by ECBs that are chained together and processed in order when the probe is fired. The order is dictated by the sequence in which they appear in a D script and by the time at which that the instrumentation occurs (for example, new ECBs are put at the end of existing ECBs).

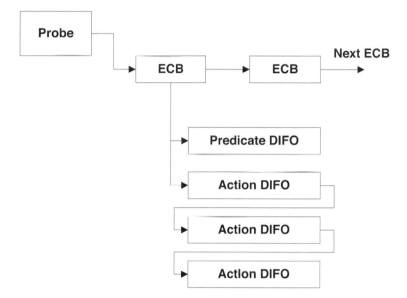

**Figure 10.3** Enabling Control Blocks (ECBs)

The majority of the DTrace subsystem is implemented as a series of kernel modules with the core framework being implemented in dtrace(7d). The framework itself performs no actual instrumentation; that is the responsibility of loadable kernel modules called providers. The providers have intimate knowledge of specific subsystems: how they are instrumented and exactly what can be instrumented (these individual sites being identified by a probe). When a consumer instructs a provider to enable a probe, the provider modifies the system appropriately. The modifications are specific to the provider, but all instrumentation methods achieve the same goal of transferring control into the DTrace framework to carry out the tracing directives for the given probe. This is achieved by execution of the dtrace_probe() function.

As an example of instrumentation, let's look at how the entry point to the ufs_write() kernel function is instrumented by the fbt provider on the SPARC platform. A function begins with a well-known sequence of instructions, which the fbt provider looks for and modifies.

```
sol10# mdb -k
Loading modules: [ unix krtld genunix dtrace specfs ufs ip sctp usba uhci fctl s1394 nca
lofs audiosup nfs random sppp crypto ptm ipc ]
> ufs_write::dis -n 1
ufs_write:                          save        %sp, -0x110, %sp
ufs_write+4:                        stx         %i4, [%sp + 0x8af]
```

The `save` instruction on the SPARC machine allocates stack space for the function to use, and most functions begin with this. If we enable `fbt::ufs_write:entry` in another window, `ufs_write()` now looks like this:

```
> ufs_write::dis -n 1
ufs_write:                          ba,a        +0x2bb388       <dt=0x3d96>
ufs_write+4:                        stx         %i4, [%sp + 0x8af]
```

The `save` instruction has been replaced with a branch to a different location. In this case, the location is the address of the first instruction in `ufs_write + 0x2bb388`. So, looking at the contents of that location, we see the following:

```
> ufs_write+0x2bb388::dis
0x14b36ec:                          save        %sp, -0x110, %sp
0x14b36f0:                          sethi       %hi(0x3c00), %o0
0x14b36f4:                          or          %o0, 0x196, %o0
0x14b36f8:                          mov         %i0, %o1
0x14b36fc:                          mov         %i1, %o2
0x14b3700:                          mov         %i2, %o3
0x14b3704:                          mov         %i3, %o4
0x14b3708:                          mov         %i4, %o5
0x14b370c:                          sethi       %hi(0x11f8000), %g1
0x14b3710:                          call        -0xe7720        <dtrace_probe>
0x14b3714:                          or          %g1, 0x360, %o7
```

The `save` instruction that was replaced is executed first. The next seven instructions set up the input arguments for the call to `dtrace_probe()`, which transfers control to the DTrace framework. The first argument loaded into register o0 is the probe ID for `ufs_write`, which is used to find the ECBs to be executed for this probe. The next five `mov` instructions copy the five input arguments for `ufs_write` so that they appear as arguments to `dtrace_probe()`. They can then be used when probe processing occurs.

This example illustrates how a kernel function's entry point is instrumented. Instrumenting, for example, a system call entry point requires a very different instrumentation method. Placing the domain-specific knowledge in provider modules makes DTrace easily extensible in terms of instrumenting different software subsystems and different hardware architectures.

When a probe is fired, the instrumentation inserted by the provider transfers control into the DTrace framework and we are now in what is termed "probe context." Interrupts are disabled for the executing CPU. The ECBs that are registered for the firing probe are iterated over, and each DIF instruction in each DIFO is interpreted. Data generated from the ECB processing is buffered in a set of per-consumer, per-CPU buffers that are read periodically by the consumer.

When a tracing session is terminated, all instrumentation carried out by providers is removed and the system returns to its original state.

## 10.5  Summary

DTrace is a revolutionary framework for instrumenting and observing the behaviour of systems, and the applications they run. The limits to what can be learned with DTrace are bound only by the users knowledge of the system and application, but it is not necessary to be an operating systems expert or software developer to make effective use of DTrace. The usability of DTrace allows for users at any level to make effective use of the tool, gaining insight into performance and general application behaviour.

## 10.6  Probe Reference

### 10.6.1  The I/O Provider

The io probes are listed in Table 10.2, and the arguments are described in Sections 10.6.1.1 through 10.6.1.3.

**Table 10.2** io Probes

| Probe | Description |
| --- | --- |
| start | Probe that fires when an I/O request is about to be made either to a peripheral device or to an NFS server. The bufinfo_t corresponding to the I/O request is pointed to by args[0]. The devinfo_t of the device to which the I/O is being issued is pointed to by args[1]. The fileinfo_t of the file that corresponds to the I/O request is pointed to by args[2]. Note that file information availability depends on the filesystem making the I/O request. See fileinfo_t for more information. |

*continues*

**Table 10.2** `io` Probes (*continued*)

| Probe | Description |
|---|---|
| done | Probe that fires after an I/O request has been fulfilled. The `bufinfo_t` corresponding to the I/O request is pointed to by `args[0]`. The done probe fires after the I/O completes, but before completion processing has been performed on the buffer. As a result `B_DONE` is not set in `b_flags` at the time the done probe fires. The `devinfo_t` of the device to which the I/O was issued is pointed to by `args[1]`. The `fileinfo_t` of the file that corresponds to the I/O request is pointed to by `args[2]`. |
| wait-start | Probe that fires immediately before a thread begins to wait pending completion of a given I/O request. The `buf(9S)` structure corresponding to the I/O request for which the thread will wait is pointed to by `args[0]`. The `devinfo_t` of the device to which the I/O was issued is pointed to by `args[1]`. The `fileinfo_t` of the file that corresponds to the I/O request is pointed to by `args[2]`. Some time after the `wait-start` probe fires, the `wait-done` probe will fire in the same thread. |
| wait-done | Probe that fires when a thread is done waiting for the completion of a given I/O request. The `bufinfo_t` corresponding to the I/O request for which the thread will wait is pointed to by `args[0]`. The `devinfo_t` of the device to which the I/O was issued is pointed to by `args[1]`. The `fileinfo_t` of the file that corresponds to the I/O request is pointed to by `args[2]`. The `wait-done` probe fires only after the `wait-start` probe has fired in the same thread. |

### 10.6.1.1 `bufinfo_t` structure

The `bufinfo_t` structure is the abstraction that describes an I/O request. The buffer corresponding to an I/O request is pointed to by `args[0]` in the `start`, `done`, `wait-start`, and `wait-done` probes. The `bufinfo_t` structure definition is as follows:

```
typedef struct bufinfo {
          int b_flags;              /* flags */
          size_t b_bcount;          /* number of bytes */
          caddr_t b_addr;           /* buffer address */
          uint64_t b_blkno;         /* expanded block # on device */
          uint64_t b_lblkno;        /* block # on device */
          size_t b_resid;           /* # of bytes not transferred */
          size_t b_bufsize;         /* size of allocated buffer */
          caddr_t b_iodone;         /* I/O completion routine */
          dev_t b_edev;             /* extended device */
} bufinfo_t;
```
                                              *See /usr/lib/dtrace/io.d*

The b_flags member indicates the state of the I/O buffer, and consists of a bit-wise-or of different state values. The valid state values are in Table 10.3.

**Table 10.3** b_flags Values

| Flag | Description |
| --- | --- |
| B_DONE | Indicates that the data transfer has completed. |
| B_ERROR | Indicates an I/O transfer error. It is set in conjunction with the b_error field. |
| B_PAGEIO | Indicates that the buffer is being used in a paged I/O request. See the description of the b_addr field for more information. |
| B_PHYS | Indicates that the buffer is being used for physical (direct) I/O to a user data area. |
| B_READ | Indicates that data is to be read from the peripheral device into main memory. |
| B_WRITE | Indicates that the data is to be transferred from main memory to the peripheral device. |
| B_ASYNC | The I/O request is asynchronous, and will not be waited upon. The wait-start and wait-done probes don't fire for asynchronous I/O requests. Note that some I/Os directed to be asynchronous might not have B_ASYNC set: the asynchronous I/O subsystem might implement the asynchronous request by having a separate worker thread perform a synchronous I/O operation. |

The structure members are as follows:

- **b_bcount** is the number of bytes to be transferred as part of the I/O request.
- **b_addr** is the virtual address of the I/O request, unless B_PAGEIO is set. The address is a kernel virtual address unless B_PHYS is set, in which case it is a user virtual address. If B_PAGEIO is set, the b_addr field contains kernel private data. Exactly one of B_PHYS and B_PAGEIO can be set, or neither flag will be set.
- **b_lblkno** identifies which logical block on the device is to be accessed. The mapping from a logical block to a physical block (such as the cylinder, track, and so on) is defined by the device.
- **b_resid** is set to the number of bytes not transferred because of an error.
- **b_bufsize** contains the size of the allocated buffer.

- **b_iodone** identifies a specific routine in the kernel that is called when the I/O is complete.

- **b_error** may hold an error code returned from the driver in the event of an I/O error. b_error is set in conjunction with the B_ERROR bit set in the b_flags member.

- **b_edev** contains the major and minor device numbers of the device accessed. Consumers may use the D subroutines getmajor() and getminor() to extract the major and minor device numbers from the b_edev field.

## 10.6.1.2 devinfo_t

The devinfo_t structure provides information about a device. The devinfo_t structure corresponding to the destination device of an I/O is pointed to by args[1] in the start, done, wait-start, and wait-done probes. The members of devinfo_t are as follows:

```
typedef struct devinfo {
            int dev_major;                  /* major number */
            int dev_minor;                  /* minor number */
            int dev_instance;               /* instance number */
            string dev_name;                /* name of device */
            string dev_statname;            /* name of device + instance/minor */
            string dev_pathname;            /* pathname of device */
} devinfo_t;
                                                 See /usr/lib/dtrace/io.d
```

- **dev_major.** The major number of the device. See getmajor(9F) for more information.

- **dev_minor.** The minor number of the device. See getminor(9F) for more information.

- **dev_instance.** The instance number of the device. The instance of a device is different from the minor number. The minor number is an abstraction managed by the device driver. The instance number is a property of the device node. You can display device node instance numbers with prtconf(1M).

- **dev_name.** The name of the device driver that manages the device. You can display device driver names with the -D option to prtconf(1M).

- **dev_statname.** The name of the device as reported by iostat(1M). This name also corresponds to the name of a kernel statistic as reported by kstat(1M). This field is provided so that aberrant iostat or kstat output can be quickly correlated to actual I/O activity.

- **dev_pathname.** The full path of the device. This path may be specified as an argument to prtconf(1M) to obtain detailed device information. The path specified by dev_pathname includes components expressing the device node, the instance number, and the minor node. However, all three of these elements aren't necessarily expressed in the statistics name. For some devices, the statistics name consists of the device name and the instance number. For other devices, the name consists of the device name and the number of the minor node. As a result, two devices that have the same dev_statname may differ in dev_pathname.

### 10.6.1.3 `fileinfo_t`

The fileinfo_t structure provides information about a file. The file to which an I/O corresponds is pointed to by args[2] in the start, done, wait-start, and wait-done probes. The presence of file information is contingent upon the filesystem providing this information when dispatching I/O requests. Some filesystems, especially third-party filesystems, might not provide this information. Also, I/O requests might emanate from a filesystem for which no file information exists. For example, any I/O to filesystem metadata will not be associated with any one file. Finally, some highly optimized filesystems might aggregate I/O from disjoint files into a single I/O request. In this case, the filesystem might provide the file information either for the file that represents the majority of the I/O or for the file that represents some of the I/O. Alternately, the filesystem might provide no file information at all in this case.

The definition of the fileinfo_t structure is as follows:

```
typedef struct fileinfo {
            string fi_name;            /* name (basename of fi_pathname) */
            string fi_dirname;         /* directory (dirname of fi_pathname) */
            string fi_pathname;        /* full pathname */
            offset_t fi_offset;        /* offset within file */
            string fi_fs;              /* filesystem */
            string fi_mount;           /* mount point of file system */
} fileinfo_t;
                                       See /usr/lib/dtrace/io.d
```

- **fi_name.** Contains the name of the file but does not include any directory components. If no file information is associated with an I/O, the fi_name field will be set to the string <none>. In some rare cases, the pathname associated with a file might be unknown. In this case, the fi_name field will be set to the string <unknown>.

- **fi_dirname.** Contains only the directory component of the file name. As with fi_name, this string may be set to <none> if no file information is present, or <unknown> if the pathname associated with the file is not known.

- **fi_pathname.** Contains the full pathname to the file. As with fi_name, this string may be set to <none> if no file information is present, or <unknown> if the pathname associated with the file is not known.

- **fi_offset.** Contains the offset within the file , or -1 if either file information is not present or if the offset is otherwise unspecified by the filesystem.

## 10.6.2 Virtual Memory Provider Probes

The vminfo provider probes correspond to the fields in the "vm" named kstat: A probe provided by vminfo fires immediately before the corresponding vm value is incremented. Table 10.4 lists the probes available from the VM provider. A probe takes the following arguments:

- **arg0.** The value by which the statistic is to be incremented. For most probes, this argument is always 1, but for some it may take other values; these probes are noted in Table 10.4.

- **arg1.** A pointer to the current value of the statistic to be incremented. This value is a 64-bit quantity that is incremented by the value in arg0. Dereferencing this pointer allows consumers to determine the current count of the statistic corresponding to the probe.

For example, if you should see the following paging activity with vmstat, indicating page-in from the swap device, you could drill down to investigate.

```
# vmstat -p 3
        memory            page           executable      anonymous       filesystem
    swap    free  re  mf   fr  de  sr  epi  epo  epf  api  apo  apf  fpi  fpo  fpf
 1512488  837792 160  20   12   0   0    0    0    0 8102    0    0   12   12   12
 1715812  985116   7  82    0   0   0    0    0    0 7501    0    0   45    0    0
 1715784  983984   0   2    0   0   0    0    0    0 1231    0    0   53    0    0
 1715780  987644   0   0    0   0   0    0    0    0 2451    0    0   33    0    0

$ dtrace -n anonpgin'{@[execname] = count()}'
dtrace: description 'anonpgin' matched 1 probe
  svc.startd                                                        1
  sshd                                                              2
  ssh                                                               3
  dtrace                                                            6
  vmstat                                                           28
  filebench                                                       913
```

The VM probes are described in Table 10.4.

**Table 10.4** DTrace VM Provider Probes and Descriptions

| Probe Name | Description |
| --- | --- |
| anonfree | Fires whenever an unmodified anonymous page is freed as part of paging activity. Anonymous pages are those that are not associated with a file; memory containing such pages include heap memory, stack memory, or memory obtained by explicitly mapping `zero(7D)`. |
| anonpgin | Fires whenever an anonymous page is paged in from a swap device. |
| anonpgout | Fires whenever a modified anonymous page is paged out to a swap device. |
| as_fault | Fires whenever a fault is taken on a page and the fault is neither a protection fault nor a copy-on-write fault. |
| cow_fault | Fires whenever a copy on-write fault is taken on a page. `arg0` contains the number of pages that are created as a result of the copy-on-write. |
| dfree | Fires whenever a page is freed as a result of paging activity. Whenever `dfree` fires, exactly one of `anonfree`, `execfree`, or `fsfree` will also subsequently fire. |
| execfree | Fires whenever an unmodified executable page is freed as a result of paging activity. |
| execpgin | Fires whenever an executable page is paged in from the backing store. |
| execpgout | Fires whenever a modified executable page is paged out to the backing store. If it occurs at all, most paging of executable pages will occur in terms of `execfree`; `execpgout` can only fire if an executable page is modified in memory—an uncommon occurrence in most systems. |
| fsfree | Fires whenever an unmodified file system data page is freed as part of paging activity. |
| fspgin | Fires whenever a file system page is paged in from the backing store. |
| fspgout | Fires whenever a modified file system page is paged out to the backing store. |
| kernel_asflt | Fires whenever a page fault is taken by the kernel on a page in its own address space. Whenever `kernel_asflt` fires, it will be immediately preceded by a firing of the `as_fault` probe. |
| maj_fault | Fires whenever a page fault is taken that results in I/O from a backing store or swap device. Whenever `maj_fault` fires, it will be immediately preceded by a firing of the `pgin` probe. |
| pgfrec | Fires whenever a page is reclaimed off of the free page list. |

## 10.6.3 The Sched Provider

The sched probes are described in Table 10.5.

**Table 10.5** `sched` Probes

| Probe | Description |
|---|---|
| `change-pri` | Probe that fires whenever a thread's priority is about to be changed. The `lwpsinfo_t` of the thread is pointed to by `args[0]`. The thread's current priority is in the `pr_pri` field of this structure. The `psinfo_t` of the process containing the thread is pointed to by `args[1]`. The thread's new priority is contained in `args[2]`. |
| `dequeue` | Probe that fires immediately before a runnable thread is dequeued from a run queue. The `lwpsinfo_t` of the thread being dequeued is pointed to by `args[0]`. The `psinfo_t` of the process containing the thread is pointed to by `args[1]`. The `cpuinfo_t` of the CPU from which the thread is being dequeued is pointed to by `args[2]`. If the thread is being dequeued from a run queue that is not associated with a particular CPU, the `cpu_id` member of this structure will be `-1`. |
| `enqueue` | Probe that fires immediately before a runnable thread is enqueued to a run queue. The `lwpsinfo_t` of the thread being enqueued is pointed to by `args[0]`. The `psinfo_t` of the process containing the thread is pointed to by `args[1]`. The `cpuinfo_t` of the CPU to which the thread is being enqueued is pointed to by `args[2]`. If the thread is being enqueued from a run queue that is not associated with a particular CPU, the `cpu_id` member of this structure will be `-1`. The value in `args[3]` is a boolean indicating whether the thread will be enqueued to the front of the run queue. The value is non-zero if the thread will be enqueued at the front of the run queue, and zero if the thread will be enqueued at the back of the run queue. |
| `off-cpu` | Probe that fires when the current CPU is about to end execution of a thread. The curcpu variable indicates the current CPU. The curlwpsinfo variable indicates the thread that is ending execution. The curpsinfo variable describes the process containing the current thread. The `lwpsinfo_t` structure of the thread that the current CPU will next execute is pointed to by `args[0]`. The `psinfo_t` of the process containing the next thread is pointed to by `args[1]`. |

*continues*

**Table 10.5** `sched` Probes (*continued*)

| Probe | Description |
|-------|-------------|
| `on-cpu` | Probe that fires when a CPU has just begun execution of a thread. The `curcpu` variable indicates the current CPU. The `curlwpsinfo` variable indicates the thread that is beginning execution. The `curpsinfo` variable describes the process containing the current thread. |
| `preempt` | Probe that fires immediately before the current thread is preempted. After this probe fires, the current thread will select a thread to run and the `off-cpu` probe will fire for the current thread. In some cases, a thread on one CPU will be preempted, but the preempting thread will run on another CPU in the meantime. In this situation, the `preempt` probe will fire, but the dispatcher will be unable to find a higher priority thread to run and the `remain-cpu` probe will fire instead of the `off-cpu` probe. |
| `remain-cpu` | Probe that fires when a scheduling decision has been made, but the dispatcher has elected to continue to run the current thread. The `curcpu` variable indicates the current CPU. The `curlwpsinfo` variable indicates the thread that is beginning execution. The `curpsinfo` variable describes the process containing the current thread. |
| `schedctl-nopreempt` | Probe that fires when a thread is preempted and then re-enqueued at the front of the run queue due to a preemption control request. See `schedctl_init(3C)` for details on preemption control. As with preempt, either `off-cpu` or `remain-cpu` will fire after `schedctl-nopreempt`. Because `schedctl-nopreempt` denotes a re-enqueuing of the current thread at the front of the run queue, `remain-cpu` is more likely to fire after `schedctl-nopreempt` than `off-cpu`. The `lwpsinfo_t` of the thread being preempted is pointed to by `args[0]`. The `psinfo_t` of the process containing the thread is pointed to by `args[1]`. |
| `schedctl-preempt` | Probe that fires when a thread that is using preemption control is nonetheless preempted and re-enqueued at the back of the run queue. See `schedctl_init(3C)` for details on preemption control. As with `preempt`, either `off-cpu` or `remain-cpu` will fire after `schedctl-preempt`. Like `preempt` (and unlike `schedctl-nopreempt`), `schedctl-preempt` denotes a re-enqueuing of the current thread at the back of the run queue. As a result, `off-cpu` is more likely to fire after `schedctl-preempt` than `remain-cpu`. The `lwpsinfo_t` of the thread being preempted is pointed to by `args[0]`. The `psinfo_t` of the process containing the thread is pointed to by `args[1]`. |

*continues*

**Table 10.5** `sched` Probes (*continued*)

| Probe | Description |
|---|---|
| `schedctl-yield` | Probe that fires when a thread that had preemption control enabled and its time slice artificially extended executed code to yield the CPU to other threads. |
| `sleep` | Probe that fires immediately before the current thread sleeps on a synchronization object. The type of the synchronization object is contained in the `pr_stype` member of the `lwpsinfo_t` pointed to by `curlwpsinfo`. The address of the synchronization object is contained in the `pr_wchan` member of the `lwpsinfo_t` pointed to by `curlwpsinfo`. The meaning of this address is a private implementation detail, but the address value may be treated as a token unique to the synchronization object. |
| `surrender` | Probe that fires when a CPU has been instructed by another CPU to make a scheduling decision—often because a higher-priority thread has become runnable. |
| `tick` | Probe that fires as a part of clock tick-based accounting. In clock tick-based accounting, CPU accounting is performed by examining which threads and processes are running when a fixed-interval interrupt fires. The `lwpsinfo_t` that corresponds to the thread that is being assigned CPU time is pointed to by `args[0]`. The `psinfo_t` that corresponds to the process that contains the thread is pointed to by `args[1]`. |
| `wakeup` | Probe that fires immediately before the current thread wakes a thread sleeping on a synchronization object. The `lwpsinfo_t` of the sleeping thread is pointed to by `args[0]`. The `psinfo_t` of the process containing the sleeping thread is pointed to by `args[1]`. The type of the synchronization object is contained in the `pr_stype` member of the `lwpsinfo_t` of the sleeping thread. The address of the synchronization object is contained in the `pr_wchan` member of the `lwpsinfo_t` of the sleeping thread. The meaning of this address is a private implementation detail, but the address value may be treated as a token unique to the synchronization object. |

## 10.6.3.1 Arguments

The argument types for the sched probes are listed in Table 10.5; the arguments are described in Table 10.6.

**Table 10.6** sched Probe Arguments

| Probe | args[0] | args[1] | args[2] | args[3] |
|---|---|---|---|---|
| change-pri | lwpsinfo_t * | psinfo_t * | pri_t | — |
| dequeue | lwpsinfo_t * | psinfo_t * | cpuinfo_t * | — |
| enqueue | lwpsinfo_t * | psinfo_t * | cpuinfo_t * | int |
| off-cpu | lwpsinfo_t * | psinfo_t * | — | — |
| on-cpu | — | — | — | — |
| preempt | — | — | — | — |
| remain-cpu | — | — | — | — |
| schedctl-nopreempt | lwpsinfo_t * | psinfo_t * | — | — |
| schedctl-preempt | lwpsinfo_t * | psinfo_t * | — | — |
| schedctl-yield | lwpsinfo_t * | psinfo_t * | — | — |
| sleep | — | — | — | — |
| surrender | lwpsinfo_t * | psinfo_t * | — | — |
| tick | lwpsinfo_t * | psinfo_t * | — | — |
| wakeup | lwpsinfo_t * | psinfo_t * | — | — |

As Table 10.6 indicates, many sched probes have arguments consisting of a pointer to an lwpsinfo_t and a pointer to a psinfo_t, indicating a thread and the process containing the thread, respectively. These structures are described in detail in lwpsinfo_t and psinfo_t, respectively.

The cpuinfo_t structure defines a CPU. As Table 10.6 indicates, arguments to both the enqueue and dequeue probes include a pointer to a cpuinfo_t. Additionally, the cpuinfo_t corresponding to the current CPU is pointed to by the curcpu variable.

```
typedef struct cpuinfo {
        processorid_t cpu_id;         /* CPU identifier */
        psetid_t cpu_pset;            /* processor set identifier */
        chipid_t cpu_chip;            /* chip identifier */
        lgrp_id_t cpu_lgrp;           /* locality group identifer */
        processor_info_t cpu_info;    /* CPU information */
} cpuinfo_t;
```

The definition of the `cpuinfo_t` structure is as follows:

- **cpu_id.** The processor identifier, as returned by `psrinfo(1M)` and `p_online(2)`.
- **cpu_pset.** The processor set that contains the CPU, if any. See `psrset(1M)` for more details on processor sets.
- **cpu_chip.** The identifier of the physical chip. Physical chips may contain several CPUs. See `psrinfo(1M)` for more information.
- **The cpu_lgrp.** The identifier of the latency group associated with the CPU. See `liblgrp(3LIB)` for details on latency groups.
- **The cpu_info.** The `processor_info_t` structure associated with the CPU, as returned by `processor_info(2)`.

## 10.6.4 DTrace Lockstat Provider

The lockstat provider makes available probes that can be used to discern lock contention statistics or to understand virtually any aspect of locking behavior. The `lockstat(1M)` command is actually a DTrace consumer that uses the lockstat provider to gather its raw data.

The lockstat provider makes available two kinds of probes: content-event probes and hold-event probes.

- **Contention-event probes.** Correspond to contention on a synchronization primitive; they fire when a thread is forced to wait for a resource to become available. Solaris is generally optimized for the noncontention case, so prolonged contention is not expected. These probes should be used to understand those cases where contention does arise. Because contention is relatively rare, enabling contention-event probes generally doesn't substantially affect performance.
- **Hold-event probes.** Correspond to acquiring, releasing, or otherwise manipulating a synchronization primitive. These probes can be used to answer arbitrary questions about the way synchronization primitives are manipulated. Because Solaris acquires and releases synchronization primitives very often (on the order of millions of times per second per CPU on a busy system), enabling hold-event probes has a much higher probe effect than does enabling contention-event probes. While the probe effect induced by enabling them can be substantial, it is not pathological; they may still be enabled with confidence on production systems.

The lockstat provider makes available probes that correspond to the different synchronization primitives in Solaris; these primitives and the probes that correspond to them are discussed in the remainder of this chapter.

### 10.6.4.1 Adaptive Lock Probes

The four lockstat probes pertaining to adaptive locks are in Table 10.7. For each probe, arg0 contains a pointer to the kmutex_t structure that represents the adaptive lock.

**Table 10.7** Adaptive Lock Probes

| Probe Name | Description |
| --- | --- |
| adaptive-acquire | Hold-event probe that fires immediately after an adaptive lock is acquired. |
| adaptive-block | Contention-event probe that fires after a thread that has blocked on a held adaptive mutex has reawakened and has acquired the mutex. If both probes are enabled, adaptive-block fires before adaptive-acquire. At most one of adaptive-block and adaptive-spin fires for a single lock acquisition. arg1 for adaptive-block contains the sleep time in nanoseconds. |
| adaptive-spin | Contention-event probe that fires after a thread that has spun on a held adaptive mutex has successfully acquired the mutex. If both are enabled, adaptive-spin fires before adaptive-acquire. At most one of adaptive-spin and adaptive-block fires for a single lock acquisition. arg1 for adaptive-spin contains the spin count: the number of iterations that were taken through the spin loop before the lock was acquired. The spin count has little meaning on its own but can be used to compare spin times. |
| adaptive-release | Hold-event probe that fires immediately after an adaptive lock is released. |

### 10.6.4.2 Spin Lock Probes

The three probes pertaining to spin locks are in Table 10.8.

**Table 10.8**  Spin Lock Probes

| Probe Name | Description |
|---|---|
| `spin-acquire` | Hold-event probe that fires immediately after a spin lock is acquired. |
| `spin-spin` | Contention-event probe that fires after a thread that has spun on a held spin lock has successfully acquired the spin lock. If both are enabled, `spin-spin` fires before `spin-acquire`. `arg1` for `spin-spin` contains the spin count: the number of iterations that were taken through the spin loop before the lock was acquired. The spin count has little meaning on its own but can be used to compare spin times. |
| `spin-release` | Hold-event probe that fires immediately after a spin lock is released. |

### 10.6.4.3 Thread Locks

Thread lock hold events are available as spin lock hold-event probes (that is, `spin-acquire` and `spin-release`), but contention events have their own probe specific to thread locks. The thread lock hold-event probe is described in Table 10.9.

**Table 10.9**  Thread Lock Probes

| Probe Name | Description |
|---|---|
| `thread-spin` | Contention-event probe that fires after a thread has spun on a thread lock. Like other contention-event probes, if both the contention-event probe and the hold-event probe are enabled, `thread-spin` fires before `spin-acquire`. Unlike other contention-event probes, however, `thread-spin` fires *before* the lock is actually acquired. As a result, multiple `thread-spin` probe firings may correspond to a single `spin-acquire` probe firing. |

### 10.6.4.4 Readers/Writer Lock Probes

The probes pertaining to readers/writer locks are in Table 10.10. For each probe, arg0 contains a pointer to the `krwlock_t` structure that represents the adaptive lock.

**Table 10.10** Readers/Writer Lock Probes

| Probe Name | Description |
| --- | --- |
| rw-acquire | Hold-event probe that fires immediately after a readers/writer lock is acquired. arg1 contains the constant RW_READER if the lock was acquired as a reader, and RW_WRITER if the lock was acquired as a writer. |
| rw-block | Contention-event probe that fires after a thread that has blocked on a held readers/writer lock has reawakened and has acquired the lock. arg1 contains the length of time (in nanoseconds) that the current thread had to sleep to acquire the lock. arg2 contains the constant RW_READER if the lock was acquired as a reader, and RW_WRITER if the lock was acquired as a writer. arg3 and arg4 contain more information on the reason for blocking. arg3 is nonzero if and only if the lock was held as a writer when the current thread blocked. arg4 contains the readers count when the current thread blocked. If both the rw-block and rw-acquire probes are enabled, rw-block fires *before* rw-acquire. |
| rw-upgrade | Hold-event probe that fires after a thread has successfully upgraded a readers/writer lock from a reader to a writer. Upgrades do not have an associated contention event because they are only possible through a nonblocking interface, rw_tryupgrade(TRYUPGRADE.9F). |
| rw-downgrade | Hold-event probe that fires after a thread had downgraded its ownership of a readers/writer lock from writer to reader. Downgrades do not have an associated contention event because they always succeed without contention. |
| rw-release | Hold-event probe that fires immediately after a readers/writer lock is released. arg1 contains the constant RW_READER if the released lock was held as a reader, and RW_WRITER if the released lock was held as a writer. Due to upgrades and downgrades, the lock may *not* have been released as it was acquired. |

### 10.6.5 The Java Virtual Machine Provider

This following section lists all probes published by the hotspot provider.

#### 10.6.5.1 VM Life Cycle Probes

Three probes are available related to the VM life cycle, as shown in Table 10.11.

**Table 10.11**  VM Life Cycle Probes

| Probe | Description |
|---|---|
| vm-init-begin | This probe fires just as the VM initialization begins. It occurs just after JNI_CreateVM() is called, as the VM is initializing. |
| vm-init-end | This probe fires when the VM initialization finishes, and the VM is ready to start running application code. |
| vm-shutdown | Probe that fires as the VM is shutting down due to program termination or error |

#### 10.6.5.2 Thread Life Cycle Probes

Two probes are available for tracking thread start and stop events, as shown in Table 10.12.

**Table 10.12**  Thread Life Cycle Probes

| Probe | Description |
|---|---|
| thread-start | Probe that fires as a thread is started |
| thread-stop | Probe that fires when the thread has completed |

Each of these probes has the arguments shown in Table 10.13.

**Table 10.13**  Thread Life Cycle Probe Arguments

| Argument | Description |
|---|---|
| args[0] | A pointer to mUTF-8 string data which contains the thread name |
| args[1] | The length of the thread name (in bytes) |

*continues*

**Table 10.13** Thread Life Cycle Probe Arguments (*continued*)

| Argument | Description |
|---|---|
| args[2] | The Java thread ID. This is the value that will match other hotspot probes that contain a thread argument. |
| args[3] | The native/OS thread ID. This is the ID assigned by the host operating system. |
| args[4] | A boolean value that indicates if this thread is a daemon or not. A value of 0 indicates a non-daemon thread. |

### 10.6.5.3 Class-Loading Probes

Two probes are available for tracking class loading and unloading activity, as shown in Table 10.14.

**Table 10.14** Class-Loading Probes

| Probe | Description |
|---|---|
| class-loaded | Probe that fires after the class has been loaded |
| class-unloaded | Probe that fires after the class has been unloaded from the system |

Each of these probes has the arguments shown in Table 10.15.

**Table 10.15** Class-Loading Probe Arguments

| Argument | Description |
|---|---|
| args[0] | A pointer to mUTF-8 string data which contains the name of the class begin loaded |
| args[1] | The length of the class name (in bytes) |
| args[2] | The class loader ID, which is a unique identifier for a class loader in the VM. This is the class loader that has loaded or is loading the class |
| args[3] | A boolean value which indicates if the class is a shared class (if the class was loaded from the shared archive) |

### 10.6.5.4 Garbage Collection Probes

The following probes measure the duration of a system-wide garbage collection cycle (for those garbage collectors that have a defined begin and end), and each memory pool can be tracked independently. The probes for individual pools pass the memory manager's name, the pool name, and pool usage information at both the begin and end of pool collection.

The provider's GC-related probes are shown in Table 10.16.

**Table 10.16** Garbage Collection Probes

| Probe | Description |
|---|---|
| gc-begin | Probe that fires when system-wide collection is about to start. Its one argument (arg[0]) is a boolean value that indicates if this is to be a Full GC. |
| gc-end | Probe that fires when system-wide collection has completed. No arguments. |
| mem-pool-gc-begin | Probe that fires when an individual memory pool is about to be collected. Provides the arguments listed in Table 10.17. |
| mem-pool-gc-end | Probe that fires after an individual memory pool has been collected. |

The memory pool probe arguments are as follows:

**Table 10.17** Garbage Collection Probe Arguments

| Argument | Description |
|---|---|
| args[0] | A pointer to mUTF-8 string data that contains the name of the manager which manages this memory pool |
| args[1] | The length of the manager name (in bytes) |
| args[2] | A pointer to mUTF-8 string data that contains the name of the memory pool |
| args[3] | The length of the memory pool name (in bytes) |
| args[4] | The initial size of the memory pool (in bytes) |
| args[5] | The amount of memory in use in the memory pool (in bytes) |
| args[6] | The number of committed pages in the memory pool |
| args[7] | The maximum size of the memory pool |

### 10.6.5.5 Method Compilation Probes

The following probes indicate which methods are being compiled and by which compiler. Then, when the method compilation has completed, it can be loaded and possibly unloaded later. Probes are available to track these events as they occur.

Probes that mark the begin and end of method compilation are shown in Table 10.18.

**Table 10.18** Method Compilation Probes

| Probe | Description |
|---|---|
| method-compile-begin | Probe that fires as method compilation begins. Provides the arguments listed below |
| method-compile-end | Probe that fires when method compilation completes. In addition to the arguments listed below, argv[8] is a boolean value which indicates if the compilation was successful |

Method compilation probe arguments are shown in Table 10.19.

**Table 10.19** Method Compilation Probe Arguments

| Argument | Description |
|---|---|
| args[0] | A pointer to mUTF-8 string data which contains the name of the compiler which is compiling this method |
| args[1] | The length of the compiler name (in bytes) |
| args[2] | A pointer to mUTF-8 string data which contains the name of the class of the method being compiled |
| args[3] | The length of the class name (in bytes) |
| args[4] | A pointer to mUTF-8 string data which contains the name of the method being compiled |
| args[5] | The length of the method name (in bytes) |
| args[6] | A pointer to mUTF-8 string data which contains the signature of the method being compiled |
| args[7] | The length of the signature(in bytes) |

When compiled methods are installed for execution, the probes shown in Table 10.20 are fired.

**Table 10.20** Compiled Method Install Probes

| Probe | Description |
|-------|-------------|
| compiled-method-load | Probe that fires when a compiled method is installed. In addition to the arguments listed below, `argv[6]` contains a pointer to the compiled code, and `argv[7]` is the size of the compiled code. |
| compiled-method-unload | Probe that fires when a compiled method is uninstalled. Provides the arguments listed in Table 10.21. |

Compiled method loading probe arguments are as follows:

**Table 10.21** Compiled Method Install Probe Arguments

| Argument | Description |
|----------|-------------|
| args[0] | A pointer to mUTF-8 string data which contains the name of the class of the method being installed |
| args[1] | The length of the class name (in bytes) |
| args[2] | A pointer to mUTF-8 string data which contains the name of the method being installed |
| args[3] | The length of the method name (in bytes) |
| args[4] | A pointer to mUTF-8 string data which contains the signature of the method being installed |
| args[5] | The length of the signature(in bytes) |

### 10.6.5.6 Monitor Probes

As an application runs, threads will enter and exit monitors, wait on objects, and perform notifications. Probes are available for all wait and notification events, as well as for contended monitor entry and exit events. A contended monitor entry is the situation where a thread attempts to enter a monitor when another thread is already in the monitor. A contended monitor exit event occurs when a thread leaves a monitor and other threads are waiting to enter to the monitor. Thus, contended enter and contended exit events may not match up to each other in relation to the thread that encounters these events, though it is expected that a contended exit from one thread should match up to a contended enter on another thread (the thread waiting for the monitor).

All monitor events provide the thread ID, a monitor ID, and the type of the class of the object as arguments. It is expected that the thread and the class will help map back to the program, while the monitor ID can provide matching information between probe firings.

Since the existance of these probes in the VM causes performance degradation, they will only fire if the VM has been started with the command-line option `-XX:+ExtendedDtraceProbes`. By default they are present in any listing of the probes in the VM, but are dormant without the flag. It is intended that this restriction be removed in future releases of the VM, where these probes will be enabled all the time with no impact to performance.

The available probes are shown in Table 10.22.

**Table 10.22** Monitor Probes

| Probe | Description |
| --- | --- |
| `monitor-contended-enter` | Probe that fires as a thread attempts to enter a contended monitor. |
| `monitor-contended-entered` | Probe that fires when the thread successfully enters the contended monitor. |
| `monitor-contended-exit` | Probe that fires when the thread leaves a monitor and other threads are waiting to enter. |
| `monitor-wait` | Probe that fires as a thread begins a wait on an object via `Object.wait()`. The probe has an additional argument, args[4] which is a "long" value which indicates the timeout being used. |
| `monitor-waited` | Probe that fires when the thread completes an `Object.wait()` and has been either been notified, or timed out. |
| `monitor-notify` | Probe that fires when a thread calls `Object.notify()` to notify waiters on a monitor monitor-notifyAll Probe that fires when a thread calls `Object.notifyAll()` to notify waiters on a monitor. |

Monitor probe arguments are shown in Table 10.23.

**Table 10.23** Monitor Probe Arguments

| Argument | Description |
| --- | --- |
| `args[0]` | The Java thread identifier for the thread peforming the monitor operation |
| `args[1]` | A unique, but opaque identifier for the specific monitor that the action is performed upon |

*continues*

**Table 10.23**  Monitor Probe Arguments (*continued*)

| Argument | Description |
|---|---|
| args[2] | A pointer to mUTF-8 string data which contains the name of the class of the object being acted upon |
| args[3] | The length of the class name (in bytes) |

### 10.6.5.7 Application Tracking Probes

A few probes are provided to allow fine-grained examination of the Java thread execution. These consist of probes that fire anytime a method in entered or returned from, as well as a probe that fires whenever a Jav object has been allocated.

Since the existance of these probes in the VM causes performance degradation, they will only fire if the VM has been started with the command-line option `-XX:+ExtendedDtraceProbes`. By default they are present in any listing of the probes in the VM, but are dormant without the flag. It is intended that this restriction be removed in future releases of the VM, where these probes will be enabled all the time with no impact to performance.

The method entry and return probes are shown in Table 10.24.

**Table 10.24**  Application Tracking Probes

| Probe | Description |
|---|---|
| method-entry | Probe which fires when a method is begin entered. Only fires if the VM was created with the `ExtendedDtraceProbes` command-line argument. |
| method-return | Probe which fires when a method returns normally or due to an exception. Only fires if the VM was created with the `Extended-DtraceProbes` command-line argument. |

Method probe arguments are shown in Table 10.25.

**Table 10.25**  Application Tracking Probe Arguments

| Argument | Description |
|---|---|
| args[0] | The Java thread ID of the thread that is entering or leaving the method |
| args[1] | A pointer to mUTF-8 string data which contains the name of the class of the method |

*continues*

**Table 10.25** Application Tracking Probe Arguments (*continued*)

| Argument | Description |
|----------|-------------|
| args[2] | The length of the class name (in bytes) |
| args[3] | A pointer to mUTF-8 string data which contains the name of the method |
| args[4] | The length of the method name (in bytes) |
| args[5] | A pointer to mUTF-8 string data which contains the signature of the method |
| args[6] | The length of the signature(in bytes) |

The available allocation probe is shown in Table 10.26.

**Table 10.26** Allocation Probe

| Probe | Description |
|-------|-------------|
| object-alloc | Probe that fires when any object is allocated, provided that the VM was created with the ExtendedDtraceProbes command-line argument. |

The object allocation probe has the arguments shown in Table 10.27.

**Table 10.27** Allocation Probe Arguments

| Argument | Description |
|----------|-------------|
| args[0] | The Java thread ID of the thread that is allocating the object |
| args[1] | A pointer to mUTF-8 string data which contains the name of the class of the object being allocated |
| args[2] | The length of the class name (in bytes) |
| args[3] | The size of the object being allocated |

## 10.6.5.8 The hotspot_jni Provider

The JNI provides a number of methods for invoking code written in the Java Programming Language, and for examining the state of the VM. DTrace probes are provided at the entry point and return point for each of these methods. The probes are provided by the hotspot_jni provider. The name of the probe is the name of the JNI method, appended with "_entry" for enter probes, and "_return" for return probes. The arguments available at each entry probe are the arguments that were provided to the function (with the exception of the `Invoke*` methods, which omit the arguments that are passed to Java method). The return probes have the return value of the method as an argument (if available).

## 10.7 MDB Reference

**Table 10.28** MDB Reference for DTrace

| `dcmd` or `walker` | Description |
| --- | --- |
| dcmd difinstr | Disassemble a DIF instruction |
| dcmd difo | Print a DIF object |
| dcmd dof_actdesc | Print a DOF actdesc |
| dcmd dof_ecbdesc | Print a DOF ecbdesc |
| dcmd dof_hdr | Print a DOF header |
| dcmd dof_probedesc | Print a DOF probedesc |
| dcmd dof_relodesc | Print a DOF relodesc |
| dcmd dof_relohdr | Print a DOF relocation header |
| dcmd dof_sec | Print a DOF section header |
| dcmd dofdump | Dump DOF |
| dcmd dtrace | Print dtrace(1M)-like output |
| dcmd dtrace_aggstat | Print DTrace aggregation hash statistics |
| dcmd dtrace_dynstat | Print DTrace dynamic variable hash statistics |
| dcmd dtrace_errhash | Print DTrace error hash |
| dcmd dtrace_helptrace | Print DTrace helper trace |
| dcmd dtrace_state | Print active DTrace consumers |
| dcmd id2probe | Translate a dtrace_id_t to a dtrace_probe_t |
| walk dof_sec | Walk DOF section header table given header address |
| walk dtrace_aggkey | Walk DTrace aggregation keys |
| walk dtrace_dynvar | Walk DTrace dynamic variables |
| walk dtrace_errhash | Walk hash of DTrace error messasges |
| walk dtrace_helptrace | Walk DTrace helper trace entries |
| walk dtrace_state | Walk DTrace per-consumer softstate |

# Kernel Statistics

*With contributions from Peter Boothby*

The Solaris kernel provides a set of functions and data structures for device drivers and other kernel modules to export module-specific statistics to the outside world. This infrastructure, referred to as kstat, provides the following to the Solaris software developer:

- C-language functions for device drivers and other kernel modules to present statistics
- C-language functions for applications to retrieve statistics data from Solaris without needing to directly read kernel memory
- Perl-based command-line program /usr/bin/kstat to access statistics data interactively or in shell scripts (introduced in Solaris 8)
- Perl library interface for constructing custom performance-monitoring utilities

## 11.1 C-Level Kstat Interface

The Solaris libkstat library contains the C-language functions for accessing kstats from an application. These functions utilize the pseudo-device /dev/kstat to provide a secure interface to kernel data, obviating the need for programs that are setuid to root.

Since many developers are interested in accessing kernel statistics through C programs, this chapter focuses on libkstat. The chapter explains the data structures and functions, and provides example code to get you started using the library.

## 11.1.1  Data Structure Overview

Solaris kernel statistics are maintained in a linked list of structures referred to as the kstat chain. Each kstat has a common header section and a type-specific data section, as shown in Figure 11.1.

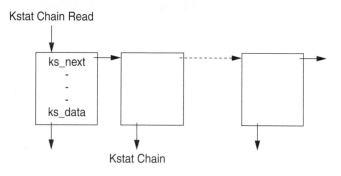

**Figure 11.1**   Kstat Chain

The chain is initialized at system boot time, but since Solaris is a dynamic operating system, this chain may change over time. Kstat entries can be added and removed from the system as needed by the kernel. For example, when you add an I/O board and all of its attached components to a running system by using Dynamic Reconfiguration, the device drivers and other kernel modules that interact with the new hardware will insert kstat entries into the chain.

The structure member `ks_data` is a pointer to the kstat's data section. Multiple data types are supported: raw, named, timer, interrupt, and I/O. These are explained in Section 11.1.3.

The following header contains the full `kstat` header structure.

```
typedef struct kstat {
     /*
      * Fields relevant to both kernel and user
      */
     hrtime_t       ks_crtime;                 /* creation time */
     struct kstat  *ks_next;                    /* kstat chain linkage */
     kid_t          ks_kid;                     /* unique kstat ID */
     char           ks_module[KSTAT_STRLEN];    /* module name */
     uchar_t        ks_resv;                    /* reserved */
     int            ks_instance;                /* module's instance */
     char           ks_name[KSTAT_STRLEN];      /* kstat name */
     uchar_t        ks_type;                    /* kstat data type */
```

*continues*

```
        char            ks_class[KSTAT_STRLEN];   /* kstat class */
        uchar_t         ks_flags;                 /* kstat flags */
        void            *ks_data;                 /* kstat type-specific data */
        uint_t          ks_ndata;                 /* # of data records */
        size_t          ks_data_size;             /* size of kstat data section */
        hrtime_t        ks_snaptime;              /* time of last data snapshot */
        /*
         * Fields relevant to kernel only
         */
        int (*ks_update)(struct kstat *, int);
        void            *ks_private;
        int (*ks_snapshot)(struct kstat *, void *, int);
        void            *ks_lock;
} kstat_t;
```

The significant members are described below.

- **ks_crtime.** This member reflects the time the kstat was created. Using the value, you can compute the rates of various counters since the kstat was created ("rate since boot" is replaced by the more general concept of "rate since kstat creation").

  All times associated with kstats, such as creation time, last snapshot time, kstat_timer_t, kstat_io_t timestamps, and the like, are 64-bit nanosecond values.

  The accuracy of kstat timestamps is machine-dependent, but the precision (units) is the same across all platforms. Refer to the gethrtime(3C) man page for general information about high-resolution timestamps.

- **ks_next.** kstats are stored as a NULL-terminated linked list or a chain. ks_next points to the next kstat in the chain.

- **ks_kid.** This member is a unique identifier for the kstat.

- **ks_module and ks_instance.** These members contain the name and instance of the module that created the kstat. In cases where there can only be one instance, ks_instance is 0. Refer to Section 11.1.4 for more information.

- **ks_name.** This member gives a meaningful name to a kstat. For additional kstat namespace information, see Section 11.1.4.

- **ks_type.** This member identifies the type of data in this kstat. Kstat data types are covered in Section 11.1.3.

- **ks_class.** Each kstat can be characterized as belonging to some broad class of statistics, such as bus, disk, net, vm, or misc. This field can be used as a filter to extract related kstats.

The following values are currently in use by Solaris:

| bus | hat | met | rpc |
|---|---|---|---|
| controller | kmem_cache | nfs | ufs |
| device_error | kstat | pages | vm |
| taskq | mib2 | crypto | errorq |
| disk | misc | partition | vmem |

- **ks_data, ks_ndata, and ks_data_size.** ks_data is a pointer to the kstat's data section. The type of data stored there depends on ks_type. ks_ndata indicates the number of data records. Only some kstat types support multiple data records. The following kstats support multiple data records.

  - KSTAT_TYPE_RAW

  - KSTAT_TYPE_NAMED

  - KSTAT_TYPE_TIMER

  The following kstats support only one data record:

  - KSTAT_TYPE_INTR

  - KSTAT_TYPE_IO

  ks_data_size is the total size of the data section, in bytes.

- **ks_snaptime.** Timestamp for the last data snapshot. With it, you can compute activity rates based on the following computational method:

  *rate = (new_count – old_count) / (new_snaptime – old_snaptime)*

## 11.1.2 Getting Started

To use kstats, a program must first call kstat_open(), which returns a pointer to a kstat control structure. The following header shows the structure members.

```
typedef struct kstat_ctl {
        kid_t      kc_chain_id;    /* current kstat chain ID */
        kstat_t    *kc_chain;      /* pointer to kstat chain */
        int        kc_kd;          /* /dev/kstat descriptor */
} kstat_ctl_t;
```

kc_chain points to the head of your copy of the kstat chain. You typically walk the chain or use kstat_lookup() to find and process a particular kind of kstat. kc_chain_id is the kstat chain identifier, or KCID, of your copy of the kstat chain. Its use is explained in Section 11.1.4.

To avoid unnecessary overhead in accessing kstat data, a program first searches the kstat chain for the type of information of interest, then uses the kstat_read() and kstat_data_lookup() functions to get the statistics data from the kernel.

The following code fragment shows how you might print out all kstat entries with information about disk I/O. It traverses the entire chain looking for kstats of ks_type KSTAT_TYPE_IO, calls kstat_read() to retrieve the data, and then processes the data with my_io_display(). How to implement this sample function is shown in <ref>.

```
kstat_ctl_t    *kc;
kstat_t        *ksp;
kstat_io_t      kio;
kc = kstat_open();
for (ksp = kc->kc_chain; ksp != NULL; ksp = ksp->ks_next) {
  if (ksp->ks_type == KSTAT_TYPE_IO) {
      kstat_read(kc, ksp, &kio);
      my_io_display(kio);
  }
}
```

## 11.1.3 Data Types

The data section of a kstat can hold one of five types, identified in the ks_type field. The following kstat types can hold multiple records. The number of records is held in ks_ndata.

- KSTAT_TYPE_RAW
- KSTAT_TYPE_NAMED
- KSTAT_TYPE_TIMER

The other two types are KSTATE_TYPE_INTR and KSTATE_TYPE_IO.
The field ks_data_size holds the size, in bytes, of the entire data section.

### 11.1.3.1 KSTAT_TYPE_RAW

The "raw" kstat type is treated as an array of bytes and is generally used to export well-known structures, such as vminfo (defined in /usr/include/sys/sysinfo.h). The following example shows one method of printing this information.

```
static void print_vminfo(kstat_t *kp)
{
    vminfo_t *vminfop;
    vminfop = (vminfo_t *)(kp->ks_data);

    printf("Free memory: %dn", vminfop->freemem);
    printf("Swap reserved: %dn" , vminfop->swap_resv);
    printf("Swap allocated: %dn" , vminfop->swap_alloc);
    printf("Swap available: %dn", vminfop->swap_avail);
    printf("Swap free: %dn", vminfop->swap_free);
}
```

## 11.1.3.2 `KSTAT_TYPE_NAMED`

This type of kstat contains a list of arbitrary *name=value* statistics. The following example shows the data structure used to hold named kstats.

```
typedef struct kstat_named {
        char    name[KSTAT_STRLEN];     /* name of counter */
        uchar_t data_type;              /* data type */
        union {
                char            c[16]; /* enough for 128-bit ints */
                int32_t         i32;
                uint32_t        ui32;
                struct {
                        union {
                                char            *ptr;   /* NULL-term string */
#if defined(_KERNEL) && defined(_MULTI_DATAMODEL)
                                caddr32_t       ptr32;
#endif
                                char            __pad[8]; /* 64-bit padding */
                        } addr;
                        uint32_t        len;    /* # bytes for strlen + '\0' */
                } str;
#if defined(_INT64_TYPE)
                int64_t         i64;
                uint64_t        ui64;
#endif
                long            l;
                ulong_t         ul;

                /* These structure members are obsolete */

                longlong_t      ll;
                u_longlong_t    ull;
                float           f;
                double          d;
        } value;                        /* value of counter */
} kstat_named_t;

#define KSTAT_DATA_CHAR         0
#define KSTAT_DATA_INT32        1
#define KSTAT_DATA_UINT32       2
#define KSTAT_DATA_INT64        3
#define KSTAT_DATA_UINT64       4

#if !defined(_LP64)
#define KSTAT_DATA_LONG         KSTAT_DATA_INT32
#define KSTAT_DATA_ULONG        KSTAT_DATA_UINT32
#else
#if !defined(_KERNEL)
#define KSTAT_DATA_LONG         KSTAT_DATA_INT64
#define KSTAT_DATA_ULONG        KSTAT_DATA_UINT64
#else
#define KSTAT_DATA_LONG         7       /* only visible to the kernel */
#define KSTAT_DATA_ULONG        8       /* only visible to the kernel */
#endif  /* !_KERNEL */
#endif  /* !_LP64 */
```

*See sys/kstat.h*

The program in the above example uses a function `my_named_display()` to show how one might display named kstats.

Note that if the type is KSTAT_DATA_CHAR, the 16-byte value field is not guaranteed to be null-terminated. This is important to remember when you are printing the value with functions like printf().

### 11.1.3.3 KSTAT_TYPE_TIMER

This kstat holds event timer statistics. These provide basic counting and timing information for any type of event.

```
typedef struct kstat_timer {
        char          name[KSTAT_STRLEN];    /* event name */
        uchar_t       resv;                  /* reserved */
        u_longlong_t  num_events;            /* number of events */
        hrtime_t      elapsed_time;          /* cumulative elapsed time */
        hrtime_t      min_time;              /* shortest event duration */
        hrtime_t      max_time;              /* longest event duration */
        hrtime_t      start_time;            /* previous event start time */
        hrtime_t      stop_time;             /* previous event stop time */
} kstat_timer_t;
```
*See sys/kstat.h*

### 11.1.3.4 KSTAT_TYPE_INTR

This type of kstat holds interrupt statistics. Interrupts are categorized as listed in Table 11.1 and as shown below the table.

#### Table 11.1 Types of Interrupt Kstats

| Interrupt Type | Definition |
| --- | --- |
| Hard | Sourced from the hardware device itself |
| Soft | Induced by the system by means of some system interrupt source |
| Watchdog | Induced by a periodic timer call |
| Spurious | An interrupt entry point was entered but there was no interrupt to service |
| Multiple Service | An interrupt was detected and serviced just before returning from any of the other types |

```
#define KSTAT_INTR_HARD       0
#define KSTAT_INTR_SOFT       1
#define KSTAT_INTR_WATCHDOG   2
#define KSTAT_INTR_SPURIOUS   3
#define KSTAT_INTR_MULTSVC    4
#define KSTAT_NUM_INTRS       5
typedef struct kstat_intr {
    uint_t intrs[KSTAT_NUM_INTRS]; /* interrupt counters */
} kstat_intr_t;
```
*See sys/kstat.h*

### 11.1.3.5 `KSTAT_TYPE_IO`

This kstat counts I/O's for statistical analysis.

```
typedef struct kstat_io {
    /*
     * Basic counters.
     */
    u_longlong_t    nread;          /* number of bytes read */
    u_longlong_t    nwritten;       /* number of bytes written */
    uint_t          reads;          /* number of read operations */
    uint_t          writes;         /* number of write operations */


    /*
     * Accumulated time and queue length statistics.
     */
    hrtime_t    wtime;              /* cumulative wait (pre-service) time */
    hrtime_t    wlentime;           /* cumulative wait length*time product*/
    hrtime_t    wlastupdate;        /* last time wait queue changed */
    hrtime_t    rtime;              /* cumulative run (service) time */
    hrtime_t    rlentime;           /* cumulative run length*time product */
    hrtime_t    rlastupdate;        /* last time run queue changed */
    uint_t      wcnt;               /* count of elements in wait state */
    uint_t      rcnt;               /* count of elements in run state */
} kstat_io_t;
```
*See sys/kstat.h*

**Accumulated Time and Queue Length Statistics.**   Time statistics are kept as a running sum of "active" time. Queue length statistics are kept as a running sum of the product of queue length and elapsed time at that length. That is, a Riemann sum for queue length integrated against time. Figure 11.2 illustrates a sample graphical representation of queue vs. time.

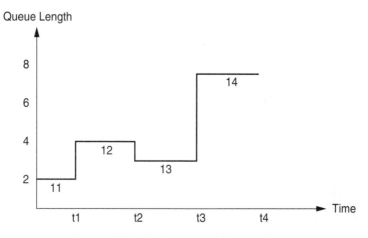

**Figure 11.2** Queue Length Sampling

At each change of state (either an entry or exit from the queue), the elapsed time since the previous state change is added to the active time (`wlen` or `rlen` fields) if the queue length was non-zero during that interval.

The product of the elapsed time and the queue length is added to the running sum of the length (`wlentime` or `rlentime` fields) multiplied by the time.

Stated programmatically:

```
if (queue length != 0) {
    time += elapsed time since last state change;
    lentime +=  (elapsed time since last state change * queue length);
}
```

You can generalize this method to measure residency in any defined system. Instead of queue lengths, think of "outstanding RPC calls to server X."

A large number of I/O subsystems have at least two basic lists of transactions they manage:

- A list for transactions that have been accepted for processing but for which processing has yet to begin
- A list for transactions that are actively being processed but that are not complete

For these reasons, two cumulative time statistics are defined:

- Pre-service (wait) time
- Service (run) time

The units of cumulative busy time are accumulated nanoseconds.

## 11.1.4 Kstat Names

The kstat namespace is defined by three fields from the `kstat` structure:

- `ks_module`
- `ks_instance`
- `ks_name`

The combination of these three fields is guaranteed to be unique.

For example, imagine a system with four FastEthernet interfaces. The device driver module for Sun's FastEthernet controller is called `"hme"`. The first Ethernet interface would be instance 0, the second instance 1, and so on. The `"hme"` driver provides two types of kstat for each interface. The first contains named kstats with performance statistics. The second contains interrupt statistics.

The kstat data for the first interface's network statistics is found under `ks_module == "hme"`, `ks_instance == 0`, and `ks_name == "hme0"`. The interrupt statistics are contained in a kstat identified by `ks_module == "hme"`, `ks_instance == 0`, and `ks_name == "hmec0"`.

In that example, the combination of module name and instance number to make the `ks_name` field (`"hme0"` and `"hmec0"`) is simply a convention for this driver. Other drivers may use similar naming conventions to publish multiple kstat data types but are not required to do so; the module is required to make sure that the combination is unique.

How do you determine what kstats the kernel provides? One of the easiest ways with Solaris 8 is to run `/usr/bin/kstat` with no arguments. This command prints nearly all the current kstat data. The Solaris `kstat` command can dump most of the known kstats of type `KSTAT_TYPE_RAW`.

## 11.1.5 Functions

The following functions are available to C programs for accessing kstat data from user programs:

```
kstat_ctl_t * kstat_open(void);
```

Initializes a kstat control structure to provide access to the kernel statistics library. It returns a pointer to this structure, which must be supplied as the kc argument in subsequent libkstat function calls.

```
kstat_t * kstat_lookup(kstat_ctl_t *kc, char *ks_module, int ks_instance,
                       char *ks_name);
```

Traverses the kstat chain searching for a kstat with a given ks_module, ks_instance, and ks_name fields. If the ks_module is NULL, ks_instance is -1, or if ks_name is NULL, then those fields are ignored in the search. For example, kstat_lookup(kc, NULL, -1, "foo") simply finds the first kstat with the name "foo".

```
void * kstat_data_lookup(kstat_t *ksp, char *name);
```

Searches the kstat's data section for the record with the specified name. This operation is valid only for kstat types that have named data records. Currently, only the KSTAT_TYPE_NAMED and KSTAT_TYPE_TIMER kstats have named data records. You must first call kstat_read() to get the data from the kernel. This routine then finds a particular record in the data section.

```
kid_t kstat_read(kstat_ctl_t *kc, kstat_t *ksp, void *buf);
```

Gets data from the kernel for a particular kstat.

*continues*

```
kid_t kstat_write(kstat_ctl_t *kc, kstat_t *ksp, void *buf);
```

Writes data to a particular kstat in the kernel. Only the superuser can use kstat_write().

```
kid_t kstat_chain_update(kstat_ctl_t *kc);
```

Synchronizes the user's kstat header chain with that of the kernel.

```
int kstat_close(kstat_ctl_t *kc);
```

Frees all resources that were associated with the kstat control structure. This is done automatically on exit(2) and execve(). (For more information on exit(2) and execve(), see the exec(2) man page.)

## 11.1.6 Management of Chain Updates

Recall that the kstat chain is dynamic in nature. The libkstat library function kstat_open() returns a copy of the kernel's kstat chain. Since the content of the kernel's chain may change, your program should call the kstat_chain_update() function at the appropriate times to see if its private copy of the chain is the same as the kernel's. This is the purpose of the KCID (stored in kc_chain_id in the kstat control structure).

Each time a kernel module adds or removes a kstat from the system's chain, the KCID is incremented. When your program calls kstat_chain_update(), the function checks to see if the kc_chain_id in your program's control structure matches the kernel's. If not, kc_chain_update() rebuilds your program's local kstat chain and returns the following:

- The new KCID if the chain has been updated
- 0 if no change has been made
- -1 if some error was detected

If your program has cached some local data from previous calls to the kstat library, then a new KCID acts as a flag to indicate that you have up-to-date information. You can search the chain again to see if data that your program is interested in has been added or removed.

A practical example is the system command iostat. It caches some internal data about the disks in the system and needs to recognize that a disk has been brought on-line or off-line. If iostat is called with an interval argument, it prints I/O statistics every interval second. Each time through the loop, it calls kstat_chain_update() to see if something has changed. If a change took place, it figures out if a device of interest has been added or removed.

## 11.1.7 Putting It All Together

Your C source file must contain:

```
#include <kstat.h>
```

When your program is linked, the compiler command line must include the argument -lkstat.

```
$ cc -o print_some_kstats -lkstat print_some_kstats.c
```

The following is a short example program. First, it uses kstat_lookup() and kstat_read() to find the system's CPU speed. Then it goes into an infinite loop to print a small amount of information about all kstats of type KSTAT_TYPE_IO. Note that at the top of the loop, it calls kstat_chain_update() to check that you have current data. If the kstat chain has changed, the program sends a short message on stderr.

```c
/*  print_some_kstats.c:
 *  print out a couple of interesting things
 */
#include <kstat.h>
#include <stdio.h>
#include <inttypes.h>
#define SLEEPTIME 10

void my_named_display(char *, char *, kstat_named_t *);
void my_io_display(char *, char *, kstat_io_t);

main(int argc, char **argv)
{
    kstat_ctl_t     *kc;
    kstat_t         *ksp;
    kstat_io_t       kio;
    kstat_named_t *knp;

    kc = kstat_open();

    /*
     * Print out the CPU speed. We make two assumptions here:
     * 1) All CPUs are the same speed, so we'll just search for the
     *    first one;
     * 2) At least one CPU is online, so our search will always
     *    find something. :)
     */
    ksp = kstat_lookup(kc, "cpu_info", -1, NULL);
    kstat_read(kc, ksp, NULL);
    /* lookup the CPU speed data record */
    knp = kstat_data_lookup(ksp, "clock_MHz");
    printf("CPU speed of system is ");
    my_named_display(ksp->ks_name, ksp->ks_class, knp);
    printf("n");
```

*continues*

```
      /* dump some info about all I/O kstats every
         SLEEPTIME seconds  */
      while(1) {
         /* make sure we have current data */
         if(kstat_chain_update(kc))
             fprintf(stderr, "<<State Changed>>n");
         for (ksp = kc->kc_chain; ksp != NULL; ksp = ksp->ks_next) {
           if (ksp->ks_type == KSTAT_TYPE_IO) {
              kstat_read(kc, ksp, &kio);
              my_io_display(ksp->ks_name, ksp->ks_class, kio);
           }
         }
         sleep(SLEEPTIME);
      } /* while(1) */

}

void my_io_display(char *devname, char *class, kstat_io_t k)
{
      printf("Name: %s Class: %sn",devname,class);
      printf("tnumber of bytes read %lldn", k.nread);
      printf("tnumber of bytes written %lldn", k.nwritten);
      printf("tnumber of read operations %dn", k.reads);
      printf("tnumber of write operations %dnn", k.writes);
}
void
my_named_display(char *devname, char *class, kstat_named_t *knp)
{
      switch(knp->data_type) {
      case KSTAT_DATA_CHAR:
          printf("%.16s",knp->value.c);
          break;
      case KSTAT_DATA_INT32:
          printf("%" PRId32,knp->value.i32);
          break;
      case KSTAT_DATA_UINT32:
          printf("%" PRIu32,knp->value.ui32);
          break;
      case KSTAT_DATA_INT64:
          printf("%" PRId64,knp->value.i64);
          break;
      case KSTAT_DATA_UINT64:
          printf("%" PRIu64,knp->value.ui64);
      }
}
```

## 11.2 Command-Line Interface

In this section, we explain tools with which you access kstat information with shell scripts. Included are a few examples to introduce the kstat(1m) program and the Perl language module it uses to extract kernel statistics.

The Solaris 8 OS introduced a new method to access kstat information from the command line or in custom-written scripts. You can use the command-line tool /usr/bin/kstat interactively to print all or selected kstat information from a system. This program is written in the Perl language, and you can use the Perl XS extension module to write your own custom Perl programs. Both facilities are documented in the pages of the online manual.

## 11.2.1 The `kstat` Command

You can invoke the `kstat` command on the command line or within shell scripts to selectively extract kernel statistics. Like many other Solaris OS commands, `kstat` takes optional interval and count arguments for repetitive, periodic output. Its command options are quite flexible.

The first form follows standard UNIX command-line syntax, and the second form provides a way to pass some of the arguments as colon-separated fields. Both forms offer the same functionality. Each of the module, instance, name, or statistic specifiers may be a shell glob pattern or a Perl regular expression enclosed by "/" characters. You can use both specifier types within a single operand. Leaving a specifier empty is equivalent to using the "*" glob pattern for that specifier. Running `kstat` with no arguments will print out nearly all kstat entries from the running kernel (most, but not all kstats of KSTAT_TYPE_RAW are decoded).

The tests specified by the options are logically ANDed, and all matching kstats are selected. The argument for the `-c`, `-i`, `-m`, `-n`, and `-s` options can be specified as a shell glob pattern, or a Perl regular expression enclosed in "/" characters.

If you pass a regular expression containing shell metacharacters to the command, you must protect it from the shell by enclosing it with the appropriate quotation marks. For example, to show all kstats that have a statistics name beginning with `intr` in the module name `cpu_stat`, you could use the following script:

```
$ kstat -p -m cpu_stat -s 'intr*'
cpu_stat:0:cpu_stat0:intr       878951000
cpu_stat:0:cpu_stat0:intrblk    21604
cpu_stat:0:cpu_stat0:intrthread 668353070
cpu_stat:1:cpu_stat1:intr       211041358
cpu_stat:1:cpu_stat1:intrblk    280
cpu_stat:1:cpu_stat1:intrthread 209879640
```

The `-p` option used in the preceding example displays output in a parsable format. If you do not specify this option, `kstat` produces output in a human-readable, tabular format. In the following example, we leave out the `-p` flag and use the *module:instance:name:statistic* argument form and a Perl regular expression.

```
$ $ kstat cpu_stat:::/^intr/
module: cpu_stat                        instance: 0
name:   cpu_stat0                       class:    misc
        intr                            879131909
        intrblk                         21608
        intrthread                      668490486
module: cpu_stat                        instance: 1
name:   cpu_stat1                       class:    misc
        intr                            211084960
        intrblk                         280
        intrthread                      209923001
```

Sometimes you may just want to test for the existence of a kstat entry. You can use the -q flag, which returns the appropriate exit status for matches against given criteria. The exit codes are as follows:

- 0: One or more statistics were matched.
- 1: No statistics were matched.
- 2: Invalid command-line options were specified.
- 3: A fatal error occurred.

Suppose that you have a Bourne shell script gathering network statistics, and you want to see if the NFS server is configured. You might create a script such as the one in the following example.

```
#!/bin/sh
# ... do some stuff
# Check for NFS server
kstat -q nfs::nfs_server:
if [ $? = 0 ]; then
    echo "NFS Server configured"
else
    echo "No NFS Server configured"
fi
# ... do some more stuff
exit 0
```

## 11.2.2 Real-World Example That Uses kstat and nawk

If you are adept at writing shell scripts with editing tools like sed or awk, here is a simple example to create a network statistics utility with kstats.

The /usr/bin/netstat command has a command-line option -I interface by which you can to print out statistics about a particular network interface. Optionally, netstat takes an interval argument to print out the statistics every interval seconds. The following example illustrates that option.

```
$ netstat -I qfe0 5
    input   qfe0      output            input  (Total)    output
packets errs  packets errs  colls  packets errs  packets errs  colls
2971681 0     1920781 0     0      11198281 0    10147381 0     0
9       0     7       0     0      31       0    29       0     0
4       0     5       0     0      24       0    25       0     0
...
```

Unfortunately, this command accepts only one -I flag argument. What if you want to print statistics about multiple interfaces simultaneously, similar to what iostat does for disks? You could devise a Bourne shell script using `kstat` and `nawk` to provide this functionality. You want your output to look like the following example.

```
$ netstatMulti.sh ge0 ge2 ge1 5
              input                output
            packets    errs    packets    errs   colls
ge0        111702738   10     82259260    0      0
ge2        28475869    0      61288614    0      0
ge1        25542766    4      55587276    0      0
ge0        1638        0      1075        0      0
ge2        518         0      460         0      0
ge1        866         0      7688        0      0
...
```

The next example is the statistics script. Note that extracting the kstat information is simple, and most of the work goes into parsing and formatting the output. The script uses `kstat -q` to check the user's arguments for valid interface names and then passes a list of formatted *module:instance:name:statistic* arguments to `kstat` before piping the output to `nawk`

```
#!/bin/sh
# netstatMulti.sh: print out netstat-like stats for
# multiple interfaces
#    using /usr/bin/kstat and nawk
USAGE="$0: interface_name ... interval"

INTERFACES="" # args list for kstat

while [ $# -gt 1 ]
do
    kstat -q -c net ::$1:    # test for valid interface
                             # name
    if [ $? != 0 ]; then
        echo $USAGE
        echo "  Interface $1 not found"
        exit 1
    fi
    INTERFACES="$INTERFACES ::$1:" # add to list
    shift
done

interval=$1

# check interval arg for int
if [ X`echo $interval | tr -d [0-9]` != X"" ]; then
        echo $USAGE
        exit 1
fi

kstat -p $INTERFACES $interval | nawk '
function process_stat(STATNAME, VALUE) {
    found = 0
```

*continues*

```
    for(i=1;i<=5;i++) {
        if(STATNAME == FIELDS[i]) {
            found = 1
            break
        }
    }

    if ( found == 0 ) return

    kstat = sprintf("%s:%s", iface, STATNAME)

    if(kstat in b_kstats) {
        kstats[kstat] = VALUE - b_kstats[kstat]
    } else {
        b_kstats[kstat] = VALUE
        kstats[kstat] = VALUE
    }
}

function print_stats() {
    printf("%-10s",iface)
    for(i=1;i<=5;i++) {
        kstat = sprintf("%s:%s",iface,FIELDS[i])
        printf(FORMATS[i],kstats[kstat])
        printf(" ")
    }
    print " "
}

BEGIN {
    print "                 input            output       "
    print "              packets    errs  packets   errs
      colls"
    split("ipackets,ierrors,opackets,oerrors,collisions",
      FIELDS,",")
    split("%-10u %-5u %-10u %-5u %-6u",FORMATS," ")
}

NF == 1 {
    if(iface) {
        print_stats()
    }
    split($0,t,":")
    iface = t[3]
    next
}

{
    split($1,stat,":")
    process_stat(stat[4], $2)
}
```

## 11.3  Using Perl to Access kstats

The previous example illustrates how simple it is to extract the information you need from the kernel; however, it also shows how tedious it can be to format the output in a shell script. Fortunately, the Perl extension module that /usr/bin/kstat uses is documented so that you can write custom Perl programs. Because

Perl is a "real programming language" and is ideally suited for text formatting, you can write solutions that are quite robust and comprehensive.

## 11.3.1 The Tied-Hash Interface to the `kstat` Facility

Access to kstats is made through a Perl extension in the XSUB interface module called `Sun::Solaris::Kstat`. To access Solaris kernel statistics in a Perl program, you use `Sun::Solaris::Kstat`; to import the module

The module contains two methods, `new()` and `update()`, correlating with the `libkstat` C functions `kstat_open()` and `kstat_chain_update()`. The module provides kstat data through a tree of hashes based on a three-part key, consisting of the module, instance, and name (`ks_module`, `ks_instance`, and `ks_name` are members of the C-language `kstat struct`). Following is a synopsis.

```
Sun::Solaris::Kstat->new();
Sun::Solaris::Kstat->update();
Sun::Solaris::Kstat->{module}{instance}{name}{statistic}
```

The lowest-level "statistic" member of the hierarchy is a tied hash implemented in the XSUB module and holds the following elements from `struct kstat`:

- **ks_crtime.** Creation time, which is presented as the statistic `crtime`
- **ks_snaptime.** Time of last data snapshot, which is presented as the statistic `snaptime`
- **ks_class.** The kstat class, which is presented as the statistic `class`
- **ks_data.** Kstat type-specific data decoded into individual statistics (the module produces one statistic per member of whatever structure is being decoded)

Because the module converts all kstat types, you need not worry about the different data structures for named and raw types. Most of the Solaris OS raw kstat entries are decoded by the module, giving you easy access to low-level data about things such as kernel memory allocation, swap, NFS performance, etc.

## 11.3.2 The `update()` Method

The `update()` method updates all the statistics you have accessed so far and adds a bit of functionality on top of the `libkstat kstat_chain_update()` function. If called in scalar context, it acts the same as `kstat_chain_update()`. It returns 0 if the kstat chain has not changed and 1 if it has. However, if update() is called in list context, it returns references to two arrays. The first array holds the keys of any kstats that have been added since the call to new() or the last call to update(); the second holds a list of entries that have been deleted. The entries in the arrays are strings of the form *module:instance:name*. This is useful for implementing programs that cache state information about devices, such as disks, that you can dynamically add or remove from a running system.

Once you access a kstat, it will always be read by subsequent calls to update(). To stop it from being reread, you can clear the appropriate hash. For example:

```
$kstat->{$module}{$instance}{$name} = ();
```

### 11.3.3 64-Bit Values

At the time the kstat tied-hash interface was first released on the Solaris 8 OS, Perl 5 could not yet internally support 64-bit integers, so the kstat module approximates these values.

- **Timer.** Values ks_crtime and ks_snaptime in struct kstat are of type hrtime_t, as are values of timer kstats and the wtime, wlentime, wlastupdate, rtime, rlentime, and rlastupdate fields of the kstat I/O statistics structures. This is a C-type definition used for the Solaris high-resolution timer, which is a 64-bit integer value. These fields are measured by the kstat facility in nanoseconds, meaning that a 32-bit value would represent approximately four seconds. The alternative is to store the values as floating-point numbers, which offer approximately 53 bits of precision on present hardware. You can store 64-bit intervals and timers as floating-point values expressed in seconds, meaning that this module rounds up time-related kstats to approximately microsecond resolution.

- **Counters.** Because it is not useful to store these values as 32-bit values and because floating-point values offer 53 bits of precision, all 64-bit counters are also stored as floating-point values.

### 11.3.4 Getting Started with Perl

As in our first example, the following example shows a Perl program that gives the same output as obtained by calling /usr/sbin/psrinfo without arguments.

```
#!/usr/bin/perl -w

# psrinfo.perl: emulate the Solaris psrinfo command
use strict;
use Sun::Solaris::Kstat;

my $kstat = Sun::Solaris::Kstat->new();

my $mh = $kstat->{cpu_info};

foreach my $cpu (keys(%$mh)) {
    my ($state, $when) = @{$kstat->{cpu_info}{$cpu}
        {"cpu_info".$cpu}}{qw(state state_begin)};
    my ($sec,$min,$hour,$mday,$mon,$year) =
        (localtime($when))[0..5];
    printf("%d\t%-8s  since %.2d/%.2d/%.2d %.2d:%.2d:%.2d\n",
        $cpu,$state,$mon + 1,$mday,$year - 100,$hour,$min,$sec);

}
```

This program produces the following output:

```
$ psrinfo.perl
0        on-line  since 07/09/01 08:29:00
1        on-line  since 07/09/01 08:29:07
```

The psrinfo command has a -v (verbose) option that prints much more detail about the processors in the system. The output looks like the following example:

```
$ psrinfo -v
Status of processor 0 as of: 08/17/01 16:52:44
  Processor has been on-line since 08/14/01 16:27:56.
  The sparcv9 processor operates at 400 MHz,
        and has a sparcv9 floating point processor.
Status of processor 1 as of: 08/17/01 16:52:44
  Processor has been on-line since 08/14/01 16:28:03.
  The sparcv9 processor operates at 400 MHz,
        and has a sparcv9 floating point processor.
```

All the information in the psrinfo command is accessible through the kstat interface. As an exercise, try modifying the simple psrinfo.perl example script to print the verbose information, as in this example.

## 11.3.5 netstatMulti Implemented in Perl

The Perl script in the following example has the same function as our previous example (in Section 11.2.2 ) that used the kstat and nawk commands. Note that we have to implement our own search methods to find the kstat entries that we want to work with. Although this script is not shorter than our first example, it is certainly easier to extend with new functionality. Without much work, you could create a generic search method, similar to how /usr/bin/kstat works, and import it into any Perl scripts that need to access Solaris kernel statistics.

```perl
#!/usr/bin/perl -w
# netstatMulti.perl: print out netstat-like stats for multiple interfaces
#  using the kstat tied hash facility

use strict;
use Sun::Solaris::Kstat;

my $USAGE = "usage: $0  ... interval";

######
# Main
######
sub interface_exists($);
sub get_kstats();
sub print_kstats();

# process args

my $argc = scalar(@ARGV);
my @interfaces = ();
my $fmt = "%-10s %-10u %-10u %-10u %-10u %-10u\n";

if ($argc < 2) {
  print "$USAGE\n";
  exit 1;
} elsif  ( !($ARGV[-1] =~ /^\d+$/) ) {
  print "$USAGE\n";
  print "   interval must be an integer.\n";
  exit 1;
}

# get kstat chain a la kstat_open()
my $kstat = Sun::Solaris::Kstat->new();

# Check for interfaces
foreach my $interface (@ARGV[-($argc)..-2]) {
  my $iface;
  if(! ($iface = interface_exists($interface)) ){
    print "$USAGE\n";
    print "   interface $interface not found.\n";
    exit 1;
  }
  push @interfaces, $iface;
}

my $interval = $ARGV[-1];
# print header
print "                input                  output     \n";
print "   packets   errs      packets   errs       colls\n";

# loop forever printing stats
while(1) {
  get_kstats();
  print_kstats();
  sleep($interval);
  $kstat->update();
}
```

*continues*

```
#############
# Subroutines
#############

# search for the first kstat with given name
sub interface_exists($) {
  my ($name) = @_;
  my ($mod, $inst) = $name =~ /^(.+?)(\d+)$/;
  return(exists($kstat->{$mod}{$inst}{$name})
        ? { module => $mod, instance => $inst, name => $name }
        : undef);
}

                      # get kstats for given interface
sub get_kstats() {
  my (@statnames) = ('ipackets','ierrors','opackets',
    'oerrors','collisions');
  my ($m, $i, $n);
  foreach my $interface (@interfaces) {
    $m = $interface->{module};
    $i = $interface->{instance};
    $n = $interface->{name};
    foreach my $statname (@statnames) {
      my $stat = $kstat->{$m}{$i}{$n}{$statname};
      die "kstat not found: $m:$i:$n:$statname" unless defined $stat;
      my $begin_stat = "b_" . $statname; # name of first sample
      if(exists $interface->{$begin_stat}) {
        $interface->{$statname} = $stat -
          $interface->{$begin_stat};
      }else { # save first sample to calculate deltas
        $interface->{$statname} =  $stat;
        $interface->{$begin_stat} = $stat;
      }
    }
  }
}

# print out formatted information a la netstat
sub print_kstats() {
  foreach my $i (@interfaces) {
    printf($fmt,$i->{name},$i->{ipackets},$i->{ierrors},
      $i->{opackets},$i->{oerrors},$i->{collisions});
  }
}
```

In the subroutine `interface_exists()`, you cache the members of the key if an entry is found. This way, you need not do another search in `get_kstats()`. You could fairly easily modify the script to display all network interfaces on the system (rather than take command-line arguments) and use the `update()` method to discover if interfaces are added or removed from the system (with `ifconfig`, for example). This exercise is left up to you.

## 11.4 Snooping a Program's `kstat` Use with DTrace

Using DTrace, it is possible to examine the `kstat` instances that a program uses. The following DTrace script shows how this could be done.

```
#!/usr/sbin/dtrace -s

#pragma D option quiet

dtrace:::BEGIN
{
        printf("%-16s %-16s %-6s %s\n",
            "CMD", "CLASS", "TYPE", "MOD:INS:NAME");
}

fbt::read_kstat_data:entry
{
        self->uk = (kstat_t *)copyin((uintptr_t)arg1, sizeof (kstat_t));
        printf("%-16s %-16s %-6s %s:%d:%s\n", execname, self->uk->ks_class,
            self->uk->ks_type == 0 ? "raw"
          : self->uk->ks_type == 1 ? "named"
          : self->uk->ks_type == 2 ? "intr"
          : self->uk->ks_type == 3 ? "io"
          : self->uk->ks_type == 4 ? "timer" : "?",
            self->uk->ks_module, self->uk->ks_instance, self->uk->ks_name);
}
```

When we run the DTrace script above, it prints out the commands and their use of `kstat`.

```
# kstat_types.d
CMD             CLASS         TYPE    MOD:INS:NAME
vmstat          misc          named   cpu_info:0:cpu_info0
vmstat          misc          named   cpu:0:vm
vmstat          misc          named   cpu:0:sys
vmstat          disk          io      cmdk:0:cmdk0
vmstat          disk          io      sd:0:sd0
vmstat          misc          raw     unix:0:sysinfo
vmstat          vm            raw     unix:0:vminfo
vmstat          misc          named   unix:0:dnlcstats
vmstat          misc          named   unix:0:system_misc
```

## 11.5 Adding Statistics to the Solaris Kernel

The `kstat` mechanism provides lightweight statistics that are a stable part of kernel code. The `kstat` interface can provide standard information that would be reported from a user-level tool. For example, if you wanted to add your own device driver I/O statistics into the statistics pool reported by the `iostat` command, you would add a `kstat` provider.

The statistics reported by vmstat, iostat, and most of the other Solaris tools are gathered by a central kernel statistics subsystem, known as "kstat." The kstat facility is an all-purpose interface for collecting and reporting named and typed data.

A typical scenario will have a kstat producer and a kstat reader. The kstat reader is a utility in user mode that reads, potentially aggregates, and then reports the results. For example, the vmstat utility is a kstat reader that aggregates statistics provided by the vm system in the kernel.

Statistics are named and accessed by a four-tuple: class, module, name, instance. Solaris 8 introduced a new method to access kstat information from the command line or in custom-written scripts. You can use the command-line tool /usr/bin/kstat interactively to print all or selected kstat information from a system. This program is written in the Perl language, and you can use the Perl XS extension module to write your own custom Perl programs. Both facilities are documented in the pages of the Perl online manual.

## 11.5.1 A kstat Provider Walkthrough

To add your own statistics to your Solaris kernel, you need to create a kstat provider, which consists of an initialization function to create the statistics group and then create a callback function that updates the statistics before they are read. The callback function is often used to aggregate or summarize information before it is reported to the reader. The kstat provider interface is defined in kstat(3KSTAT) and kstat(9S). More verbose information can be found in usr/src/uts/common/sys/kstat.h.

The first step is to decide on the type of information you want to export. The two primary types are RAW and NAMED or IO. The RAW interface exports raw C data structures to userland; its use is strongly discouraged, since a change in the C structure will cause incompatibilities in the reader. The NAMED mechanisms are preferred since the data is typed and extensible. Both the NAMED and IO types use typed data.

The NAMED type provides single or multiple records of data and is the most common choice. The IO record provides I/O statistics only. It is collected and reported by the iostat command and therefore should be used only for items that can be viewed and reported as I/O devices (we do this currently for I/O devices and NFS file systems).

A simple example of NAMED statistics is the virtual memory summaries provided by system_pages.

```
$ kstat -n system_pages
module: unix                              instance: 0
name:    system_pages                     class:    pages
         availrmem                        343567
         crtime                           0
         desfree                          4001
         desscan                          25
         econtig                          4278190080
         fastscan                         256068
         freemem                          248309
         kernelbase                       3556769792
         lotsfree                         8002
         minfree                          2000
         nalloc                           11957763
         nalloc_calls                     9981
         nfree                            11856636
         nfree_calls                      6689
         nscan                            0
         pagesfree                        248309
         pageslocked                      168569
         pagestotal                       512136
         physmem                          522272
         pp_kernel                        64102
         slowscan                         100
         snaptime                         6573953.83957897
```

These are first declared and initialized by the following C structs in usr/src/uts/common/os/kstat_fr.c.

```
struct {
        kstat_named_t physmem;
        kstat_named_t nalloc;
        kstat_named_t nfree;
        kstat_named_t nalloc_calls;
        kstat_named_t nfree_calls;
        kstat_named_t kernelbase;
        kstat_named_t econtig;
        kstat_named_t freemem;
        kstat_named_t availrmem;
        kstat_named_t lotsfree;
        kstat_named_t desfree;
        kstat_named_t minfree;
        kstat_named_t fastscan;
        kstat_named_t slowscan;
        kstat_named_t nscan;
        kstat_named_t desscan;
        kstat_named_t pp_kernel;
        kstat_named_t pagesfree;
        kstat_named_t pageslocked;
        kstat_named_t pagestotal;
} system_pages_kstat = {
        { "physmem",            KSTAT_DATA_ULONG },
        { "nalloc",             KSTAT_DATA_ULONG },
        { "nfree",              KSTAT_DATA_ULONG },
        { "nalloc_calls",       KSTAT_DATA_ULONG },
        { "nfree_calls",        KSTAT_DATA_ULONG },
        { "kernelbase",         KSTAT_DATA_ULONG },
```

*continues*

```
        { "econtig",              KSTAT_DATA_ULONG },
        { "freemem",              KSTAT_DATA_ULONG },
        { "availrmem",            KSTAT_DATA_ULONG },
        { "lotsfree",             KSTAT_DATA_ULONG },
        { "desfree",              KSTAT_DATA_ULONG },
        { "minfree",              KSTAT_DATA_ULONG },
        { "fastscan",             KSTAT_DATA_ULONG },
        { "slowscan",             KSTAT_DATA_ULONG },
        { "nscan",                KSTAT_DATA_ULONG },
        { "desscan",              KSTAT_DATA_ULONG },
        { "pp_kernel",            KSTAT_DATA_ULONG },
        { "pagesfree",            KSTAT_DATA_ULONG },
        { "pageslocked",          KSTAT_DATA_ULONG },
        { "pagestotal",           KSTAT_DATA_ULONG },
};
```

These statistics are the simplest type, merely a basic list of 64-bit variables. Once declared, the kstats are registered with the subsystem.

```
static int system_pages_kstat_update(kstat_t *, int);

...

        kstat_t *ksp;

        ksp = kstat_create("unix", 0, "system_pages", "pages", KSTAT_TYPE_NAMED,
                sizeof (system_pages_kstat) / sizeof (kstat_named_t),
                KSTAT_FLAG_VIRTUAL);
        if (ksp) {
                ksp->ks_data = (void *) &system_pages_kstat;
                ksp->ks_update = system_pages_kstat_update;
                kstat_install(ksp);
        }

...
```

The kstat create function takes the 4-tuple description and the size of the kstat and provides a handle to the created kstats. The handle is then updated to include a pointer to the data and a callback function which will be invoked when the user reads the statistics.

The callback function when invoked has the task of updating the data structure pointed to by ks_data. If you choose not to update, simply set the callback function to default_kstat_update(). The system pages kstat preamble looks like this:

```
static int
system_pages_kstat_update(kstat_t *ksp, int rw)
{

        if (rw == KSTAT_WRITE) {
                return (EACCES);
        }
```

This basic preamble checks to see if the user code is trying to read or write the structure. (Yes, it's possible to write to some statistics if the provider allows it.) Once basic checks are done, the update callback simply stores the statistics into the predefined data structure, and then returns.

```
...
        system_pages_kstat.freemem.value.ul      = (ulong_t)freemem;
        system_pages_kstat.availrmem.value.ul    = (ulong_t)availrmem;
        system_pages_kstat.lotsfree.value.ul     = (ulong_t)lotsfree;
        system_pages_kstat.desfree.value.ul      = (ulong_t)desfree;
        system_pages_kstat.minfree.value.ul      = (ulong_t)minfree;
        system_pages_kstat.fastscan.value.ul     = (ulong_t)fastscan;
        system_pages_kstat.slowscan.value.ul     = (ulong_t)slowscan;
        system_pages_kstat.nscan.value.ul        = (ulong_t)nscan;
        system_pages_kstat.desscan.value.ul      = (ulong_t)desscan;
        system_pages_kstat.pagesfree.value.ul    = (ulong_t)freemem;
...


        return (0);
}
```

That's it for a basic named `kstat`.

## 11.5.2 I/O Statistics

In this section, we can see an example of how I/O stats are measured and recorded. As discussed in Section 11.1.3.5, there is special type of kstat for I/O statistics.

I/O devices are measured as a queue, using Reimann Sum—which is a count of the visits to the queue and a sum of the "active" time. These two metrics can be used to determine the average service time and I/O counts for the device. There are typically two queues for each device, the wait queue and the active queue. This represents the time spent after the request has been accepted and enqueued, and then the time spent active on the device.

An I/O device driver has a similar declare and create section, as we saw with the NAMED statistics. For instance, the floppy disk device driver (usr/src/uts/sun/io/fd.c) shows `kstat_create()` in the device driver attach function.

```
static int
fd_attach(dev_info_t *dip, ddi_attach_cmd_t cmd)
{
...
        fdc->c_un->un_iostat = kstat_create("fd", 0, "fd0", "disk",
            KSTAT_TYPE_IO, 1, KSTAT_FLAG_PERSISTENT);
        if (fdc->c_un->un_iostat) {
                fdc->c_un->un_iostat->ks_lock = &fdc->c_lolock;
                kstat_install(fdc->c_un->un_iostat);
        }
...
}
```

The per-I/O statistics are updated when the device driver strategy function and the location where the I/O is first received and queued. At this point, the I/O is marked as waiting on the wait queue.

```
#define KIOSP    KSTAT_IO_PTR(un->un_iostat)

static int
fd_strategy(register struct buf *bp)
{
        struct fdctlr *fdc;
        struct fdunit *un;

        fdc = fd_getctlr(bp->b_edev);
        un = fdc->c_un;
...
        /* Mark I/O as waiting on wait q */
        if (un->un_iostat) {
                kstat_waitq_enter(KIOSP);
        }


...
}
```

The I/O spends some time on the wait queue until the device is able to process the request. For each I/O the `fdstart()` routine moves the I/O from the wait queue to the run queue with the `kstat_waitq_to_runq()` function.

```
static void
fdstart(struct fdctlr *fdc)
{

...
                /* Mark I/O as active, move from wait to active q */
                if (un->un_iostat) {
                        kstat_waitq_to_runq(Kiosp);
                }
...

                /* Do I/O... */
...
```

When the I/O is complete (still in the `fdstart()` function), it is marked with `kstat_runq_exit()` as leaving the active queue. This updates the last part of the statistic, leaving us with the number of I/Os and the total time spent on each queue.

```
                 /* Mark I/O as complete */
                 if (un->un_iostat) {
                         if (bp->b_flags & B_READ) {
                                 KIOSP->reads++;
                                 KIOSP->nread +=
                                         (bp->b_bcount - bp->b_resid);
                         } else {
                                 KIOSP->writes++;
                                 KIOSP->nwritten += (bp->b_bcount - bp->b_resid);
                         }
                         kstat_runq_exit(KIOSP);
                 }
                 biodone(bp);

        ...

}
```

These statistics provide us with our familiar metrics, where `actv` is the average length of the queue of active I/Os and `asvc_t` is the average service time in the device. The wait queue is represented accordingly with `wait` and `wsvc_t`.

```
$ iostat -xn 10
                  extended device statistics
    r/s    w/s   kr/s   kw/s wait actv wsvc_t asvc_t  %w  %b device
    1.2    0.1    9.2    1.1  0.1  0.5    0.1   10.4   1   1 fd0
```

## 11.6  Additional Information

Much of the information in this chapter derives from various SunSolve InfoDocs, Solaris white papers, and Solaris man pages (section 3KSTAT). For detailed information on the APIs, refer to the *Solaris 8 Reference Manual Collection* and *Writing Device Drivers*. Both publications are available at `docs.sun.com`.

# PART THREE

# Debugging

# 12

# The Modular Debugger

*Contributions from Mike Shapiro*

This chapter introduces the Modular Debugger, MDB. The subsequent chapters serve as a guide to learn basic MDB capabilities.

## 12.1 Introduction to the Modular Debugger

If you were a detective investigating the scene of a crime, you might interview witnesses and ask them to describe what happened and who they saw. However, if there were no witnesses or these descriptions proved insufficient, you might consider collecting fingerprints and forensic evidence that could be examined for DNA to help solve the case. Often, software program failures divide into analogous categories: problems that can be solved with source-level debugging tools; and problems that require low-level debugging facilities, examination of core files, and knowledge of assembly language to diagnose and correct. The MDB environment facilitates analysis of this second class of problems.

It might not be necessary to use MDB in every case, just as a detective doesn't need a microscope and DNA evidence to solve every crime. However, when programming a complex low-level software system such as an operating system, you might frequently encounter these situations. That's why MDB is designed as a debugging framework that lets you construct your own custom analysis tools to aid in the diagnosis of these problems. MDB also provides a powerful set of built-in commands with which you can analyze the state of your program at the assembly language level.

## 12.1.1 MDB

MDB provides a completely customizable environment for debugging programs, including a dynamic module facility that programmers can use to implement their own debugging commands to perform program-specific analysis. Each MDB module can examine the program in several different contexts, including live and postmortem. The Solaris Operating System includes a set of MDB modules that assist programmers in debugging the Solaris kernel and related device drivers and kernel modules. Third-party developers might find it useful to develop and deliver their own debugging modules for supervisor or user software.

## 12.1.2 MDB Features

MDB offers an extensive collection of features for analyzing the Solaris kernel and other target programs. Here's what you can do:

- **Perform postmortem analysis of Solaris kernel crash dumps and user process core dumps.**

    MDB includes a collection of debugger modules that facilitate sophisticated analysis of kernel and process state, in addition to standard data display and formatting capabilities. The debugger modules allow you to formulate complex queries to do the following:

    – Locate all the memory allocated by a particular thread

    – Print a visual picture of a kernel STREAM

    – Determine what type of structure a particular address refers to

    – Locate leaked memory blocks in the kernel

    – Analyze memory to locate stack traces

- **Use a first-class programming API to implement your own debugger commands and analysis tools without having to recompile or modify the debugger itself.**

    In MDB, debugging support is implemented as a set of loadable modules (shared libraries on which the debugger can run dlopen(3C)), each of which provides a set of commands that extends the capabilities of the debugger itself. The debugger in turn provides an API of core services, such as the ability to read and write memory and access symbol table information. MDB provides a framework for developers to implement debugging support for their own drivers and modules; these modules can then be made available for everyone to use.

- **Learn to use MDB if you are already familiar with the legacy debugging tools `adb` and `crash`.**

  MDB is backward compatible with these existing debugging solutions. The MDB language itself is designed as a superset of the adb language; all existing adb macros and commands work within MDB, so developers who use adb can immediately use MDB without knowing any MDB-specific commands. MDB also provides commands that surpass the functionality available from the crash utility.

- **Benefit from enhanced usability features. MDB provides a host of usability features:**

  - Command-line editing
  - Command history
  - Built-in output pager
  - Syntax error checking and handling
  - Online help
  - Interactive session logging

The MDB infrastructure was first added in Solaris 8. Many new features have been added throughout Solaris releases, as shown in Table 12.1.

**Table 12.1** MDB History

| Solaris Revision | Annotation |
|---|---|
| Solaris 8 | MDB introduced |
| Solaris 9 | Kernel type information (e.g., `::print`) |
| Solaris 10 | User-level type information (Common Type Format) `kmdb` replaces `kadb` |

## 12.1.3 Terms

Throughout this chapter, MDB is used to describe the common debugger core—the set of functionality common to both `mdb` and `kmdb`. `mdb` refers to the userland debugger. `kmdb` refers to the in-situ kernel debugger.

## 12.2 MDB Concepts

This section discusses the significant aspects of MDB's design and the benefits derived from this architecture.

### 12.2.1 Building Blocks

MDB has several different types of building blocks which, when combined provide a flexible and extensible architecture. They include:

- Targets: the object to be inspected, such as kernel crash dumps and process core files.
- Debugger commands or dcmnds.
- Walkers: routines to "walk" the examined object's structures.
- Debugger modules or dmods.
- Macros: sets of debugger commands.

The following section describes each of these objects in more detail.

### 12.2.2 Targets

The target is the program being inspected by the debugger. MDB currently provides support for the following types of targets:

- User processes
- User process core files
- Live operating system without kernel execution control (through /dev/kmem and /dev/ksyms)
- Live operating system with kernel execution control (through kmdb(1))
- Operating system crash dumps
- User process images recorded inside an operating system crash dump
- ELF object files
- Raw data files

Each target exports a standard set of properties, including one or more address spaces, one or more symbol tables, a set of load objects, and a set of threads. Figure 12.1 shows an overview of the MDB architecture, including two of the built-in targets and a pair of sample modules.

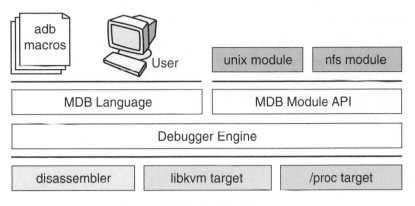

**Figure 12.1** MDB Architecture

## 12.2.3 Debugger Commands

A debugger command, or *dcmd* (pronounced dee-command) in MDB terminology, is a routine in the debugger that can access any of the properties of the current target. MDB parses commands from standard input, then executes the corresponding dcmds. Each dcmd can also accept a list of string or numerical arguments, as shown in Section 13.2. MDB contains a set of built-in dcmds described in Section 13.2.5, that are always available. The programmer can also extend the capabilities of MDB itself by writing dcmds, using a programming API provided with MDB.

## 12.2.4 Walker

A *walker* is a set of routines that describe how to walk, or iterate, through the elements of a particular program data structure. A walker encapsulates the data structure's implementation from dcmds and from MDB itself. You can use walkers interactively or as a primitive to build other dcmds or walkers. As with dcmds, you can extend MDB by implementing additional walkers as part of a debugger module.

## 12.2.5 Debugger Modules

A debugger module, or *dmod* (pronounced dee-mod), is a dynamically loaded library containing a set of dcmds and walkers. During initialization, MDB attempts to load dmods corresponding to the load objects present in the target. You can subsequently load or unload dmods at any time while running MDB. MDB provides a set of standard dmods for debugging the Solaris kernel.

## 12.2.6 Macros

A macro file is a text file containing a set of commands to execute. Macro files typically automate the process of displaying a simple data structure. MDB provides complete backward compatibility for the execution of macro files written for `adb`. The set of macro files provided with the Solaris installation can therefore be used with either tool.

## 12.2.7 Modularity

The benefit of MDB's modular architecture extends beyond the ability to load a module containing additional debugger commands. The MDB architecture defines clear interface boundaries between each of the layers shown in Figure 12.2. Macro files execute commands written in the MDB or adb language. Dcmds and walkers in debugger modules are written with the MDB Module API, and this forms the basis of an application binary interface that allows the debugger and its modules to evolve independently.

The MDB namespace of walkers and dcmds also defines a second set of layers between debugging code that maximizes code sharing and limits the amount of code that must be modified as the target program itself evolves. For example, imagine you want to determine the processes that were running when a kernel crash dump file was produced. One of the primary data structures in the Solaris kernel is the list of `proc_t` structures representing active processes in the system. To read this listing we use the `::ps` dcmd, which must iterate over this list to produce its output.The procedure to iterate over the list is is encapsulated in the genunix module's proc walker.

MDB provides both `::ps` and `::ptree` dcmds, but neither has any knowledge of how `proc_t` structures are accessed in the kernel. Instead, they invoke the proc walker programmatically and format the set of returned structures appropriately. If the data structure used for `proc_t` structures ever changed, MDB could provide a new proc walker and none of the dependent dcmds would need to change. You can also access the proc walker interactively with the `::walk` dcmd to create novel commands as you work during a debugging session.

In addition to facilitating layering and code sharing, the MDB Module API provides dcmds and walkers with a single stable interface for accessing various properties of the underlying target. The same API functions access information from user process or kernel targets, simplifying the task of developing new debugging facilities.

In addition, a custom MDB module can perform debugging tasks in a variety of contexts. For example, you might want to develop an MDB module for a user program you are developing. Once you have done so, you can use this module when

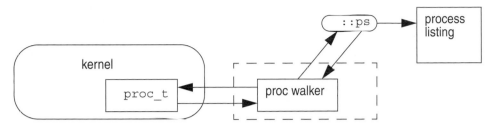

**Figure 12.2**  Example of MDB Modularity

MDB examines a live process executing your program, a core dump of your program, or even a kernel crash dump taken on a system on which your program was executing.

The Module API provides facilities for accessing the following target properties:

- **Address spaces.** The module API provides facilities for reading and writing data from the target's virtual address space. Functions for reading and writing using physical addresses are also provided for kernel debugging modules.

- **Symbol table.** The module API provides access to the static and dynamic symbol tables of the target's primary executable file, its runtime link editor, and a set of load objects (shared libraries in a user process or loadable modules in the Solaris kernel).

- **External data.** The module API provides a facility for retrieving a collection of named external data buffers associated with the target. For example, MDB provides programmatic access to the proc(4) structures associated with a user process or user core file target.

In addition, you can use built-in MDB dcmds to access information about target memory mappings, to load objects, to obtain register values, and to control the execution of user process targets.

# An MDB Tutorial

*Contributions from Mike Shapiro, Matthew Simmons, and Eric Schrock*

In this chapter, we take a tour of MDB basics, from startup through elements (command syntax, expressions, symbols, and other core concepts), via simple procedures illustrated by examples.

## 13.1 Invoking MDB

MDB is available on Solaris systems as two commands that share common features: mdb and kmdb. You can use the mdb command interactively or in scripts to debug live user processes, user process core files, kernel crash dumps, the live operating system, object files, and other files. You can use the kmdb command to debug the live operating system kernel and device drivers when you also need to control and halt the execution of the kernel. To start mdb, execute the mdb(1) command.

The following example shows how mdb can be started to examine a live kernel.

```
sol8# mdb -k
Loading modules: [ unix krtld genunix specfs dtrace ufs ip sctp usba uhci s1394 fcp fctl
emlxs nca lofs zfs random nfs audiosup sppp crypto md fcip logindmux ptm ipc ]
>
```

To start mdb with a kernel crash image, specify the namelist and core image names on the command line.

```
sol8# cd /var/crash/myserver

sol8# ls /var/crash/*
bounds    unix.1    unix.3    unix.5    unix.7    vmcore.1  vmcore.3  vmcore.5  vmcore.7
unix.0    unix.2    unix.4    unix.6    vmcore.0  vmcore.2  vmcore.4  vmcore.6

sol8# mdb -k unix.1 vmcore.1
Loading modules: [ unix krtld genunix specfs dtrace ufs ip sctp usba uhci s1394 fcp fctl
emlxs nca lofs zfs random nfs audiosup sppp crypto md fcip logindmux ptm ipc ]
>
```

To start `mdb` with a process target, enter either a command to execute or a process ID with the `-p` option.

```
# mdb /usr/bin/ls
>

# mdb -p 121
Loading modules: [ ld.so.1 libumem.so.1 libc.so.1 libuutil.so.1 ]
```

To start `kmdb`, boot the system or execute the `mdb` command with the `-K` option as described in Chapter 14.

## 13.1.1 Logging Output to a File

It's often useful to log output to a file, so arrange for that early on by using the `::log` dcmd.

```
> ::log mymdb.out
mdb: logging to "mymdb.out"
```

## 13.2 MDB Command Syntax

The MDB debugger lets us interact with the target program and the memory image of the target. The syntax is an enhanced form of that used with debuggers like `adb`, in which basic form is expressed as value and a command.

```
[value] [,count ] command
```

The language syntax is designed around the concept of computing the *value* of an *expression* (typically a memory address in the target), and applying a *command* to that expression. A command in MDB can be of several forms. It can be a *macro file*, a *metacharacter*, or a dcmd *pipeline*. A simple command is a metacharacter or dcmd followed by a sequence of zero or more blank-separated words. The words are typically passed as arguments. Each command returns an exit status that indicates it succeeded, failed, or was invoked with invalid arguments.

For example, if we wanted to display the contents of the word at address fec4b8d0, we could use the / metacharacter with the word X as a format specifier, and optionally a count specifying the number of iterations.

```
> fec4b8d0 /X
lotsfree:
lotsfree:       f5e
> fec4b8d0,4 /X
lotsfree:
lotsfree:       f5e         7af         3d7         28
```

MDB retains the notion of dot (.) as the current address or value, retained from the last successful command. A command with no supplied expression uses the value of dot for its argument.

```
> /X
lotsfree:
lotsfree:       f5e

> . /X
lotsfree:
lotsfree:       f5e
```

A pipeline is a sequence of one or more simple commands separated by |. Unlike the shell, dcmds in MDB pipelines are not executed as separate processes. After the pipeline has been parsed, each dcmd is invoked in order from left to right. The full definition of a command involving pipelines is as follows.

```
[expr] [,count ] pipeline [words...]
```

Each dcmd's output is processed and stored as described in "dcmd Pipelines" in Section 13.2.8. After the left-hand dcmd is complete, its processed output is used as input for the next dcmd in the pipeline. If any dcmd does not return a successful exit status, the pipeline is aborted.

For reference, Table 13.1 lists the full set of expression and pipeline combinations that form commands.

**Table 13.1**  General MDB Command Syntax

| Command | Description |
|---|---|
| `pipeline [!word...] [;]` | basic |
| `expr pipeline [!word...] [;]` | set dot, run once |
| `expr, expr pipeline [!word...] [;]` | set dot, repeat |
| `,expr pipeline [!word...] [;]` | repeat |
| `expr [!word...] [;]` | set dot, last pipeline, run once |
| `,expr [!word...] [;]` | last pipeline, repeat |
| `expr, expr [!word...] [;]` | set dot, last pipeline, repeat |
| `!word... [;]` | shell escape |

## 13.2.1 Expressions

Arithmetic expansion is performed when an MDB command is preceded by an optional *expression* representing a numerical argument for a dcmd. A list of common expressions is summarized in Tables 13.2, 13.3, and 13.4.

**Table 13.2**  Arithmetic Expressions

| Operator | Expression |
|---|---|
| `integer` | `0i` binary<br>`0o` octal<br>`0t` decimal<br>`0x` hex |
| `0t[0-9]+\.[0-9]+` | IEEE floating point |
| `'cccccccc'` | little-endian character const |
| `<identifier` | variable lookup |
| `identifier` | symbol lookup |
| `(expr)` | the value of expr |
| `.` | the value of dot |
| `&` | last dot used by dcmd |
| `+` | dot+increment |
| `^` | dot-increment (increment is effected by the last formatting dcmd) |

**Table 13.3** Unary Operators

| Operator | Expression |
|---|---|
| `#expr` | logical NOT |
| `~expr` | bitwise NOT |
| `-expr` | integer negation |
| `%expr` | object-file pointer dereference |
| `%/[csil]/expr` | object-file typed dereference |
| `%/[1248]/expr` | object-file sized dereference |
| `*expr` | virtual-address pointer dereference |
| `*/[csil]/expr` | virtual-address typed dereference |
| `*/[1248]/expr` | virtual-address sized dereference |
| *[csil] is char-, short-, int-, or long-sized* | |

**Table 13.4** Binary Operators

| Operator | Description |
|---|---|
| `expr * expr` | integer multiplication |
| `expr % expr` | integer division |
| `left # right` | left rounded up to next right multiple |
| `expr + expr` | integer addition |
| `expr - expr` | integer subtraction |
| `expr << expr` | bitwise left shift |
| `expr >> expr` | bitwise right shift (logical) |
| `expr == expr` | logical equality |
| `expr != expr` | logical inequality |
| `expr & expr` | bitwise AND |
| `expr ^ expr` | bitwise XOR |
| `expr | expr` | bitwise OR |

An example of a simple expression is adding an integer to an address.

```
> d7c662e0+0t8/X
0xd7c662e8:     d2998b80
> d7c662e0+0t8::print int
0xd7c662e8:     d2998b80
```

## 13.2.2 Symbols

MDB can reference memory or objects according to the value of a symbol of the target. A symbol is the name of either a function or a global variable in the target.

For example, you compute the address of the kernel's global variable `lotsfree` by entering it as an expression, and display it by using the = metacharacter. You display the value of the `lotsfree` symbol by using the / metacharacter.

```
> lotsfree=X
                fec4b8d0

> lotsfree/D
lotsfree:
lotsfree:       3934
```

Symbol names can be resolved from kernel and userland process targets. In the kernel, the resolution of the symbol names can optionally be defined with a scope by specifying the module or object file name. In a process, symbols' scope can be defined by library or object file names. They take the form shown in Table 13.5.

**Table 13.5** Resolving Symbol Names

| Target | Form |
| --- | --- |
| kernel | {module`}{file`}symbol |
| process | {LM[0-9]+`}{library`}{file`}symbol |

The target typically searches the primary executable's symbol tables first, then one or more of the other symbol tables. Notice that ELF symbol tables contain only entries for external, global, and static symbols; automatic symbols do not appear in the symbol tables processed by MDB.

Additionally, MDB provides a private user-defined symbol table that is searched before any of the target symbol tables are searched. The private symbol table is initially empty and can be manipulated with the ::nmadd and ::nmdel dcmds.

The ::nm -P option displays the contents of the private symbol table. The private symbol table allows the user to create symbol definitions for program functions or data that were either missing from the original program or stripped out.

```
> ::nm
Value      Size       Type  Bind  Other Shndx   Name
0x00000000|0x00000000|NOTY |LOCL |0x0  |UNDEF  |
0xfec40038|0x00000000|OBJT |LOCL |0x0  |14     |_END_
0xfe800000|0x00000000|OBJT |LOCL |0x0  |1      |_START_
0xfec00000|0x00000000|NOTY |LOCL |0x0  |10     |__return_from_main
...
```

These definitions are then used whenever MDB converts a symbolic name to an address, or an address to the nearest symbol. Because targets contain multiple symbol tables and each symbol table can include symbols from multiple object files, different symbols with the same name can exist. MDB uses the backquote " ` " character as a symbol-name scoping operator to allow the programmer to obtain the value of the desired symbol in this situation.

### 13.2.3 Formatting Metacharacters

The /, \, ?, and = metacharacters denote the special output formatting dcmds. Each of these dcmds accepts an argument list consisting of one or more format characters, repeat counts, or quoted strings. A format character is one of the ASCII characters shown in Table 13.6.

**Table 13.6** Formatting Metacharacters

| Metacharacter | Description |
| --- | --- |
| / | Read or write virtual address from . (dot) |
| \ | Read or write physical address from . |
| ? | Read or write primary object file, using virtual address from . |
| = | Read or write the value of . |

### 13.2.4 Formatting Characters

Format characters read or write and format data from the target. They are combined with the formatting metacharacters to read, write, or search memory. For example, if we want to display or set the value of a memory location, we could represent that location by its hexadecimal address or by its symbol name. Typically, we use a *metacharacter* with a *format* or a *dcmd* to indicate what we want MDB to do with the memory at the indicated address.

In the following example, we display the address of the kernel's lotsfree symbol. We use the = metacharacter to display the absolute value of the symbol, lotsfree and the X format to display the address in 32-bit hexadecimal notation.

```
> lotsfree=X
fec4b8d0
```

In a more common example, we can use the / metacharacter to format for display the value at the *address* of the lotsfree symbol.

```
> lotsfree/D
lotsfree:
lotsfree:        4062
```

Optionally, a repeat count can be supplied with a format. A repeat count is a positive integer preceding the format character and is always interpreted in base 10 (decimal). A repeat count can also be specified as an expression enclosed in square brackets preceded by a dollar sign ($ [ ]). A string argument must be enclosed in double-quotes (" "). No blanks are necessary between format arguments.

```
> lotsfree/4D
lotsfree:
lotsfree:        3934            1967           983              40
```

If MDB is started in writable (-w) mode, then write formats are enabled. Note that this should be considered MDB's dangerous mode, especially if operating on live kernels or applications. For example, if we wanted to rewrite the value indicated by lotsfree to a new value, we could use the W write format with a valid MDB value or arithmetic expression as shown in the summary at the start of this section. For example, the W format writes the 32-bit value to the given address. In this example, we use an integer value, represented by the 0t arithmetic expression prefix.

```
> lotsfree/W 0t5000
lotsfree:
lotsfree:        f5e
```

A complete list of format strings can be found with the ::formats dcmd.

```
> ::formats
+ - increment dot by the count (variable size)
- - decrement dot by the count (variable size)
B - hexadecimal int (1 byte)
C - character using C character notation (1 byte)
D - decimal signed int (4 bytes)
E - decimal unsigned long long (8 bytes)
...
```

A summary of the common formatting characters and the required metacharacters is shown in Table 13.7 through Table 13.9.

**Table 13.7** Metacharacters and Formats for Reading

| Metacharacter | | | Description |
|---|---|---|---|
| `[/\?=] [BCVbcdhoquDHOQ+-^NnTrtaIiSsE]` | | | value is immediate or `$[expr]` |
| `/` | | | format VA from . (dot) |
| `\` | | | format PA from . |
| `?` | | | format primary object file, using VA from . |
| `=` | | | format value of . |

| Format | Description | Format | Description |
|---|---|---|---|
| B (1) | hex | + | dot += increment |
| C (1) | char (C-encoded) | - | dot -= increment |
| V (1) | unsigned | ^ (var) | dot -= incr*count |
| b (1) | octal | N | newline |
| c (1) | char (raw) | n | newline |
| d (2) | signed | T | tab |
| h (2) | hex, swap endianness | r | whitespace |
| o (2) | octal | t | tab |
| q (2) | signed octal | a | dot as symbol+offset |
| u (2) | decimal | I (var) | address and instruction |
| D (4) | signed | i (var) | instruction |
| H (4) | hex, swap endianness | S (var) | string (C-encoded) |
| O (4) | octal | s (var) | string (raw) |
| Q (4) | signed octal | E (8) | unsigned |
| U (4) | unsigned | F (8) | double |
| X (4) | hex | G (8) | octal |
| Y (4) | decoded `time32_t` | J (8) | hex |
| f (4) | float | R (8) | binary |
| K (4\|8) | hex `uintptr_t` | e (8) | signed |
| P (4\|8) | symbol | g (8) | signed octal |
| p (4\|8) | symbol | y (8) | decoded `time64_t` |

**Table 13.8** Metacharacters and Formats for Writing

| Metacharacter | Description |
| --- | --- |
| `[/\?][vwWZ] value...` | value is immediate or `$[expr]` |
| `/` | write virtual addresses |
| `\` | write physical addresses |
| `?` | write object file |

| **Format** | **Description** |
| --- | --- |
| `v (1)` | write low byte of each value, starting at dot |
| `w (2)` | write low 2 bytes of each value, starting at dot |
| `W (4)` | write low 4 bytes of each value, starting at dot |
| `Z (8)` | write all 8 bytes of each value, starting at dot |

**Table 13.9** Metacharacters and Formats for Searching

| Metacharacter | Description |
| --- | --- |
| `[/\?][lLM] value [mask]` | value and mask are immediate or `$[expr]` |
| `/` | search virtual addresses |
| `\` | search physical addresses |
| `?` | search object file |

| Format | Description |
| --- | --- |
| l (2) | search for 2-byte value, optionally masked |
| L (4) | search for 4-byte value, optionally masked |
| M (8) | search for 8-byte value, optionally masked |

## 13.2.5 dcmds

The metacharacters we explored in the previous section are actually forms of dcmds. The more general form of a dcmd is `::name`, where name is the command name, as summarized by the following:

```
::{module`}d
expr>var        write the value of expr into var
```

A list of dcmds can be obtained with ::dcmds. Alternatively, the ::dmods command displays information about both dcmds and walkers, conveniently grouped per MDB module.

```
> ::dmods -1
genunix
...
  dcmd pfiles              - print process file information
  dcmd pgrep               - pattern match against all processes
  dcmd pid2proc            - convert PID to proc_t address
  dcmd pmap                - print process memory map
  dcmd project             - display kernel project(s)
  dcmd prtconf             - print devinfo tree
  dcmd ps                  - list processes (and associated thr,lwp)
  dcmd ptree               - print process tree
...
```

Help on individual dcmds is available with the help dcmd. Yes, almost everything in MDB is implemented as a dcmd!

```
> ::help ps

NAME
  ps - list processes (and associated thr,lwp)

SYNOPSIS
  ..ps [-flrzTP]

ATTRIBUTES

  Target: kvm
  Module: genunix
  Interface Stability: Unstable
```

For example, we can optionally use ::ps as a simple dcmd with no arguments.

```
> ::ps
S    PID  PPID  PGID   SID  UID      FLAGS              ADDR NAME
R      0     0     0     0    0 0x00000001 ffffffffbc23640 sched
R      3     0     0     0    0 0x00020001 ffffffff812278f8 fsflush
R      2     0     0     0    0 0x00020001 ffffffff81228520 pageout
R      1     0     0     0    0 0x42004000 ffffffff81229148 init
R   1782     1  1782  1782    1 0x42000000 ffffffff8121cc38 lockd
R    524     1   524   524    0 0x42000000 ffffffff8b7fd548 dmispd
R    513     1   513   513    0 0x42010000 ffffffff87bd2878 snmpdx
R    482     1     7     7    0 0x42004000 ffffffff87be90b8 intrd
R    467     1   466   466    0 0x42010000 ffffffff87bd8020 smcboot
```

Optionally, we could use the same ::ps dcmd with an address supplied in hexa-decimal.

```
> ffffffff87be90b8::ps
S     PID    PPID    PGID    SID    UID      FLAGS         ADDR NAME
R     482      1       7      7       0 0x42004000 ffffffff87be90b8 intrd

> ffffffff87be90b8::ps -ft
S     PID    PPID    PGID    SID    UID      FLAGS         ADDR NAME
R     482      1       7      7       0 0x42004000 ffffffff87be90b8 /usr/perl5/bin/perl /
usr/lib/intrd
          T   0xffffffff8926d4e0 <TS_SLEEP>
```

## 13.2.6 Walkers

A *walker* is used to traverse a connect set of data. Walkers are a type of plugin that is coded to iterate over the specified type of data. In addition to the ::dcmds dcmd, the ::walkers dcmd lists walkers.

```
> ::walkers
Client_entry_cache          - walk the Client_entry_cache cache
DelegStateID_entry_cache    - walk the DelegStateID_entry_cache cache
File_entry_cache            - walk the File_entry_cache cache
HatHash                     - walk the HatHash cache
...
```

For example, the ::proc walker could be used to traverse set of process struc-tures (proc_ts). Many walkers also have a default data item to walk if none is specified.

```
> ::walk proc
ffffffffffbc23640
ffffffff812278f8
ffffffff81228520
...
```

There are walkers to traverse common generic data structure indexes. For example, simple linked lists can be traversed with the ::list walker, and AVL trees with the ::avl walker.

```
> ffffffff9a647ae0::walk avl
ffffffff9087a990
fffffe85ad8aa878
fffffe85ad8aa170
...
> ffffffffffbc23640::list proc_t p_prev
ffffffffffbc23640
ffffffff81229148
ffffffff81228520
...
```

## 13.2.7 Macros

MDB provides a compatibility mode that can interpret macros built for `adb`. A macro file is a text file containing a set of commands to execute. Macro files typically automate the process of displaying a simple data structure. These older macros can therefore be used with either tool. The development of macros is discouraged, since they are difficult to construct and maintain. Following is an example of using a macro to display a data structure.

```
> d8126310$<ce
            ce instance structure
0xd8126310:   dip                instance        dev_regs
              d8c8e840           d84b65c8        d2999900
...
```

## 13.2.8 Pipelines

Walkers and dcmds can build on each other, combining to do more powerful things by placement into an mdb "pipeline."

The purpose of a pipeline is to pass a list of values, typically virtual addresses, from one dcmd or walker to another. Pipeline stages might map a pointer from one type of data structure to a pointer to a corresponding data structure, sort a list of addresses, or select the addresses of structures with certain properties.

MDB executes each dcmd in the pipeline in order from left to right. The leftmost dcmd executes with the current value of dot or with the value specified by an explicit expression at the start of the command. When a | operator is encountered, MDB creates a pipe (a shared buffer) between the output of the dcmd to its left and the MDB parser, and an empty list of values.

To give you a taste of the power of pipelines, here's an example, running against the live kernel. The `::pgrep` dcmd allows you to find all processes matching a pattern, the thread walker walks all of the threads in a process, and the `::findstack` dcmd gets a stack trace for a given thread. Connecting them into a pipeline, you can yield the stack traces of all sshd threads on the system (note that the middle one is swapped out). MDB pipelines are quite similar to standard UNIX pipelines and afford debugger users a similar level of power and flexibility.

```
> ::pgrep sshd
S     PID   PPID  PGID    SID    UID      FLAGS            ADDR NAME
R 100174       1 100174 100174      0 0x42000000 0000030009216790 sshd
R 276948 100174 100174 100174      0 0x42010000 000003002d9a9860 sshd
R 276617 100174 100174 100174      0 0x42010000 0000030013943010 sshd
> ::pgrep sshd | ::walk thread
3000c4f0c80
311967e9660
30f2ff2c340
> ::pgrep sshd | ::walk thread | ::findstack
stack pointer for thread 3000c4f0c80: 2a10099d071
[ 000002a10099d071 cv_wait_sig_swap+0x130() ]
  000002a10099d121 poll_common+0x530()
  000002a10099d211 pollsys+0xf8()
  000002a10099d2f1 syscall_trap32+0x1e8()
stack pointer for thread 311967e9660: 2a100897071
[ 000002a100897071 cv_wait_sig_swap+0x130() ]
stack pointer for thread 30f2ff2c340: 2a100693071
[ 000002a100693071 cv_wait_sig_swap+0x130() ]
  000002a100693121 poll_common+0x530()
  000002a100693211 pollsys+0xf8()
  000002a1006932f1 syscall_trap32+0x1e8()
```

The full list of built-in dcmds can be obtained with the ::dmods dcmd.

```
> ::dmods -l mdb

mdb
   dcmd $<              - replace input with macro
   dcmd $<<             - source macro
   dcmd $>              - log session to a file
   dcmd $?              - print status and registers
   dcmd $C              - print stack backtrace
...
```

## 13.2.9  Piping to UNIX Commands

MDB can pipe output to UNIX commands with the ! pipe. A common task is to use grep to filter output from a dcmd. We've shown the output from ::ps for illustration; actually, a handy ::pgrep command handles this common task.

```
> ::ps !grep inet
R    255       1    255    255      0 0x42000000 ffffffff87be9ce0 inetd
```

## 13.2.10 Obtaining Symbolic Type Information

The MDB environment exploits the Compact Type Format (CTF) information in debugging targets. This provides symbolic type information for data structures in the target; such information can then be used within the debugging environment.

Several dcmds consume CTF information, most notably ::print. The ::print dcmd displays a target data type in native C representation. The following example shows ::print in action.

```
/* process ID info */

struct pid {
        unsigned int pid_prinactive :1;
        unsigned int pid_pgorphaned :1;
        unsigned int pid_padding :6;      /* used to be pid_ref, now an int */
        unsigned int pid_prslot :24;
        pid_t pid_id;
        struct proc *pid_pglink;
        struct proc *pid_pgtail;
        struct pid *pid_link;
        uint_t pid_ref;
};
                                                              See sys/proc.h

> ::print -t "struct pid"
{
    unsigned pid_prinactive :1
    unsigned pid_pgorphaned :1
    unsigned pid_padding :6
    unsigned pid_prslot :24
    pid_t pid_id
    struct proc *pid_pglink
    struct proc *pid_pgtail
    struct pid *pid_link
    uint_t pid_ref
}
```

The ::print dcmd is most useful to print data structures in their typed format. For example, using a pipeline we can look up the address of the p_pidp member of the supplied proc_t structure and print its structure's contents.

```
> ::pgrep inet
S      PID    PPID    PGID     SID    UID        FLAGS      ADDR NAME
R     1595       1    1595    1595      0 0x42000400 d7c662e0 inetd

> d7c662e0::print proc_t p_pidp |::print -t "struct pid"
{
    unsigned pid_prinactive :1 = 0
    unsigned pid_pgorphaned :1 = 0x1
    unsigned pid_padding :6 = 0
    unsigned pid_prslot :24 = 0xae
    pid_t pid_id = 0x63b
```

*continues*

```
    struct proc *pid_pglink = 0xd7c662e0
    struct proc *pid_pgtail = 0xd7c662e0
    struct pid *pid_link = 0
    uint_t pid_ref = 0x3
}
```

The ::print command also understands how to traverse more complex data structures. For example, here we traverse an element of an array.

```
> d7c662e0::print proc_t p_user.u_auxv[9]
{
    p_user.u_auxv[9].a_type = 0x6
    p_user.u_auxv[9].a_un = {
        a_val = 0x1000
        a_ptr = 0x1000
        a_fcn = 0x1000
    }
}
```

Several other dcmds, listed below, use the CTF information. Starting with Solaris 9, the kernel is compiled with CTF information, making type information available by default. Starting with Solaris 10, CTF information is also available in userland, and by default some of the core system libraries contain CTF. The CTF-related commands are summarized in Table 13.10.

### Table 13.10 CTF-Related dcmds

| dcmd | Description |
|---|---|
| addr::print [type] [field...] | Use CTF info to print out a full structure or particular fields thereof. |
| ::sizeof type<br>::offsetof type field<br>::enum enumname | Get information about a type. |
| addr::array [type count] [var] | Walk the count elements of an array of type type, starting at addr. |
| addr::list type field [var] | Walk a circular or NULL-terminated list of type type, which starts at addr and uses field as its linkage. |
| ::typegraph<br>addr::whattype<br>addr::istype type<br>addr::notype | Use the type inference engine—works on non-debug text. |

## 13.2.11 Variables

A *variable* is a variable name, a corresponding integer value, and a set of attributes. A variable name is a sequence of letters, digits, underscores, or periods. A variable can be assigned a value with > dcmd and read with < dcmd. Additionally, the variable can be the ::typeset dcmd, and its attributes can be manipulated with the ::typeset dcmd. Each variable's value is represented as a 64-bit unsigned integer. A variable can have one or more of the following attributes:

- Read-only (cannot be modified by the user)
- Persistent (cannot be unset by the user)
- Tagged (user-defined indicator)

The following examples shows assigning and referencing a variable.

```
> 0t27>myvar

> <myvar=D
                 27
> $v
myvar = 1b
 . = 1b
 0 = f5e
 b = fec00000
 d = 85737
 e = fe800000
 m = 464c457f
 t = 1a3e70
```

The CPU's registers are also exported as variables.

```
> ::vars
uesp = 0
eip = 0
myvar = 1b
cs = 0
savfp = 0
ds = 0
trapno = 0
es = 0
 . = 1b
 0 = f5e
 1 = 0
 2 = 0
ss = 0
 9 = 0
fs = 0
gs = 0
 _ = 0
```

*continues*

```
eax = 0
b = fec00000
d = 85737
e = fe800000
eflags = 0
ebp = 0
m = 464c457f
ebx = 0
t = 1a3e70
ecx = 0
hits = 0
edi = 0
edx = 0
err = 0
esi = 0
esp = 0
savpc = 0
thread = 0
```

Commands for working with variables are summarized in Table 13.11.

**Table 13.11**  Variables

| Variable | Description |
|----------|-------------|
| 0 | Most recent value [ / \ ? = ] ed |
| 9 | Most recent count for $< dcmd |
| b | Base VA of the data section |
| d | Size of the data |
| e | VA of entry point |
| hits | Event callback match count |
| m | Magic number of primary object file, or zero |
| t | Size of text section |
| thread | TID of current representative thread |

## 13.2.12 Walkers, Variables, and Expressions Combined

Variables can be combined with arithmetic expressions and evaluated to construct more complex pipelines, in which data is manipulated between stages. In a simple example, we might want to iterate only over processes that have a uid of zero. We can easily iterate over the processes by using a pipeline consisting of a walker and type information, which prints the cr_uids for every process.

```
> ::walk proc | ::print proc_t p_cred->cr_uid
cr_uid = 0
cr_uid = 0x19
cr_uid = 0x1
cr_uid = 0
...
```

Adding an expression allows us to select only those that match a particular condition. The `::walk` dcmd takes an optional variable name, in which to place the value of the walk. In this example, the walker sets the value of `myvar` and also pipes the output of the same addresses into `::print`, which extracts the value of `proc_t->p_cred->cr_uid`. The `::eval` dcmd prints the variable `myvar` only when the expression is true; in this case when the result of the previous dcmd (the printed value of `cr_uid`) is equal to 1. The statement given to `::eval` to execute retrieves the value of the variable `myvar` and formats it with the K format (`uint_ptr_t`).

```
> ::walk proc myvar |::print proc_t p_cred->cr_uid |::grep .==1 |::eval <myvar=K
fec1d280
d318d248
d318daa8
d318e308
...
> ::walk proc myvar | ::print proc_t p_cred->cr_uid |::grep .==1 |::eval <myvar=K
|::print -d proc_t p_pidp->pid_id
p_pidp->pid_id = 0t4189
p_pidp->pid_id = 0t4187
p_pidp->pid_id = 0t4067
p_pidp->pid_id = 0t4065
...
```

## 13.3 Working with Debugging Targets

MDB can control and interact with live `mdb` processes or `kmdb` kernel targets. Typical debugging operations include starting, stopping, and stepping the target. We discuss more about controlling `kmdb` targets in Chapter 14. The common commands for controlling targets are summarized in Table 13.12.

### Table 13.12 Debugging Target dcmds

| dcmd | Description |
| --- | --- |
| `::status` | Print summary of current target. |
| `$r` `::regs` | Display current register values for target. |

*continues*

**Table 13.12** Debugging Target dcmds (*continued*)

| dcmd | Description |
|---|---|
| `$c`<br>`::stack`<br>`$C` | Print current stack trace (`$C`: with frame pointers). |
| `addr[,b]`<br>`::dump [-g sz] [-e]` | Dump at least `b` bytes starting at address `addr`. `-g` sets the group size; for 64-bit debugging, `-g 8` is useful. |
| `addr::dis` | Disassemble text, starting around `addr`. |
| `[ addr ] :b`<br>`[ addr ] ::bp [+/-dDestT] [-c cmd]`<br>`[-n count] sym ...  addr  [cmd ... ]` | Set breakpoint at `addr`. |
| `$b`<br>`::events [-av] $b [-av]` | Display all breakpoints. |
| `addr ::delete [id | all]`<br>`addr :d [id | all]` | Delete a breakpoint at `addr`. |
| `:z` | Delete all breakpoints. |
| `::cont [SIG]`<br>`:c [SIG]` | Continue the target program, and wait for it to terminate. |
| `id ::evset [+/-dDestT] [-c cmd]`<br>`[-n count] id ...` | Modify the properties of one or more software event specifiers. |
| `::next [SIG]`<br>`:e [SIG]` | Step the target program one instruction, but step over subroutine calls. |
| `::step [branch | over | out] [SIG]`<br>`:s SIG`<br>`:u SIG` | Step the target program one instruction. |
| `addr [,len]::wp [+/-dDestT] [-rwx]`<br>`[-ip] [-c cmd] [-n count]`<br><br>`addr [,len]:a [cmd... ]`<br>`addr [,len]:p [cmd... ]`<br>`addr [,len]:w [cmd... ]` | Set a watchpoint at the specified address. |

## 13.3.1 Displaying Stacks

We can print a stack of the current address with the $c command or with $C, which also prints the stack frame address for each stack level.

```
> $c
atomic_add_32+8(0)
nfs4_async_inactive+0x3b(dc1c29c0, 0)
nfs4_inactive+0x41()
fop_inactive+0x15(dc1c29c0, 0)
vn_rele+0x4b(dc1c29c0)
snf_smap_desbfree+0x59(dda94080)

> $C
d2a58828 atomic_add_32+8(0)
d2a58854 nfs4_async_inactive+0x3b(dc1c29c0, 0)
d2a58880 nfs4_inactive+0x41()
d2a5889c fop_inactive+0x15(dc1c29c0, 0)
d2a588b0 vn_rele+0x4b(dc1c29c0)
d2a588c0 snf_smap_desbfree+0x59(dda94080)
```

## 13.3.2 Displaying Registers

We can print a stack of the current address with the $c command or with $C, which also prints the stack frame address for each stack level.

```
> ::regs (or $r)
%cs = 0x0158            %eax = 0x00000000
%ds = 0xd9820160           %ebx = 0xde453000
%ss = 0x0000           %ecx = 0x00000001
%es = 0xfe8d0160           %edx = 0xd2a58de0
%fs = 0xfec30000           %esi = 0xdc062298
%gs = 0xfe8301b0           %edi = 0x00000000

%eip = 0xfe82ca58 atomic_add_32+8
%ebp = 0xd2a58828
%esp = 0xd2a58800

%eflags = 0x00010282
  id=0 vip=0 vif=0 ac=0 vm=0 rf=1 nt=0 iopl=0x0
  status=<of,df,IF,tf,SF,zf,af,pf,cf>

  %uesp = 0xfe89ab0d
%trapno = 0xe
   %err = 0x2
```

## 13.3.3 Disassembling the Target

We can dissasemble instructions in the target with the `::dis` dcmd.

```
> atomic_add_32+8::dis
atomic_add_32:                        movl    0x4(%esp),%eax
atomic_add_32+4:                      movl    0x8(%esp),%ecx
atomic_add_32+8:                      lock addl %ecx,(%eax)
atomic_add_32+0xb:                    ret
```

Note that in this example combined with the registers shown in Section 13.3.2, the contents of `%eax` from `$r` is zero, causing the `movl` instruction to trap with a `NULL` pointer reference at `atomic_add_32+4`.

## 13.3.4 Setting Breakpoints

We can set breakpoints in MDB by using `:b`. Typically, we pass a symbol name to `:b` (the name of the function of interest).

We can start the target program and then set a breakpoint for the `printf` function.

```
> printf:b

> :r

mdb: stop at 0x8050694
mdb: target stopped at:
PLT:printf:        jmp    *0x8060980
```

In this example, we stopped at the first symbol matching "`printf`", which is actually in the procedure linkage table (PLT) (see the *Linker and Libraries* manual for a description of how dynamic linking works in Solaris). To match the `printf` we likely wanted, we can increase the scope of the symbol lookup. The `:c` command continues execution until the next breakpoint or until the program finishes.

```
> libc`printf:b

> :c
mdb: stop at libc.so.1`printf
mdb: target stopped at:
libc.so.1`printf:        pushl  %ebp
```

## 13.4 GDB-to-MDB Reference

**Table 13.13** GDB-to-MDB Migration

| GDB | MDB | Description |
|---|---|---|
| **Starting Up** | | |
| `gdb program` | `mdb path mdb -p pid` | Start debugging a command or running process. GDB will treat numeric arguments as pids, while MDB explicitly requires the `-p` option. |
| `gdb program core` | `mdb [ program ] core` | Debug a corefile associated with `program`. For MDB, the program is optional and is generally unnecessary given the corefile enhancements made during Solaris 10. |
| **Exiting** | | |
| `quit` | `::quit` | Both programs also exit on Ctrl-D. |
| **Getting Help** | | |
| `help` | | |
| `help command` | `::help ::help dcmd ::dcmds ::walkers` | List all the available walkers or dcmds, as well as get help on a specific dcmd (MDB). Another useful trick is `::dmods -l` module, which lists walkers and dcmds provided by a specific module. |
| **Running Programs** | | |
| `run arglist` | `::run arglist` | Run the program with the given arguments. If the target is currently running or is a corefile, MDB will restart the program if possible. |
| `kill` | `::kill` | Forcibly kill and release target. |
| `show env` | `::getenv` | Display current environment. |
| `set env var string` | `::setenv var=string` | Set an environment variable. |
| `get env var` | `::getenv var` | Get a specific environment variable. |

*continues*

**Table 13.13** GDB-to-MDB Migration (*continued*)

| GDB | MDB | Description |
|---|---|---|
| **Shell Commands** | | |
| shell cmd | ! cmd | Execute the given shell command. |
| **Breakpoints and Watchpoints** | | |
| break func | | |
| break *addr | addr::bp | Set a breakpoint at the given address or function. |
| break file:line | — | Break at the given line of the file. MDB does not support source-level debugging. |
| break ... if expr | — | Set a conditional breakpoint. MDB doesn't support conditional breakpoints, though you can get a close approximation with the -c option (though its complicated enough to warrant its own post). |
| watch expr | addr::wp -rwx [-L size] | Set a watchpoint on the given region of memory. |
| info break | | |
| info watch | ::events | Display active watchpoints and breakpoints. MDB shows you signal events as well. |
| delete [n] | ::delete n | Delete the given breakpoint or watchpoints. |
| **Program Stack** | | |
| backtrace n | ::stack $C | Display stack backtrace for the current thread. |
| — | thread:: findstack -v | Display a stack for a given thread. In the kernel, thread is the address of kthread_t. In userland, it's the thread identifier. |
| info ... | — | Display information about the current frame. MDB doesn't support the debugging data necessary to maintain the frame abstraction. |
| **Execution Control** | | |
| continue | | |
| c | :c | Continue target. |

*continues*

**Table 13.13** GDB-to-MDB Migration (*continued*)

| GDB | MDB | Description |
|---|---|---|
| stepi | | |
| si | ::step ] | Step to the next machine instruction. MDB does not support stepping by source lines. |
| nexti ni | ::step over [ | Step over the next machine instruction, skipping any function calls. |
| finish | ::step out | Continue until returning from the current frame. |
| jump *address | address>reg | Jump to the given location. In MDB, reg depends on your platform. For SPARC it's pc, for i386 its eip, and for amd64 it's rip. |
| **DIsplay** | | |
| print expr | addr::print expr | Print the given expression. In GDB you can specify variable names as well as addresses. For MDB, you give a particular address and then specify the type to display (which can include dereferencing of members, etc.). |
| print /f | addr/f | Print data in a precise format. See ::formats for a list of MDB formats. |
| disassem addr | addr::dis | Disassemble text at the given address or the current PC if no address is specified. |

## 13.5 dcmd and Walker Reference

### 13.5.1 Commands

```
pipeline [!word...] [;]                    basic
expr pipeline [!word...] [;]               set dot, run once
expr, expr pipeline [!word...] [;]         set dot, repeat
,expr pipeline [!word...] [;]              repeat
expr [!word...] [;]                        set dot, last pipeline, run once
,expr [!word...] [;]                       last pipeline, repeat
expr, expr [!word...] [;]                  set dot, last pipeline, repeat
!word... [;]                               shell escape
```

### 13.5.2 Comments

```
//                                  Comment to end of line
```

## 13.5.3 Expressions

```
Arithmetic
        integer                 0i binary, 0o octal, 0t decimal, 0x hex
        0t[0-9]+\.[0-9]+        IEEE floating point
        'cccccccc'              Little-endian character const
        <identifier             variable lookup
        identifier              symbol lookup
        (expr)                  the value of expr
        .                       the value of dot
        &                       last dot used by dcmd
        +                       dot+increment
        ^                       dot-increment
        increment is effected by the last formatting dcmd.

Unary Ops
        #expr                   logical NOT
        ~expr                   bitwise NOT
        -expr                   integer negation
        %expr                   object file pointer dereference
        %/[csil]/expr           object file typed dereference
        %/[1248]/expr           object file sized dereference
        *expr                   virtual address pointer dereference
        */[csil]/expr           virtual address typed dereference
        */[1248]/expr           virtual address sized dereference

        [csil] is char-, short-, int-, or long-sized

Binary Ops
        expr *   expr           integer multiplication
        expr %   expr           integer division
        left #   right          left rounded up to next right multiple
        expr +   expr           integer addition
        expr -   expr           integer subtraction
        expr <<  expr           bitwise left shift
        expr >>  expr           bitwise right shift (logical)
        expr ==  expr           logical equality
        expr !=  expr           logical inequality
        expr &   expr           bitwise AND
        expr ^   expr           bitwise XOR
        expr |   expr           bitwise OR
```

## 13.5.4 Symbols

```
kernel          {module`}{file`}symbol
proc            {LM[0-9]+`}{library`}{file`}symbol
```

## 13.5.5 dcmds

```
::{module`}d
expr>var        write the value of expr into var
```

## 13.5.6 Variables

```
0               Most recent value [/\?=]ed.
9               Most recent count for $< dcmd
b               base VA of the data section
d               size of the data
e               VA of entry point
hits            Event callback match count
```

```
m               magic number of primary object file, or zero
t               size of text section
thread          TID of current representative thread.

registers are exported as variables (g0, g1, ...)
```

## 13.5.7 Read Formats

```
/               format VA from .
\               format PA from .
?               format primary object file, using VA from .
=               format value of .

B (1)   hex                     +       dot += increment
C (1)   char (C-encoded)        -       dot -= increment
V (1)   unsigned                ^ (var) dot -= incr*count
b (1)   octal                   N       newline
c (1)   char (raw)              n       newline
d (2)   signed                  T       tab
h (2)   hex, swap endianness    r       whitespace
o (2)   octal                   t       tab
q (2)   signed octal            a       dot as symbol+offset
u (2)   decimal                 I (var) address and instruction
D (4)   signed                  i (var) instruction
H (4)   hex, swap endianness    S (var) string (C-encoded)
O (4)   octal                   s (var) string (raw)
Q (4)   signed octal            E (8)   unsigned
U (4)   unsigned                F (8)   double
X (4)   hex                     G (8)   octal
Y (4)   decoded time32_t        J (8)   hex
f (4)   float                   R (8)   binary
K (4|8) hex uintptr_t           e (8)   signed
P (4|8) symbol                  g (8)   signed octal
p (4|8) symbol                  y (8)   decoded time64_t
```

## 13.5.8 Write Formats

```
[/\?][vwWZ] value...            value is immediate or $[expr]

/       write virtual addresses
\       write physical addresses
?       write object file

v (1)   write low byte of each value, starting at dot
w (2)   write low 2 bytes of each value, starting at dot
W (4)   write low 4 bytes of each value, starting at dot
Z (8)   write all 8 bytes of each value, starting at dot
```

## 13.5.9 Search Formats

```
[/\?][lLM] value [mask]         value and mask are immediate or $[expr]

/       search virtual addresses
\       search physical addresses
?       search object file

l (2)   search for 2-byte value, optionally masked
L (4)   search for 4-byte value, optionally masked
M (8)   search for 8-byte value, optionally masked
```

## 13.5.10 General dcmds

```
::help dcmd
        Give help text for 'dcmd.'
::dmods -l [module...]
        List dcmds and walkers grouped by the dmod which provides them.
::log -e file
        Log session to file.
::quit / $q
        Quit.
```

## 13.5.11 Target-Related dcmds

```
::status
        Print summary of current target.
$r / ::regs
        Display current register values for target.
$c / ::stack / $C
        Print current stack trace ($C: with frame pointers).
addr[,b]::dump [-g sz] [-e]
        Dump at least b bytes starting at address addr.  -g sets
        the group size -- for 64-bit debugging, '-g 8' is useful.
addr::dis
        Disassemble text, starting around addr.

[ addr ] :b
[ addr ] ::bp [+/-dDestT] [-c cmd] [-n count] sym ...  addr  [cmd ... ]
        Set breakpoint at addr.
$b
::events [-av]
$b [-av]
        Display all the breakpoints.
addr ::delete [id | all]
addr :d [id | all]
        Delete a breakpoint at addr.
:z
        Deletes all breakpoints
::cont [SIG]
:c [SIG]
        Continue the target program, and wait for it to terminate
id ::evset [+/-dDestT] [-c cmd] [-n count] id ...
        Modify the properties of one or more software event specifiers.
::next [SIG]
:e [SIG]
        Step the target program one instruction, but step over subroutine calls.
::step [branch | over | out] [SIG]
:s SIG
:u SIG
        Step the target program one instruction.
addr [,len]::wp [+/-dDestT] [-rwx] [-ip] [-c cmd] [-n count]
addr [,len]:a [cmd... ]
addr [,len]:p [cmd... ]
addr [,len]:w [cmd... ]
        Set a watchpoint at the specified address.
```

## 13.5.12 CTF-Related

```
addr::print [type] [field...]
        Use CTF info to print out a full structure, or
        particular fields thereof.
::sizeof type / ::offsetof type field / ::enum enumname
        Get information about a type
```

```
addr::array [type count] [var]
        Walk the count elements of an array of type 'type'
        starting at address.
addr::list type field [var]
        Walk a circular or NULL-terminated list of type 'type',
        which starts at addr and uses 'field' as its linkage.
::typegraph / addr::whattype / addr::istype type / addr::notype
        bmc's type inference engine -- works on non-debug
```

## 13.5.13  Kernel: proc-Related

```
0tpid::pid2proc
        Convert the process ID 'pid' (in decimal) into a proc_t ptr.
as::as2proc
        Convert a 'struct as' pointer to its associated proc_t ptr.
vn::whereopen
        Find all processes with a particular vnode open.
::pgrep pattern
        Print out proc_t ptrs which match pattern.
[procp]::ps
        Process table, or (with procp) the line for particular proc_t.
::ptree
        Print out a ptree(1)-like indented process tree.
procp::pfiles
        Print out information on a process' file descriptors.

[procp]::walk proc
        walks all processes, or the tree rooted at procp
```

## 13.5.14  Kernel: Thread-Related

```
threadp::findstack
        Print out a stack trace (with frame pointers) for threadp.
[threadp]::thread
        Give summary information about all threads or a particular thread.

[procp]::walk thread
        Walk all threads, or all threads in a process (with procp).
```

## 13.5.15  Kernel: Synchronization-Related

```
[sobj]::wchaninfo [-v]
        Get information on blocked-on condition variables.  With
        sobj, info about that wchan.  With -v, lists all threads
        blocked on the wchan.
sobj::rwlock
        Dump out a rwlock, including detailed blocking information.

sobj::walk blocked
        Walk all threads blocked on sobj, a synchronization object.
```

## 13.5.16  Kernel: CPU-Related

```
::cpuinfo [-v]
        Give information about CPUs on the system and what they
        are doing.  With '-v', show threads on the run queues.
::cpupart
        Give information about CPU partitions (psrset(1m)s).
```

```
addr::cpuset
        Print out a cpuset as a list of included CPUs.
[cpuid]::ttrace
        Dump out traptrace records, which are generated in DEBUG
        kernels.  These include all traps and various other events of
        interest.

::walk cpu
        Walk all cpu_ts on the system.
```

## 13.5.17  Kernel: Memory-Related

```
::memstat
        Display memory usage summary.
pattern::kgrep [-d dist|-m mask|-M invmask]
        Search the kernel heap for pointers equal to pattern.
addr::whatis [-b]
        Try to identify what a given kernel address is.  With
        '-b', give bufctl address for the buffer (see
        $<bufctl_audit, below).
```

## 13.5.18  Kernel: kmem-Related

```
::kmastat
        Give statistics on the kmem caches and vmem arenas in the system
::kmem_cache
        Information about the kmem caches on the system
[cachep]::kmem_verify
        Validate all buffers in the system, checking for corruption.
        With cachep, shows the details of a particular cache.
threadp::allocdby / threadp::freedby
        Show buffers that were last allocated/freed by a particular
        thread, and are still in that state.
::kmalog [fail | slab]
        Dump out the transaction log, showing recent kmem activity.
        With fail/slab, outputs records of allocation failures and
        slab creations (which are always enabled)
::findleaks [-dvf]
        Find memory leaks, coalesced by stack trace.
::bufctl [-v]
        Print a summary line for a bufctl -- can also filter them
        -v dumps out a kmem_bufctl_audit_t.

::walk cachename
        Print out all allocated buffers in the cache named cachename.

[cp]::walk kmem/[cp]::walk freemem/[cp]::walk bufctl/[cp]::walk freectl
        Walk {allocated,freed}{buffers,bufctls} for all caches,
        or the particular kmem_cache_t cp.
```

## 13.5.19  Process: Target-Related

```
flt ::fltbp [+/-dDestT] [-c cmd] [-n count] flt ...
        Trace the specified machine faults.
signal :i
        Ignore the specified signal and allow it to be delivered
        transparently to the target.
$i
        Display the list of signals that are ignored by the debugger and
        will be handled directly by the target.
```

```
$1
        Print the LWPID of the representative thread if the target is a user process.

$L
        Print the LWPIDs of each LWP in the target if the target is a user
        process.
::kill
:k
        Forcibly terminate the target if it is a live user process.
::run [args ... ]
:r [args ... ]
        Start a new target program running with the specified arguments and
        attach to it.
[signal] ::sigbp [+/-dDestT] [-c cmd] [-n count] SIG ...
[signal] :t [+/-dDestT] [-c cmd] [-n count] SIG ...
        Trace delivery of the specified signals.
::step [branch | over | out] [SIG]
:s SIG
:u SIG
        Step the target program one instruction.
[syscall] ::sysbp [+/-dDestT] [-io] [-c cmd] [-n count] syscall ...
        Trace entry to or exit from the specified system calls.
```

## 13.5.20 Kernel: kmdb-Related

```
::help dcmd
        gives help text for 'dcmd'
::dmods -l [module...]
        Lists dcmds and walkers grouped by the dmod which provides them

::status
        Print summary of current target.
$r
::regs
        Display current register values for target.
$c
::stack
$C
        Print current stack trace ($C: with frame pointers).
addr[,b]
::dump [-q sz] [-e]
        Dump at least b bytes starting at address addr.  -g sets the group size;
        for 64-bit debugging, -g 8 is useful.
addr::dis
        Disassemble text, starting around addr.
[ addr ] :b
[ addr ] ::bp [+/-dDestT] [-n count] sym ...  addr
        Set breakpoint at addr.
$b
        Display all the breakpoints.
::branches
        Display the last branches taken by the CPU. (x86 only)
addr ::delete [id | all]
addr :d [id | all]
        Delete a breakpoint at addr.
:z
        Delete all breakpoints.
function ::call [arg [arg ...]]
        Call the specified function, using the specified arguments.
[cpuid] ::cpuregs [-c cpuid]
        Display the current general-purpose register set.
[cpuid] ::cpustack [-c cpuid]
        Print a C stack backtrace for the specified CPU.
::cont
```

```
:c
        Continue the target program.
$M
        List the macro files that are cached by kmdb for use with the $< dcmd
::next
:e
        Step the target program one instruction, but step over subroutine calls.
::step [branch | over | out]
        Step the target program one instruction.
$<systemdump
        Initiate a panic/dump.
::quit [-u]
$q
        Cause the debugger to exit. When the -u option is used,
        the system is resumed and the debugger is unloaded.
        addr [,len]::wp [+/-dDestT] [-rwx] [-ip] [-n count]

addr [,len]:a [cmd ...]
addr [,len]:p [cmd ...]
addr [,len]:w [cmd ...]
        Set a watchpoint at the specified address.
```

# 14

# Debugging Kernels

In this chapter we explore the rudimentary facilities within MDB for analyzing kernel crash images and debugging live kernels. The objective is not to provide an all-encompassing kernel crash analysis tutorial, but rather to introduce the most relevant MDB dcmds and techniques.

A more comprehensive guide to crash dump analysis can be found in some of the recommended reference texts, for example, *Panic!* by Chris Drake and Kimberly Brown for SPARC [8], and "Crash Dump Analysis" by Frank Hoffman for x86/x64 [12].

## 14.1 Working with Kernel Cores

The most common type of kernel debug target is a core file, saved from a prior system crash. In the following sections, we highlight some of the introductory steps as used with mdb to explore a kernel core image.

### 14.1.1 Locating and Attaching the Target

If a system has crashed, then we should have a core image saved in /var/crash on the target machine. The mdb debugger should be invoked from a system with the same architecture and Solaris revision as the crash image. The first steps are to locate the appropriate saved image and then to invoke mdb.

```
# cd /var/crash/nodename

# ls
bounds    unix.1    unix.3    unix.5    unix.7    vmcore.1  vmcore.3  vmcore.5  vmcore.7
unix.0    unix.2    unix.4    unix.6    vmcore.0  vmcore.2  vmcore.4  vmcore.6

# mdb -k unix.7 vmcore.7
Loading modules: [ unix krtld$c
 genunix specfs dtrace ufs ip sctp usba uhci s1394 fcp fctl nca lofs zfs random nfs
audiosup sppp crypto md fcip logindmux ptm ipc ]
>
```

## 14.1.2  Examining Kernel Core Summary Information

The kernel core contains important summary information from which we can
extract the following:

- Revision of the kernel
- Hostname
- CPU and platform architecture of the system
- Panic string
- Module causing the panic

We can use the ::showrev and ::status dcmds to extract this information.

```
> ::showrev
Hostname: zones-internal
Release: 5.11
Kernel architecture: i86pc
Application architecture: i386
Kernel version: SunOS 5.11 i86pc snv_27
Platform: i86pc
> ::status
debugging crash dump vmcore.2 (32-bit) from zones-internal
operating system: 5.11 snv_27 (i86pc)
panic message: BAD TRAP: type=e (#pf Page fault) rp=d2a587c8 addr=0 occurred in module
"unix" due to a NULL pointer dereference
dump content: kernel pages only
> ::panicinfo
             cpu        0
          thread d2a58de0
         message BAD TRAP: type=e (#pf Page fault) rp=d2a587c8 addr=0 occurred in module
"unix" due to a NULL pointer dereference
              gs fe8301b0
              fs fec30000
              es fe8d0160
              ds d9820160
             edi        0
             esi dc062298
             ebp d2a58828
             esp d2a58800
             ebx de453000
```

*continues*

```
        edx  d2a58de0
        ecx         1
        eax         0
     trapno         e
        err         2
        eip  fe82ca58
         cs       158
     eflags     10282
       uesp  fe89ab0d
         ss         0
        gdt  fec1f2f002cf
        idt  fec1f5c007ff
        ldt       140
       task       150
        cr0  8005003b
        cr2         0
        cr3  4cb3000
        cr4       6d8
```

### 14.1.3  Examining the Message Buffer

The kernel keeps a cyclic buffer of the recent kernel messages. In this buffer we can observe the messages up to the time of the panic. The ::msgbuf dcmd shows the contents of the buffer.

```
> ::msgbuf
MESSAGE
/pseudo/zconsnex@1/zcons@5 (zcons5) online
/pseudo/zconsnex@1/zcons@6 (zcons6) online
/pseudo/zconsnex@1/zcons@7 (zcons7) online
pseudo-device: ramdisk1024
...
panic[cpu0]/thread=d2a58de0:
BAD TRAP: type=e (#pf Page fault) rp=d2a587c8 addr=0 occurred in module "unix" due to a
NULL pointer dereference


sched:
#pf Page fault
Bad kernel fault at addr=0x0
pid=0, pc=0xfe82ca58, sp=0xfe89ab0d, eflags=0x10282
cr0: 8005003b<pg,wp,ne,ct,ts,mp,pe> cr4: 6d8<xmme,fxsr,pge,mce,pse,de>
cr2: 0 cr3: 4cb3000
        gs: fe8301b0  fs: fec30000  es: fe8d0160  ds: d9820160
       edi:         0 esi: dc062298 ebp: d2a58828 esp: d2a58800
       ebx: de453000 edx: d2a58de0 ecx:        1 eax:        0
       trp:         e err:        2 eip: fe82ca58  cs:      158
       efl:     10282 usp: fe89ab0d  ss:        0
...
```

### 14.1.4  Obtaining a Stack Trace of the Running Thread

We can obtain a stack backtrace of the current thread by using the $C command. Note that the displayed arguments to each function are not necessarily accurate. On each platform, the meaning of the shown arguments is as follows:

- **SPARC.** The values of the arguments if they are available from a saved stack frame, assuming they are not overwritten by use of registers during the called function. With SPARC architectures, a function's input argument registers are sometimes saved on the way out of a function—if the input registers are reused during the function, then values of the input arguments are overwritten and lost.

- **x86.** Accurate values of the input arguments. Input arguments are always saved onto the stack and can be accurately displayed

- **x64.** The values of the arguments, assuming they are available. As with the SPARC architectures, input arguments are passed in registers and may be overwritten.

```
> $C
d2a58828 atomic_add_32+8(0)
d2a58854 nfs4_async_inactive+0x3b(dc1c29c0, 0)
d2a58880 nfs4_inactive+0x41()
d2a5889c fop_inactive+0x15(dc1c29c0, 0)
d2a588b0 vn_rele+0x4b(dc1c29c0)
d2a588c0 snf_smap_desbfree+0x59(dda94080)
d2a588dc dblk_lastfree_desb+0x13(de45b520, d826fb40)
d2a588f4 dblk_decref+0x4e(de45b520, d826fb40)
d2a58918 freemsg+0x69(de45b520)
d2a5893c FreeTxSwPacket+0x3b(d38b84f0)
d2a58968 CleanTxInterrupts+0xb4(d2f9cac0)
d2a589a4 e1000g_send+0xf6(d2f9cac0, d9ffba00)
d2a589c0 e1000g_m_tx+0x22()
d2a589dc dls_tx+0x16(d4520f68, d9ffba00)
d2a589f4 str_mdata_fastpath_put+0x1e(d3843f20, d9ffba00)
d2a58a40 tcp_send_data+0x62d(db0ecac0, d97ee250, d9ffba00)
d2a58aac tcp_send+0x6b6(d97ee250, db0ecac0, 564, 28, 14, 0)
d2a58b40 tcp_wput_data+0x622(db0ecac0, 0, 0)
d2a58c28 tcp_rput_data+0x2560(db0ec980, db15bd20, d2d45f40)
d2a58c40 tcp_input+0x3c(db0ec980, db15bd20, d2d45f40)
d2a58c78 squeue_enter_chain+0xe9(d2d45f40, db15bd20, db15bd20, 1, 1)
d2a58cec ip_input+0x658(d990e554, d3164010, 0, e)
d2a58d40 i_dls_link_ether_rx+0x156(d4523db8, d3164010, db15bd20)
d2a58d70 mac_rx+0x56(d3520200, d3164010, db15bd20)
d2a58dac e1000g_intr+0xa6(d2f9cac0, 0)
d2a58ddc intr_thread+0x122()
```

## 14.1.5  Which Process?

If the stack trace is of a kernel housekeeping or interrupt thread, the process reported for the thread will be that of p0—"sched." The process pointer for the thread can be obtained with ::thread, and ::ps will then display summary information about that process. In this example, the thread is an interrupt thread (as indicated by the top entry in the stack from $C), and the process name maps to sched.

```
> d2a58de0::thread -p
    ADDR      PROC      LWP     CRED
d2a58de0 fec1d280          0 d9d1cf38
> fec1d280::ps -t
S    PID   PPID   PGID    SID    UID     FLAGS    ADDR NAME
R      0      0      0      0      0 0x00000001 fec1d280 sched
        T          t0 <TS_STOPPED>
```

## 14.1.6  Disassembling the Suspect Code

Once we've located the thread of interest, we often learn more about what happened by disassembling the target and looking at the instruction that reportedly
caused the panic. MDB's ::dis dcmd will disassemble the code around the target
instruction that we extract from the stack backtrace.

```
> $C
d2a58828 atomic_add_32+8(0)
d2a58854 nfs4_async_inactive+0x3b(dc1c29c0, 0)
d2a58880 nfs4_inactive+0x41()
d2a5889c fop_inactive+0x15(dc1c29c0, 0)
d2a588b0 vn_rele+0x4b(dc1c29c0)
...
> nfs4_async_inactive+0x3b::dis
nfs4_async_inactive+0x1a:       pushl    $0x28
nfs4_async_inactive+0x1c:       call     +0x51faa30        <kmem_alloc>
nfs4_async_inactive+0x21:       addl     $0x8,%esp
nfs4_async_inactive+0x24:       movl     %eax,%esi
nfs4_async_inactive+0x26:       movl     $0x0,(%esi)
nfs4_async_inactive+0x2c:       movl     -0x4(%ebp),%eax
nfs4_async_inactive+0x2f:       movl     %eax,0x4(%esi)
nfs4_async_inactive+0x32:       movl     0xc(%ebp),%edi
nfs4_async_inactive+0x35:       pushl    %edi
nfs4_async_inactive+0x36:       call     +0x51b7cdc        <crhold>
nfs4_async_inactive+0x3b:       addl     $0x4,%esp
nfs4_async_inactive+0x3e:       movl     %edi,0x8(%esi)
nfs4_async_inactive+0x41:       movl     $0x4,0xc(%esi)
nfs4_async_inactive+0x48:       leal     0xe0(%ebx),%eax
nfs4_async_inactive+0x4e:       movl     %eax,-0x8(%ebp)
nfs4_async_inactive+0x51:       pushl    %eax
nfs4_async_inactive+0x52:       call     +0x51477f4        <mutex_enter>
nfs4_async_inactive+0x57:       addl     $0x4,%esp
nfs4_async_inactive+0x5a:       cmpl     $0x0,0xd4(%cbx)
nfs4_async_inactive+0x61:       je       +0x7e     <nfs4_async_inactive+0xdf>
nfs4_async_inactive+0x63:       cmpl     $0x0,0xd0(%ebx)
> crhold::dis
crhold:                         pushl    %ebp
crhold+1:                       movl     %esp,%ebp
crhold+3:                       andl     $0xfffffff0,%esp
crhold+6:                       pushl    $0x1
crhold+8:                       movl     0x8(%ebp),%eax
crhold+0xb:                      pushl    %eax
crhold+0xc:                      call     -0x6e0b8 <atomic_add_32>
crhold+0x11:                     movl     %ebp,%esp
crhold+0x13:                     popl     %ebp
crhold+0x14:                     ret
> atomic_add_32::dis
atomic_add_32:                  movl     0x4(%esp),%eax
atomic_add_32+4:                movl     0x8(%esp),%ecx
atomic_add_32+8:                lock addl %ecx,(%eax)
atomic_add_32+0xb:              ret
```

### 14.1.7  Displaying General-Purpose Registers

In this example, the system had a NULL pointer reference at `atomic_add_32+8(0)`. The faulting instruction was atomic, referencing the memory at the location pointed to by `%eax`. By looking at the registers at the time of the panic, we can see that `%eax` was indeed NULL. The next step is to attempt to find out *why* `%eax` was NULL.

```
> ::regs
%cs = 0x0158            %eax = 0x00000000
%ds = 0xd9820160          %ebx = 0xde453000
%ss = 0x0000            %ecx = 0x00000001
%es = 0xfe8d0160          %edx = 0xd2a58de0
%fs = 0xfec30000          %esi = 0xdc062298
%gs = 0xfe8301b0          %edi = 0x00000000

%eip = 0xfe82ca58 atomic_add_32+8
%ebp = 0xd2a58828
%esp = 0xd2a58800

%eflags = 0x00010282
  id=0 vip=0 vif=0 ac=0 vm=0 rf=1 nt=0 iopl=0x0
  status=<of,df,IF,tf,SF,zf,af,pf,cf>

  %uesp = 0xfe89ab0d
%trapno = 0xe
   %err = 0x2
```

### 14.1.8  Navigating the Stack Backtrace

The function prototype for `atomic_add_32()` reveals that the first argument is a pointer to the memory location to be added. Since this was an x86 machine, the arguments reported by the stack backtrace are known to be useful, and we can look to see where the NULL pointer was handed down—in this case `nfs4_async_inactive()`.

```
void
atomic_add_32(volatile uint32_t *target, int32_t delta)
{
        *target += delta;
}


> atomic_add_32::dis
atomic_add_32:                  movl   0x4(%esp),%eax
atomic_add_32+4:                movl   0x8(%esp),%ecx
atomic_add_32+8:                lock addl %ecx,(%eax)
atomic_add_32+0xb:              ret
> $C
d2a58828 atomic_add_32+8(0)
d2a58854 nfs4_async_inactive+0x3b(dc1c29c0, 0)
d2a58880 nfs4_inactive+0x41()
d2a5889c fop_inactive+0x15(dc1c29c0, 0)
d2a588b0 vn_rele+0x4b(dc1c29c0)
...
```

```
> $C
d2a58828 atomic_add_32+8(0)
d2a58854 nfs4_async_inactive+0x3b(dc1c29c0, 0)
d2a58880 nfs4_inactive+0x41()
d2a5889c fop_inactive+0x15(dc1c29c0, 0)
d2a588b0 vn_rele+0x4b(dc1c29c0)
...
> nfs4_async_inactive+0x3b::dis
nfs4_async_inactive+0x1a:        pushl     $0x28
nfs4_async_inactive+0x1c:        call      +0x51faa30        <kmem_alloc>
nfs4_async_inactive+0x21:        addl      $0x8,%esp
nfs4_async_inactive+0x24:        movl      %eax,%esi
nfs4_async_inactive+0x26:        movl      $0x0,(%esi)
nfs4_async_inactive+0x2c:        movl      -0x4(%ebp),%eax
nfs4_async_inactive+0x2f:        movl      %eax,0x4(%esi)
nfs4_async_inactive+0x32:        movl      0xc(%ebp),%edi
nfs4_async_inactive+0x35:        pushl     %edi
nfs4_async_inactive+0x36:        call      +0x51b7cdc        <crhold>
nfs4_async_inactive+0x3b:        addl      $0x4,%esp
nfs4_async_inactive+0x3e:        movl      %edi,0x8(%esi)
nfs4_async_inactive+0x41:        movl      $0x0,0xc(%esi)
nfs4_async_inactive+0x48:        leal      0xe0(%ebx),%eax
nfs4_async_inactive+0x4e:        movl      %eax,-0x8(%ebp)
nfs4_async_inactive+0x51:        pushl     %eax
nfs4_async_inactive+0x52:        call      +0x51477f4        <mutex_enter>
nfs4_async_inactive+0x57:        addl      $0x4,%esp
nfs4_async_inactive+0x5a:        cmpl      $0x0,0xd4(%ebx)
nfs4_async_inactive+0x61:        je        +0x7e     <nfs4_async_inactive+0xdf>
nfs4_async_inactive+0x63:        cmpl      $0x0,0xd0(%ebx)
...
```

Looking at the disassembly, it appears that there is an additional function call, which is omitted from the stack backtrack (typically due to tail call compiler optimization). The call is to crhold(), passing the address of a credential structure from the arguments to nfs4_async_inactive(). Here we can see that crhold() does in fact call atomic_add_32().

```
/*
 * Put a hold on a cred structure.
 */
void
crhold(cred_t *cr)
{
        atomic_add_32(&cr->cr_ref, 1);
}


> crhold::dis
crhold:                          pushl     %ebp
crhold+1:                        movl      %esp,%ebp
crhold+3:                        andl      $0xfffffff0,%esp
crhold+6:                        pushl     $0x1
crhold+8:                        movl      0x8(%ebp),%eax
crhold+0xb:                      pushl     %eax
crhold+0xc:                      call      -0x6e0b8 <atomic_add_32>
crhold+0x11:                     movl      %ebp,%esp
crhold+0x13:                     popl      %ebp
crhold+0x14:                     ret
```

Next, we look into the situation in which `nfs4_async_inactive()` was called. The first argument is a `vnode` pointer, and the second is our suspicious credential pointer. The `vnode` pointer can be examined with the CTF information and the `::print` dcmd. We can see that we were performing an `nfs4_async_inactive` function on the `vnode` referencing a pdf file in this case.

```
 */
void
nfs4_async_inactive(vnode_t *vp, cred_t *cr)
{



> $C
d2a58828 atomic_add_32+8(0)
d2a58854 nfs4_async_inactive+0x3b(dc1c29c0, 0)
> dc1c29c0::print vnode_t
{
...
    v_type = 1 (VREG)
    v_rdev = 0
...
    v_path = 0xdc3de800 "/zones/si/root/home/ftp/book/solarisinternals_projtaskipc.pdf"
...
}
```

Looking further at the stack backtrace and the code, we can try to identify where the credentials were derived from. `nfs4_async_inactive()` was called by `nfs4_inactive()`, which is one of the standard `VOP` methods (`VOP_INACTIVE`).

```
> $C
d2a58828 atomic_add_32+8(0)
d2a58854 nfs4_async_inactive+0x3b(dc1c29c0, 0)
d2a58880 nfs4_inactive+0x41()
d2a5889c fop_inactive+0x15(dc1c29c0, 0)
d2a588b0 vn_rele+0x4b(dc1c29c0)
```

The credential can be followed all the way up to `vn_rele()`, which derives the pointer from `CRED()`, which references the current thread's `t_cred`.

```
vn_rele(vnode_t *vp)
{
        if (vp->v_count == 0)
                cmn_err(CE_PANIC, "vn_rele: vnode ref count 0");
        mutex_enter(&vp->v_lock);
        if (vp->v_count == 1) {
                mutex_exit(&vp->v_lock);
                VOP_INACTIVE(vp, CRED());
...

#define CRED()              curthread->t_cred
```

We know which thread called `vn_rele()`—the interrupt thread with a thread pointer of `d2a58de0`. We can use `::print` to take a look at the thread's `t_cred`.

```
> d2a58de0::print kthread_t t_cred
t_cred = 0xd9d1cf38
```

Interestingly, it's not NULL! A further look around the code gives us some clues as to what's going on. In the initialization code during the creation of an interrupt thread, the `t_cred` is set to NULL:

```
/*
 * Create and initialize an interrupt thread.
 *       Returns non-zero on error.
 *       Called at spl7() or better.
 */
void
thread_create_intr(struct cpu *cp)
{
 ...
        /*
         * Nobody should ever reference the credentials of an interrupt
         * thread so make it NULL to catch any such references.
         */
        tp->t_cred = NULL;
```

Our `curthread->t_cred` is not NULL, but NULL was passed in when `CRED()` accessed it in the not-too-distant past—an interesting situation indeed. It turns out that the NFS client code wills credentials to the interrupt thread's `t_cred`, so what we are in fact seeing is a race condition, where `vn_rele()` is called from the interrupt thread with no credentials. In this case, a bug was logged accordingly and the problem was fixed!

## 14.1.9 Looking at the Status of the CPUs

Another good source of information is the `::cpuinfo` dcmd. It shows a rich set of information of the processors in the system. For each CPU, the details of the thread currently running on each processor are shown. If the current CPU is handling an interrupt, then the thread running the interrupt and the preempted thread are shown. In addition, a list of threads waiting in the run queue for this processor is shown.

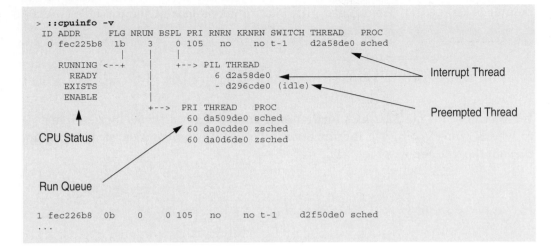

```
> ::cpuinfo -v
  ID ADDR       FLG NRUN BSPL PRI RNRN KRNRN SWITCH THREAD     PROC
   0 fec225b8   1b    3    0 105   no    no   t-1   d2a58de0 sched

      RUNNING <--+    |    +--> PIL THREAD                                   Interrupt Thread
      READY           |           6 d2a58de0
      EXISTS          |           - d296cde0 (idle)
      ENABLE          |                                                     Preempted Thread

                      +--> PRI THREAD   PROC
                           60 da509de0 sched
                           60 da0cdde0 zsched
  CPU Status             60 da0d6de0 zsched



  Run Queue

   1 fec226b8   0b    0    0 105   no    no   t-1   d2f50de0 sched
   ...
```

In this example, we can see that the idle thread was preempted by a level 6
interrupt. Three threads are on the run queue: the thread that was running immediately before preemption and two other threads waiting to be scheduled on the
run queue. We can traverse these manually, by traversing the stack of the thread
pointer with ::findstack.

```
> :da509de0:findstack
stack pointer for thread da509de0: da509d08
  da509d3c swtch+0x165()
  da509d60 cv_timedwait+0xa3()
  da509dc8 taskq_d_thread+0x149()
  da509dd8 thread_start+8()
```

The CPU containing the thread that caused the panic will, we hope, be reported
in the panic string and, furthermore, will be used by MDB as the default thread for
other dcmds in the core image. Once we determine the status of the CPU, we can
observe which thread was involved in the panic.

Additionally, we can use the CPU's run queue (cpu_dispq) to provide a stack
list for other threads queued up to run. We might do this just to gather a little
more information about the circumstance in which the panic occurred.

```
> fec225b8::walk cpu_dispq |::thread
  ADDR      STATE   FLG PFLG SFLG  PRI  EPRI PIL   INTR DISPTIME BOUND PR
da509de0 run         8    0   13   60     0   0    n/a  7e6f9c    -1  0
da0cdde0 run         8 2000   13   60     0   0    n/a  7e8452    -1  0
da0d6de0 run         8 2000   13   60     0   0    n/a  7e8452    -1  0
```

*continues*

```
> fec225b8::walk cpu_dispq |::findstack
stack pointer for thread da509de0: da509d08
  da509d3c swtch+0x165()
  da509d60 cv_timedwait+0xa3()
  da509dc8 taskq_d_thread+0x149()
  da509dd8 thread_start+8()
stack pointer for thread da0cdde0: da0cdd48
  da0cdd74 swtch+0x165()
  da0cdd84 cv_wait+0x4e()
  da0cddc8 nfs4_async_manager+0xc9()
  da0cddd8 thread_start+8()
stack pointer for thread da0d6de0: da0d6d48
  da0d6d74 swtch+0x165()
  da0d6d84 cv_wait+0x4e()
  da0d6dc8 nfs4_async_manager+0xc9()
  da0d6dd8 thread_start+8()
```

## 14.1.10 Traversing Stack Frames in SPARC Architectures

We briefly mentioned in Section 14.1.4 some of the problems we encounter when trying to glean argument values from stack backtraces. In the SPARC architecture, the values of the input arguments' registers are saved into register windows at the exit of each function. In most cases, we can traverse the stack frames to look at the values of the registers as they are saved in register windows. Historically, this was done by manually traversing the stack frames (as illustrated in *Panic!*). Conveniently, MDB has a dcmd that understands and walks SPARC stack frames. We can use the ::stackregs dcmd to display the SPARC input registers and locals (%10-%17) for each frame on the stack.

```
> ::stackregs
000002a100d074c1 vpanic(12871f0, e, e, fffffffffffffffe, 1, 185d400)
  %10-%13:             0     2a100d07f10    2a100d07f40         ffffffff
  %14-%17: fffffffffffffffe           0        1845400          1287000
  px_err_fabric_intr+0xbc: call    -0x1946c0      <fm_panic>

000002a100d07571 px_err_fabric_intr+0xbc(600024f9880, 31, 340, 600024d75d0,
30000842020, 0)
  %10-%13:             0     2a100d07f10    2a100d07f40         ffffffff
  %14-%17: fffffffffffffffe           0        1845400          1287000
  px_msiq_intr+0x1ac:      call    -0x13b0        <px_err_fabric_intr>

000002a100d07651 px_msiq_intr+0x1ac(60002551db8, 0, 127dcc8, 6000252e9e0, 30000828a58,
30000842020)
  %10-%13:             0     2a100d07f10    2a100d07f40      2a100d07f10
  %14-%17:             0              31    30000842020      600024d21d8
  current_thread+0x174:    jmpl    %o5, %o7

000002a100d07751 current_thread+0x174(16, 2000, ddf7dfff, ddf7ffff, 2000, 12)
  %10-%13:       100994c     2a100cdf021              e               7b9
  %14-%17:             0               0              0       2a100cdf8d0
  cpu_halt+0x134:          call    -0x29dcc       <enable_vec_intr>
```

*continues*

```
000002a100cdf171 cpu_halt+0x134(16, d, 184bbd0, 30001334000, 16, 1)
   %l0-%l3:        60001db16c8           0        60001db16c8 ffffffffffffffff
   %l4-%l7:                0             0                  0         10371d0
   idle+0x124:               jmpl       %l7, %o7

000002a100cdf221 idle+0x124(1819800, 0, 30001334000, ffffffffffffffff, e, 1818400)
   %l0-%l3:        60001db16c8          1b                  0 ffffffffffffffff
   %l4-%l7:                0             0                  0         10371d0
   thread_start+4:           jmpl       %i7, %o7

000002a100cdf2d1 thread_start+4(0, 0, 0, 0, 0, 0)
   %l0-%l3:                 0             0                  0               0
   %l4-%l7:                 0             0                  0               0
```

SPARC input registers become output registers, which are then saved on the stack. The common technique when trying to qualify registers as valid arguments is to ascertain, before the registers are saved in the stack frame, whether they have been overwritten during the function. A common technique is to disassemble the target function, looking to see if the input registers (%i0-%i7) are reused in the function's code body. A quick and dirty way to look for register usage is to use ::dis piped to a UNIX grep; however, at this stage, examining the code for use of input registers is left as an exercise for the reader. For example, if we are looking to see if the values of the first argument to cpu_halt() are valid, we could see if %i0 is reused during the cpu_halt() function, before we branch out at cpu_halt+0x134.

```
> cpu_halt::dis !grep i0
cpu_halt+0x24:                     ld         [%g1 + 0x394], %i0
cpu_halt+0x28:                     cmp        %i0, 1
cpu_halt+0x90:                     add        %i2, 0x120, %i0
cpu_halt+0xd0:                     srl        %i4, 0, %i0
cpu_halt+0x100:                    srl        %i4, 0, %i0
cpu_halt+0x144:                    ldub       [%i3 + 0xf9], %i0
cpu_halt+0x150:                    and        %i0, 0xfd, %l7
cpu_halt+0x160:                    add        %i2, 0x120, %i0
```

As we can see in this case, %i0 is reused very early in cpu_halt() and would be invalid in the stack backtrace.

## 14.1.11 Listing Processes and Process Stacks

We can obtain the list of processes by using the ::ps dcmd. In addition, we can search for processes by using the pgrep(1M)-like ::pgrep dcmd.

```
> ::ps -f
S      PID   PPID    PGID     SID    UID       FLAGS      ADDR NAME
R        0      0       0       0      0 0x00000001 fec1d280 sched
R        3      0       0       0      0 0x00020001 d318d248 fsflush
R        2      0       0       0      0 0x00020001 d318daa8 pageout
R        1      0       0       0      0 0x42004000 d318e308 /sbin/init
R     9066      1    9066    9066      1 0x52000400 da2b7130 /usr/lib/nfs/nfsmapid
R     9065      1    9063    9065      1 0x52000400 d965a978 /usr/lib/nfs/nfs4cbd
R     4125      1    4125    4125      0 0x42000400 d9659420 /local/local/bin/httpd -k start
R     9351   4125    4125    4125  40000 0x52000000 da2c0428 /local/local/bin/httpd -k start
R     4118      1    4117    4117      1 0x42000400 da2bc988 /usr/lib/nfs/nfs4cbd
R     4116      1    4116    4116      1 0x52000400 d8da7240 /usr/lib/nfs/nfsmapid
R     4105      1    4105    4105      0 0x42000400 d9664108 /usr/apache/bin/httpd
R     4263   4105    4105    4105  60001 0x52000000 da2bf368 /usr/apache/bin/httpd
...
> ::ps -t
S      PID   PPID    PGID     SID    UID       FLAGS      ADDR NAME
R        0      0       0       0      0 0x00000001 fec1d280 sched
         T            t0 <TS_STOPPED>
R        3      0       0       0      0 0x00020001 d318d248 fsflush
         T    0xd3108a00 <TS_SLEEP>
R        2      0       0       0      0 0x00020001 d318daa8 pageout
         T    0xd3108c00 <TS_SLEEP>
R        1      0       0       0      0 0x42004000 d318e308 init
         T    0xd3108e00 <TS_SLEEP>
R     9066      1    9066    9066      1 0x52000400 da2b7130 nfsmapid
         T    0xd942be00 <TS_SLEEP>
         T    0xda68f000 <TS_SLEEP>
         T    0xda4e8800 <TS_SLEEP>
         T    0xda48f800 <TS_SLEEP>
...

::pgrep httpd
> ::pgrep http
S      PID   PPID    PGID     SID    UID       FLAGS      ADDR NAME
R     4125      1    4125    4125      0 0x42000400 d9659420 httpd
R     9351   4125    4125    4125  40000 0x52000000 da2c0428 httpd
R     4105      1    4105    4105      0 0x42000400 d9664108 httpd
R     4263   4105    4105    4105  60001 0x52000000 da2bf368 httpd
R     4111   4105    4105    4105  60001 0x52000000 da2b2138 httpd
...
```

We can observe several aspects of the user process by using the *ptool-like* dcmds.

```
> ::pgrep nscd
S      PID   PPID    PGID     SID    UID       FLAGS            ADDR NAME
R      575      1     575     575      0 0x42000000 ffffffff866f1878 nscd

> 0t575 |::pid2proc |::walk thread |::findstack
(or)
> ffffffff82f5f860::walk thread |::findstack
stack pointer for thread ffffffff866cb060: fffffe8000c7fdd0
[ fffffe8000c7fdd0 _resume_from_idle+0xde() ]
  fffffe8000c7fe10 swtch+0x185()
  fffffe8000c7fe80 cv_wait_sig_swap_core+0x17a()
  fffffe8000c7fea0 cv_wait_sig_swap+0x1a()
  fffffe8000c7fec0 pause+0x59()
  fffffe8000c7ff10 sys_syscall32+0x101()
...
```

*continues*

```
> ffffffff866f1878::ptree
fffffffffbc23640  sched
     ffffffff82f6b148  init
          ffffffff866f1878  nscd

> ffffffff866f1878::pfiles
FD    TYPE         VNODE INFO
  0   CHR ffffffff833d4700 /devices/pseudo/mm@0:null
  1   CHR ffffffff833d4700 /devices/pseudo/mm@0:null
  2   CHR ffffffff833d4700 /devices/pseudo/mm@0:null
  3 DOOR ffffffff86a0eb40 [door to 'nscd' (proc=ffffffff866f1878)]
  4 SOCK ffffffff835381c0

> ffffffff866f1878::pmap
           SEG          BASE       SIZE      RES PATH
ffffffff85e416c0 0000000008046000      8k       8k [ anon ]
ffffffff866ab5e8 0000000008050000     48k          /usr/sbin/nscd
ffffffff839b1950 000000000806c000      8k       8k /usr/sbin/nscd
ffffffff866ab750 000000000806e000    520k     480k [ anon ]
...
```

## 14.1.12  Global Memory Summary

The major buckets of memory allocation are available with the ::memstat dcmd.

```
> ::memstat
Page Summary               Pages              MB    %Tot
------------        -----------------   -----------------  ----
Kernel                     49022              191   19%
Anon                       68062              265   27%
Exec and libs               3951               15    2%
Page cache                  4782               18    2%
Free (cachelist)            7673               29    3%
Free (freelist)           118301              462   47%

Total                     251791              983
Physical                  251789              983
```

## 14.1.13  Listing Network Connections

We can use the ::netstat dcmd to obtain the list of network connections.

```
> ::netstat
TCPv4    St   Local Address      Remote Address       Zone
da348600  6     10.0.5.104.63710      10.0.5.10.38189      7
da348a80  0     10.0.5.106.1016       10.0.5.10.2049       2
da34fc40  0     10.0.5.108.1018       10.0.5.10.2049       3
da3501c0  0     10.0.4.106.22        192.18.42.17.64836    2
d8ed2800  0     10.0.4.101.22        192.18.42.17.637
...
```

## 14.1.14 Listing All Kernel Threads

A stack backtrace of all threads in the kernel can be obtained with the `::threadlist` dcmd. (If you are familiar with adb, this is a modern version of adb's `$<threadlist` macro). With this dcmd, we can quickly and easily capture a useful snapshot of all current activity in text form, for deeper analysis.

```
> ::threadlist
    ADDR      PROC       LWP CMD/LWPID
fec1dae0 fec1d280 fec1fdc0 sched/1
d296cde0 fec1d280        0 idle()
d2969de0 fec1d280        0 taskq_thread()
d2966de0 fec1d280        0 taskq_thread()
d2963de0 fec1d280        0 taskq_thread()
d2960de0 fec1d280        0 taskq_thread()
d29e3de0 fec1d280        0 taskq_thread()
d29e0de0 fec1d280        0 taskq_thread()
...
> ::threadlist -v
    ADDR      PROC       LWP CLS PRI    WCHAN
fec1dae0 fec1d280 fec1fdc0   0  96        0
  PC: 0xfe82b507    CMD: sched
  stack pointer for thread fec1dae0: fec33df8
    swtch+0x165()
    sched+0x3aa()
    main+0x365()

d296cde0 fec1d280        0   0  -1        0
  PC: 0xfe82b507    THREAD: idle()
  stack pointer for thread d296cde0: d296cd88
    swtch+0x165()
    idle+0x32()
    thread_start+8()
...

# echo "::threadlist" |mdb -k >mythreadlist.txt
```

## 14.1.15 Other Notable Kernel dcmds

The `::findleaks` dcmd efficiently detects memory leaks in kernel crash dumps when the full set of kmem debug features has been enabled. The first execution of `::findleaks` processes the dump for memory leaks (this can take a few minutes), then coalesces the leaks by the allocation stack trace. The findleaks report shows a bufctl address and the topmost stack frame for each memory leak that was identified. See Section 11.4.9.1 in *Solaris™ Internals* for more information on `::findleaks`.

```
> ::findleaks
CACHE     LEAKED    BUFCTL  CALLER
70039ba8       1  703746c0  pm_autoconfig+0x708
70039ba8       1  703748a0  pm_autoconfig+0x708
7003a028       1  70d3b1a0  sigaddq+0x108
7003c7a8       1  70515200  pm_ioctl+0x187c
------------------------------------------------------
   Total       4 buffers, 376 bytes
```

If the -v option is specified, the dcmd prints more verbose messages as it executes. If an explicit address is specified prior to the dcmd, the report is filtered and only leaks whose allocation stack traces contain the specified function address are displayed.

The ::vatopfn dcmd translates virtual addresses to physical addresses, using the appropriate platform translation tables.

```
> fec4b8d0::vatopfn
        level=1 htable=d9d53848 pte=30007e3
Virtual fec4b8d0 maps Physical 304b8d0
```

The ::whatis dcmd attempts to determine if the address is a pointer to a kmem-managed buffer or another type of special memory region, such as a thread stack, and reports its findings. When the -a option is specified, the dcmd reports all matches instead of just the first match to its queries. When the -b option is specified, the dcmd also attempts to determine if the address is referred to by a known kmem bufctl. When the -v option is specified, the dcmd reports its progress as it searches various kernel data structures. See Section 11.4.9.2 in *Solaris™ Internals* for more information on ::whatis.

```
> 0x705d8640::whatis
705d8640 is 705d8640+0, allocated from streams_mblk
```

The ::kgrep dcmd lets you search the kernel for occurrences of a supplied value. This is particularly useful when you are trying to debug software with multiple instances of a value.

```
> 0x705d8640::kgrep
400a3720
70580d24
7069d7f0
706a37ec
706add34
```

## 14.2 Examining User Process Stacks within a Kernel Image

A kernel crash dump can save memory pages of user processes in Solaris. We explain how to save process memory pages and how to examine user processes by using the kernel crash dump.

## 14.2.1 Enabling Process Pages in a Dump

We must modify the dump configuration to save process pages. We confirm the dump configuration by running dumpadm with no option.

```
# /usr/sbin/dumpadm
         Dump content: all pages
          Dump device: /dev/dsk/c0t0d0s1 (swap)
   Savecore directory: /var/crash/example
     Savecore enabled: yes
```

If Dump content is not all pages or curproc, no process memory page will be dumped. In that case, we run dumpadm -c all or dumpadm -c curproc.

## 14.2.2 Invoking MDB to Examine the Kernel Image

We gather a crash dump and confirm that user pages are contained.

```
# /usr/bin/mdb unix.0 vmcore.0
   Loading modules: [ unix krtld genunix ufs_log ip nfs random ptm
   logindmux ]

> ::status
debugging crash dump vmcore.0 (64-bit) from rmcferrari
operating system: 5.11 snv_31 (i86pc)
panic message: forced crash dump initiated at user request
dump content: all kernel and user pages
```

The dump content line shows that this dump includes user pages.

## 14.2.3 Locating the Target Process

Next, we search for process information with which we are concerned. We use nscd as the target of this test case. The first thing to find is the address of the process.

```
> ::pgrep nscd
S     PID   PPID   PGID    SID    UID      FLAGS          ADDR NAME
R     575      1    575    575      0 0x42000000 ffffffff866f1878 nscd
```

The address of the process is ffffffff866f1878. As a sanity check, we can look at the kernel thread stacks for each process—we'll use these later to double-check that the user stack matches the kernel stack, for those threads blocked in a system call.

```
> 0t575::pid2proc |::print proc_t p_tlist |::list kthread_t t_forw |::findstack
stack pointer for thread ffffffff866cb060: fffffe8000c7fdd0
[ fffffe8000c7fdd0 _resume_from_idle+0xde() ]
  fffffe8000c7fe10 swtch+0x185()
  fffffe8000c7fe80 cv_wait_sig_swap_core+0x17a()
  fffffe8000c7fea0 cv_wait_sig_swap+0x1a()
  fffffe8000c7fec0 pause+0x59()
  fffffe8000c7ff10 sys_syscall32+0x101()
stack pointer for thread ffffffff866cc140: fffffe8000c61d70
[ fffffe8000c61d70 _resume_from_idle+0xde() ]
  fffffe8000c61db0 swtch+0x185()
  fffffe8000c61e10 cv_wait_sig+0x150()
  fffffe8000c61e50 door_unref+0x94()
  fffffe8000c61ec0 doorfs32+0x90()
  fffffe8000c61f10 sys_syscall32+0x101()
stack pointer for thread ffffffff866cba80: fffffe8000c6dd10
[ fffffe8000c6dd10 _resume_from_idle+0xde() ]
  fffffe8000c6dd50 swtch_to+0xc9()
  fffffe8000c6ddb0 shuttle_resume+0x376()
  fffffe8000c6de50 door_return+0x228()
  fffffe8000c6dec0 doorfs32+0x157()
  fffffe8000c6df10 sys_syscall32+0x101()
stack pointer for thread ffffffff866cb720: fffffe8000c73cf0
[ fffffe8000c73cf0 _resume_from_idle+0xde() ]
  fffffe8000c73d30 swtch+0x185()
  fffffe8000c73db0 cv_timedwait_sig+0x1a3()
  fffffe8000c73e30 cv_waituntil_sig+0xab()
  fffffe8000c73ec0 nanosleep+0x141()
  fffffe8000c73f10 sys_syscall32+0x101()
...
```

It appears that the first few threads on the process are blocked in the pause(), door(), and nanosleep() system calls. We'll double-check against these later when we traverse the user stacks.

## 14.2.4 Extracting the User-Mode Stack Frame Pointers

The next things to find are the stack pointers for the user threads, which are stored in each thread's lwp.

```
> ffffffff866f1878::walk thread |::print kthread_t t_lwp->lwp_regs|::print "struct
regs" r_rsp |=X
            8047d54         fecc9f80        febbac08        fea9df78        fe99df78
fe89df78            fe79df78
            fe69df78        fe59df78        fe49df78        fe39df58        fe29df58
fe19df58            fe09df58
            fdf9df58        fde9df58        fdd9df58        fdc9df58        fdb9df58
fda9df58            fd99df58
            fd89d538            fd79bc08
```

Each entry is a thread's stack pointer in the user process's address space. We can use these to traverse the stack in the user process's context.

## 14.3 Switching MDB to Debug a Specific Process

An mdb command, <proc address>::context, switches a context to a specified user process.

```
> ffffffff866f1878::context
debugger context set to proc ffffffff866f1878
```

After the context is switched, several mdb commands return process information rather than kernel information. For example:

```
> ::nm
Value                Size               Type  Bind  Other Shndx    Name
0x0000000000000000 | 0x0000000000000000 | NOTY | LOCL | 0x0  | UNDEF  |
0x0000000008056c29 | 0x0000000000000076 | FUNC | GLOD | 0x0  | 10     | gethost_revalidate
0x0000000008056ad2 | 0x0000000000000024 | FUNC | GLOB | 0x0  | 10     | getgr_uid_reaper
0x000000000805be5f | 0x0000000000000000 | OBJT | GLOB | 0x0  | 14     | _etext
0x0000000008052778 | 0x0000000000000000 | FUNC | GLOB | 0x0  | UNDEF  | strncpy
0x0000000008052788 | 0x0000000000000000 | FUNC | GLOB | 0x0  | UNDEF  | _uncached_getgrnam_r
0x000000000805b364 | 0x000000000000001b | FUNC | GLOB | 0x0  | 12     | _fini
0x0000000008058f54 | 0x0000000000000480 | FUNC | GLOB | 0x0  | 10     | nscd_parse
0x0000000008052508 | 0x0000000000000000 | FUNC | GLOB | 0x0  | UNDEF  | pause
0x00000000080554e0 | 0x0000000000000076 | FUNC | GLOB | 0x0  | 10     | getpw_revalidate
...

> ::mappings
        BASE            LIMIT           SIZE NAME
     8046000         8048000           2000 [ anon ]
     8050000         805c000           c000 /usr/sbin/nscd
     806c000         806e000           2000 /usr/sbin/nscd
     806e000         80f0000          82000 [ anon ]
     fd650000        fd655000           5000 /lib/nss_files.so.1
     fd665000        fd666000           1000 /lib/nss_files.so.1
     fd680000        fd690000          10000 [ anon ]
     fd6a0000        fd79e000          fe000 [ anon ]
     fd7a0000        fd89e000          fe000 [ anon ]
...
```

### 14.3.1 Constructing the Process Stack

Unlike examining the kernel, where we would ordinarily use the stack-related mdb commands like ::stack or ::findstack, we need to use stack pointers to traverse a process stack. In this case, nscd is an x86 32-bit application. So a "stack pointer + 0x38" and a "stack pointer + 0x3c" shows the stack pointer and the program counter of the previous frame.

```
/*
 * In the Intel world, a stack frame looks like this:
 *
 * %fp0->|                              |
 *       |------------------------------|
 *       |    Args to next subroutine   |
 *       |------------------------------|-\
 * %sp0->|  One-word struct-ret address | |
 *       |------------------------------| > minimum stack frame
 * %fp1->|  Previous frame pointer (%fp0)| |
 *       |------------------------------|-/
 *       |    Local variables           |
 * %sp1->|------------------------------|
 *
 * For amd64, the minimum stack frame is 16 bytes and the frame pointer must
 * be 16-byte aligned.
 */

struct frame {
        greg_t  fr_savfp;                    /* saved frame pointer */
        greg_t  fr_savpc;                    /* saved program counter */
};

#ifdef _SYSCALL32

/*
 * Kernel's view of a 32-bit stack frame.
 */
struct frame32 {
        greg32_t fr_savfp;                   /* saved frame pointer */
        greg32_t fr_savpc;                   /* saved program counter */
};
```
*See sys/stack.h*

Each individual stack frame is defined as follows:

```
/*
 * In the x86 world, a stack frame looks like this:
 *
 *                |--------------------------|
 * 4n+8(%ebp) ->| argument word n          |
 *                | ...                      |       (Previous frame)
 *    8(%ebp) ->| argument word 0          |
 *                |--------------------------|--------------------
 *    4(%ebp) ->| return address           |
 *                |--------------------------|
 *    0(%ebp) ->| previous %ebp (optional) |
 *                |--------------------------|
 *   -4(%ebp) ->| unspecified              |       (Current frame)
 *                | ...                      |
 *    0(%esp) ->| variable size            |
 *                |--------------------------|
 */
```
*See sys/stack.h*

We can explore the stack frames from Section 14.2.4.

```
> ffffffff866f1878::walk thread |::print kthread_t t_lwp->lwp_regs|::print "struct
regs" r_rsp |=X
                8047d54         fecc9f80        febbac08        fea9df78        fe99df78
fe89df78        fe79df78
                fe69df78        fe59df78        fe49df78        fe39df58        fe29df58
fe19df58        fe09df58
                fdf9df58        fde9df58        fdd9df58        fdc9df58        fdb9df58
fda9df58        fd99df58
                fd89d538        fd79bc08
```

```
> 8047d54/X
0x8047d54:      fedac74f
> fedac74f/
libc.so.1`pause+0x67:           8e89c933        = xorl    %ecx,%ecx

> febbac08/X
0xfebbac08:     feda83ec
> feda83ec/
libc.so.1`_door_return+0xac:    eb14c483        = addl    $0x14,%esp

> fea9df78/X
0xfea9df78:     fedabe4c
> fedabe4c/
libc.so.1`_sleep+0x88:          8908c483        = addl    $0x8,%esp
```

Thus, we observe user stacks of pause(), door_return(), and sleep(), as we expected.

## 14.3.2 Examining the Process Memory

In the process context, we can examine process memory as usual. For example, we can dissasemble instructions from a processes's address space:

```
> libc.so.1`_sleep+0x88::dis
libc.so.1`_sleep+0x67:          pushq   $-0x13
libc.so.1`_sleep+0x69:          call    -0x5cb59 <0xfed4f2d4>
libc.so.1`_sleep+0x6e:          addl    $0x4,%esp
libc.so.1`_sleep+0x71:          movl    %esp,%eax
libc.so.1`_sleep+0x73:          movl    %eax,0x22c(%rsi)
libc.so.1`_sleep+0x79:          leal    0x14(%rsp),%eax
libc.so.1`_sleep+0x7d:          pushq   %rax
libc.so.1`_sleep+0x7e:          leal    0x10(%rsp),%eax
libc.so.1`_sleep+0x82:          pushq   %rax
libc.so.1`_sleep+0x83:          call    +0xc419  <0xfedb8260>
libc.so.1`_sleep+0x88:          addl    $0x8,%esp
libc.so.1`_sleep+0x8b:          movl    %edi,0x22c(%rsi)
libc.so.1`_sleep+0x91:          movb    0xb3(%rsi),%cl
libc.so.1`_sleep+0x97:          movb    %cl,0xb2(%rsi)
libc.so.1`_sleep+0x9d:          jmp     +0x14    <libc.so.1`_sleep+0xb1>
libc.so.1`_sleep+0x9f:          leal    0x14(%rsp),%eax
libc.so.1`_sleep+0xa3:          pushq   %rax
libc.so.1`_sleep+0xa4:          leal    0x10(%rsp),%eax
libc.so.1`_sleep+0xa8:          pushq   %rax
libc.so.1`_sleep+0xa9:          call    +0xc3f3  <0xfedb8260>
libc.so.1`_sleep+0xae:          addl    $0x8,%esp
```

## 14.4 `kmdb`, the Kernel Modular Debugger

The userland debugger, `mdb`, debugs the running kernel and kernel crash dumps. It can also control and debug live user processes as well as user core dumps. `kmdb` extends the debugger's functionality to include instruction-level execution control of the kernel. `mdb`, by contrast, can only observe the running kernel.

The goal for `kmdb` is to bring the advanced debugging functionality of `mdb`, to the maximum extent practicable, to in-situ kernel debugging. This includes loadable-debugger module support, debugger commands, ability to process symbolic debugging information, and the various other features that make `mdb` so powerful.

`kmdb` is often compared with tracing tools like DTrace. DTrace is designed for tracing in the large—for safely examining kernel and user process execution at a function level, with minimal impact upon the running system. `kmdb`, on the other hand, grabs the system by the throat, stopping it in its tracks. It then allows for micro-level (per-instruction) analysis, allowing users observe the execution of individual instructions and allowing them to observe and change processor state. Whereas DTrace spends a great deal of energy trying to be safe, `kmdb` scoffs at safety, letting developers wreak unpleasantness upon the machine in furtherance of the debugging of their code.

### 14.4.1 Diagnosing with `kmdb` and `moddebug`

Diagnosing problems with `kmdb` builds on the techniques used with `mdb`. In this section, we cover some basic examples of how to use `kmdb` to boot the system.

#### 14.4.1.1 Starting `kmdb` from the Console

`kmdb` can be started from the command line of the console login with `mdb` and the -K option.

```
# mdb -K

Welcome to kmdb
Loaded modules: [ audiosup cpc uppc ptm ufs unix zfs krtld s1394 sppp nca lofs
genunix ip logindmux usba specfs pcplusmp nfs md random sctp ]
[0]> $c
kmdbmod`kaif_enter+8()
kdi_dvec_enter+0x13()
kmdbmod`kctl_modload_activate+0x112(0, fffffe85ad938000, 1)
kmdb`kdrv_activate+0xfa(4c6450)
kmdb`kdrv_ioctl+0x32(ab00000000, db0001, 4c6450, 202001, ffffffff8b483570,
fffffe8000c48edc)
cdev_ioctl+0x55(ab00000000, db0001, 4c6450, 202001, ffffffff8b483570,
fffffe8000c48edc)
specfs`spec_ioctl+0x99(fffffffffbc4cc880, db0001, 4c6450, 202001,
ffffffff8b483570, fffffe8000c48edc)
```

*continues*

```
fop_ioctl+0x2d(fffffffbc4cc880, db0001, 4c6450, 202001, ffffffff8b483570,
fffffe8000c48edc)
ioctl+0x180(4, db0001, 4c6450)
sys_syscall+0x17b()
[0] > :c
```

## 14.4.2  Booting with the Kernel Debugger

If you experience hangs or panics during Solaris boot, whether during installation
or after you've already installed, using the kernel debugger can be a big help in
collecting the first set of "what happened" information.

You invoke the kernel debugger by supplying the -k switch in the kernel boot
arguments. So a common request from a kernel engineer starting to examine a
problem is often "try booting with kmdb."

Sometimes it's useful either to set a breakpoint to pause the kernel startup and
examine something, or to just set a kernel variable to enable or disable a feature or
to enable debugging output. If you use -k to invoke kmdb but also supply the -d
switch, the debugger will be entered before the kernel really starts to do anything
of consequence, so you can set kernel variables or breakpoints.

To enter the debugger at boot with Solaris 10, enter b -kd at the appropriate
prompt; this is slightly different whether you're installing or booting an already
installed system.

```
ok boot kmdb -d
Loading kmdb...

Welcome to kmdb
[0] >
```

If, instead, you're doing this with a system where GRUB boots Solaris, you add
the -kd to the "kernel" line in the GRUB menu entry (you can edit GRUB menu
entries for this boot by using the GRUB menu interface, and the "c" (for edit) key).

```
kernel /platform/i86pc/multiboot -kd -B console=ttya
```

Either way, you'll drop into the kernel debugger in short order, which will
announce itself with this prompt:

```
[0] >
```

Now we're in the kernel debugger. The number in square brackets is the CPU that is running the kernel debugger; that number might change for later entries into the debugger.

### 14.4.3  Configuring a tty Console on x86

Solaris uses a bitmap screen and keyboard by default. To facilitate remote debugging, it is often desirable to configure the system to use a serial tty console. To do this, change the `bootenv.rc` and grub boot configuration.

```
setprop ttya-rts-dtr-off true
setprop console 'text'
                                                        See /boot/solaris/bootenv.rc
```

Edit the grub boot configuration to include `-B console=ttya` via the grub menu at boot time, or via `bootadm(1M)`.

```
kernel /platform/i86pc/multiboot -kd -B console=ttya
```

### 14.4.4  Investigating Hangs

For investigating hangs, try turning on module debugging output. You can set the value of a kernel variable by using the `/W` command ("write a 32-bit value"). Here's how you set `moddebug` to 0x80000000 and then continue execution of the kernel.

```
[0]> moddebug/W 80000000
[0]> :c
```

This command gives you debug output for each kernel module that loads. The bit masks for `moddebug` are shown below. Often, `0x80000000` is sufficient for the majority of initial exploratory debugging.

```
/*
 * bit definitions for moddebug.
 */
#define MODDEBUG_LOADMSG        0x80000000      /* print "[un]loading..." msg */
#define MODDEBUG_ERRMSG         0x40000000      /* print detailed error msgs */
#define MODDEBUG_LOADMSG2       0x20000000      /* print 2nd level msgs */
#define MODDEBUG_FINI_EBUSY     0x00020000      /* pretend fini returns EBUSY */
#define MODDEBUG_NOAUL_IPP      0x00010000      /* no Autounloading ipp mods */
```

*continues*

```
#define MODDEBUG_NOAUL_DACF       0x00008000    /* no Autounloading dacf mods */
#define MODDEBUG_KEEPTEXT         0x00004000    /* keep text after unloading */
#define MODDEBUG_NOAUL_DRV        0x00001000    /* no Autounloading Drivers */
#define MODDEBUG_NOAUL_EXEC       0x00000800    /* no Autounloading Execs */
#define MODDEBUG_NOAUL_FS         0x00000400    /* no Autounloading File sys */
#define MODDEBUG_NOAUL_MISC       0x00000200    /* no Autounloading misc */
#define MODDEBUG_NOAUL_SCHED      0x00000100    /* no Autounloading scheds */
#define MODDEBUG_NOAUL_STR        0x00000080    /* no Autounloading streams */
#define MODDEBUG_NOAUL_SYS        0x00000040    /* no Autounloading syscalls */
#define MODDEBUG_NOCTF            0x00000020    /* do not load CTF debug data */
#define MODDEBUG_NOAUTOUNLOAD     0x00000010    /* no autounloading at all */
#define MODDEBUG_DDI_MOD          0x00000008    /* ddi_mod{open,sym,close} */
#define MODDEBUG_MP_MATCH         0x00000004    /* dev_minorperm */
#define MODDEBUG_MINORPERM        0x00000002    /* minor perm modctls */
#define MODDEBUG_USERDEBUG        0x00000001    /* bpt after init_module() */
                                                  See sys/modctl.h
```

## 14.4.5 Collecting Information about Panics

When the kernel panics, it drops into the debugger and prints some interesting information; usually, however, the most interesting thing is the stack backtrace; this shows, in reverse order, all the functions that were active at the time of panic. To generate a stack backtrace, use the following:

```
[0]> $c
```

A few other useful information commands during a panic are ::msgbuf and ::status, as shown in Section 14.1.

```
[0]> ::msgbuf    - which will show you the last things the kernel printed onscreen, and
[0]> ::status    - which shows a summary of the state of the machine in panic.
```

If you're running the kernel while the kernel debugger is active and you experience a hang, you may be able to break into the debugger to examine the system state; you can do this by pressing the <F1> and <A> keys at the same time (a sort of "F1-shifted-A" keypress). (On SPARC systems, this key sequence is <Stop>-<A>.) This should give you the same debugger prompt as above, although on a multi-CPU system you may see that the CPU number in the prompt is something other than 0. Once in the kernel debugger, you can get a stack backtrace as above; you can also use ::switch to change the CPU and get stack backtraces on the different CPU, which might shed more light on the hang. For instance, if you break into the debugger on CPU 1, you could switch to CPU 0 with the following:

```
[1]> 0::switch
```

## 14.4.6 Working with Debugging Targets

For the most part, the execution control facilities provided by kmdb for the kernel mirror those provided by the mdb process target. Breakpoints (:bp), watchpoints (::wp), ::continue, and the various flavors of ::step can be used.

We discuss more about debugging targets in Section 13.3 and Section 14.1. The common commands for controlling kmdb targets are summarized in Table 14.1.

**Table 14.1**  Core kmdb dcmds

| dcmd | Description |
|---|---|
| ::status | Print summary of current target. |
| $r<br>::regs | Display current register values for target. |
| $c<br>::stack<br>$C | Print current stack trace ($C: with frame pointers). |
| addr[,b]<br>::dump [-g sz] [-e] | Dump at least b bytes starting at address addr. -g sets the group size; for 64-bit debugging, -g 8 is useful. |
| addr::dis | Disassemble text, starting around addr. |
| [ addr ] :b<br>[ addr ] ::bp [+/-dDestT] [-n count]<br>sym ...  addr | Set breakpoint at addr. |
| $b | Display all breakpoints. |
| ::branches | Display the last branches taken by the CPU. (x86 only) |
| addr ::delete [id \| all]<br>addr :d [id \| all] | Delete a breakpoint at addr. |
| :z | Delete all breakpoints. |
| function ::call [arg [arg ...]] | Call the specified function, using the specified arguments. |
| [cpuid] ::cpuregs [-c cpuid] | Display the current general-purpose register set. |
| [cpuid] ::cpustack [-c cpuid] | Print a C stack backtrace for the specified CPU. |

*continues*

**Table 14.1** Core `kmdb` dcmds (*continued*)

| dcmd | Description |
|---|---|
| `::cont`<br>`:c` | Continue the target program. |
| `$M` | List the macro files that are cached by `kmdb` for use with the `$<` dcmd. |
| `::next`<br>`:e` | Step the target program one instruction, but step over subroutine calls. |
| `::step [branch | over | out]` | Step the target program one instruction. |
| `$<systemdump` | Initiate a panic/dump. |
| `::quit [-u]`<br>`$q` | Cause the debugger to exit. When the `-u` option is used, the system is resumed and the debugger is unloaded. |
| `addr [,len]::wp [+/-dDestT] [-rwx]`<br>`[-ip] [-n count]`<br><br>`addr [,len]:a [cmd ...]`<br>`addr [,len]:p [cmd ...]`<br>`addr [,len]:w [cmd ...]` | Set a watchpoint at the specified address. |

## 14.4.7 Setting Breakpoints

Setting breakpoints with `kmdb` is done in the same way as with generic `mdb` targets, using the `:b` dcmd. Refer to Table 13.12 for a complete list of debugger dcmds.

```
# mdb -K
Loaded modules: [ crypto ]
kmdb: target stopped at:
kmdbmod`kaif_enter+8:    popfq
[0]> resume:b
[0]> :c
kmdb: stop at resume
kmdb: target stopped at:
resume:          movq    %gs:0x18,%rax
[0]> :z
[0]> :c
#
```

## 14.4.8  Forcing a Crash Dump with `halt -d`

The following example shows how to force a crash dump and reboot of the x86-based system by using the `halt -d` and boot commands. Use this method to force a crash dump of the system. Afterwards, reboot the system manually.

```
# halt -d
4ay 30 15:35:15 wacked.Central.Sun.COM halt: halted by user

panic[cpu0]/thread=ffffffff83246ec0: forced crash dump initiated at user request

fffffe80006bbd60 genunix:kadmin+4c1 ()
fffffe80006bbec0 genunix:uadmin+93 ()
fffffe80006bbf10 unix:sys_syscall32+101 ()

syncing file systems... done
dumping to /dev/dsk/c1t0d0s1, offset 107675648, content: kernel
NOTICE: adpu320: bus reset
100% done: 38438 pages dumped, compression ratio 4.29, dump succeeded

Welcome to kmdb
Loaded modules: [ audiosup crypto ufs unix krtld s1394 sppp nca uhci lofs
genunix ip usba specfs nfs md random sctp ]
[0]>
kmdb: Do you really want to reboot? (y/n) y
```

## 14.4.9  Forcing a Dump with `kmdb`

If you cannot use the `reboot -d` or the `halt -d` command, you can use the kernel debugger, `kmdb`, to force a crash dump. The kernel debugger must have been loaded, either at boot or with the `mdb -k` command, for the following procedure to work. Enter `kmdb` by using L1–A on SPARC, F1-A on x86, or break on a tty.

```
[0]> $<systemdump
panic[cpu0]/thread=ffffffff83246ec0: forced crash dump initiated at user request

fffffe80006bbd60 genunix:kadmin+4c1 ()
fffffe80006bbec0 genunix:uadmin+93 ()
fffffe80006bbf10 unix:sys_syscall32+101 ()

syncing file systems... done
dumping to /dev/dsk/c1t0d0s1, offset 107675648, content: kernel
NOTICE: adpu320: bus reset
100% done: 38438 pages dumped, compression ratio 4.29, dump succeeded
```

## 14.5  Kernel Built-In MDB dcmds

```
dcmd $<              - replace input with macro
dcmd $<<             - source macro
dcmd $>              - log session to a file
dcmd $?              - print status and registers
dcmd $C              - print stack backtrace
dcmd $G              - enable/disable C++ demangling support
dcmd $M              - list macro aliases
dcmd $P              - set debugger prompt string
dcmd $Q              - quit debugger
dcmd $V              - get/set disassembly mode
dcmd $W              - reopen target in write mode
dcmd $X              - print floating-point registers
dcmd $Y              - print floating- point registers
dcmd $b              - list traced software events
dcmd $c              - print stack backtrace
dcmd $d              - get/set default output radix
dcmd $e              - print listing of global symbols
dcmd $f              - print listing of source files
dcmd $g              - get/set C++ demangling options
dcmd $i              - print signals that are ignored
dcmd $l              - print the representative thread's lwp id
dcmd $m              - print address space mappings
dcmd $p              - change debugger target context
dcmd $q              - quit debugger
dcmd $r              - print general-purpose registers
dcmd $s              - get/set symbol matching distance
dcmd $v              - print non-zero variables
dcmd $w              - get/set output page width
dcmd $x              - print floating-point registers
dcmd $y              - print floating-point registers
dcmd /               - format data from virtual as
dcmd :A              - attach to process or core file
dcmd :R              - release the previously attached process
dcmd :a              - set read access watchpoint
dcmd :b              - set breakpoint at the specified address
dcmd :c              - continue target execution
dcmd :d              - delete traced software events
dcmd :e              - step target over next instruction
dcmd :i              - ignore signal (delete all matching events)
dcmd :k              - forcibly kill and release target
dcmd :p              - set execute access watchpoint
dcmd :r              - run a new target process
dcmd :s              - single-step target to next instruction
dcmd :t              - stop on delivery of the specified signals
dcmd :u              - step target out of current function
dcmd :w              - set write access watchpoint
dcmd :z              - delete all traced software events
dcmd =               - format immediate value
dcmd >               - assign variable
dcmd ?               - format data from object file
dcmd @               - format data from physical as
dcmd \               - format data from physical as
dcmd array           - print each array element's address
dcmd attach          - attach to process or corefile
dcmd bp              - set breakpoint at the specified addresses or symbols
dcmd cat             - concatenate and display files
dcmd cont            - continue target execution
dcmd context         - change debugger target context
dcmd dcmds           - list available debugger commands
dcmd delete          - delete traced software events
dcmd dem             - demangle C++ symbol names
dcmd dis             - disassemble near addr
```

```
        dcmd disasms           - list available disassemblers
        dcmd dismode           - get/set disassembly mode
        dcmd dmods             - list loaded debugger modules
        dcmd dump              - dump memory from specified address
        dcmd echo              - echo arguments
        dcmd enum              - print an enumeration
        dcmd eval              - evaluate the specified command
        dcmd events            - list traced software events
        dcmd evset             - set software event specifier attributes
        dcmd files             - print listing of source files
        dcmd fltbp             - stop on machine fault
        dcmd formats           - list format specifiers
        dcmd fpregs            - print floating point registers
        dcmd grep              - print dot if expression is true
        dcmd head              - limit number of elements in pipe
        dcmd help              - list commands/command help
        dcmd kill              - forcibly kill and release target
        dcmd list              - walk list using member as link pointer
        dcmd load              - load debugger module
        dcmd log               - log session to a file
        dcmd map               - print dot after evaluating expression
        dcmd mappings          - print address space mappings
        dcmd next              - step target over next instruction
        dcmd nm                - print symbols
        dcmd nmadd             - add name to private symbol table
        dcmd nmdel             - remove name from private symbol table
        dcmd objects           - print load objects information
        dcmd offsetof          - print the offset of a given struct or union member
        dcmd print             - print the contents of a data structure
        dcmd quit              - quit debugger
        dcmd regs              - print general-purpose registers
        dcmd release           - release the previously attached process
        dcmd run               - run a new target process
        dcmd set               - get/set debugger properties
        dcmd showrev           - print version information
        dcmd sigbp             - stop on delivery of the specified signals
        dcmd sizeof            - print the size of a type
        dcmd stack             - print stack backtrace
        dcmd stackregs         - print stack backtrace and registers
        dcmd status            - print summary of current target
        dcmd step              - single-step target to next instruction
        dcmd sysbp             - stop on entry or exit from system call
        dcmd term              - display current terminal type
        dcmd typeset           - set variable attributes
        dcmd unload            - unload debugger module
        dcmd unset             - unset variables
        dcmd vars              - print listing of variables
        dcmd version           - print debugger version string
        dcmd vtop              - print physical mapping of virtual address
        dcmd walk              - walk data structure
        dcmd walkers           - list available walkers
        dcmd whence            - show source of walk or dcmd
        dcmd which             - show source of walk or dcmd
        dcmd wp                - set a watchpoint at the specified address
        dcmd xdata             - print list of external data buffers

krtld
        dcmd ctfinfo           - list module CTF information
        dcmd modctl            - list modctl structures
        dcmd modhdrs           - given modctl, dump module ehdr and shdrs
        dcmd modinfo           - list module information
        walk modctl            - list modctl structures
```

```
mdb_kvm
  ctor 0x8076f20          - target constructor
  dcmd $?                 - print status and registers
  dcmd $C                 - print stack backtrace
  dcmd $c                 - print stack backtrace
  dcmd $r                 - print general-purpose registers
  dcmd regs               - print general-purpose registers
  dcmd stack              - print stack backtrace
  dcmd stackregs          - print stack backtrace and registers
  dcmd status             - print summary of current target
```

# APPENDICES

# A

# Tunables and Settings

As with most complex systems, parameters for overall control of the system can have a dramatic effect on performance. In the past much of a UNIX System Administrator's time would be spent "tuning" the kernel parameters of a system to achieve greater performance, tighten security, or control a system more closely such as by limiting logins or processes per user. These days, the modern Solaris operating environment is reasonably well tuned out of the box and much of the kernel "tweaking" is generally not needed. That being said, some system parameters still need to be set for specific tasks and for changing the Solaris environment from that of generalized computing to one specialized for the customer's environment.

## A.1 Tunable Parameters in Solaris

Historically, Solaris parameters have typically been found in various locations. These include the /etc/system file, running commands like ndd(1) and the /etc/default directory. In more recent Solaris versions, additional features such as resource management and container technology has allowed for a more flexible system of task-based controls and even distributed level of tunables using directory services, not specific to a single system.

The following subsections present an overview of the key locations.

## A.1.1 `/etc/default` Directory

This directory contains configuration files for many Solaris services. With each major release of Solaris, more configuration files have been migrated to this consistent location. Following is a list of these files on Solaris 10.

```
# ls /etc/default
autofs        inetinit      lu             passwd        tar
cron          init          metassist.xml  power         telnetd
devfsadm      ipsec         mpathd         rpc.nisd      utmpd
dhcpagent     kbd           nfs            su            webconsole
fs            keyserv       nfslogd        sys-suspend   yppasswdd
ftp           login         nss            syslogd
```

It is useful to become familiar with which configuration files exist in this directory. They are usually well commented and easy to edit, and some have man pages.

## A.1.2 `prctl` Command

The new framework enables us to dynamically configure tunable parameters by using the resource control framework. Ideally, we want these to be statically defined for our applications. We can also put these definitions within a network database (LDAP) to remove any per-machine settings.

The following example shows how to observe the System V Shared memory max parameter for a given login instance by using the `prctl` command.

```
sol10$ id -p
uid=0(root) gid=0(root) projid=3(default)
sol10# prctl -n project.max-shm-memory -i project 3
project: 3: default
NAME    PRIVILEGE       VALUE    FLAG   ACTION                    RECIPIENT
project.max-shm-memory
        privileged      246MB      -    deny                              -
        system         16.0EB     max   deny                              -
```

The shared memory maximum for this login has defaulted to 246 Mbytes. The following example shows how we can dynamically raise the shared memory limit.

```
sol10# prctl -n project.max-shm-memory -r -v 500mb -i project 3
sol10# prctl -n project.max-shm-memory -i project 3
project: 3: default
NAME    PRIVILEGE       VALUE    FLAG   ACTION                    RECIPIENT
project.max-shm-memory
        privileged      500MB      -    deny                              -
        system         16.0EB     max   deny                              -
```

To make this permanent, we would create a project entry for the user or project in question.

```
sol10# projadd -c "My database" -U oracle user.oracle
sol10# projmod -sK "project.max-shm-memory=(privileged,64G,deny)" user.oracle
sol10# su - oracle
oracle$ prctl -n project.max-shm-memory -i project user.oracle
project: 101: user.oracle
NAME      PRIVILEGE      VALUE     FLAG   ACTION                        RECIPIENT
project.max-shm-memory
          privileged     64.0GB      -    deny                                -
          system         16.0EB     max   deny                                -
```

## A.1.3 /etc/system File

The system configuration file customizes various parameters in the kernel. This file is read-only at boot time, so changes require a reboot to take effect. The following are example configuration lines.

```
set autoup=600
set nfs:nfs4_nra=16
```

This first line sets the parameter `autoup` to be 600. `autoup` is a `fsflush` parameter that defines the age in seconds at which dirty pages are written to disk. The second line sets the `nfs4_nra` variable from the `nfs` module to be 16, which is the NFSv4 read-ahead block parameter.

A common reason that /etc/system was modified was to tune kernel parameters such as the maximum shared memory, the number of semaphores, and the number of `pts` devices. In recent versions of Solaris, some of these commonly tuned parameters have been made dynamic or dynamically changeable, as described in Section A.1.2. You must still edit /etc/system for less commonly used parameters.

Table A.1 lists the various commands that can be placed in /etc/system. These are also listed in the default comments (which start with either "*" or "#").

When changing settings in /etc/system, be sure to carefully study the *Tunable Parameters Reference Manual* for that release of Solaris. The manual, which is available on docs.sun.com, lists crucial details for each parameter, such as *description, data type, default, range, units, dynamic or static behavior, validity checks that are performed, suggestions for when to change,* and *commitment level.*

Another reference for /etc/system is system(4).

**Table A.1** `/etc/system` Commands

| Command | Description |
|---|---|
| `moddir` | The search path for modules |
| `rootfs` | The root file system type (ufs) |
| `rootdev` | The root device—often customized when root is mirrored |
| `exclude` | Modules that should not be loaded—sometimes used as a workaround to skip a faulty module |
| `forceload` | Modules that must be loaded at boot |
| `set` | Parameter to set |

## A.1.4 `driver.conf` File

Individual configuration files for drivers (kernel modules) may reside in `/kernel/drv`, `/usr/kernel/drv` and under `/platform`. These files allow drivers to be customized in advanced ways.

However, editing `/etc/system` is often sufficient since the `set` command can modify driver parameters, as was shown with `nfs:nfs4_nra`; the `set` command also places driver settings in one file for easy maintenance. Editing `driver.conf` files instead is usually only done under the direction of a Sun engineer.

## A.1.5 `ndd` Command

The `ndd`[1] command gets and sets TCP/IP driver parameters and makes temporary live changes. Permanent changes to driver parameters usually need to be listed in `/etc/system`.

The following example demonstrates the use of `ndd` to list the parameters from the `arp` driver, to list the value of `arp_cleanup_interval`, and finally to set the value to 60,000 and check that this worked.

---

1. There is a popular belief that ndd stands for Network Device Driver, which sounds vaguely meaningful. We're not sure what it stands for, nor does the source code say; however, the data types used suggest ndd may mean *Name Dispatch Debugger*. An Internet search returns zero hits on this.

```
# ndd /dev/arp \?
?                              (read only)
arp_cache_report               (read only)
arp_debug                      (read and write)
arp_cleanup_interval           (read and write)
arp_publish_interval           (read and write)
arp_publish_count              (read and write)
# ndd /dev/arp arp_cleanup_interval
300000
# ndd -set /dev/arp arp_cleanup_interval 60000
# ndd -get /dev/arp arp_cleanup_interval
60000
```

The `arp_cleanup_interval` is the timeout milliseconds for the `arp` cache.

### A.1.6 `routeadm(1)`

Solaris 10 provides a new command, `routeadm`, that sets `ip_forwarding` for network interfaces in a permanent (that is, survives reboots) way. The following command enables `ip_forwarding` for all network interface and configures `routed` to broadcast RIP and answer RDISC, both now and after reboots:,

```
# routeadm -e ipv4-routing -e ipv4-forwarding -u
```

## A.2 System V IPC Tunables for Databases

In Solaris 10, we enhanced the System V IPC implementation to do away with as much administrative hand-holding (removing unnecessary tunables) and, by the use of task-based resource controls, to limit users' access to the System V IPC facilities (replacing the remaining tunables). At the same time, we raised the default values for those limits that remained to more reasonable values. For information on the System V Tunables, see the discussion on Section 4.2.1 in *Solaris™ Internals*.

# B

# DTrace One-Liners

## B.1 DTrace One-Liners

```
# New processes with arguments,
dtrace -n 'proc:::exec-success { trace(curpsinfo->pr_psargs); }'

# Files opened by process name,
dtrace -n 'syscall::open*:entry { printf("%s %s",execname,copyinstr(arg0)); }'

# Files created using creat() by process name,
dtrace -n 'syscall::creat*:entry { printf("%s %s",execname,copyinstr(arg0)); }'

# Syscall count by process name,
dtrace -n 'syscall:::entry { @num[execname] = count(); }'

# Syscall count by syscall,
dtrace -n 'syscall:::entry { @num[probefunc] = count(); }'

# Syscall count by process ID,
dtrace -n 'syscall:::entry { @num[pid,execname] = count(); }'

# Read bytes by process name,
dtrace -n 'sysinfo:::readch { @bytes[execname] = sum(arg0); }'

# Write bytes by process name,
dtrace -n 'sysinfo:::writech { @bytes[execname] = sum(arg0); }'

# Read size distribution by process name,
dtrace -n 'sysinfo:::readch { @dist[execname] = quantize(arg0); }'

# Write size distribution by process name,
dtrace -n 'sysinfo:::writech { @dist[execname] = quantize(arg0); }'

# Disk size by process ID,
dtrace -n 'io:::start { printf("%d %s %d",pid,execname,args[0]->b_bcount); }'
```

```
# Disk size aggregation
dtrace -n 'io:::start { @size[execname] = quantize(args[0]->b_bcount); }'

# Pages paged in by process name,
dtrace -n 'vminfo:::pgpgin { @pg[execname] = sum(arg0); }'

# Minor faults by process name,
dtrace -n 'vminfo:::as_fault { @mem[execname] = sum(arg0); }'

# Interrupts by CPU,
dtrace -n 'sdt:::interrupt-start { @num[cpu] = count(); }'

# CPU cross calls by process name,
dtrace -n 'sysinfo:::xcalls { @num[execname] = count(); }'

# Lock time by process name,
dtrace -n 'lockstat:::adaptive-block { @time[execname] = sum(arg1); }'

# Lock distribution by process name,
dtrace -n 'lockstat:::adaptive-block { @time[execname] = quantize(arg1); }'

# Kernel funtion calls by module
dtrace -n 'fbt:::entry { @calls[probemod] = count(); }'

# Stack size for processes
dtrace -n 'sched:::on-cpu { @[execname] = max(curthread->t_procp->p_stksize);}'
```

## B.2  DTrace Longer One-Liners

```
# New processes with arguments and time,
dtrace -qn 'syscall::exec*:return { printf("%Y %s\n",walltimestamp,curpsinfo->pr_psargs); }'

# Successful signal details,
dtrace -n 'proc:::signal-send /pid/ { printf("%s -%d %d",execname,args[2],args[1]->pr_pid);
}'
```

# C

Java DTrace Scripts

## C.1 `dvm_probe_test.d`

```
#!/usr/sbin/dtrace -s

/* #pragma D option quiet */

dvm$1:::vm-init
{
    printf("  vm-init");
}

dvm$1:::vm-death
{
    printf("  vm-death");
}

dvm$1:::thread-start
{
    printf("  tid=%d, thread-start: %s  ", tid, copyinstr(arg0));
}

dvm$1:::thread-end
{
    printf("  tid=%d, thread-end  ", tid);
}

dvm$1:::class-load
{
    printf("  tid=%d, class-load: %s  ", tid, copyinstr(arg0));
}

dvm$1:::class-unload
{
    printf("  tid=%d, class-unload: %s  ", tid, copyinstr(arg0));
}
```

```
dvm$1:::gc-start
{
    printf("  tid=%d, gc-start  ", tid);
}

dvm$1:::gc-finish
{
    printf("  tid=%d, gc-finish  ", tid);
}

dvm$1:::gc-stats
{
    printf("  tid=%d, gc-stats: used objects: %ld, used object space: %ld  ",
            tid, arg0, arg1);
}

dvm$1:::object-alloc
{
    printf("  tid=%d, object-alloc: class name: %s, size: %ld  ",
            tid, copyinstr(arg0), arg1);
}

dvm$1:::object-free
{
    printf("  tid=%d, object-free:  class name: %s  ",
            tid, copyinstr(arg0));
}

dvm$1:::monitor-contended-enter
{
    printf("  tid=%d, monitor-contended-enter:   thread name: %s  ",
            tid, copyinstr(arg0));
}

dvm$1:::monitor-contended-entered
{
    printf("  tid=%d, monitor-contended-entered: thread name: %s  ",
            tid, copyinstr(arg0));
}

dvm$1:::monitor-wait
{
    printf("  tid=%d, monitor-wait:   thread name: %s, time-out: %ld  ",
            tid, copyinstr(arg0), arg1);
}

dvm$1:::monitor-waited
{
    printf("  tid=%d, monitor-waited: thread name: %s, time-out: %ld  ",
            tid, copyinstr(arg0), arg1);
}

dvm$1:::method-entry
{
    printf("  tid=%d, method-entry:  %s:%s %s  ",
            tid, copyinstr(arg0), copyinstr(arg1), copyinstr(arg2));
}

dvm$1:::method-return
{
    printf("  tid=%d, method-return: %s:%s %s  ",
            tid, copyinstr(arg0), copyinstr(arg1), copyinstr(arg2));
}
```

```
pid$1::exit:entry
/execname == "java"/
{
    printf("  tid=%d, D-script exited: pid=%d  \n", tid, pid);
    exit(0);
}
```

## C.2  DVM Agent Provider Interface

```
provider dvm {
  probe vm__init();
  probe vm__death();
  probe thread__start(char *thread_name);
  probe thread__end();
  probe class__load(char *class_name);
  probe class__unload(char *class_name);
  probe gc__start();
  probe gc__finish(),
  probe gc__stats(long used_objects, long used_object_space);
  probe object__alloc(char *class_name, long size);
  probe object__free(char *class_name);
  probe monitor__contended__enter(char *thread_name);
  probe monitor__contended__entered(char *thread_name);
  probe monitor__wait(char *thread_name, long timeout);
  probe monitor__waited(char *thread_name, long timeout);
  probe method__entry(char *class_name, char *method_name, char *method_signature);
  probe method__return(char *class_name, char *method_name, char *method_signature);
};
```

# Sample Perl Kstat Utilities

## D.1 A Simple Kstat Walker

```perl
#!/usr/bin/perl -w
#
# kgrep - walk the Kstat tree, grepping names.
#
# This is a simple demo of walking the Kstat tree in Perl. The output
# is similar to a "kstat -p", however an argument can be provided to
# grep the full statistic name (joined by ":").
#
# USAGE:    kgrep [pattern]
#    eg,    kgrep hme0

use strict;
use Sun::Solaris::Kstat;
my $Kstat = Sun::Solaris::Kstat->new();
my $pattern = defined $ARGV[0] ? $ARGV[0] : ".";
die "USAGE: kgrep [pattern]\n" if $pattern eq "-h";

# loop over all kstats
foreach my $module (keys(%$Kstat)) {
    my $Modules = $Kstat->{$module};
    foreach my $instance (keys(%$Modules)) {
        my $Instances = $Modules->{$instance};
        foreach my $name (keys(%$Instances)) {
            my $Names = $Instances->{$name};
            foreach my $stat (keys(%$Names)) {
                my $value = $$Names{$stat};
                # print kstat name and value
                printf "%-50s %s\n", "$module:$instance:$name:$stat", $value
                    if "$module:$instance:$name:$stat" =~ /$pattern/;
            }
        }
    }
}
```

## D.2  A Perl Version of Uptime

```perl
#!/usr/bin/perl -w
#
# uptime - Perl Kstat version of uptime. Solaris 8+.
#
# This program fetches similar statistics to the /usr/bin/uptime command,
# as a demonstation of the Perl Kstat module.
#
# USAGE:    uptime
#

use strict;
use Sun::Solaris::Kstat;

### Create Kstat object
my $Kstat = Sun::Solaris::Kstat->new();

### Fetch load averages
my $load1  = $Kstat->{unix}->{0}->{system_misc}->{avenrun_1min};
my $load5  = $Kstat->{unix}->{0}->{system_misc}->{avenrun_5min};
my $load15 = $Kstat->{unix}->{0}->{system_misc}->{avenrun_15min};

### Fetch boot time
my $boot = $Kstat->{unix}->{0}->{system_misc}->{boot_time};

### Processing
$load1  /= 256;
$load5  /= 256;
$load15 /= 256;
my $days = (time() - $boot) / (60 * 60 * 24);

### Print output
print scalar localtime();
printf ",  up %.2f days", $days ;
printf ",  load averages: %.2f, %.2f, %.2f\n", $load1, $load5, $load15;
```

## D.3  A Network Statistics Utility

```perl
#!/usr/bin/perl -w
#
# nicstat - print network traffic, Kb/s read and written.
#           Solaris 8+, Perl (Sun::Solaris::Kstat).
#
# "netstat -i" only gives a packet count, this program gives Kbytes.
#
# 23-Jan-2006, ver 0.98
#
# USAGE:    nicstat [-hsz] [-i int[,int...]] | [interval [count]]
#           -h              # help
#           -s              # print summary output
#           -z              # skip zero lines
#           -i int[,int...] # print these instances only
#   eg,
#           nicstat         # print summary since boot
#           nicstat 1       # print continually, every 1 second
#           nicstat 1 5     # print 5 times, every 1 second
#           nicstat -i hme0 # only examine hme0
#
```

```
# This prints out the Kb/s transferred for all the network cards (NICs),
# including packet counts and average sizes. The first line is the summary
# data since boot.
#
# FIELDS:
#          Int          Interface
#          rKb/s        read Kbytes/s
#          wKb/s        write Kbytes/s
#          rPk/s        read Packets/s
#          wPk/s        write Packets/s
#          rAvs         read Average size, bytes
#          wAvs         write Average size, bytes
#          %Util        %Utilisation (r+w/ifspeed)
#          Sat          Saturation (defer, nocanput, norecvbuf, noxmtbuf)
#
# Author: Brendan Gregg   [Sydney, Australia]
#

use strict;
use Getopt::Std;
use Sun::Solaris::Kstat;
my $Kstat = Sun::Solaris::Kstat->new();


#
#   Process command line args
#
usage() if defined $ARGV[0] and $ARGV[0] eq "--help";
getopts('hi:sz') or usage();
usage() if defined $main::opt_h;
my $STYLE    = defined $main::opt_s ? $main::opt_s : 0;
my $SKIPZERO = defined $main::opt_z ? $main::opt_z : 0;

# process [interval [count]],
my ($interval, $loop_max);
if (defined $ARGV[0]) {
    $interval = $ARGV[0];
    $loop_max = defined $ARGV[1] ? $ARGV[1] : 2**32;
    usage() if $interval == 0;
}
else {
    $interval = 1;
    $loop_max = 1;
}

# check for -i,
my %NetworkOnly;                # network interfaces to print
my $NETWORKONLY = 0;            # match on network interfaces
if (defined $main::opt_i) {
    foreach my $net (split /,/, $main::opt_i) {
        $NetworkOnly{$net} = 1;
    }
    $NETWORKONLY = 1;
}

# globals,
my $loop = 0;                   # current loop number
my $PAGESIZE = 20;              # max lines per header
my $line = $PAGESIZE;           # counter for lines printed
my %NetworkNames;               # Kstat network interfaces
my %NetworkData;                # network interface data
my %NetworkDataOld;             # network interface data
$main::opt_h = 0;
$| = 1;                         # autoflush
```

```perl
### Determine network interfaces
unless (find_nets()) {
    if ($NETWORKONLY) {
        print STDERR "ERROR1: $main::opt_i matched no network interfaces.\n";
    }
    else {
        print STDERR "ERROR1: No network interfaces found!\n";
    }
    exit 1;
}

#
#   Main
#
while (1) {

    ### Print Header
    if ($line >= $PAGESIZE) {
        if ($STYLE == 0) {
            printf "%8s %5s %7s %7s %7s %7s %7s %7s %7s %7s\n",
                    "Time", "Int", "rKb/s", "wKb/s", "rPk/s", "wPk/s", "rAvs",
                    "wAvs", "%Util", "Sat";
        }
        elsif ($STYLE == 1) {
            printf "%8s %8s %14s %14s\n", "Time", "Int", "rKb/s", "wKb/s";
        }

        $line = 0;
    }

    ### Get new data
    my (@NetworkData) = fetch_net_data();

    foreach my $network_data (@NetworkData) {

        ### Extract values
        my ($int, $rbytes, $wbytes, $rpackets, $wpackets, $speed, $sat, $time)
            = split /:/, $network_data;

        ### Retrieve old values
        my ($old_rbytes, $old_wbytes, $old_rpackets, $old_wpackets, $old_sat,
            $old_time);
        if (defined $NetworkDataOld{$int}) {
            ($old_rbytes, $old_wbytes, $old_rpackets, $old_wpackets,
             $old_sat, $old_time) = split /:/, $NetworkDataOld{$int};
        }
        else {
            $old_rbytes = $old_wbytes = $old_rpackets = $old_wpackets
                = $old_sat = $old_time = 0;
        }

        #
        #   Calculate statistics
        #

        # delta time
        my $tdiff = $time - $old_time;

        # per second values
        my $rbps = ($rbytes - $old_rbytes) / $tdiff;
        my $wbps = ($wbytes - $old_wbytes) / $tdiff;
        my $rkps = $rbps / 1024;
        my $wkps = $wbps / 1024;
        my $rpps = ($rpackets - $old_rpackets) / $tdiff;
        my $wpps = ($wpackets - $old_wpackets) / $tdiff;
        my $ravs = $rpps > 0 ? $rbps / $rpps : 0;
        my $wavs = $wpps > 0 ? $wbps / $wpps : 0;
```

```
            # skip zero lines if asked
            next if $SKIPZERO and ($rbps + $wbps) == 0;

            # % utilisation
            my $util;
            if ($speed > 0) {
                # the following has a mysterious "800", it is 100
                # for the % conversion, and 8 for bytes2bits.
                $util = ($rbps + $wbps) * 800 / $speed;
                $util = 100 if $util > 100;
            }
            else {
                $util = 0;
            }

            # saturation per sec
            my $sats = ($sat - $old_sat) / $tdiff;

            #
            #  Print statistics
            #
            if ($rbps ne "") {
                my @Time = localtime();

                if ($STYLE == 0) {
                    printf "%02d:%02d:%02d %5s " .
                            "%7.2f %7.2f %7.2f %7.2f %7.2f %7.2f %7.2f %7.2f\n",
                            $Time[2], $Time[1], $Time[0], $int, $rkps, $wkps,
                            $rpps, $wpps, $ravs, $wavs, $util, $sats;
                }
                elsif ($STYLE == 1) {
                    printf "%02d:%02d:%02d %8s %14.3f %14.3f\n",
                            $Time[2], $Time[1], $Time[0], $int, $rkps, $wkps;
                }

                $line++;

                # for multiple interfaces, always print the header
                $line += $PAGESIZE if @NetworkData > 1;
            }

            ### Store old values
            $NetworkDataOld{$int}
                = "$rbytes:$wbytes:$rpackets:$wpackets:$sat:$time";
    }

    ### Check for end
    last if ++$loop == $loop_max;

    ### Interval
    sleep $interval;
}


# find_nets - walk Kstat to discover network interfaces.
#
# This walks %Kstat and populates a %NetworkNames with discovered
# network interfaces.
#
sub find_nets {
    my $found = 0;

    ### Loop over all Kstat modules
    foreach my $module (keys %$Kstat) {
        my $Modules = $Kstat->{$module};
```

```perl
        foreach my $instance (keys %$Modules) {
            my $Instances = $Modules->{$instance};

            foreach my $name (keys %$Instances) {

                ### Skip interface if asked
                if ($NETWORKONLY) {
                    next unless $NetworkOnly{$name};
                }

                my $Names = $Instances->{$name};

                # Check this is a network device.
                # Matching on ifspeed has been more reliable than "class"
                if (defined $$Names{ifspeed} and $$Names{ifspeed}) {

                    ### Save network interface
                    $NetworkNames{$name} = $Names;
                    $found++;
                }
            }
        }
    }

    return $found;
}

# fetch - fetch Kstat data for the network interfaces.
#
# This uses the interfaces in %NetworkNames and returns useful Kstat data.
# The Kstat values used are rbytes64, obytes64, ipackets64, opackets64
# (or the 32 bit versions if the 64 bit values are not there).
#
sub fetch_net_data {
    my ($rbytes, $wbytes, $rpackets, $wpackets, $speed, $time);
    my @NetworkData = ();

    $Kstat->update();

    ### Loop over previously found network interfaces
    foreach my $name (keys %NetworkNames) {
        my $Names = $NetworkNames{$name};

        if (defined $$Names{obytes} or defined $$Names{obytes64}) {

            ### Fetch write bytes
            if (defined $$Names{obytes64}) {
                $rbytes = $$Names{rbytes64};
                $wbytes = $$Names{obytes64};
            }
            else {
                $rbytes = $$Names{rbytes};
                $wbytes = $$Names{obytes};
            }

            ### Fetch read bytes
            if (defined $$Names{opackets64}) {
                $rpackets = $$Names{ipackets64};
                $wpackets = $$Names{opackets64};
            }
            else {
                $rpackets = $$Names{ipackets};
                $wpackets = $$Names{opackets};
            }
```

```perl
                ### Fetch interface speed
                if (defined $$Names{ifspeed}) {
                    $speed = $$Names{ifspeed};
                }
                else {
                    # if we can't fetch the speed, print the
                    # %Util as 0.0 . To do this we,
                    $speed = 2 ** 48;
                }

                ### Determine saturation value
                my $sat = 0;
                if (defined $$Names{nocanput} or defined $$Names{norcvbuf}) {
                    $sat += defined $$Names{defer} ? $$Names{defer} : 0;
                    $sat += defined $$Names{nocanput} ? $$Names{nocanput} : 0;
                    $sat += defined $$Names{norcvbuf} ? $$Names{norcvbuf} : 0;
                    $sat += defined $$Names{noxmtbuf} ? $$Names{noxmtbuf} : 0;
                }

                ### use the last snaptime value,
                $time = $$Names{snaptime};

                ### store data
                push @NetworkData, "$name:$rbytes:$wbytes:" .
                 "$rpackets:$wpackets:$speed:$sat:$time";
            }
        }

    return @NetworkData;
}

# usage - print usage and exit.
#
sub usage {
        print STDERR <<END;
USAGE: nicstat [-hsz] [-i int[,int...]] | [interval [count]]
   eg, nicstat                 # print summary since boot
       nicstat 1               # print continually every 1 second
       nicstat 1 5             # print 5 times, every 1 second
       nicstat -s              # summary output
       nicstat -i hme0         # print hme0 only
END
        exit 1;
}
```

# D.4  A Performance Utility for CPU, Memory, Disk, and Net

```perl
#!/usr/bin/perl -w
#
# sysperfstat - System Performance Statistics. Solaris 8+, Perl.
#
# This displays utilisation and saturation for CPU, memory, disk and network.
# This can be useful to get an overall view of system performance, the
# "view from 20,000 feet".
#
# 19-Mar-2006, ver 0.85
#
# USAGE:    sysperfstat [-h] | [interval [count]]
#    eg,
#           sysperfstat                 # print summary since boot only
#           sysperfstat 5               # print continually, every 5 seconds
```

```
#          sysperfstat 1 5          # print 5 times, every 1 second
#          sysperfstat -h           # print help
#
# This program prints utilisation and saturation values from four areas
# on one line. The first line printed is the summary since boot.
# The values represent,
#
# Utilisation,
#          CPU               # usr + sys time across all CPUs
#          Memory            # free RAM. freemem from availrmem
#          Disk              # %busy. r+w times across all Disks
#          Network           # throughput. r+w bytes across all NICs
#
# Saturation,
#          CPU               # threads on the run queue
#          Memory            # scan rate of the page scanner
#          Disk              # operations on the wait queue
#          Network           # errors due to buffer saturation
#
# The utilisation values for CPU and Memory have maximum values of 100%,
# Disk and Network don't. 100% CPU means all CPUs are running at 100%, however
# 100% Disk means perhaps 1 disk is running at 100%, or 2 disks at 50%;
# a similar calculation is used for Network. There are some sensible
# reasons behind this decision that I hope to document at some point.
#
# The saturation values have been tuned to be similar to system load averages;
# A value of 1.00 indicates moderate saturation of the resource (usually bad),
# a value of 4.00 would indicate heavy saturation or demand for the resource.
# A value of 0.00 does not indicate idle or unused - rather not saturated.
#
# See other Solaris commands for further details on utilisation or saturation.
#
# NOTE: For new physical disk types, add their module name to the @Disk
# tunable in the code below.
#
# Author: Brendan Gregg  [Sydney, Australia]
#

use strict;
use Sun::Solaris::Kstat;
my $Kstat = Sun::Solaris::Kstat->new();

#
#  Tunables
#

#
# Default tick rate. use 1000 if hires_tick is on
#
my $HERTZ = 100;

#
# Default NIC speed (if detection fails). 100 Mbits/sec
#
my $NIC_SPEED = 100_000_000;

#
# Disk module names
# these are deliberatly hard-coded, so that we match physical
# disks and not metadevices (which from kstat look like disks).
# matching metadevices would overcount disk statistics.
#
my @Disk = qw(cmdk dad sd ssd);
```

```
#
#   Process command line args
#
usage() if defined $ARGV[0] and $ARGV[0] =~ /^(-h|--help|0)$/;

# process [interval [count]],
my ($interval, $loop_max);
if (defined $ARGV[0]) {
    $interval = $ARGV[0];
    $loop_max = defined $ARGV[1] ? $ARGV[1] : 2**32;
    usage() if $interval == 0;
}
else {
    $interval = 1;
    $loop_max = 1;
}


#
#   Variables
#
my $loop = 0;               # current loop number
my $PAGESIZE = 20;          # max lines per header
my $lines = $PAGESIZE;      # counter for lines printed
my $cycles  = 0;            # CPU ticks usr + sys
my $freepct = 0;            # Memory free
my $busy    = 0;            # Disk busy
my $thrput  = 0;            # Network r+w bytes
my $runque  = 0;            # CPU total run queue length
my $scan    = 0;            # Memory scan rate
my $wait    = 0;            # Disk wait sum
my $error   = 0;            # Network errors
$| = 1;
my ($update1, $update2, $update3, $update4);

### Set Disk and Network identify hashes
my (%Disk, %Network);
$Disk{$_} = 1 foreach (@Disk);
discover_net();



#
#   Main
#

while (1) {

    ### Print header
    if ($lines++ >= $PAGESIZE) {
        $lines = 0;
        printf "%8s %28s %28s\n", "", "------ Utilisation ------",
            "------ Saturation ------";
        printf "%8s %7s %6s %6s %6s %7s %6s %6s %6s\n", "Time", "%CPU",
            "%Mem", "%Disk", "%Net", "CPU", "Mem", "Disk", "Net";
    }

    #
    #   Store old values
    #
    my $oldupdate1 = $update1;
    my $oldupdate2 = $update2;
    my $oldupdate3 = $update3;
    my $oldupdate4 = $update4;
    my $oldcycles  = $cycles;
    my $oldbusy    = $busy;
    my $oldthrput  = $thrput;
    my $oldrunque  = $runque;
```

```perl
        my $oldscan    = $scan;
        my $oldwait    = $wait;
        my $olderror   = $error;

        #
        #  Get new values
        #
        $Kstat->update();
        ($cycles, $runque, $update1) = fetch_cpu();
        ($freepct, $scan, $update2)  = fetch_mem();
        ($busy, $wait, $update3)     = fetch_disk();
        ($thrput, $error, $update4)  = fetch_net();

        #
        #  Calculate utilisation
        #
        my $ucpu  = ratio($cycles, $oldcycles, $update1, $oldupdate1, 100);
        my $umem  = sprintf("%.2f", $freepct);
        my $udisk = ratio($busy, $oldbusy, $update3, $oldupdate3);
        my $unet  = ratio($thrput, $oldthrput, $update4, $oldupdate4);

        #
        #  Calculate saturation
        #
        my $scpu  = ratio($runque, $oldrunque, $update1, $oldupdate1);
        my $smem  = ratio($scan, $oldscan, $update2, $oldupdate2);
        my $sdisk = ratio($wait, $oldwait, $update3, $oldupdate3);
        my $snet  = ratio($error, $olderror, $update4, $oldupdate4);

        #
        #  Print utilisation and saturation
        #
        my @Time = localtime();
        printf "%02d:%02d:%02d %7s %6s %6s %6s %7s %6s %6s %6s\n",
                $Time[2], $Time[1], $Time[0], $ucpu, $umem, $udisk, $unet,
                $scpu, $smem, $sdisk, $snet;

        ### Check for end
        last if ++$loop == $loop_max;

        ### Interval
        sleep $interval;
}


#
#  Subroutines
#

# fetch_cpu - fetch current usr + sys times, and the runque length.
#
sub fetch_cpu {

    ### Variables
    my ($runqueue, $time, $usr, $sys, $util, $numcpus);
    $usr = 0; $sys = 0;

    ### Loop over all CPUs
    my $Modules = $Kstat->{cpu_stat};
    foreach my $instance (keys(%$Modules)) {
        my $Instances = $Modules->{$instance};

        foreach my $name (keys(%$Instances)) {
```

```
                ### Utilisation - usr + sys
                my $Names = $Instances->{$name};
                if (defined $$Names{user}) {
                    $usr += $$Names{user};
                    $sys += $$Names{kernel};
                    # use last time seen
                    $time = $$Names{snaptime};
                }
            }
        }
    }

    ### Saturation - runqueue length
    $runqueue = $Kstat->{unix}->{0}->{sysinfo}->{runque};

    ### Utilisation - usr + sys
    $numcpus = $Kstat->{unix}->{0}->{system_misc}->{ncpus};
    $numcpus = 1 if $numcpus == 0;
    $util = ($usr + $sys) / $numcpus;
    $util = $util * 100/$HERTZ if $HERTZ != 100;

    ### Return
    return ($util, $runqueue, $time);
}

# fetch_mem - return memory percent utilised and scanrate.
#
# To determine the memory utilised, we use availrmem as the limit of
# usable RAM by the VM system, and freemem as the amount of RAM
# currently free.
#
sub fetch_mem {

    ### Variables
    my ($scan, $time, $pct, $freemem, $availrmem);
    $scan = 0;

    ### Loop over all CPUs
    my $Modules = $Kstat->{cpu_stat};
    foreach my $instance (keys(%$Modules)) {
        my $Instances = $Modules->{$instance};

        foreach my $name (keys(%$Instances)) {
            my $Names = $Instances->{$name};

            ### Saturation - scan rate
            if (defined $$Names{scan}) {
                $scan += $$Names{scan};
                # use last time seen
                $time = $$Names{snaptime};
            }
        }
    }

    ### Utilisation - free RAM (freemem from availrmem)
    $availrmem = $Kstat->{unix}->{0}->{system_pages}->{availrmem};
    $freemem = $Kstat->{unix}->{0}->{system_pages}->{freemem};

    #
    # Process utilisation.
    # this is a little odd, most values from kstat are incremental
    # however these are absolute. we calculate and return the final
    # value as a percentage. page conversion is not necessary as
    # we divide that value away.
    #
    $pct = 100 - 100 * ($freemem / $availrmem);
```

```
    #
    # Process Saturation.
    # Divide scanrate by slowscan, to create sensible saturation values.
    # Eg, a consistant load of 1.00 indicates consistantly at slowscan.
    # slowscan is usually 100.
    #
    $scan = $scan / $Kstat->{unix}->{0}->{system_pages}->{slowscan};

    ### Return
    return ($pct, $scan, $time);
}

# fetch_disk - fetch kstat values for the disks.
#
# The values used are  the r+w times for utilisation, and wlentime
# for saturation.
#
sub fetch_disk {

    ### Variables
    my ($wait, $time, $rtime, $wtime, $disktime);
    $wait = $rtime = $wtime = 0;

    ### Loop over all Disks
    foreach my $module (keys(%$Kstat)) {

        # Check that this is a physical disk
        next unless $Disk{$module};
        my $Modules = $Kstat->{$module};

        foreach my $instance (keys(%$Modules)) {
            my $Instances = $Modules->{$instance};

            foreach my $name (keys(%$Instances)) {

                # Check that this isn't a slice
                next if $name =~ /,/;

                my $Names = $Instances->{$name};

                ### Utilisation - r+w times
                if (defined $$Names{rtime} or defined $$Names{rtime64}) {
                    # this is designed to be future safe
                    if (defined $$Names{rtime64}) {
                        $rtime += $$Names{rtime64};
                        $wtime += $$Names{wtime64};
                    }
                    else {
                        $rtime += $$Names{rtime};
                        $wtime += $$Names{wtime};
                    }
                }

                ### Saturation - wait queue
                if (defined $$Names{wlentime}) {
                    $wait += $$Names{wlentime};
                    $time = $$Names{snaptime};
                }
            }
        }
    }

    ### Process Utilisation
    $disktime = 100 * ($rtime + $wtime);
```

```
        ### Return
        return ($disktime, $wait, $time);
}

# fetch_net - fetch kstat values for the network interfaces.
#
# The values used are r+w bytes, defer, nocanput, norcvbuf and noxmtbuf.
# These error statistics aren't ideal, as they are not always triggered
# for network satruation. Future versions may pull this from the new tcp
# mib2 or net class kstats in Solaris 10.
#
sub fetch_net {

        ### Variables
        my ($err, $time, $speed, $util, $rbytes, $wbytes);
        $err = $util = 0;

        ### Loop over all NICs
        foreach my $module (keys(%$Kstat)) {

            # Check this is a network device
            next unless $Network{$module};
            my $Modules = $Kstat->{$module};

            foreach my $instance (keys(%$Modules)) {
                my $Instances = $Modules->{$instance};

                foreach my $name (keys(%$Instances)) {
                    my $Names = $Instances->{$name};

                    # Check that this is a network device
                    next unless defined $$Names{ifspeed};

                    ### Utilisation - r+w bytes
                    if (defined $$Names{obytes} or defined $$Names{obytes64}) {
                        if (defined $$Names{obytes64}) {
                            $rbytes = $$Names{rbytes64};
                            $wbytes = $$Names{obytes64};
                        }
                        else {
                            $rbytes = $$Names{rbytes};
                            $wbytes = $$Names{obytes};
                        }

                        if (defined $$Names{ifspeed} and $$Names{ifspeed}) {
                            $speed = $$Names{ifspeed};
                        }
                        else {
                            $speed = $NIC_SPEED;
                        }

                        #
                        # Process Utilisation.
                        # the following has a mysterious "800", it is 100
                        # for the % conversion, and 8 for bytes2bits.
                        # $util is cumulative, and needs further processing.
                        #
                        $util += 800 * ($rbytes + $wbytes) / $speed;
                    }

                    ### Saturation - errors
                    if (defined $$Names{nocanput} or defined $$Names{norcvbuf}) {
                        $err += defined $$Names{defer} ? $$Names{defer} : 0;
                        $err += defined $$Names{nocanput} ? $$Names{nocanput} : 0;
                        $err += defined $$Names{norcvbuf} ? $$Names{norcvbuf} : 0;
```

```perl
                          $err += defined $$Names{noxmtbuf} ? $$Names{noxmtbuf} : 0;
                          $time = $$Names{snaptime};
                  }
              }
          }
      }

      #
      # Process Saturation.
      # Divide errors by 200. This gives more sensible load averages,
      # such as 4.00 meaning heavily saturated rather than 800.00.
      #
      $err = $err / 200;

      ### Return
      return ($util, $err, $time);
}

# discover_net - discover network modules, populate %Network.
#
# This could return an array of pointers to Kstat objects, but for
# now I've kept things simple.
#
sub discover_net {

    ### Loop over all NICs
    foreach my $module (keys(%$Kstat)) {

        my $Modules = $Kstat->{$module};
        foreach my $instance (keys(%$Modules)) {

            my $Instances = $Modules->{$instance};
            foreach my $name (keys(%$Instances)) {

                my $Names = $Instances->{$name};

                # Check this is a network device.
                # Matching on ifspeed has been more reliable than "class"
                if (defined $$Names{ifspeed}) {
                    $Network{$module} = 1;
                }
            }
        }
    }
}

# ratio - calculate the ratio of a count delta over time delta.
#
# Takes count and oldcount, time and oldtime. Returns a string
# of the value, or a null string if not enough data was provided.
#
sub ratio {

    my ($count, $oldcount, $time, $oldtime, $max) = @_;

    # Calculate deltas
    my $countd = $count - (defined $oldcount ? $oldcount : 0);
    my $timed = $time - (defined $oldtime ? $oldtime : 0);

    # Calculate ratio
    my $ratio = $timed > 0 ? $countd / $timed : 0;

    # Maximum cap
    if (defined $max) {
        $ratio = $max if $ratio > $max;
    }
```

```
        # Return as rounded string
        return sprintf "%.2f", $ratio;
}

# usage - print usage and exit.
#
sub usage {
        print STDERR <<END;
USAGE: sysperfstat [-h] | [interval [count]]
   eg, sysperfstat                 # print summary since boot only
        sysperfstat 5               # print continually every 5 seconds
        sysperfstat 1 5             # print 5 times, every 1 second
END
        exit 1;
}
```

# Bibliography

1. Bach, M. J., *The Design of the UNIX Operating System*, Prentice Hall, 1986.

2. Bonwick, J., *The Slab Allocator: An Object-Caching Kernel Memory Allocator*. Sun Microsystems, Inc. White paper.

3. Bourne, S. R., *The UNIX System*, Addison-Wesley, 1983.

4. Catanzaro, B., *Multiprocessor System Architectures*, Prentice Hall, 1994.

5. Cockcroft, A., *Sun Performance and Tuning—Java and the Internet,* 2nd Edition, Sun Microsystems Press/Prentice Hall, 1998.

6. Cockcroft, A., *CPU Time Measurement Errors*, Computer Measurement Group Paper 2038, 1998.

7. Cypress Semiconductor, *The CY7C601 SPARC RISC Users Guide*, Ross Technology, 1990.

8. Drake, C. and Brown, K., *Panic! UNIX System Crash Dump Analysis*, Prentice Hall, 1995.

9. Eykholt, J. R., et al., *Beyond Multiprocessing—Multithreading the SunOS Kernel*, Summer '92 USENIX Conference Proceedings.

10. Gingell, R. A., Moran, J. P., Shannon, W. A., *Virtual Memory Architecture in SunOS*, Proceedings of the Summer 1987 USENIX Conference.

11. Goodheart, B., Cox, J., *The Magic Garden Explained—The Internals of UNIX System V Release 4*, Prentice Hall, 1994.

12. Hoffman, F. "Crash Dump Analysis for x86/x64," http://www.genunix.org, 2005.

13. Hwang, K., Xu, Z., *Scalable Parallel Computing*, McGraw-Hill, 1998.

14. Intel Corp., *The Intel Architecture Software Programmers Manual, Volumes 1, 2 and 3*, Intel Part Numbers 243190, 24319102, and 24319202, 1993.

15. Johnstone, Mark S. and Wilson, Paul R. *The Memory Fragmentation Problem: Solved?* ISMM'98 Proceedings of the ACM SIGPLAN International Symposium on Memory Management, pp. 26-36. Available at ftp://ftp.dcs.gla.ac.uk/pub/drastic/gc/wilson.ps.

16. Kleiman, S. R., *Vnodes: An Architecture for Multiple File System Types in Sun UNIX*, Proceedings of Summer 1986 Usenix Conference.

17. Kleiman, S., Shah, D., Smaalders, B., *Programming with Threads*, Prentice Hall, SunSoft Press, 1996.

18. Knuth, D., *The Art of Computer Programming: Fundamental Algorithms*, Addison Wesley, 1973.

19. Leffler, S. J., McKusick, M. K., Karels, M. J., Quarterman, J. S., *The Design and Implementation of the 4.3BSD UNIX Operating System*, Addison-Wesley, 1989.

20. Lewis, B., Berg, D. J., *Threads Primer. A Guide to Multithreaded Programming*, SunSoft Press/Prentice Hall, 1996.

21. Lewis, B., Berg, D. J., *Multithreaded Programming with Pthreads*. Sun Microsystems Press/Prentice Hall. 1998

22. McKusick, M. K., Bostic, K., Karels, M. J., Quarterman, J. S., *The Design and Implementation of the 4.4 BSD Operating System*, Addison-Wesley, 1996.

23. McKusick, M. K., Joy, W., Leffler, S., Fabry, R., *A Fast File System for UNIX*, ACM Transactions on Computer Systems, 2(3):181–197, August 1984.

24. Moran, J. P., *SunOS Virtual Memory Implementation*, Proceedings of 1988 EUUG Conference.

25. Pfister, G., *In Search of Clusters*, Prentice Hall, 1998.

26. Rosenthal, David S., *Evolving the Vnode Interface*, Proceedings of Summer 1990 USENIX Conference.

27. Schimmel, C., *UNIX Systems for Modern Architectures*, Addison-Wesley, 1994.

28. Seltzer, M., Bostic, K., McKusick, M., Staelin, C. *An Implementation of a Log-Structured File System for UNIX*, Proceedings of the Usenix Winter Conference, January 1993.

29. Shah, D. K., Zolnowsky, J., *Evolving the UNIX Signal Model for Lightweight Threads*, Sun Proprietary/Confidential Internal Use Only, White paper, SunSoft TechConf '96.

30. Snyder, P., *tmpfs: A Virtual Memory File System*, Sun Microsystems White paper.

31. SPARC International, *System V Application Binary Interface—SPARC Version 9 Processor Supplement*, 1997.

32. Sun Microsystems, *Writing Device Drivers—Part Number 805-3024-10*, Sun Microsystems, 1998

33. Sun Microsystems, *STREAMS Programming Guide—Part Number 805-4038-10*, Sun Microsystems, 1998

34. Sun Microsystems, *UltraSPARC Microprocessor Users Manual—Part Number 802-7220*, Sun Microsystems, 1995.

35. Stevens, W. R., *Advanced Programming in the UNIX Environment*, Addison-Wesley, 1992.

36. Stevens, W. R., *UNIX Network Programming, Volume 2. Interprocess Communication, Second Edition*. Addison-Wesley, 1998.

37. Swain, P., Softway. Personal communication.

38. Talluri, M., *Use of Superpages and subblOcking in the Address Translation Hierarchy*, Thesis for the doctorate of computer science, University of Wisconsin, 1995.

39. Tanenbaum, A. *Operating Systems: Design and Implementation*. Prentice Hall, 1987.

40. Taylor, R., Veritas Software. Personal communication.

41. Tucker, A., *Scheduler Activations*, PSARC 1996/021, Sun Internal Proprietary Document. March, 1996.

42. Tucker, A., *Scheduler Activations in Solaris,* SunSoft TechConf '96. Sun Proprietary/Confidential—Internal Use Only Document.

43. Tucker, A., Private Communication.

44. UNIX Software Operation, *System V Application Binary Interface—UNIX System V*. Prentice Hall/UNIX Press. 1990.

45. Vahalia, U., *UNIX Internals—The New Frontiers,* Prentice Hall, 1996.

46. Van der Linden, P., *Expert C Programming—Deep C Secrets*, SunSoft Press/Prentice Hall, 1994.

47. Weaver, D., Germond, T. (editors), *The SPARC Architecture Manual, Version 9*, Prentice Hall, 1994.

48. Weinstock, C. B. and Wulf, W. A., *QuickFit: An Efficient Algorithm for Heap Storage Allocation*. ACM SIGPLAN Notices, v.23, no. 10, pp. 141–144 (1988).

49. Wilson, P. R, Johnstone, M. S., Neely, M., Boles D., *Dynamic Storage Allocation: A Survey and Critical Review. Proceedings of the International Workshop on MemoryManagement*, September 1995. Available at `http://citeseer.nj.nec.com/wilson95dynamic.html`.

50. Wong, B., *Configuration and Capacity Planning on Sun Solaris Servers*, Sun Microsystems Press/Prentice Hall, 1996.

51. Zaks, R., *Programming the Z80*, Sybex Computer Books, 1982.

# Index

## TEN MOVES AHEAD

1. APPLICATIONS CAN RUN UP TO 30 TIMES FASTER

2. ACCESS TO OPENSOLARIS™ AND OVER 1,600 PATENTS

3. IP INDEMNIFICATION

4. REAL TIME APPLICATION DEBUGGING WITH SOLARIS™ DYNAMIC TRACING

5. AUTOMATED WORKLOAD MANAGEMENT WITH SOLARIS CONTAINERS

6. AUTOMATED AVAILABILITY SERVICES WITH PREDICTIVE SELF-HEALING

7. WORLD'S MOST ADVANCED SECURITY FEATURES— BUILT IN

8. SAME OS ON MORE THAN 360 SPARC,® AMD OPTERON,™ AND INTEL SYSTEMS

9. ACCESS TO 85% OF FORTUNE 500 IT ORGANIZATIONS, RUNNING THE SOLARIS OS

10. APPLICATIONS GUARANTEED FROM RELEASE TO RELEASE, PLATFORM TO PLATFORM*

MOVE AHEAD TODAY AT:
SUN.COM/SOLARIS10

**FOR MORE INFORMATION ON SUN MICROSYSTEMS PRESS, VISIT WWW.SUN.COM/BOOKS**

# informIT

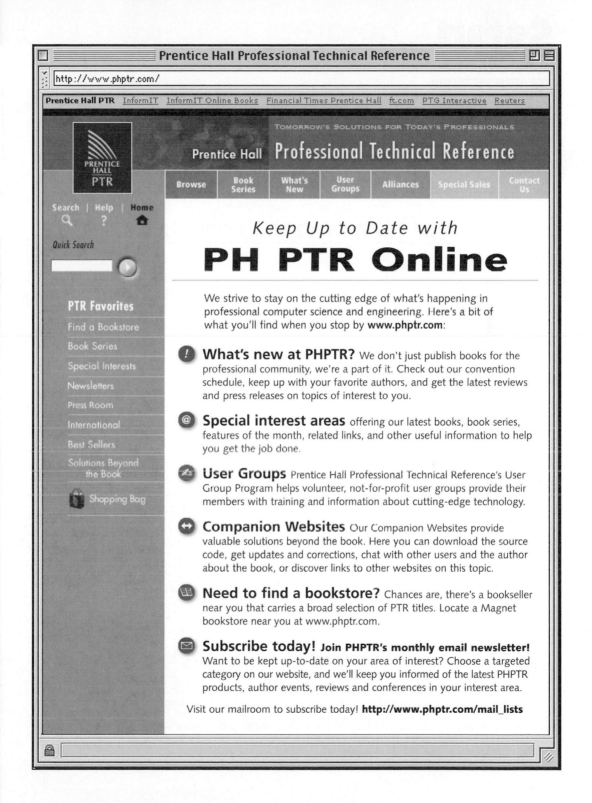